Tourism and the Less Developed World

Issues and Case Studies

For Asha and Ian

Tourism and the Less Developed World

Issues and Case Studies

_____

Edited by

David Harrison

Professor of Tourism
Culture and Development
University of North London
UK

CABI *Publishing*

CABI Publishing is a division of CAB International

CABI Publishing
CAB International
Wallingford
Oxon OX10 8DE
UK

Tel: +44 (0)1491 832111
Fax: +44 (0)1491 833508
Email: cabi@cabi.org
Web site: www.cabi-publishing.org

CABI Publishing
875 Massachusetts Avenue
7th Floor
Cambridge, MA 02139
USA

Tel: +1 617 395 4056
Fax: +1 617 354 6875
Email: cabi-nao@cabi.org

A catalogue record for this book is available from the British Library, London, UK

The Library of Congress has cataloged the hardcover edition as follows:
Tourism and the less developed world : issues and case studies / edited by David Harrison.
   p.   cm.
Includes bibliographical references (p.).
ISBN 0-85199-433-4 (alk. paper)
   1.   Tourism–Developing countries. I. Harrison, David.

   G155.D44 T687 2001
   338.4'791'091724--dc21   00-054723

HB ISBN 0 85199 433 4
PB ISBN 0 85199 830 5

Hardback edition first published 2001
Reprinted 2004
Paperback edition 2004

Typeset in 9/11 Optima by Columns Design Ltd, Reading.
Printed and bound in the UK by Cromwell Press, Trowbridge

Contents

Notes on Contributors

Garth Allen is Professor and Director of the School of Social and Educational Development at the College of St Mark and St John, Plymouth, England, and co-Director of a research unit at the University of Natal, South Africa. He is interested in applying political economic theory to the study of tourism, and is author, with Frank Brennan, of *Tourism in the New South Africa: Conflict, Community and Development* (I.B. Tauris, 2001).

Heba Aziz is a lecturer at the University of Alexandria, Egypt. She received her PhD from the University of Surrey, which was based on fieldwork, carried out in the Sinai, on the impact of Bedouin communities. Her publications on gender issues in tourism, on the relationship of tourism and terrorism, on backpacking and on employment among Bedouin communities have been well received in academic circles and in the popular media.

Frank Brennan lectures in the Anthropology of Development Studies at the College of St Mark and St John, Plymouth, England, where he is also Research Associate at the Centre for Social and Educational Research. His main research interests are in the anthropology of tourist motivation and he is co-author, with Garth Allen, of *Tourism in the New South Africa: Conflict, Community and Development* (I.B. Tauris, 2001).

Kelly S. Bricker received her PhD in Leisure Studies from Pennsylvania State University, USA. She has worked in the field of nature-based, adventure and incentive tourism since 1981, taught at the University of the South Pacific in Suva, Fiji, and now teaches at West Virginia University. Her research interests include ecotourism and ecotourists, linkages between sense of place and the management of natural resources, and tourism as a tool for conservation.

Peter U.C. Dieke is Senior Lecturer in Tourism at the Scottish Hotel School, University of Strathclyde, Glasgow, Scotland. He has research and teaching interests in tourism development, focusing on planning, policy, and implementation strategies for less developed countries generally, with a regional interest in sub-Saharan Africa. He has written extensively on these topics.

C. Michael Hall is Professor and Head of the Department of Tourism at the University of Otago in New Zealand. He is also Visiting Professor in Tourism Management at Sheffield Hallam University in the United Kingdom. He has written widely in the areas of tourism, heritage and environmental history and is currently focusing on tourism's role in economic restructuring and regional development policy, particularly with respect to cool-climate wine regions.

Derek R. Hall is head of the Leisure and Tourism Management Department at the Scottish Agricultural College (SAC), Auchincruive, and has a personal chair in Regional Development. Recent work has included: *Europe goes East: EU Enlargement, Diversity and Uncertainty* (Stationery Office, 2000), a text jointly edited with Darrick Danta; and *Rural Tourism and Recreation: Principles to Practice* (CAB *International*, 2001), which is jointly edited with Lesley Roberts.

David Harrison has written on tourism's impacts in the Caribbean, southern Africa, Bulgaria and the South Pacific. After teaching at the Universities of Sussex and the South Pacific, he became Professor of Tourism, Culture and Development at the University of North London, in 1998. Author of *The Sociology of Modernization and Development* (1988), he also edited *Tourism and the Less Developed Countries* (1992), and coedited *Sustainable Tourism in Islands and Small States: Case Studies* (1996).

Brian King is Professor and Head of School of Hospitality, Tourism and Marketing at Victoria University, Australia. He has written *Creating Island Resorts, Tourism Marketing in Australia, Developing Products* and *Sales Supervision*, and has coedited *Asia-Pacific Tourism: Regional Co-operation, Planning and Development*. He is Joint Editor-in-Chief of the journal *Tourism, Culture and Communication*. His research interests include planning for tourism in developing countries and island microstates, resort and destination marketing, tourism education and migrant tourism consumption.

Alan A. Lew is Professor of Geography and Public Planning at Northern Arizona University, USA, where he teaches classes on tourism, urban planning and geography. His research interests focus on tourism in East and South-East Asia, and on American Indian lands in the western USA. He is also founding editor of the journal, *Tourism Geographies.*

Heather Montgomery is a Lecturer in Childhood Studies at the Open University, UK. She is author of *Modern Babylon: Prostituting Children in Thailand* and other articles on child prostitution, children's rights and sex tourism.

Linda K. Richter teaches public policy as Professor of Political Science at Kansas State University. Her books and articles focus on tourism development issues, including gender, heritage preservation, health, political stability, terrorism and sustainable tourism in developing nations. She is Associate Editor of *Annals of Tourism Research* and *The Encyclopaedia of Tourism*. She was a member of the US Travel and Tourism Advisory Board and is a member of the International Academy for the Study of Tourism.

Sheryl Ross holds degrees from McGill University and the University of Waterloo (both in Canada), as well as a Diploma in Wildlife Management from the former institution. She has held a number of positions related to park planning and interpretation, and is currently employed by Parks Canada.

Guilherme Santana is a researcher and lecturer at the Centre for Technology, Earth and Marine Sciences at the Universidade do Vale do Itajaí, SC, Brazil. He holds a PhD from the International Centre for Tourism and Hospitality Research, Bournemouth University, UK, and an MSc in hotel management and marketing from the University of Surrey, UK. His research interests in tourism include crisis management, tourism safety, tourism in developing countries, marketing and sustainable tourism.

Shalini Singh is Research Professor at the Centre for Tourism Research and Development, Lucknow, India, and visiting professor at other Indian universities. An editor of *Tourism Recreation Research*, and on the editorial board of *Tourism Management*, her research is mostly on Indian tourism, and her publications include *Cultural Tourism and Heritage Management* (1994), *Profiles of Indian Tourism* (1996) and *Tourism Development in Critical Environments* (1999). She is currently working on the theme of community tourism.

Geoffrey Wall is Professor of Geography, Planning and Recreation and Leisure Studies at the University of Waterloo, Canada, where he is also Associate Dean for Graduate Studies in the Faculty of Environmental Studies. He is interested in the implications of tourism of different types for destination areas with varying characteristics. Much of his recent research, as well as that of his students, has been conducted in Asia, especially Indonesia and China.

David B. Weaver is Associate Professor in the School of Tourism and Hotel Management, Griffith University, Australia and in January 2002 will become Professor of Tourism at George Mason University, Virginia, USA. His PhD (1986) focused on tourism development in Antigua, and he has studied ecotourism, resort cycles and sustainable tourism in the Caribbean, Canada, Africa and Australia. Author or co-author of three books and many journal articles and book chapters, he is editor of *The Encyclopedia of Ecotourism* (CAB *International*, 2001) and is on the editorial boards of several tourism journals.

Preface

The preface is usually the last part of a book to be written. It is the start of a process of objectification, whereby the author distances himself or herself from the finished product, and (like the parent of a newborn child) examines it for flaws. That such are to be found in this book is undeniable, and remain the editor's responsibility. In particular, I am aware that in trying to provide an overview of tourism in less developed countries (LDCs), analytical depth has sometimes been sacrificed, but I hope that there are enough indications of the many rich veins of research possibilities to prompt others to take up the challenge.

There is also a danger that such a broad review will leave specialists unsatisfied, but here I feel less apologetic. This is not a book about tourism marketing or gender relations, for example, and was not intended to be, although it is hoped that anyone interested in these topics will find at least parts of it interesting and relevant. It is, instead, a series of chapters on tourism in LDCs interpreted from a perspective derived primarily from the sociology (and anthropology) of development. And the main argument is very simple: international tourism in LDCs at the beginning of the third millennium is the extension of a process of globalization that was well established by the middle of the 19th century, and must be understood within this historical context.

The many contributors to this volume have been exceptionally patient with editorial demands. One noted my good fortune to be on the other side of the world when he received my comments on the first draft of his chapter, and others may have felt the same. I should like to thank them for their tolerance. In addition, I am especially grateful to colleagues at two quite different institutions: the University of the South Pacific, in Fiji, and the newly formed International Institute for Culture, Tourism and Development at the University of North London. My time in Fiji, from March 1996 until December 1998, at the School of Social and Economic Development, was immensely productive and enjoyable, and I learned much from colleagues at the University and in the tourism industry. At the end of 1998, I received a similarly warm welcome (albeit more metaphorically) from the Centre for Leisure and Tourism Studies at the University of North London, which was the basis for the new Institute, and I greatly value the friendship and support of colleagues committed to furthering the study of leisure and tourism, in developed and less developed countries.

Finally, I should like to thank Tim Hardwick of CABI *Publishing*, for his patience and understanding. He never hassled me when I missed deadlines and was always quietly supportive.

David Harrison

1

Less Developed Countries and Tourism: the Overall Pattern

David Harrison

The Background

For many people in 'developed' societies, taking a holiday (or, increasingly, several holidays) every year is the norm. It is a part of the life cycle, and holidays join birthdays, religious festivals and the annual round of births, deaths and weddings as notable and noteworthy episodes that punctuate the passing of time. For business people, too, overseas trips, which may indeed contain a significant degree of sightseeing and other touristic activities, are part of a regular routine, and such travellers constitute an important and highly profitable component of the international tourist market. Travelling overseas, then, for pleasure, business or both, is now a recognized feature of everyday life in the developed world. It is part of the world we take for granted.

Destination areas have developed to accommodate all these travellers, and receiving them and catering for their needs has also become part of a daily routine. Just as in the past many communities depended on Western tastes for sugar, coffee, tea or sweets for their living, so they may now also depend on tourists for their livelihood. From the south coast of England to the markets of Morocco, from 'heritage' cities of western Europe to islands of the Pacific and the Caribbean, the globe is continuously criss-crossed by millions, by car, by air and by sea.

This book is an attempt to describe and explain the importance of these vast population movements, especially to those who live in less developed countries (LDCs). It is argued in this chapter that the pattern is not new, that it is the continuation of a long historical process that has sometimes been described as 'development'. In the first part of this introduction, this approach is discussed in some detail, and consideration is also given to other perspectives that have been employed to analyse tourism's role in the modern world. The remainder of the chapter is taken up with an examination of current patterns of tourist movement and, in particular, the extent to which LDCs rely on tourism, region by region, and the overall trends that seem to underlie the pattern. It is, in a sense, an attempt to obtain a bird's-eye view of international travel, before moving to a detailed examination of some of the social factors that prompt such a major but nevertheless regular and predictable movement of the world's population. The way is then open for other contributors to take up the challenge and examine tourism and its importance in specific countries and regions.

Tourism is certainly not a new phenomenon. Early visitors to the Egyptian pyramids

© CAB *International* 2001. *Tourism and the Less Developed World: Issues and Case Studies* (ed. D. Harrison)

indulged in graffiti, ancient Greeks made merry at the Olympic Games at Olympia, near Elis (and at similar events elsewhere), and Romans headed in large numbers for the Bay of Naples to escape the midsummer heat of the city (Casson, 1994: 143; Carroll, 2000; Grayling, 2000). By the fourth century AD, travel for religious reasons was developing among Western Christians and the anchorites, (for example) went to the wilderness to 'escape' the corruption of the everyday world or – according to their critics – to evade their economic and civic duties (Adler, 1993: 410). In the same period, growing numbers of Christian pilgrims were similarly criticized, especially for opening themselves to 'moral mischief' (Gregory of Nyssa, quoted in Coleman and Elsner, 1995: 80), an accusation which did not prevent pilgrimage from becoming increasingly popular. Indeed, by the beginning of the 16th century pilgrimages had become, for many, 'simply an excuse for a holiday' (Myers, 1952: 221). At a local level, too, visitors to medieval fairs and the festivals, held on numerous 'holy days' that punctuated the Christian calendar, were noted more for their excessive eating and drinking than for their piety (Axton, 1992: 141–153).

In the 16th century, too, the Grand Tour started to become popular among European elites, who wanted to learn foreign languages and generally improve their education (Adler, 1989: 9). Later, travellers focused on proto-academic forms of observation and empirical research (Adler 1989: 20–21) but by the beginning of the 19th century the Grand Tour had become less of an educational adventure and more of a holiday experience, catering primarily for North Americans and the European middle class (Wilson, 1935; Towner, 1996: 138). At the opposite end of the class divide, in the early 19th century, young members of the European working class went 'tramping' in search of work and overseas experiences, carrying out what was, in effect, the 19th century working-class equivalent of the Grand Tour (Adler, 1985: 345). By the mid-19th century, then, numerous influences had prompted young and old, elite and working class, ascetic and hedonist, to follow the well-established pilgrim, tramping and tourist routes that criss-crossed Europe and were

already leading further afield. Improved roads had opened up the countryside to 'domestic' tourists, and advances in sea transport provided easier access to domestic and overseas seaside resorts, which were now regarded as healthier destinations than the once-popular inland spas.

It was the railways, though, that brought *mass* tourism to Europe and enabled the beneficiaries of the industrial revolution to move out of the crowded cities. As Urry (1995: 119) remarked, they generated 'one of the most distinctive experiences of the modern world', compressing time and space, and bringing places once deemed far from the teeming cities within the reach of the prosperous middle class and (later) the more affluent working class. Seaside resorts topographically convenient to the industrial centres, and previously accessible only to the upper classes, became preferred destinations of the new middle class and (to the horror of many) the working-class day trippers. And the almost insatiable demand for, first, domestic and then international travel was ably met by a new breed of tour operators, most notably Thomas Cook (Pudney, 1954).

In 1837, visitors going by coach to the southern English coastal town of Brighton numbered about 50,000. By 1850, 9 years after the rail link had been established, it had the capacity to carry more than this number in a week, and in 1860 received an estimated quarter of a million visitors (Gilbert, 1975: 152). Similar success stories can be told of other resorts in the UK, also situated in areas that were, by the standards of the time, undeveloped, and (with due regard to numerous local and regional differences) the incorporation of peripheral coastal areas as holiday destinations for urban dwellers followed a broadly similar pattern in other parts of Europe and the USA (Towner, 1996: 167–216).

The processes by which tourist development occurred in these new (or revitalized) destination areas varied according to place and time, and changes in fashion, taste and national legislation (on working hours and paid holidays, for example) articulated with such local factors as topography, climate and land ownership patterns. Between the two world wars, the access of holidaymakers and day trippers to the countryside and seaside was increased by the extension of car ownership throughout the European and North American middle class and, just as Henry Ford transformed car production, so Billy Butlin's development of the holiday camp on Fordist lines in the UK transformed the British holiday industry after the Second World War (Butlin, 1982; Read, 1986). As a consequence of these and many other factors, from the 1850s to the 1950s mass domestic tourism was the norm, irrespective of the type of tourist involved, and large swathes of the European and North American seascape, roadscape and landscape were transformed.

International tourism also increased. In the second half of the 19th century, the construction of large and increasingly luxurious ocean-going liners expanded long-haul travel, often a by-product of colonial settlement, and by the end of the 1930s car ownership was facilitating travel across Europe and North America. By 1937, British tourists were travelling further afield; in that year, some 1.4 million trips were made from the UK, mainly to Belgium, France, Italy and Switzerland (Pimlott, 1976: 262–263).

If the mid-19th century was 'the age of the train', the mid-20th century was the 'age of the plane'. Although the Second World War curtailed much international travel, when it ended there was a surplus of aircraft. As austerity was reduced, cheap charter flights took package holidaymakers away from the UK (and the holiday camps which had been so popular in the late 1940s and 1950s) to Majorca, Sardinia, the Spanish Mainland and other parts of the Mediterranean, and North Americans flew *en masse* to Acapulco in Mexico (Turner and Ash, 1975: 93–106). In 1959, even before passenger jet aircraft were introduced, more passengers crossed the Atlantic by air than by sea, and the advent of passenger jets, followed by the introduction of wide-bodied jets in the late 1970s, meant that residents of the developed world could travel quickly and relatively comfortably not only across the Atlantic, but also to an ever-expanding tourist periphery (Heppenheimer, 1995: 183–195, 303–304).

Many of the patterns of international tourism that prompt so much debate in the new millennium were present in the 1800s. The 19th century success of seaside resorts in southern England, for example, was accompanied by much moral indignation. Even in the early development of Brighton, there were complaints that 'the habits of the visitors corrupted the working residents' (Gilbert, 1975: 104) and drunkenness, crime and prostitution accompanied the development of mass tourism (Gilbert, 1975: 193–196). By the 1860s, too, there were complaints that the local economy was benefiting but little from the visitors (Gilbert, 1975: 206):

> The native inhabitants look down with supreme contempt upon these economical festivities, for all the delicacies of the season, even including the beer and the 'drop of something short', are brought from London, and Brighton reaps no benefit save from the extra pint or pot, or warm 'go', that may be consumed as a supplementary treat in one of the numerous inferior houses of entertainment with which the town abounds.

Perspectives on Tourism

In a book where the main focus is on tourism in less developed countries, why open with a brief history of mass tourism in the developed world? Quite simply because, nearly 150 years after the introduction of package tours for large numbers of people in Europe, the debates it engendered and the processes it involved continue to be relevant. Just as tourism is not new, neither is mass tourism. Over the centuries changes in fashion, in individual and collective fortunes, and in the tides and affairs of nations, have led to a continuous ebb and flow of destination areas. Early 19th century fishing villages became urban seaside resorts, often developing as dormitory towns for the metropolises that initially provided them with tourists, only to see their economic fortunes decline as the search for the sun and improved communications (roads and air transport) facilitated travel to easily accessible and often cheaper destinations overseas. The link with 'development issues' becomes clearer when it is realized, for example, that in 1999 the Isle of Thanet, in south-east England, once so popular with London visitors, is in receipt of considerable funds from the UK's Single Regeneration Budget and the European Union's Social and Regional Development Funds (Thanet Regeneration Board, 1999).

The role of tourism as a 'tool' for development is very much the subject of this chapter, but this is by no means the only perspective employed by those who have studied tourism's causes and impacts. In what might be referred to as 'the view from the centre', MacCannell and Krippendorf, for example, related the 20th century rise of international tourism to changes in Western capitalist society (MacCannell, 1976, 1992; Krippendorf, 1987), opting to explain it by reference to a modern variant of alienation theory. Similarly, Urry and his colleagues linked tourism to a movement from organized to disorganized capitalism which *inter alia* shifts the focus from production to consumption, to the increased importance of a 'service class' in 'post-modern' society. In turn, such changes are reflected in the increasing prevalence of the 'post-tourist' who, unlike his or her Fordist predecessor, is a consumer of *difference*, as befits a member of the service class at play (Abercrombie and Urry, 1983; Lash and Urry, 1987; Urry, 1990, 1995).

Others have focused on the continued similarities of modern tourism to pilgrimage. Turner and Turner (1978: 20) coined the memorable statement that 'a tourist is half a pilgrim, if a pilgrim is half a tourist' and Graburn (1978) also referred to tourism as 'a sacred journey', later emphasizing the activities and expressions of sentiments to be found at tourism destinations (Graburn, 1983). Structural and other similarities have been noted by numerous others, including Ousby (1990: 7–8) and Smith (1992), and Coleman and Elsner (1995: 220) reflected that while much of modern tourism may be no more than a distant analogy of sacred travel, pilgrimage has indeed been 'remarkably persistent in adapting to and even appropriating the innovations of secular modernity'. It is perhaps worth noting that just as religious myths, while not literally 'true', help to situate believers in a coherent symbolic universe, so myths associated with tourist destination areas may enable tourists (and sometimes even local residents) to develop a sense of place and frame their

perceptions of the ongoing tourist experience (Selwyn, 1996: 3).

In a sense, those who link tourism to pilgrimage also put forward a view from the centre. They focus on 'escape' to a local or distant shrine, in the hope of discovering a degree of *communitas* (Turner and Turner, 1978: 250). In general, the longer and more difficult the journey, and the more different the destination, the more kudos accrues to the traveller. Once again, the incorporation of destinations in LDCs serves the interests of the Western tourist.

Somewhat different perspectives are employed by geographers analysing the impact of tourism on destination regions. Some have concentrated on changes in the urban landscape and architecture, linking them to increased numbers of tourists and developments in the transport infrastructure, but other geographers have examined the extent to which destination areas have developed spontaneously, rather than through planning, and the degree to which they have relied on the initiative of a single developer (Pearce, 1989: 16–24, 57–87). In one of the most quoted papers in tourism studies, Butler (1980) has suggested that destination areas can be considered as 'products' that evolve through fairly typical developmental stages, with corresponding changes in the extent of local and foreign ownership of facilities, in types of tourists, and in attitudes of the 'host' population. Butler's work, which can be linked to Doxey's development of an 'index of irritation' (Doxey, 1971), has been subjected to considerable scrutiny (Cooper, 1994; Baum, 1998) and is perhaps best regarded as an 'ideal type' of tourism development, against which the empirical evolution of tourist destination areas might be assessed (Harrison, 1995).

Social geography complements the interests of sociologists and anthropologists who analyse the social structures and role performances in destination areas associated with tourism, the interaction of residents with tourists, and conflicts that emerge and ways in which they are resolved. In this respect, Cohen's output is consistently impressive (e.g. 1971, 1985, 1993a, 1996) but other social scientists have also made important contributions (Smith, 1978, 1989; de Kadt, 1979; Ryan, 1991; Boissevain, 1996; Nash, 1996; Selwyn, 1996). By contrast, some social scientists, from a range of disciplines, including geography, concentrate more on the processes whereby place and landscape, nation and community, are collectively and inter-subjectively perceived from within what is largely a Western capitalist orientation (Urry, 1990, 1995; Dann, 1996; Hutnyk, 1996), a perspective that returns us to the complex relationship and interplay of modernity or post-modernity with travel, tourism and cultural identity in a world increasingly characterized by mobility, not only of people, but also of objects. As Rojek and Urry (1997: 10) pointedly remind us, '"cultures" travel too'.

Development and LDCs

It is suggested, then, that the *processes* by which tourism crosses international boundaries are much the same as those which, in the 19th century, brought less developed regions in developed societies closer to the urban metropolises which were the source of most 'domestic' tourists. Now, as then, improvements in standards of living and communications prompt a mass but largely temporary and seasonal movement to areas promoted by entrepreneurs, both in and outside the destination regions, who offer appropriate and profitable accommodation and attractions to increasing numbers of visitors. Now, as then, local residents are encouraged to see these visitors as the means by which their own lives can be improved. In short, now as then, tourism is considered a tool for 'development'.

But 'development' is a highly contested concept and since the Second World War debates over what it is, and how it is achieved, have gone through a number of phases. These have been discussed in detail elsewhere (Harrison, 1988, 1992: 8–11, 1994) and in this context it is necessary only to outline the main themes. Up to the 1980s there were two broadly competing social scientific perspectives on how development was to occur in 'the third world'. Modernization theorists favoured a path based largely on Western capitalism, advocating close links with 'devel-

oped' societies and the import, if necessary, of capital, skills, ideas and institutions which would allow 'developing' societies to overcome the constraints of tradition and replicate patterns of economic and social change that had so benefited the West.

Even while modernization theory was being articulated, however, opposition was being expressed from a very different ideological standpoint (Harrison, 1988: 70–99). Experience in post-colonial Latin America and elsewhere suggested to neo-Marxist critics that, far from encouraging 'development', close relations with Western capitalism actively 'under developed' societies with a colonial past, increased their economic backwardness, and led to a social and cultural impoverishment that was wrongly attributed to their inability to adopt capitalist methods of production. Such an argument, much welcomed by governments in newly 'independent' nations, pointed the finger of blame at Western capitalism and stipulated economic policies of de-linking from Western colonial and post-colonial institutions.

During the 1970s and 1980s, proponents of modernization theory and underdevelopment theory acrimoniously debated the benefits or otherwise of global capitalism. However, these economically orientated approaches to development were increasingly challenged from a set of perspectives that focused less on economic growth *per se* and more on the ramifications it had for the natural environment. In effect, 'environmentalism' was joining the fray as a separate but vital strand in the development debate.

In the West, concern for the natural environment dates back at least to the second half of the 19th century, when national institutions were created to conserve historic buildings and landscapes considered to be under threat (Yale, 1991: 157–192). At about the same time, colonialists once responsible for the destruction of vast numbers of wild animals were belatedly turning to wildlife conservation (Reilly and Reilly, 1979; Yale, 1991: 178–179; Adams, 1995: 92). As Adams notes (1995: 90–92), while influences are complex and varied, environmentalism can also be traced to the development of the science of ecology, which prompted increased biological research (for example, the *Man and Biosphere* programme set up by UNESCO in 1968) and led, through the 1972 United Nations (UN) Conference on the Human Environment in Stockholm, to the UN Environmental Programme (UNEP). Other international initiatives followed, including the World Conservation Strategy of 1980, set up by the International Union for the Conservation of Nature, UNEP and the World Wildlife Fund (now World Wide Fund for Nature) and, perhaps most famously, the World Commission on Environment and Development, The Brundtland Commission, which defined 'sustainable development' as 'development that meets the needs of the present without compromising the ability of future generations to meet their own needs' (1987: 43).

Further impetus to the international conservation movement was provided at the 1992 UN Conference on Environment and Development at Rio de Janeiro. One outcome of the conference was an agenda for action ('Agenda 21'), which urged governments, in particular, but also other sectors of society, to promote environmentally sustainable development (Mowforth and Munt, 1998: 23, 113–115).

By the end of the 1990s, then, the rise of environmentalism had prompted a series of different questions. Whereas in modernization theory, development was seen primarily in terms of economic growth (albeit aided by appropriate and complementary social structures and cultural imperatives), and by underdevelopment theory as something akin to a state of economic and national independence, environmentalists focused on development that was *sustainable*. As Adams put it, 'Technocentric colonial science' and '1970s environmentalism' contributed to a discourse on sustainable development which has been joined, somewhat uneasily, by a variety of social movements and ideologies. These include non-Western opponents of capitalism, the marginalized and dehumanized in Western society, and educated groups of young 'post materialists' who 'focus on the desirability of non-hierarchical and decentralized structures of decision-making, and reject Fordist industrialization and consumerism' (Adams, 1995: 92, 95).

Throughout the post-war period, then, sev-eral perspectives on the nature of development competed for the attention of academics and practitioners alike. However, by the mid-1980s, the lines between bourgeois and neo-Marxist approaches were becoming blurred. Once the straitjackets of fixed ideological positions were loosened, it was evident that there was at least a 'limited commensurability' between the two major approaches (Harrison, 1988: 167–175). Experience away from university lecture halls, especially in LDCs, increasingly indicated that neither form of analysis was entirely satisfactory. Despite modernization theory, empirical evidence clearly indicated that the structural relations of LDCs with the West were crucially significant to their economic development, but it was also clear that underdevelopment theory was wrong in suggesting that class, ethnic, cultural and political configurations within LDCs were ultimately dependent on external factors.

While signs of dissatisfaction with neo-Marxist approaches to LDCs were already evident in the mid-1980s (Booth, 1985, 1987; Kitching, 1985), the fall of the Berlin Wall at the end of 1989 dealt a body blow from which Marxist scholarship in general has yet to recover. Arguably, it was this event, rather than any attack from post-modernism, that signalled the end of 'the Grand Narrative'. Scholarly responses varied, but notably featured the advocacy of smaller-scale empirical studies, a closer examination of the links between agency, structure and social action (Booth, 1994), as well as re-analysis of development discourses and the role of new social movements, along with closer attention to individual biographies and voices (Crush, 1995).

Whether this recent reluctance to engage in grand theorizing and comprehensive world solutions is to be deplored or applauded depends on one's perspective. However, while the apparently exclusive 'paradigms' of modernization theory, underdevelopment theory and environmentalism no longer dominate, their core concerns have been incorporated into the wider, more loose-knit conceptual framework of globalization theory. This has been much discussed in recent years, but in essence is an overarching perspective that facilitates description and analyses of economic, cultural, political and social processes whereby local and national institutions and actors are differentially incorporated into the wider global environment, with which they interact and against which frequently react (Albrow and King, 1990; King, 1991; Robertson, 1992; Pieterse, 1994; Waters, 1995; Scott, 1997; Scholte, 2000). Put more pithily, globalization is nothing less than the continuous integration, disintegration and reintegration of the modern world.

The focus on globalization rather than modernization or underdevelopment has undoubtedly led to a less coherent body of knowledge about the nature and processes of development. However, it has also meant that social processes linking communities, societies and nations continue to be legitimate areas of research, but without the requirement that those who study them become fully paid-up members of any one ideological camp.

Development Theory and Tourism

Inevitably, the study of international tourism was caught up in debates over the nature of development. As has been indicated elsewhere, 'tourism can be seen as a form of modernization, transferring capital, technology, expertise and "modern" values from the West to LDCs' (Harrison, 1992: 10), and supporters and critics of tourism have long debated the advantages and disadvantages of international tourism from within a framework derived (often implicitly) from modernization theory. When MacCannell (1976) referred to the tourist as 'modern man' and Graburn (1984) and Cohen (1993b) discussed tourism's role in the development of arts and crafts in tourist-receiving societies, for example, they did so in terms perfectly compatible with modernization theory. This applies equally to those analysing the complex interplay of tourism with tradition (Nunez, 1963; Greenwood, 1972), the role of tourism in bringing about change (Michaud, 1993, 1997), the activities of indigenous and foreign entrepreneurs (Ioannides, 1992), or the influence of hotels on social life in LDCs (Wood, 1984). Recent studies indicate that the experience of modernity continues to be important in tourism, transforming people

'into touristic subjects,' thus operating as a new motivating force in Western tourism (Wang, 2000: 215) or by providing the central plank in both the policy of the modernizing state and in the negotiated and adaptive response of those it seeks to dominate (Oakes, 1998: 229).

Those who have utilized underdevelopment theory in their analyses (e.g. Perez, 1975; Geshekter, 1978; Nash, 1978; Hoivik and Heiberg, 1980; Britton, 1982; Erisman, 1983; Oglethorpe, 1984) tended to be more critical of tourism, and suggested it is a mixed blessing which, like other economic sectors, is best run (or at least closely controlled) by the state, which could develop 'social tourism' for the benefit of its nationals and attract international tourists from similarly orientated socialist societies. Such a policy operated throughout the Eastern bloc until the 1960s, when the demand for 'hard' currency came to outweigh the risks of cultural pollution from Western tourists (Hall, 1991: 80–81). More generally, too, academic studies of tourism, even if not explicitly taking a neo-Marxist approach, tended to betray a degree of suspicion about the impacts of tourism development, especially in societies or communities with a recent history of colonialism.

The influence of environmentalist concerns in tourism studies is more recent and perhaps more diffused. As Mowforth and Munt (1998: 84) indicated, in tourism

> the term 'sustainability' can be and has been hijacked by many to give moral rectitude and 'green' credentials to tourist activities. And it is by no means just the tour operator and other profit-making companies standing to gain from the activity who have used the term for their own ends. Conservationists, government officials, politicians, local community organizations and tourists themselves have all misused and/or abused the term.

Arguably, the same might be said of some academic treatments of the issue, and there is little doubt that the notion of sustainable development is 'intensely synthetic' and adaptive (Adams, 1990: 66). This is hardly surprising, given its origin in such contentious topics as 'development' and 'sustainability'. Nevertheless, the importation of 'sustainable development' from the environmentalist discourse led to a focus on different 'development' criteria and to dozens of publications on the theory and practice of sustainable tourism, ecotourism (perhaps best seen as a sub-sector of sustainable tourism) and numerous types of alternative tourism. Publications often cross several categories, but range from texts that are primarily academic (Smith and Eadington, 1992; Cater and Lowman, 1994; Briguglio *et al.*, 1996a,b; Price, 1996; Wahab and Pigram, 1997; Mowforth and Munt, 1998; Weaver, 1998; Fennell, 1999; Honey, 1999), through exhortation by individuals and pressure groups critical of mass tourism (Eber, 1992; Croall, 1995; McLaren, 1998) to those dispensing practical advice to the tourism industry about how sustainable tourism should be planned, implemented and managed, often on the grounds that such measures not only benefit the environment, but also attract more tourists and cut costs (Lindberg and Hawkins, 1993; Linderg *et al.*, 1998; Middleton, 1998). The tourism industry itself has joined in the rush to go 'green', setting up such joint initiatives as the International Hotel Environment Initiative (IHEI) (1993) and Green Globe, along with many others (Neale, 1998: 27–71; WTO, 1995: 1–2), while tour operators and travel writers have not been slow to publicize holidays defined by them, at least, as environmentally friendly (Wood and House, 1991; Elkington and Hailes, 1992).

In fact, the notion of 'sustainable tourism' is at best ambiguous and more often than not virtually useless. There is little agreement about what it is, let alone how it can be operationalized, and it is quite clear that the tourism *industry* can be sustained for long periods, albeit at the cost of specific destination areas, environments and communities (Harrison, 1996: 73; Butler, 1999). And when discussing the extent to which tourism can sustain communities or their cultures, it is frequently forgotten that they are, by their very nature, adaptive. As has been indicated elsewhere (Harrison, 1996: 79):

> Culture is highly flexible and, even where tradition may be regarded as an important guide to current behaviour, specific traditions change and are replaced by others, to which people become equally committed; the king is dead: long live the king.

In addition, benefits from 'sustainable' tourism are likely to be limited if obtained by reducing alternative sources of income, employment and development in any specific community. Clearly, tourism is one of many factors involved in the development process and should be considered in the wider environmental, social and economic context. Nevertheless, despite problems in utilizing the notion of sustainability in tourism studies, it performs a valuable role in sensitizing scholars and all involved in tourism to a range of issues that might hitherto have been neglected.

Finally, tourism is both a feature and a cause of globalization. As Waters (1995: 151–156) suggests, once Western notions of leisure and travel became generally established, the way was open for tourism itself to be a global influence. Road, sea, rail and air networks may not have been initiated to take tourists from one place to another, but over the centuries they have certainly been improved to facilitate tourist travel. And in the very act of leaving home, tourists became agents of social change, frequently transmitting their languages, tastes and customs to their 'hosts' and, at least sometimes, themselves adopting habits and customs first encountered away from home. Waters (1995: 155) may be less correct, though, in suggesting that globalized tourism reflects tourist perceptions of the world 'as a single place, without internal geographical boundaries'. They may be sensitized to material and cultural difference, and inward and outward acculturation may indeed occur, but most tourists do not travel great distances, either across space or across cultures. When travelling to LDCs, especially, their experience of foreign culture may well be accompanied by an increased appreciation of life at home.

Tourism and Less Developed Countries: the Backdrop

It was suggested earlier that international tourism has been a global phenomenon for centuries, but that packaging of tourism for mass consumption dates back to the mid-19th century, when a specific service sector devoted to the mass consumption of travel emerged, roughly parallel to the development of mass production in the industrial sector. The chapters in this book together represent an attempt to describe the current significance of tourism to many of the world's LDCs, and some of the substantive issues they raise are discussed in the Afterword. In the remainder of this chapter, however, the overall patterns of tourist movement are highlighted, along with key general features of the relationship of international tourism to LDCs, and an attempt is made to show how processes of tourism development are linked to wider aspects of economic and social change in the global system.

Importantly, what constitutes a 'less developed' (or 'developing' or 'underdeveloped') country remains a matter of continued debate, as is the importance of less developed regions within developed societies. In 1992, it was suggested (perhaps somewhat disingenuously) that 'irrespective of the criteria used, the list will be much the same and most countries of the world will be on it' (Harrison, 1992: 1), but it has to be recognized that the category 'less developed' remains very much a residual one. A criterion commonly used is to regard as 'developing' or 'less developed' all countries listed by the World Bank as not falling into the 'high income' category (World Bank, 1997). Others prefer to take a more rounded view of 'development' and focus on countries considered by the United Nations Development Programme (UNDP) to have either a 'medium' or 'low' ranking in the Human Development Index (HDI) (UNDP, 1999: 134–137).

At the time of writing, the World Tourism Organization (WTO) is revising its classifications. However, until recently, it distinguished between 'developing' societies (roughly along the lines of the World Bank classification) and economies 'in transition' (WTO, 1997a: 139–141, 1999a: 4–5), the countries of the former Soviet bloc, a division apparently based on their reluctance (despite not enjoying 'high income' status) to be associated with the 'Third World.' This position is held despite increasing evidence to the contrary. Indeed, it has been estimated that in eastern Europe in 1996 the average monthly wage was

US$40.00 and that rural life, in particular, was characterized by an alarming loss of human resources, malnutrition and abject poverty (Anon., 2000: 29). The WTO also diverges from the World Bank by treating 20 'high income' countries as 'developing' (including Bermuda, Greenland, Guam, Hong Kong, Kuwait, Saudi Arabia, Singapore and the US Virgin Islands).

There can be no denying the limitations of a category that includes Singapore, a city state with a per capita income the purchasing equivalent of US$22,770, (South) Cyprus, where more than 80% of households have a car, 7% have more than three cars, and one in four people own a mobile phone (Karsera, 2000: 3), Mozambique and Zaire, with US$810 and US$490, respectively, and Poland, with the equivalent of US$5,400 (World Bank, 1997: 6–9, 18). However, faced with the choice of using the WTO classifications or retabulating all the tourism statistics of some 150 countries, the value of the WTO listing is substantially enhanced, and the isolation and analysis of trends need not be greatly affected by individual anomalies, which are always likely to be present in some form. For better or for worse, unless otherwise indicated, in this chapter 'LDCs' will be taken to indicate those classed by the WTO as 'developing' or as economies 'in transition.'

Tourism statistics constitute a minefield not to be entered lightly, and it is also necessary to be circumspect in the use of other tourism data. Short flights across the Mediterranean from southern Europe to North Africa are examples of inter-regional travel, while a journey from north-west to eastern Europe may take considerably longer but remains within the region. Similarly, a US citizen resident in New York taking a holiday in Hawaii is a domestic tourist. Even within the WTO categories, which are essentially geographical, there is considerable divergence. 'The Americas', for instance, includes the islands of the Caribbean as well as many mainland Latin American territories generally considered less developed (WTO, 1998a: 15), and 'Europe' includes not only the 'transition economies' of central and eastern Europe (WTO, 1999b: 101) but also Turkey, Israel and Cyprus (WTO, 1999b: 101).

Who Goes Where? Patterns of Tourist Movement

Statistical analyses of tourist movements do not necessarily make for thrilling reading, but they do provide a necessary backdrop for under-standing the impact of tourism. Throughout the 1990s, international tourism continued to grow, and whereas in 1990 international arrivals numbered 458 million, and brought in US$269 billion (WTO, 1999a: 2), by 1999 there were an estimated 663 million arrivals and receipts of US$453 billion (WTO, 2000a:1).

The first travel patterns to note are that (as in the past) most tourists go from developed societies to developed societies, and that prominent destination areas also tend to pro-vide tourists for other countries, as indicated in Table 1.1. Indeed, of the top ten destination areas in 1997, seven were also among the top ten tourist spenders, with China the sole rep-resentative of LDCs in both elite groups. Indeed, over the period 1989–1997, there has been a remarkable consistency in these league tables. No fewer than 18 of the top 20 desti-nation areas in 1989 were also there in 1997, as were 16 of the top 20 spenders. In 1997, however, such newly important spenders as China, Mexico, Poland and the Russian Federation appeared in the table for the first time.

Table 1.1. Top tourism destinations and spenders (1997).

	Top destination areas			Top tourism spenders		
	Rank			Rank		
Country	1997	(1989)	Share (%)	1997	(1989)	Share (%)
France	1	(1)	11.2	6	(5)	4.4
Spain	2	(3)	7.6	21	(15)	1.2
USA	3	(2)	7.5	1	(1)	13.6
Italy	4	(4)	5.6	5	(7)	4.4
UK	5	(6)	4.1	4	(4)	7.3
China	6	(11)	3.8	10	(39)	2.7
Mexico	7	(17)	3.1	22	(13)	1.0
Poland	8	(29)	3.0	14	(48)	1.8
Canada	9	(7)	3.0	7	(6)	3.0
Austria	10	(5)	2.8	8	(9)	2.9
Germany	11	(8)	2.6	2	(2)	12.2
Czech Republic	12	(14)	2.6	31	–	0.6
Russian Federation	13	(15)[a]	2.5	11	–	2.7
Hungary	14	(9)	2.3	–	(28)	
Portugal	15	(16)	1.9	34	(33)	0.6
Greece	16	(13)	1.8	–	(27)	–
Switzerland	17	(10)	1.8	13	(10)	1.8
China (Hong Kong)	18	(18)	1.5	–	–	
Turkey	19	(24)	1.5	39	(38)	0.5
Thailand	20	(20)	1.2	37	(30)	0.5
Netherlands	22	(25)	1.0	9	(8)	2.7
Belgium	23		1.0	12	(12)	2.2
Japan	32	(32)	0.7	3	(3)	8.7
Brazil	39	(45)	0.5	15	(29)	1.7
Sweden				16	(11)	1.7
Taiwan				17	–	1.7
Korean Republic				18	(18)	1.7
Australia				19	(14)	1.6
Norway				20	(17)	1.2
Total of top 20			71.8			80.0

[a]USSR.
Sources: WTO (1990: 130–132; 1999a: 14, 16).

Secondly, most tourist travel is intra-regional. In 1996, for instance, most visitors to European destinations were from other parts of Europe, North Americans tended to visit other parts of North America, and Japanese went to other parts of East Asia (WTO, 1997c: 18, 27, 32–33). Only in South Asia did arrivals from outside the region (including 45% from Europe) exceed the 25% from within the area (WTO, 1999b: 21, 67, 92, 118, 128). Similar conclusions are reached by Pearce (1995: 34), who noted the importance in 1990 of visitors from the USA to the Americas and to Europe, and the prevalence of intra-regional tourism travel generally.

Thirdly, during the 1990s, tourism to LDCs was both significant and increasing. In 1989, LDCs accounted for 85.3 million international arrivals (21% of all tourist trips) and received more than US$54 billion (26%) from all receipts, excluding the cost of travel to destinations (WTO, 1990: 2, 97 and 109). By 1997, the equivalent percentages were 30.5% and 30% (WTO, 1999b: 9), and these figures would be considerably higher if account were also taken of central and eastern European economies 'in transition,' several of which since 1989 have re-orientated their tourism to appeal to tourists from western and northern Europe. In 1997, they accounted for a further 13% of arrivals and nearly 6% of international receipts (WTO, 1999b: 2, 6, 101). Indeed, as indicated in Table 1.1, of the nine LDCs or economies 'in transition' in the top 20 destination areas, six (China, Mexico, Poland, the Czech Republic, the Russian Federation and Turkey) have increased their position in the table, two (Hong Kong and Thailand) have retained their ranking, and only Hungary has lowered its position.

The increased importance of LDCs is also reflected in the declining market share of Europe and the Americas, as indicated in Table 1.2. Although Europe continues to take nearly 60% of all tourist arrivals, and with the Americas accounts for nearly 80% of all arrivals, during the 1990s these two WTO regions grew relatively slowly, whereas Africa, East Asia/Pacific, the Middle East and South Asia increased their share of the market. East Asia, especially, continued to grow in importance, both as a source of tourists and as a tourism destination area, and while the 'Asian crisis', which first appeared in Thailand in 1997, led to an even greater dependence on tourism in the region, current evidence suggests that the region's major economies are experiencing a tourism revival (WTO, 2000a).

The fourth point of note, which is of far more than statistical significance, is that most tourists to LDCs are from developed countries. Putting it differently, tourism to LDCs involves people from relatively wealthy countries visiting people in relatively poor countries. Numerous statistics can be presented to demonstrate this, but it clearly has a common-sense basis: in so far as LDCs are *defined* as having relatively low per capita incomes, it is only to be expected that those who take holidays in them are likely to have a higher income. Taking holidays and receiving tourists thus involves two quite different kinds of relationships: the *structural* relationship of two countries, which might have been preceded by a history of colonialism, and *personal* relationships between 'host' and 'guest,' which may themselves have been conditioned by this historical background. Equally clearly, as countries become more 'developed' – or, at least, richer – increasing numbers of their nationals can afford to travel overseas. China is a case in point.

Table 1.2. International tourism trends (1989–1998).

Region	Arrivals 1989		Arrivals 1998		Increase 1989–1998		Average annual growth rate (%)		
	Million	Share (%)	Million	Share (%)	Million	(%)	1989–1993	1994–1998	1989–1998
Africa	13.8	3.2	24.9	4.0	11.1	80.4	7.6	6.9	6.8
Americas	87.0	20.4	120.2	19.2	33.2	38.2	4.5	3.1	3.7
East Asia/Pacific	47.8	11.2	86.9	13.9	39.1	81.8	10.5	3.1	6.9
Europe	266.3	62.4	372.5	59.6	106.2	39.9	3.9	3.0	3.8
Middle East	8.6	2.0	15.6	2.5	7.0	81.4	7.4	5.1	6.9
South Asia	3.0	0.7	5.1	0.8	2.1	70.0	3.7	7.0	5.9
World total	426.5	100.0	625.2	100.0	198.8	46.6	5.0	3.2	4.3

Source: WTO (1999a: 8–11).

Fifthly, like tourism destinations generally, many LDCs continue to rely heavily on a supply of tourists from relatively few countries of origin. At the end of the 1980s, it was clear that some LDCs had extremely high concentration ratios (that is, the percentage of tourists from the three most important source countries), with the Bahamas, Jamaica and Mexico, for example, in excess of 90% (Harrison, 1992: 12). Pearce came to similar conclusions. Basing his figures on tourist arrivals in 1990 at 127 destinations, he concluded no fewer than 59, nearly all LDCs, had concentration ratios of 60% or more, and 11, mainly in the Caribbean, had a concentration ratio of more than 90% (Pearce, 1995: 38). Arguably, the more dependent a destination area on one or two sources of tourists, the more brittle its tourism industry is likely to be. Mexico, for example, with 94% of its tourists coming from the USA, is likely to be more vulnerable to a recession or bad publicity in the USA, for example, than is Thailand, where arrivals from the USA represent only 5% of the market share, and whose sources for tourists are more diverse (WTO, 1999c: 161 and 228).

Sixthly, dependence on tourism is generally greater in islands and small states which have few natural resources other than those of the sun, sea and sand variety. Indeed, unless they also have extensive mineral deposits, the same features that make their climates attractive to tourists are likely to prevent them diversifying their economies. It is thus no surprise that the 25 countries where international tourism makes the greatest percentage contribution to gross national produce are all island states, ranging (in 1995) from 83% in the Maldives to 21% in Cyprus (WTO, 1998b: 71). By the same token, their lack of productive capacity means their tourist income multipliers are likely to be low (Harrison, 1992: 16). Money leaves the economy to purchase foodstuffs, drinks and other products for the tourists, although – as the WTO points out – this does not prevent such small economies from outperforming many better endowed territories (1998b: 70). How far this reliance on specific tourism markets for the economic benefits of tourism leads to cultural or political dependency is a much discussed but little researched question, which is discussed later in this chapter.

A Regional Review

At the end of the 1990s, it remained the case that tourists were spread unequally among LDCs. Extremely poor countries, lacking an adequate infrastructure and modern communications, do not attract tourists in any number and (however unjustified the reputation) those thought unable to protect tourists from illness, accidents, or crime and political violence are unlikely to experience a tourist boom (Harrison, 2000). However, throughout the WTO regions, some LDCs can be considered 'growth poles,' in that they have demonstrated considerable success in attracting tourists.

In Europe, only Turkey, Cyprus, Malta and Israel and the Occupied Territories might be regarded as LDCs, but tourism is important in all of them. By 1997, Turkey was one of the most important tourism-receiving countries in the world and was receiving more than 7 million holidaymakers. Malta and (Southern) Cyprus were more mature destination areas, and arrivals tended to be stable at about 1.2 million and 2.1 million, respectively, while Israel, where statistics are complicated by how pilgrims and religiously orientated tourists are categorized, seems also to attract about 1.5 million non-business visitors a year (WTO, 1999d). There are also several economies 'in transition', and Hungary, Poland, the Czech Republic, Croatia, the Russian Federation, Romania and Bulgaria all record high numbers of tourists. Only the first four attract substantial numbers of high-spending tourists from western Europe, and thus (with the Russian Federation) figure in the world's top 40 tourism earners (WTO, 1999a: 15, 1999c). According to the WTO, such growth is likely to continue, and it estimates that by 2020 one in three visitors to Europe will be going to central or eastern Europe (WTO, 2000b: 5).

In East Asia/Pacific in 1998, China, Hong Kong, Thailand, Singapore, Malaysia, Indonesia, the Korean Republic, Australia, Japan and Macau attracted some 71 billion visitors (WTO, 1999e: 27). All were affected by the 'Asian Crisis' but, except for troubled Indonesia, appear to be on the road to recovery (WTO, 2000a: 1–2); this owes much to the revival in the Japanese economy, which – as Michael Hall suggests in Chapter 8 – is crucial to tourism in the region. China, also discussed by Alan Lew in Chapter 7, dominates the East Asia/Pacific category and was the fastest growing destination in north-east Asia over the decade to 1998. As Lew has indicated elsewhere, it may indeed be the 'growth engine' for Asian tourism, and its potential impact on tourism throughout the region is enormous (Lew, 2000: 282). The other major players are best regarded as relatively mature destination areas. By contrast, up-and-coming destination areas are found mostly in South-east Asia and include Cambodia, Laos and Vietnam (WTO, 1999e: 18, 21).

Elsewhere in East Asia/Pacific, Australia and New Zealand dominate the sub-region of Oceania, attracting nearly 6 million tourists annually (WTO, 1999d: 215) but tourism (while quite insignificant in world terms) is vital to many Pacific islands, where the lion's share of these scraps, so to speak, is taken by Fiji (Melanesia), Guam and the North Marianas (Micronesia) and French Polynesia (Polynesia) (WTO, 1997c: 87). As Kelly Bricker indicates in Chapter 16, even in relatively well established destination areas such as the Fiji Islands, tourism may not have reached the hinterlands, and its subsequent expansion might meet stiff competition from such apparently more lucrative if more problematic industries as commercial logging. And as King demonstrates in Chapter 12, the development of tourist resorts in island societies and less developed countries generally may have ramifications for the relationship of such enclaves to the wider society.

As indicated in Table 1.2, in 1998 South Asia received relatively few visitors, but the importance of tourism to countries in the region varies considerably. Over the past decade, the Maldives, Iran, Nepal and Burma (despite concerted overseas opposition to its brutal regime) have increased their performance, while India and Pakistan, for instance, have made little advance in numbers (WTO, 1997c: 123). Some of the reasons for India's sluggish performance in attracting international tourists are discussed by Shalini Singh in Chapter 9. However, as Table 1.3 indicates, India continues to receive half the arrivals to the region, and Iran, as yet largely undeveloped but with immense tourism potential, is now in second place. Clearly, though, tourism is of greatest importance to the Maldives, which (despite possibly flawed statistics) clearly depends massively on the industry, especially on European visitors, for its prosperity. Indeed, South Asia generally is unusual in the role played by long-haul tourism. In 1996, no less than 45% of all arrivals to the region in 1996 were from Europe, a trend attributed by the WTO to the reduced cost (in real terms) of air travel, the importance of business visitors, and visits from friends and relatives who now live elsewhere (WTO, 1997c: 121).

In the Americas, as indicated earlier, Mexico is a major tourist-receiving country, second only to the USA and ahead of Canada, with most of its arrivals coming from the USA. Indeed, as indicated in Table 1.4, more than 70% of all international tourist trips to the Americas are to these three countries. Among the remainder, island or part-island states are well represented (Puerto Rico, the Dominican Republic, the Bahamas, Jamaica, Cuba and Aruba) and, as David Weaver indicates in Chapter 11, many Caribbean islands are highly dependent on forms of tourism that, in the long term, are likely to be unsustainable. The performance of Cuba is especially noteworthy. Since the end of its reliance on the former Soviet Union, it has made strenuous efforts to diversify its economy. Despite the US embargo, tourist arrivals doubled from 1993 to 1997 (WTO, 1999c: 303) and, as Derek Hall suggests in Chapter 6, once the US government allows its citizens free access to Cuba, further dramatic increases might be expected in tourist arrivals to that country. Indeed, at the time of writing, and for good or ill, the indicators suggest that Cuba is on track to reclaiming its role as a major Caribbean holiday destination for north Americans (Schwartz, 1997).

The position of Costa Rica in the league table is also interesting, given its emphasis on nature-based tourism and, in particular, on ecotourism. As Lumsdon and Swift (1998: 169) pointed out, now that Costa Rica has entered the stage of mass tourism, it remains to be seen how far it can retain a balance between conservation and increased tourist arrivals. In this respect, Costa Rica provides a specific study of a general problem.

Africa and the Middle East, which are comprised almost entirely of LDCs, are relatively

Table 1.3. Selected South Asia destinations (1996) by total arrivals, tourism receipts and sources of tourists.

Country	Total arrivals (000)	Rank	Share (%)	Source of tourists (%)				Receipts (US$ million)	Receipts per capita (US$)	Receipts per arrival (US$)
				Europe	South Asia	EAP	Americas			
India	2288	1	50.8	39.2	23.8	14.6	14.1	3027	2.9	1297
Iran	465	2	10.3	46.0	36.9	3.0	0.5	165	2.4	354
Nepal	404	3	9.0	35.2	35.5	20.1	8.4	130	5.3	322
Pakistan	369	4	8.2	41.5	23.8	11.9	14.6	146	0.9	302
Maldives	339	5	7.5	74.6	5.9	15.6	1.2	265[a]	777.8[a]	667
Sri Lanka	302	6	6.7	57.0	19.9	16.9	4.3	168	12.3	558
Bangladesh	166	7	3.7	30.7	39.8	18.1	8.4	32	0.2	147
Burma (Myanmar)	165	8	3.7	29.7	1.2	57.0	8.1	90	0.8	345
Bhutan	5	9	0.1	46.2	–	30.8	21.2	5	3.0	1000
Afghanistan	4	10	0.1	N/A	N/A	N/A	N/A	1	–	250
Total (1996)	4507		100.0					4029	846	

[a]With an estimated population of some 260,000, these figures appear to be inaccurate.
Sources: WTO (1997c: 117–125, 1999d).

Table 1.4. Top 20 tourism destinations in the Americas: international tourist arrivals (excluding same-day visitors) (1997).

Country	Rank 1985	Rank 1990	Rank 1997	Arrivals (000)	Change 1997/1996 (%)	Total 1997 (%)
United States	1	1	1	48,409	4.1	40.6
Mexico	3	2	2	19,351	−9.6	16.2
Canada	2	3	3	17,610	1.6	14.8
Argentina	6	4	4	4,540	5.9	3.8
Puerto Rico	5	5	5	3,332	8.7	2.8
Brazil	4	9	6	2,995	12.3	2.5
Uruguay	8	8	7	2,316	7.6	1.9
Dominican Republic	10	7	8	2,211	14.8	1.9
Chile	12	11	9	1,683	16.8	1.4
Bahamas	7	6	10	1,592	−2.5	1.3
Colombia	9	12	11	1,193	−4.8	1.0
Jamaica	11	10	12	1,192	2.6	1.0
Cuba	24	23	13	1,152	15.3	1.0
Costa Rica	21	17	14	811	3.8	0.7
Venezuela	19	14	15	796	4.9	0.7
Guadeloupe	22	22	16	660	5.6	0.6
Aruba	26	19	17	650	1.4	0.5
Peru	18	24	18	635	8.7	0.5
Guatemala	23	15	19	576	10.8	0.5
Ecuador	24	21	20	525	6.3	0.4
Total 1–20				112,239	1.8	94.1
Total Americas				119,280	2.2	100.0

Source: WTO (1998a: 29).

small players on the stage of international tourism, together taking less than 7% of all international arrivals. As indicated in Table 1.2, in 1998 Africa attracted some 25 million tourists, some 4% of all international arrivals. In general, the continent has a poor international image (Harrison, 2000) and, as Peter Dieke notes in Chapter 4, it urgently requires trained indigenous personnel at all levels in the tourism industry. With some exceptions, Africa does not appeal to mass tourists. Indeed, at the end of the 1980s, holidaymakers to the continent were outnumbered by other visitors (Harrison, 1992: 7) and even at the end of the 1990s they were unlikely to account for much more than half all tourist trips.

The top 20 African destinations are indicated in Table 1.5. Also provided – where figures are available – is a breakdown of arrivals by purpose of visit. Six countries (South Africa, Morocco, Zimbabwe, Kenya, Botswana and Tunisia) account for nearly 70% of all arrivals and, except for Botswana, are also the most popular holiday destinations. Significantly, the leading destination areas are nearly all classified by the UNDP as having a medium HDI (UNDP,

1999: 134–137). In Africa, as elsewhere, tourists visit the haves rather than the have-nots.

Since the overthrow of apartheid, the Republic of South Africa has become a major player in the continent's tourism industry and attracts nearly a quarter of all international arrivals to the continent. However, the extent to which the poor benefit from tourist arrivals is questionable. As Brennan and Allen argue, in their case study in Chapter 14, while postapartheid governments have been keen to develop community-based ecotourism, mountains must yet be climbed before local communities are to be able to set the tourism agenda for themselves.

Further north, Morocco and Tunisia are mature destinations that specialize in attracting mass (and relatively low-spending) tourists, and more than 80% of visitors to both countries come from Europe (WTO, 1999c: 469, 504). Like Kenya to the east, they are part of the European periphery. So, too, are the islands of Reunion and Mauritius, where more affluent European visitors make up 88% and 61%, respectively, of all arrivals (WTO, 1999c: 158, 200).

Table 1.5. Top 20 destinations in Africa, by total arrivals and purpose of visit (1997).

Country	Rank in total arrivals	Total arrivals (000)	Total arrivals Share (%)	Leisure, recreation and holidays	Business	Other	Rank as holiday destination
South Africa[a]	1	4,944	21.2	3,938	622	384	1
Tunisia	2	4,263	18.3	2,558[d]	1,705		2
Morocco	3	3,072	13.2	1,690	246	1,136	3
Zimbabwe[b]	4	1,549	6.7	1,075	260	214	4
Botswana[b]	5	1,083	4.6	120	191	772	10
Kenya	6	1,001	4.3	805	102	94	5
Algeria[b]	7	635		N/A	N/A	N/A	–
Nigeria	8	632		N/A	N/A	N/A	–
Mauritius[b]	9	558		503	23	32	6
Namibia	10	502		402	70	30	7
Eritrea	11	410		67	175	168	14
Reunion	12	370		186	33	151	9
Tanzania	13	360		246	81	33	8
Zambia	14	341		90	140	111	13
Ghana	15	325		N/A	N/A	N/A	–
Swaziland[a]	16	315		N/A	N/A	N/A	–
Senegal	17	313		N/A	N/A	N/A	–
Côte d'Ivoire	18	260		94	135	31	11
Malawi[a]	19	194		49	84	61	15
Uganda[c]	20	189		93	76	20	12
Total 1–20		21,316					
Total Africa (1997)		23,291					

[a]1996 figures.
[b]Includes day visitors.
[c]1995 figures.
[d]Estimated (as 60% of all arrivals).
Sources: WTO (1998c: 30; 1999d).

Finally, the Middle East is not a region strongly associated with tourism. As Heba Aziz notes in Chapter 10, its image in the West is generally unfavourable and closely associated with negative views of Arabs (often reinforced through their demonization in Hollywood films), of Islam and the perceived links of Islam with terrorism. Political instability in the region is undoubtedly unfavourable to the growth of tourism and, while parts of it may be liberally endowed with sun and sand, the temperate climate and other attractions valued by mass tourists are not necessarily present. However, holidaymaking tourism is especially important in Egypt (as indicated in Table 1.6) and in recent years some oil-rich states have recognized the usefulness of cultural tourism as a counter to falling oil prices (WTO, 1997d: 70–87).

With nearly two-thirds of its tourists coming from Europe, Egypt is part of the European periphery (with Turkey, Tunisia, Morocco, Israel and Cyprus). It is undoubtedly the major focus of international tourism in the Middle East. Although rocked in the early 1990s by a series of terrorist attacks, in 1995 it nevertheless attracted more than 3.5 million tourists, a quarter of all the region's arrivals, and earned nearly 40% of the region's tourism receipts. By 1999, traveller confidence increased further, resulting in 4.4 million visitors, an increase of 40% on the 1998 figures alone (WTO, 2000a).

Whereas the Egyptian government fully supports tourism development, that of Saudi Arabia is more circumspect, and holidaymakers are greatly outnumbered by pilgrims and business travellers. Leisure tourists who do visit the country are largely from Muslim countries in other parts of the Middle East and from East Asia (WTO, 1997d: 82; Cave, 1998: 5). For their part, Saudis and residents of other Gulf states make overnight visits to Bahrein, and intra-regional tourism is important throughout the area.

Tourists from outside the region are gener-

Table 1.6. Selected Middle East destinations (1995) by total arrivals and tourism receipts.

Country	Total arrivals (000)	Rank	Share(%)	GNP per capita (US$)	Receipts US$ million	Receipts Share (%)	Receipts per capita (US$)	Receipts per arrival (US$)
Egypt	3,528	1	24.9	768	3,200	39.9	47.3	975
Saudi Arabia	3,458	2	24.4	7,469	1,308	16.3	67.7	364
United Arab Emirates	1,768	3	12.5	26,101	–	–	–	–
Bahrein	1,757	4	12.4	7,669	300	3.7	488.1	141
Jordan	1,103	5	7.8	1,481	744	9.3	153.8	615
Syria	888	6	6.3	1,112	1,478	18.4	93.4	1,626
Oman	435	7	3.1	4,897	99	1.2	42.6	261
Lebanon	420	8	3.0	3,546	715	8.9	235.9	1,732
Iraq	345	9	2.4	978	13	0.2	0.6	38
Qatar	263	10	1.9	13,542	–	–	–	–
Libya	88	11	0.6	6,562	6	0.1	1.1	107
Yemen	74	12	0.5	279	42	0.5	2.3	541
Kuwait	33	13	0.2	18,317	109	1.4	67.7	363
Total (1995)	14,160		100.0		8,014	100.0		

Source: WTO (1997c: 107–115).

ally in a small minority. Dubai (in the United Arab Emirates) is developing its reputation as a shopping and leisure centre, especially among Russian visitors (WTO, 1997d: 85) and also attracts a significant number of business tourists. European tourists also make up an important percentage of visitors to Lebanon (about 30%) and the Yemen (68%). Qatar (by promoting sports events) and Oman are also hoping to increase international arrivals. At the same time, Jordan is benefiting from the peace process (and aiding it) through cross-border cooperation and joint marketing initiatives with Israel (WTO, 1997d: 64–88; Freedland, 2000). There are indeed some signs of change in the region, but the situation does not greatly differ from that reported by the WTO in 1997, to the effect that 'the current political situation in a number of Middle Eastern countries is not at all favourable to tourism. There is little immediate likelihood of any real industrial development' (WTO, 1997d: 64).

Conclusion

The process by which LDCs have been incorporated into the world tourism system is not new. It is the same as that which, over centuries, brought European countries closer together and which, at various times, saw Europe increasingly criss-crossed by crusaders and pilgrims, participants in the Grand Tour and 'tramps' and, from the mid-19th century, by package tourists whose travel was facilitated by steam, whether by ship or by rail.

The railways heralded the age of mass travel and led to the development of seaside resorts, in Europe and North America, that depended on metropolitan centres for their prosperity. After 1945, the development of air transport increasingly brought overseas resorts into the system, commencing with islands and hinterlands in the Mediterranean periphery and gradually moving further afield.

Analyses of the tourist phenomenon have varied. Some have associated it with changes in Western capitalist society, whereas others have linked it to religion and drawn parallels with pilgrimage and other forms of religious journey. By contrast, geographers tend to focus on topographical changes, on landscapes, the collective perception of landscapes, and on urban development, while other social scientists study tourism's relationship to changing social structures.

For many, tourism is a tool for 'development', a concept much debated by 'bourgeois' theorists of modernization and neo-Marxist advocates of underdevelopment theory. More recently, environmentalists have joined the fray, situating tourism (and development generally) in a much wider system where the social, economic, cultural and ecological are interrelated. All these perspectives have now been incorporated into globalization theory, a wide-ranging conceptual framework which, while inevitably less coherent and cohesive than its predecessors, enables the analysis and description of economic, social and other processes that link local and global institutions and, in turn, evoke countervailing responses at national and regional level. Commentators on the spread of tourism have inevitably taken up these theoretical perspectives and, in recent years, the issue of 'sustainability' has been much discussed. It has certainly added a new and welcome dimension to the debate, but is best regarded as bringing into the analysis additional criteria for 'development', rather than offering an entirely new approach. Against this theoretical backdrop, tourism is inexorably increasing, feeding on increased globalization and, in turn, contributing to it. Like other migrants, tourists are agents of social change. Looking for a change themselves, tourists themselves take change to their destinations and, at least sometimes, are changed by their experiences. As a consequence, inward and outward acculturation are major features of international tourism.

Most international travel occurs within the world's major regions, mostly to near-neighbours, and mostly from one developed country to another. Europe and the Americas are major travel regions, and tourism is growing rapidly and consistently in East Asia and the Pacific, where the Japanese (and the Japanese economy) are at the 'centre'. More generally, less developed countries are increasingly part of the tourism circuit, and islands and small states, especially, rely on tourism for their prosperity.

Tourism is rarely to the poorest LDCs. In Europe, Turkey, Cyprus, Malta and Israel and the Occupied Territories are the main recipients, along with some central and eastern European countries previously part of the Soviet bloc. In East Asia and the Pacific, such newly industrializing countries as China and Hong Kong, Thailand, Singapore and Malaysia take the bulk of tourist arrivals, and most tourists to South Asia go to India. In the Americas, Mexico – another newly industrializing country – is by far the most popular LDC, benefit-

ing from its border with the USA, and more than two-thirds of tourists visiting Africa go to South Africa, Morocco, Zimbabwe, Kenya and Tunisia. Finally, although tourism to the Middle East has not really taken off, Egypt, as part of the European periphery, is an important destination region.

Organization of this Book

Contributions are organized into four distinct but overlapping sections. General themes are raised in Part One, comprising this chapter, which outlines the global pattern of tourist movement, the second chapter, which focuses on key issues in the study of tourism to LDCs, and a review by Linda Richter of the (largely political) challenges of international tourism and the overall trends in its development which have passed from the 20th into the 21st century.

The seven chapters in Part Two constitute a review of the role and importance of international tourism throughout much of the less developed world. Africa (Dieke), South America (Brennan and Allen), eastern and central Europe, along with Cuba, North Korea and Vietnam (Derek Hall), the Middle East (Aziz), India (Singh), China (Lew), Japan and the Pacific Rim (Michael Hall) are all described and discussed at some length. Contributors to this section were encouraged to portray tourism development in their chosen region with a relatively broad brush, but specific themes do emerge.

In Part Three, six case studies of selected topics and regions are presented. These touch on a variety of issues but several focus on the role that tourism plays in physical and social environments which might be described as 'fragile,' especially in island societies, and all, to a greater or lesser extent, discuss alternatives to mass tourism. It cannot be assumed, however, that all forms of tourism that involve close interaction with members of tourist-receiving societies are necessarily preferable to mass tourism. Sex tourism is a case in point and, as Heather Montgomery's chapter shows, child sex tourism, in particular, is an unsavoury feature of tourism in Thailand (and indeed elsewhere) which is much debated, much criticized but, as yet, little understood.

Finally, Part Four contains one chapter, the Afterword, where there is a reflection on themes raised by contributors to this volume, an attempt to link them to 'key' issues raised in Chapter two, and a framework which, it is suggested, might provide a basis for the comparative study of the social and cultural impacts of international tourism. It is a task that has barely begun.

References

Abercrombie, N. and Urry, J. (1983) *Capital, Labour and the Middle Classes*. Allen and Unwin, London.

Adams, W.M. (1990) *Green Development: Environment and Sustainability in the Third World*. Routledge, London.

Adams, W.M. (1995) Green development theory? Environmentalism and sustainable development. In: Crush, J. (ed.) *Power of Development*. Routledge, London, pp. 87–99.

Adler, J. (1985) Youth on the road: reflections on the history of tramping. *Annals of Tourism Research* 12(3), 335–354.

Adler, J. (1989) Origins of Sightseeing. *Annals of Tourism Research* 16(1), 7–29.

Adler, J. (1993) Mobility and the creation of the subject: theorising movement and the self in early Christian monasticism. *Proceedings of the International Colloquium, 'International Tourism between Tradition and Modernity'*, Nice, 19–21 November 1992, pp. 407–415.

Albrow, M. and King, E. (eds) (1990) *Globalization, Knowledge and Society: Readings from International Sociology*. Sage, London.

Anon. (2000) Poverty in Eastern Europe: the land that time forgot. *The Economist* 23–29 September, pp. 29–36.

Axton, R. (1992) Festive culture in country and town. In: Ford, B. (ed.) *Medieval Britain*. Cambridge University Press, Cambridge, UK.

Baum, T. (1998) Taking the exit route: extending the tourism area life cycle model. *Current Issues in Tourism* 1(2): 167–175.

Boissevain, J. (ed.) (1996) *Coping with Tourists: European Reactions to Mass Tourism*. Berghahn Books, Providence, USA.

Booth, D. (1985) Marxism and development sociology: interpreting the impasse. *World Development* 13(7), 761–787.

Booth, D. (1987) Alternatives in the restructuring of state–society relations: research issues for Tropical Africa. *IDS Bulletin* 18(4), 23–30.

Booth, D. (1994) Rethinking social development: an overview. In: Booth, D. (ed.) *Rethinking Social Development: Theory, Research and Practice*. Longman, Harlow, UK, pp. 3–34.

Briguglio, L., Archer, B., Jafari, J. and Wall, G. (eds) (1996a) *Sustainable Tourism in Islands and Small States: Issues and Policies*. Pinter Press, London.

Briguglio, L., Butler, R., Harrison, D. and Leal Filho, W. (eds) (1996b) *Sustainable Tourism in Islands and Small States: Case Studies*. Pinter Press, London.

Britton, S.G. (1982) The political economy of tourism in the third world. *Annals of Tourism Research* 9(3), 331–358.

Butler, R. (1980) The concept of a tourism area cycle of evolution: implication for management of resources. *Canadian Geographer* 24(1), 5–12.

Butler, R. (1999) Sustainable tourism: a state-of-the-art review. *Tourism Geographies* 1(1), 7–21.

Butlin, B. (1982) *The Billy Butlin Story: 'a Showman to the End'* (with Peter Dacre). Robson Books, London.

Carroll, R. (2000) Wine, women and the poor of Pompeii. *The Guardian* 13 June, p. 16.

Casson, L. (1994) *Travel in the Ancient World*. John Hopkins University Press, Baltimore, Maryland.

Cater, E. and Lowman, G. (eds) (1994) *Ecotourism: a Sustainable Option?* John Wiley & Sons, Chichester, UK.

Cave, P. (1998) International tourism: a viable option for the Saudi Arabian economy? In: *New Horizons and Roles in Development*. Conference of Administrative Sciences, College of Industrial Management, King Faud University of Petroleum and Minerals, Dhahran, March.

Cohen, E. (1971) Arab boys and tourist girls in a mixed Jewish Arab community. *International Journal of Comparative Sociology* 12(4), 217–233.

Cohen, E. (1985) The tourist guide: the origins, structure and dynamics of a role. *Annals of Tourism Research* 12(1), 5–29.

Cohen, E. (1993a) Open-ended prostitution as a skilful game of luck: opportunity, risk and security among tourist-oriented prostitutes in a Bangkok soi. In: Hitchcock, M., King, V.T. and Parnwell, M.J.G. (eds) *Tourism in South-East Asia*. Routledge, London, pp. 155–178.

Cohen, E. (1993b) The heterogeneization of a tourist art. *Annals of Tourism Research* 20(1), 138–163.

Cohen, E. (1996) Touting tourists in Thailand: tourist-oriented crime and social structure. In: Pizam, A. and Mansfield, Y. (eds) *Tourism, Crime and International Security Issues*. John Wiley & Sons, Chichester, UK, pp. 77–90.

Coleman, S. and Elsner, J. (1995) *Pilgrimage Past and Present in the World Religions*. British Museum Press, London.

Cooper, C. (1994) The destination life cycle: an update. In: Seaton, A.V. Jenkins, C.L., Wood, R.C., Dieke, P.U.C., Bennett, M.M., MacLellan, L.R. and Smith, R. (eds) *Tourism: the State of the Art*. John Wiley & Sons, Chichester, UK, pp. 340–346.

Croall, J. (1995) *Preserve or Destroy: Tourism and the Environment*. Calouste Gulbenkian Foundation, London.

Crush, J. (1995) Introduction: imagining development. In: Crush, J. (ed.) *Power of Development*. Routledge, London, pp. 1–23.

Dann, G. (1996) *The Language of Tourism*. CAB International, Wallingford, UK.

Doxey, G.V. (1971) A causation theory of visitor–resident irritants: methodology and research inferences. *The Travel Research Association Sixth Annual conference Proceedings, 'The Impact of Tourism'*. San Diego, California, 8-11 September, pp. 195–198.

Eber, S. (ed.) (1992) *Beyond the Green Horizon: Principles for Sustainable Tourism*. World Wildlife Fund, Godalming, UK.

Elkington, J. and Hailes, J. (1992) *Holidays that Don't Cost the Earth*. Victor Gollancz, London.

Erisman, M. (1983) Tourism and Cultural Dependency in the West Indies. *Annals of Tourism Research* 10(3), 337–361.

Fennell, D.A. (1999) *Ecotourism: an Introduction*. Routledge, London and New York.

Freedland, M. (2000) The riviera built on Peace. *The Observer (Escape* section), 30 July, pp. 2–3.

Geshekter, C.L. (1978) International tourism and African underdevelopment: some reflections on Kenya. In: *Tourism and Culture Change, Studies in Third World Societies*, Publication No. 6. College of William and Mary, Williamsberg, Virginia, pp. 57–88.

Gilbert, E.M. (1975) *Brighton: Old Ocean's Bauble*. Flare Books, Hassocks, UK.

Graburn, N. (1978) Tourism: the sacred journey. In: Smith, V.L. (ed.) *Hosts and Guests: the Anthropology of Tourism*. Basil Blackwell, Oxford, pp. 17–31.

Graburn, N. (1984) The Evolution of Tourist Arts. *Annals of Tourism Research* 11(3), 393–419.

Grayling, A.C. (2000) Olympian Heights. *The Guardian (Saturday Review)* 10 June, pp. 1–2.

Greenwood, D. (1972) Tourism as an agent of change: a Spanish Basque case. *Ethnology* XI(1), 80–91.

Hall, D. (1991) Evolutionary pattern of tourism development in Eastern Europe and the Soviet Union. In: Hall, D. (ed.) *Tourism and Economic Development in Eastern Europe and the Soviet Union*. Belhaven Press, London, pp. 78–115.

Harrison, D. (1988) *The Sociology of Modernization and Development*. Routledge, London.

Harrison, D. (1992) 'International tourism and the less developed countries: the background. In: Harrison, D. (ed.) *Tourism and the Less Developed Countries*. John Wiley & Sons, Chichester, UK, pp. 1–18.

Harrison, D. (1994) Tourism, capitalism and development in less developed countries. In: Sklair, L. (ed.) *Capitalism and Development*. Routledge, London, pp. 232–257.

Harrison, D. (1995) Development of tourism in Swaziland. *Annals of Tourism Research* 22(1), 135–156.

Harrison, D. (1996) Sustainability and tourism: reflections from a muddy pool. In: Briguglio, L., Archer, B., Jafari, J. and Wall, G. (eds) *Sustainable Tourism in Islands and Small States: Issues and Policies*. Pinter Press, London, pp. 69–89.

Harrison, D. (2000) Tourism in Africa: the social and cultural framework. In: Dieke, P. (ed.) *The Political Economy of Tourism in Africa*. Cognizant, New York.

Heppenheimer, T.A. (1995) *Turbulent Skies: the History of Commercial Aviation*. John Wiley & Sons, New York.

Hoivik, T. and Heiberg, T. (1980) Centre-periphery tourism and self-reliance. *International Social Science Journal* 32(1), 69–98.

Honey, M. (1999) *Ecotourism and Sustainable Development: Who Owns Paradise?* Island Press, Washington, DC.

Hutnyk, J. (1996) *The Rumour of Calcutta: Tourism, Charity and the Poverty of Representation*. Zed Books, London.

International Hotels Environment Initiative (IHEI) (1993) *Environmental Management for Hotels: the Industry Guide to Best Practice*. Butterworth-Heinemann, London.

Ioannides, D. (1992) Tourism development agents: the Cypriot resort cycle. *Annals of Tourism Research* 19(4), 711–731.

de Kadt, E. (ed.) (1979) *Tourism: Passport to Development?* Oxford University Press, New York (for the World Bank and UNESCO).

Karsera, A. (2000) Three cars and a mobile phone: the key to happiness? *Cyprus Mail* 14 September, p. 3.

King, A.D. (ed.) (1991) *Culture, Globalization and the World-System.* Macmillan, Basingstoke, UK.

Kitching, G. (1985) Politics, method and evidence in the 'Kenya' debate. In: Bernstein, H. and Campbell, B.K. (eds) *Contradictions of Accumulation in Africa: Studies in Economy and State.* Sage, Beverly Hills, California, pp. 115–151.

Krippendorf, J. (1987) *The Holiday Makers: Understanding the Impact of Leisure and Travel.* Heinemann, Oxford, UK.

Lash, S. and Urry, J. (1987) *The End of Organised Capitalism.* Polity Press, Cambridge, UK.

Lew, A.A. (2000) China: a growth engine for Asian tourism. In: Hall, C.M. and Page, S. (eds) *Tourism in South and South East Asia.* Butterworth-Heinemann, Oxford, UK, pp. 268–285.

Lindberg, K. and Hawkins, D.E. (eds) (1993) *Ecotourism: a Guide for Planners and Managers,* Vol. 1. The Ecotourism Society, North Bennington, Vermont.

Lindberg, K., Wood, M.E. and Engeldrum, D. (eds) (1998) *Ecotourism: a Guide for Planners and Managers,* Vol. 2. Ecotourism Society, North Bennington, Vermont.

Lumsdon, L.M. and Swift, J.S. (1998) Ecotourism at the crossroads: the case of Costa Rica. *Journal of Sustainable Tourism* 6(2), 155–172.

MacCannell, D. (1976) *The Tourist: a New Theory of the Leisure Class.* Macmillan, London.

MacCannell, D. (1992) *Empty Meeting Grounds: the Tourist Papers.* Routledge, London.

Mclaren, D. (1998) *Rethinking Tourism and Ecotravel: the Paving of Paradise and What You Can Do to Stop It.* Kumarian Press, West Hartford, Connecticut.

Michaud, J. (1993) Tourism as a catalyst of economic and political change. *Internationales Asienforum* 24(1–2), 21–43.

Michaud, J. (1997) A portrait of cultural resistance: the confinement of tourism in a Hmong village of Thailand. In: Picard, M. and Wood, R.E. (eds) *Tourism, Ethnicity and the State in Asian and Pacific Societies.* University of Hawaii Press, Honolulu, pp. 128–154.

Middleton, V.T.C. (1998) *Sustainable Tourism: a Marketing Perspective* (with R. Hawkins). Butterworth-Heinemann, Oxford, UK.

Mowforth, M. and Munt, I. (1998) *Tourism and Sustainability: New Tourism in the Third World.* Routledge, London.

Myers, A.R. (1952) *England in the Late Middle Ages.* Penguin, Harmondsworth, UK.

Nash, D. (1978) Tourism as a form of imperialism. In: Smith, V. (ed.) *Hosts and Guests: the Anthropology of Tourism.* Blackwell, Oxford, UK, pp. 33–47.

Nash, D. (1996) *The Anthropology of Tourism.* Pergamon Press, Oxford, UK.

Neale, G. (1998) *The Green Travel Guide.* Earthscan, London.

Nunez, T. (1963) Tourism, tradition and acculturation: weekendismo in a Mexican village. *Ethnology* II(3), 347–352.

Oakes, T. (1998) *Tourism and Modernity in China.* Routledge, London.

Oglethorpe, M.G. (1984) Tourism in Malta: a crisis of dependence. *Leisure Studies* 3(2), 141–161.

Ousby, I. (1990) *The Englishman's England: Taste, Travel and the Rise of Tourism.* Cambridge University Press, Cambridge, UK.

Pearce, P. (1989) *Tourist Development,* 2nd edn. Longman, Harlow, UK.

Pearce, P. (1995) *Tourism Today: a Geographical Analysis,* 2nd edn. Longman, Harlow, UK.

Perez, L.A. (1975) *Underdevelopment and Dependency: Tourism in the West Indies.* Center for Inter-American Studies, University of El Paso, Texas.

Pieterse, J.N. (1994) Globalisation as Hybridisation. *International Sociology* 9(2), 161–184.

Pimlott, J.A.R. (1976) *The Englishman's Holiday: a Social History* (first published 1947). Harvester Press, Hassocks, UK.

Price, M. (ed.) (1996) *People and Tourism in Fragile Environments.* John Wiley & Sons, Chichester, UK.

Pudney, J. (1954) *The Thomas Cook Story.* The Non-fiction Book Club, London.

Read, S. (1986) *Hello Campers* (with B. Haynes). Transworld Publishers, London.

Reilly, T. and Reilly, E. (1979) The political alternative. *African Wildlife* 33(4), 18–21.

Robertson, R. (1992) *Globalization: Social Theory and Global Culture.* Sage, London.

Rojek, C. and Urry, J. (1997) Transformations of travel and theory. In: Rojek, C. and Urry, J. (eds) *Touring Cultures: Transformations of Travel and Theory.* Routledge, London, pp. 1–19.

Ryan, C. (1991) *Recreational Tourism: a Social Science Perspective*. Routledge, London.

Scholte, J.A. (2000) *Globalization: a Critical Introduction*. Palgrave, Houndmills, Basingstoke, UK.

Schwartz, R. (1997) *Pleasure Island: Tourism and Temptation in Cuba*. University of Nebraska Press, Lincoln.

Scott, A. (ed.) (1997) *The Limits of Globalization: Cases and Arguments*, Routledge, London.

Selwyn, T. (1996) Introduction. In: Selwyn, T. (ed.) *The Tourist Image: Myths and Myth-making in Tourism*. John Wiley & Sons, Chichester, UK, pp. 1–32.

Smith, V.L. (ed.) (1978) *Hosts and Guests: the Anthropology of Tourism*. Basil Blackwell, Oxford, UK.

Smith, V.L. (ed.) (1989) *Hosts and Guests: the Anthropology of Tourism*, 2nd edn. University of Pennsylvania Press, Philadephia, Pennsylvania.

Smith, V.L. (1992) Introduction: the quest in guest. *Annals of Tourism Research* 19(1), 1–17.

Smith, V.L. and Eadington, W.R. (eds) (1992) *Tourism Alternatives: Potentials and Problems in the Development of Tourism*. University of Pennsylvania Press, Philadelphia, Pennsylvania.

Thanet Regeneration Board (1999) *Isle of Thanet Regeneration Update*, Winter. Thanet Regeneration Board, Thanet District Council, Margate, UK.

Thomas, C.Y. (1988) *The Poor and the Powerless: Economic Policy and Change in the Caribbean*. Latin America Bureau, London.

Towner, J. (1996) *An Historical Geography of Recreation and Tourism in the Western World*. John Wiley & Sons, Chichester, UK.

Turner, L. and Ash, J. (1975) *The Golden Hordes: International Tourism and the Pleasure Periphery*. Constable, London.

Turner, V. and Turner, E.L.B. (1978) *Image and Pilgrimage in Christian Culture*. Columbia University Press, New York.

UNDP (1999) *Pacific Human Development Report, 1999: Creating Opportunities*. United Nations Development Programme, Suva, Fiji.

Urry, J. (1990) *The Tourist Gaze: Leisure and Travel in Contemporary Societies*. Sage, London.

Urry, J. (1995) *Consuming Places*. Routledge, London.

Wahab, S. and Pigram, J.J. (eds) (1997) *Tourism, Development and Growth: the Challenge of Sustainability*. Routledge, London.

Wang, N. (2000) *Tourism and Modernity: a Sociological Analysis*. Pergamon Press, Amsterdam.

Waters, M. (1995) *Globalization*. Routledge, London.

Weaver, D.B. (1998) *Ecotourism in the Less Developed World*. CAB International, Wallingford, Oxon, UK.

Wilson, M. (1935) The decline of the Grand Tour. In: Lambert, R.S. (ed.) *Grand Tour: a Journey in the Tracks of the Aristocracy*. Faber and Faber, London, pp. 153–167.

Wood, K. and House, S. (1991) *The Good Tourist*. Mandarin, London.

Wood, R.E. (1984) Ethnic tourism: the state and cultural change in Southeast Asia. *Annals of Tourism Research* 11(3), 353–374.

World Bank (1997) *World Development Indicators, 1997*. World Bank (International Bank of Reconstruction and Development), Washington DC.

World Commission on Environment and Development (The Brundtland Commission) (1987) *Our Common Future*. Oxford University Press, Oxford, UK.

WTO (1990) *Yearbook of Tourism Statistics*, Vol. 1, 43rd edn. World Tourism Organization, Madrid.

WTO (1995) *WTO News*, No. 5, October.

WTO (1997a) *Yearbook of Tourism Statistics*, Vol.1, 49th edn. WTO, Madrid.

WTO (1997b) *Yearbook of Tourism Statistics*, Vol. 2, 49th edn. WTO, Madrid.

WTO (1997c) *Tourism Market Trends: World, 1985–1996*. WTO, Madrid.

WTO (1997d) *Tourism Market Trends: Expanded Middle East, 1986–1996*. WTO, Madrid.

WTO (1998a) *Tourism Market Trends: Americas, 1988–1997*. WTO, Madrid.

WTO (1998b) *Tourism Economic Report*. WTO, Madrid.

WTO (1998c) *Tourism Market Trends: Africa. 1988–1997*. WTO, Madrid.

WTO (1999a) *Tourism Highlights, 1999*. WTO, Madrid.

WTO (1999b) *Yearbook of Tourism Statistics*, Vol. 1, 51st edn. WTO, Madrid.

WTO (1999c) *Yearbook of Tourism Statistics*, Vol. 2, 51st edn. WTO, Madrid.

WTO (1999d) *Compendium of Tourism Statistics, 1993–1997* 19th edn. WTO, Madrid.

WTO (1999e) *Tourism Market Trends: East Asia and the Pacific: 1999 Edition*. WTO, Madrid.

WTO (2000a) World tourism results revised upwards. http://www/world-tourism.org/pressrel/00_5_11I.htm (30 July 2000).

WTO (2000b) European tourism to nearly double in next 20 years. *WTO News* No. 2, (Second Quarter), p. 5.

Yale, P. (1991) *From Tourist Attractions to Heritage Tourism*. ELM Publications, Huntingdon.

2

Tourism and Less Developed Countries: Key Issues

David Harrison

The focus of Chapter 1 was the global movement of international tourists and, in particular, the extent to which less developed countries (LDCs) figured as their destinations. However, in themselves the numbers mean little. Using an analogy familiar to residents of the West Country in England, such collective movements of tourists can be likened to those of ants, even flying ants, moving uniformly to and from their home base to destination regions, repeatedly creating patterns that are both describable and predictable. To be understood or interpreted, these patterns must be set in a wider conceptual framework, and it was suggested in Chapter 1 that international tourism could be seen as an aspect of 'development' and as part of a process of mass movement that was already well established by the middle of the 19th century.

This chapter focuses specifically on key features of the role of international tourism in the wider development process. Inevitably, the selection is subjective. Other research areas are closely linked to the topics raised, and at the end of the discussion suggestions are given as to how they might be situated in the wider framework proposed. However, it is argued here, first, that tourism is a crucial feature of a much wider process of migration; secondly, that it is strongly associated with the expansion of capitalism; and, thirdly, that of all the major factors in the spread of international tourism, one of the most crucial is the state.

Tourism and Migration

According to Castles and Miller (1998: 20–29), general theories of migration fall into three major categories. Putting them somewhat simplistically, the neo-classical equilibrium theory focuses on 'push' and 'pull' factors that prompt individuals to move from one area to another. By contrast, historical-structural approaches, much influenced by Marxist political economy, envisage migration more as a collective response to the demand of international capital for labour. Finally, a focus on migration systems brings together elements of both (Castles and Miller, 1998: 27; emphasis in the original):

> Macro- and micro-structures are linked at all levels with each other. Together they can be examined as facets of an overarching *migratory process*. This concept sums up the complex sets of factors and interactions which lead to international migration and influence its course. No single cause is ever sufficient to explain why people decide to leave their country and settle in another.

For the record, the third position seems the most sensible, focusing as it does on the ways in which individual decision-making and social interaction are linked to wider social networks, structures and systems within which interaction occurs. Indeed, such issues are discussed in the final chapter of this book. However, for present purposes what is noteworthy is that tourism barely figures in any of these perspectives. Yet, in so far as international tourism is defined as a visit to another country for at least a night and no more than a year, it is clearly a form of temporary migration – and one that 'dwarfs all other comparable forms of transnational mobility, past or present' (Cohen and Kennedy, 2000: 214). Moreover, that is not the end of the story, for just as links with the country of origin may be retained by 'permanent' migrants, so migration for tourism purposes need not always be temporary. It may actually lead to repeat visits, holiday homes, retirement and even full migration, as indicated in Fig. 2.1. In addition, migration itself can lead to tourism, prompting either friends and relatives to make visits, or migrants themselves to make return visits to their country of origin, perhaps even returning as entrepreneurs or retirees (or both).

For destination areas, tourism is certainly not temporary in its effects. Holidaymaking by individuals in large numbers can make a dramatic and permanent impact, changing the rural to urban and bringing about equally noteworthy changes in the attitudes of residents towards visitors. Doxey (1975: 195–196) noted that mass tourism could eventually lead residents to displays of antagonism, thus requiring more tourism promotion and remedial planning to offset the inevitable bad press received by the destination area. How far this does happen is a matter for debate and empirical enquiry (and seems not to have occurred in Barbados, one of the destinations he studied). In so far as tourism continues in such circumstances, there is possibly a stage after antagonism when residents adopt a more professional, distant and unaffected approach to tourists. In this context, it might be useful to adapt an immigrant–host framework, such as that previously used by Patterson (1965: 19–35) in analysing large-scale immigration to the UK. Depending on the stage of tourism development, and prior contact and familiarity of 'host' and 'guest' cultures, processes of absorption, for instance, may range from complete assimilation, through pluralistic integration (where groups are accepted into economic and civic life but nevertheless retain important cultural attributes that separate them from the rest of the population), to accommodation, where 'a *modus vivendi* between newcomers and the receiving society' is achieved (Patterson, 1965: 24).

As one of many consequences of large-scale migration, the normative basis for inter-personal relationships may also be changed. Where tourist contacts with locals are transitory and ephemeral, it is hardly surprising that 'normal' rules of cultural and economic interchange are suspended by 'guest' and 'host' in favour of less morally constrained profit-seeking behaviour (Crick, 1994: 162). There is ample evidence, however, that tourist destinations worldwide have long relied as much on 'repeat visitors' as on attracting newcomers, and the literature on the marketing of tourism is replete with references to the importance of 'brand loyalty' (Oppermann, 1998: 131–133).

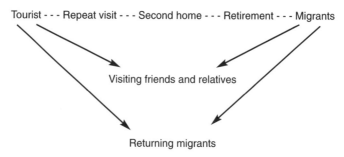

Tourist - - - Repeat visit - - - Second home - - - Retirement - - - Migrants

Visiting friends and relatives

Returning migrants

Fig. 2.1. A tourist–migrant continuum.

Anecdotal evidence and personal experience indicate that many holidaymakers prefer the known to the unknown, returning not once but many times to people and places previously visited. In one sample of tourists in Majorca, for example, no less than two-thirds were repeat visitors to the island (Ryan, 1995: 209–210), and repeat visitors were consistently more than one-third of the visitors to a luxury island resort in the Fiji Islands (Harrison, 1999). Unfortunately, little research seems to have been carried out on what this means for tourist destination areas in LDCs, on the relationships of repeat visitors with first-time visitors, or on how different types of visitor interact with members of the host society. What is evident, though, is that repeat visitors are crucial to the survival of a tourism business, and it is at least possible that their social and cultural impact differs from that of first-time visitors.

Equally importantly, repeat business can lead to second homes and retiree tourism. By the end of the 19th century, seaside resorts in the UK were already attracting second-home owners and retirees (Travis, 1993: 116) and the trend has continued to the present, with many towns on the south and south-west coast of England, for example, now known retirement areas (Underwood, 1978: 150–151). The process was extended to the rest of Europe, where second-home and retirement tourism have long been established for both domestic and international visitors (Bielckus et al., 1972; Downing and Dower, 1974; Coppock, 1977; Williams and Shaw, 1991: 48–49). In most cases, homes have been purchased for recreation and retirement purposes, and are found in areas much visited by (other) tourists. More recently, following a series of studies of international retirement migration in Europe, Williams et al. (1997: 129) concluded that 'repeat holidays can act as the stepping stone to seasonal or permanent migration, often via the purchase of a holiday home'. Of the retirees in their samples, no fewer than 90% in the Costa del Sol (Spain) and the Algarve (Portugal) had previously been to the area on holiday, with three-quarters having visited Malta and Tuscany (Italy) before investing in property in the region (King et al., 1998: 101). Similar findings were reported by O'Reilly (2000: 24) in her study of British migrants to Spain. Research in other developed countries also highlights the impact of second homes and retiree tourism on destination areas (e.g. Jordan, 1980; Jaakson, 1986; Gartner, 1987; Strapp, 1988; Girard and Gartner, 1993). The contribution of British second-home owners and retirees in many parts of France, for instance, has been well publicized, as has the response of British residents to the published adventures of Peter Mayle in France, indicating that long-established migrants do not always welcome more recent arrivals (Mayle, 1989; Martin, 1992). Communities of expatriates may be internally quite divided. O'Reilly (2000: 52–68) categorized the British on the Costa del Sol, Spain, as full residents (that is, permanent migrants), returning residents (who return periodically to the UK), seasonal visitors (who live in Spain during the winter months) and peripatetic visitors (who have second homes in the region and visit when they can). The community she describes is socially 'betwixt and between' two cultures. Marginalized in Spain primarily because of their failure to learn the local language, the British centre their lives within the English-speaking community. 'Their sense of status, self-worth and belonging derive from other Britons' (O'Reilly, 2000: 153) and status is claimed and awarded on the basis of the length of time spent in the community (O'Reilly, 2000: 126–127). A similar process seems to have occurred in Mallorca, where increasing numbers of immigrants have led to a polarization between insiders and outsiders (Waldren, 1996: 138–208).

Unfortunately, relatively little is known about the role of holiday and retirement homes in LDCs. An exception is the economies 'in transition' in the former Eastern bloc where, even under socialist regimes in the 1960s, ownership of second homes was widespread, often for recreational and holiday purposes, but also to facilitate the production of fresh food for household consumption (Hall, 1991: 86–87).

In LDCs in the southern hemisphere, second homes are purchased or rented only in territories with adequate health facilities and relatively good international communications. In some former colonies, settlers and administrators made temporary visits to more congenial places when the climate at their normal residence was deemed oppressive, as to the hill stations of India (Tyagi, 1991: 60–88). On a smaller scale, local settlers and metropolitan elites built residences in the more wealthy and accessible parts of the Caribbean. By the beginning of the 20th century, Caribbean islands were already a winter playground for the wealthy and/or the celebrated (Henshall, 1977: 75; Pattullo, 1996: 9) and in the 1920s Cuban developers 'encouraged North Americans to visit the island as tourists and to build their homes alongside friendly Cubans' (Schwartz, 1997: 38). More recently, a variety of holiday homes has emerged in many Caribbean islands, including locally owned homes rented to foreign visitors for the duration of the northern winter, houses purchased outright for second homes and retirement purposes, and condominiums, often attached to hotel and retail complexes (Henshall, 1977: 76). In some islands, enclaves of retired tourists emerged, with important effects on the social structure and the economy, as occurred in Montserrat until the idyll was brought to an abrupt end by the 1995 eruption of the island's volcano (Harrison, 1975: 60–63; Henshall, 1977: 77–83).

How far second-home ownership and retiree tourism are developing in other LDCs depends on numerous factors, not least the availability of land for foreigners (or their agents) to purchase. In the early 1990s, for example, a comparison of vacation home projects in Malaysia, Thailand, Indonesia and Singapore led to the conclusion (Economist Intelligence Unit, 1991: 40) that:

> Malaysia – with the most liberal regulatory environment for foreign ownership, the most sophisticated financial markets, the highest number of tourist arrivals and an extremely vibrant economy fuelled by foreign investment – has potentially the largest number of vacation home units. On the other hand, Indonesia – with the most restrictive ownership regulations, the least sophisticated financial markets, the fewest tourist arrivals and arguably the most uncertain economy – has the least.

Local systems of land tenure clearly affect the ability of foreigners to build holiday or retirement homes. This is most obvious, perhaps, in the Pacific islands, where land tenure arrangements vary widely (Crocombe, 1987). In the Fiji Islands, where more than 80% of the land is communally held by indigenous Fijians, holiday and retirement homes are uncommon and largely restricted to isolated pockets of freehold land or (even more rarely) to condominiums on land leased by major hotels. By contrast, condominiums are especially important in Hawaii and Guam, where much land is privately owned by large corporations (Meller and Horowitz, 1987: 32; Souder, 1987: 221; Minerbi, 1996: 195). In this context, the increasing importance of timeshare arrangements in LDCs should be noted. Following their success in Europe and the USA, timeshare resorts are rapidly increasing in Mexico and other parts of Latin America, Asia and the Caribbean (RCI Europe, 1993; British Hospitality Association, 1999: 45).

In the above examples, tourism is at the beginning of the process, and second-home ownership, retirement and migration are at the end. Conversely, the order may be reversed and 'permanent' migration may be the start of the cycle. Once migrants to the metropolitan country are established, they are likely to receive visits from friends and relatives and, in turn, visit their countries of origin at regular intervals. Research by King (1994) confirms the pattern, and he noted the crucial importance of visits by overseas Chinese to China, and of visits by friends and relatives to migrants of quite different ethnic backgrounds in Australia, New Zealand and Europe. Similarly, Kang and Page (2000: 57–60) showed that (South) Korean emigration to New Zealand prompted a pattern of 'ethnic reunion' in both directions, thus further confirming the close link between visiting friends and relatives (VFR) tourism and migration already noted by Jackson in 1990 (cited in Kang and Page, 2000: 58).

A common feature of some migration patterns is for emigrants to build a house in their country of origin, to which they plan eventually to retire. In the meantime, while awaiting the return journey (which may or may not happen), the house is let to visitors from other parts of the world. This is certainly the experience of many Caribbean migrants to the UK or North America, who regularly visit their 'home' country and harbour thoughts of a more permanent return (Byron, 1994: 169), to the extent that they have been seen as examples of the 'internationalization' of the family (Chamberlain, 1997: 6) and described as bearers of 'a global identity' (Chamberlain, 1998: 8). In particular, those who retire early and then return to the Caribbean show a notable tendency to start a business, often in the service sector. Writing of returned migrants to St Kitts/Nevis, Byron (1994: 183) remarked that:

> returning migrants are increasingly attracted to jobs in the tourism sector, in particular to work at a new 160 room luxury hotel complex ... This new concern welcomed the presence of the returnees, at times making use of skills they had gained in Britain in more senior positions within the hotel staff hierarchy ... The expanding island economy caused mainly by the growth of the tourist industry and its consequent labour demand may encourage the return of migrants who were uncertain about their ability to start their own businesses which tended to be the goal of unretired potential returnees. The changes also encourage the return of people who may wish to start businesses which would serve this sector, such as souvenir shops, or exploit another section of the market such as small guest house proprietorship.

Similar findings have come from research elsewhere. The dynamic contribution of returned migrants to the tourism industry of the Greek islands was discussed at length by Kenna (1993) and Tsartas (1992: 528), while Popelka and Littrell (1991: 394) noted the financial and cultural capital provided to village handicraft production by Mexicans returning from extended stays in the USA. By contrast, a study of Tongans and Samoans in Australia found that only a small proportion intended to return permanently to their country of origin and that those in this category had not accumulated more cultural and financial capital than those who had no intention to re-migrate (Ahlburg and Brown, 1998). When compared with much of the Caribbean, tourism is undeveloped in Tonga and Samoa, and the pattern could change if more opportunities became available, but there is clearly a case for more research on the topic. Meanwhile, the importance of returned migrants is confined neither to the Caribbean nor even to island states, and further research will cast more light on the increasingly blurred distinctions separating migrant, tourist and returnee. It will also help to reveal the continued but dynamic relationships of 'centres', which receive labour and provide tourists, and their numerous 'peripheries', where previous

colonial ties may be continually reinforced by inward and outward migration, including different kinds of tourism.

This discussion has not exhausted the links between tourism and other forms of migration, and geographers, in particular, are taking a renewed interest in them (Williams and Hall, 2000). As in developed countries, for instance, tourism development in LDCs may attract a substantial labour force from the surrounding region, if not further afield, especially at the 'development' stage of a destination area (Butler, 1980: 8). Indeed, Bianchi (2000) highlights the importance of 'tourist-workers', often white, young and well educated from developed societies, who (like many Australians and New Zealanders in the UK) work in tourist destination areas to finance their own tourist activities, thus emulating 'tramps' of the early 19th century (Adler, 1985). Furthermore, as Dieke notes in Chapter 4, LDCs may continue to depend on the managerial and technical experience of migrant labour from developed countries. Indeed, many migrants to tourism areas, in both the formal and informal sectors, and at all income levels, successfully combine business, pleasure and leisure, thus blurring the distinction between business tourists and holidaymakers.

Tourist or migrant? Returnee, visitor or resident? And who is to decide? Is it simply a matter of employing the correct analytical framework, or should we also be asking how residents and tourists define themselves? Some Cook Islanders in the South Pacific happily consider visiting military personnel and anthropologists – in fact, any white visitor – as 'tourists' (Berno, 1999: 666), and Vincentians in the eastern Caribbean similarly distiguished between white 'tourists' and 'visitors' from other Caribbean islands (Harrison, 1975: vii). In the writer's own experience, migrants returning to Trinidad for a holiday so exasperated other villagers by incessantly referring to life in St Thomas or St Croix that friends and relatives heartily wished they would 'go home', and breathed a great sigh of relief when they did so. A similar blurring of categories is reported for Greek islands (Kenna, 1993), and over the years so many expatriates have gone to live in Deià, Mallorca, that the distinction between 'insider' and 'outsider' is one of negotiation and degree rather than absolute categories (Waldren, 1997: 63). Finally, in (South) Cyprus, government encourages return migration by offering such incentives as tax-free importation of cars and capital to returning migrants, who make up an important category of entrepreneurs in tourism (and other) businesses. Nevertheless, repatriates 'complain of being made to feel like outsiders in their own home country' and have formed a Federation of Repatriated Cypriots to counter what they consider to be discriminatory treatment (Hellicar, 2000: 2).

Tourism, Capitalism and Commoditization

It is no coincidence that much tourism development is linked to migration. This can occur at the early stages of a resort's development, when migrant labour is imported to build the infrastructure, and also later, when hotels and other accommodation agencies need workers in the hospitality industry to receive yet another set of migrants – the tourists. How far any of these forms of migration is temporary is a matter for research rather than prior assumption. However, it is also the case that migration to 'growth poles' or 'centres' of development is a central feature of capitalist expansion generally and, in this respect, what occurs in tourism is part of a more general process. This has not always been recognized in the tourism literature, but there has been a focus on commoditization (or commodification) and the loss of 'authenticity,' especially in LDCs. Indeed, Boorstin's (1964: 77–117) attack on 'pseudo events' and MacCannell's (1976) eloquent (if simplistic) depiction of modern man's doomed search for authenticity in a world already lost to modernity were but opening shots in a discussion that has continued for more than three decades. The links between tourism, authenticity and commoditization have been discussed in detail elsewhere (Harrison, 1992b: 20–22, 1994: 243–244; Selwyn, 1996: 14–28; Hitchcock, 2000: 2–11) but the emphasis has shifted since the early debates. Initially, tourism was much condemned as a polluter of native cultures and a 'corrupter of innocence' (Turner and Ash, 1975: 155–167) and was said to have so

extended commoditization into the cultural sphere that culture was purchased 'by the pound' (Greenwood, 1978). More measured commentators would later note that who or what was 'authentic' depended largely upon the perspective or discipline of the onlooker or consumer (Cohen, 1988; Littrell *et al.*, 1993) and attention also moved to the role played by marketing and advertising in publicizing and/or constructing images of place and people in tourist destination regions (Silver, 1993; Dann, 1996a,b; Sternberg, 1997). Yet others focused on how tourism (and perhaps outside entrepreneurs) influenced the production and marketing of indigenously produced arts and crafts, which often retained and even gained 'artistic' value as they were 'commoditized' and sold in a much wider market (Graburn, 1984; Cohen, 1993) It was also increasingly recognized that even in obviously commercialized performances, 'authentic' experience was possible for both participant and observer (Boissevain, 1996: 116–118; Daniel, 1996). In fact, rather than being an objectively fixed property of a practice or artefact, 'authenticity' emerges as a quality invested in an item or practice which may nevertheless have been changed or adapted over an extended period of time (Ryan and Crofts, 1997: 914). Indeed, as indicated in studies of Bali by Picard (1990, 1993, 1996), modern dances produced specifically for tourists may come to be viewed by participants as 'authentic' or as 'spiritual' as traditional performances previously restricted to temple venues.

Tourism's links with authenticity, tradition and commoditization are now considered more dynamic and complicted than was felt in the 1960s and 1970s, and local accommodation to tourism is known to vary considerably. This newly recognized complexity has yet to be firmly conceptualized in an analytical framework that enables commoditization in tourist destination areas to be compared and related to wider aspects of capitalist development. However, MacCannell has linked tourism directly, even crudely, to the growth of postmodern culture (MacCannell, 2000: 457–458) and others, too, have explicitly drawn on postmodernist insights in situating tourism within a postmodern and consumerist context (Selwyn, 1996, pp. 14–28; Wang, 2000, pp. 46–71).

In the continuing study of consumer culture, attention has often focused on the tendency in capitalist production to standardize the product and the apparently countervailing need to market it as distinctive. This can be seen, for example, in the debate over the 'McDonaldization' of modern society (Ritzer, 1996, 1998). However, except for a study by Hughes (1995) on the marketing of Scottish produce, most accounts of tourism's role in the commoditization of people and place in destination areas ignore the wider historical context in which these processes occur. At a time when explicitly Marxist and neo-Marxist approaches to development are in decline, and their former adherents belatedly discovering the merits of actor-orientated, empirical research (e.g. Booth, 1994), it is worth making the rather obvious point that international tourism is part of a much wider process of social and economic change. Indeed, Marxist and neo-Marxist analyses both focus on the spread of capitalism – an economic system for profit based primarily on production by labourers who directly sell their labour power. By any stretch of the imagination, the process was well advanced by the end of the 19th century, and by the end of the 20th century it was virtually supreme. The obvious point here is that by the time international tourism developed on a mass scale, after the Second World War, capitalism had been exported, to a greater or lesser extent, to most parts of the globe.

As world systems theorists frequently pointed out, even those (few) countries with little or no history of colonialism existed in a world dominated by colonial powers (Harrison, 1988: 111), and allegiances and links dating back to colonialism still condition travel to many LDCs (Hoivik and Heiberg, 1980: 75). It is no accident, for example, that French tourists to North Africa tend to visit French-speaking Morocco and Tunisia, both former colonies, but so do as many German tourists (WTO, 1999: 169, 239). Similarly, the majority of European tourists to Sri Lanka are from the UK (WTO, 1999: 220). More generally, there can be little doubt that prior colonial association and exposure to capitalism, as well as geographical propinquity, are important features of tourism to many LDCs. In Marxist terms, what this implies is that the process of commoditization, so much a feature of the incorporation of

pre-capitalist social formations into the world capitalist system, was established many decades, in some cases centuries, before international tourism was under way, and this, in turn, conditioned the growth and specific characteristics of tourism in LDCs.

Once the spread of international tourism is seen as a continuing feature of capitalism, arguments over authenticity and commoditization take on a new light. Many alleged consequences of tourism are then seen to be features of capitalism in general. Increased independence of the young and of women from patriarchal authority (Peake, 1989; Harrison, 1992b), the spread of the cash economy, and movement from rural to urban areas, for example, are all known features of capitalist expansion and were much in evidence a century or more ago (Smith and Sender, 1986: 57). The commoditization of culture, whether of the *alarde* in Fuentarrabia, Spain (Greenwood, 1978), or of firewalking in Fiji (Stymeist, 1996), is no isolated phenomenon but a well-established feature of capitalist development.

Without wishing to labour the point unduly, other insights can be learned from what is now almost a defunct form of Marxist analysis. There is no need, for instance, to accept the economic determinism that underpinned much of the mode of production debate in the late 1970s and 1980s (Harrison, 1988: 123–138) to appreciate the value of analysing levels of incorporation (or 'articulation') of LDCs in the world capitalist system. Tourist destination areas in LDCs clearly have very different histories, cultures and social structures. When introduced to large-scale international tourism, the degree to which their economies were monetized and characterized by wage labour and commoditization varied considerably. Even in developed societies, not all trade occurs within the market economy, and agricultural production for use rather than for sale continues to be the norm in many LDCs.

How might the usefulness of this kind of analysis be demonstrated? Take as a comparison the island states of the Caribbean and those of the South Pacific. The former were subjected to colonial domination over an extended period, starting in the 15th century. Once much of the indigenous population was wiped out, slaves were imported in bulk from

West Africa, as part of the triangular trade. Later, when slavery ended, some societies (notably Trinidad and Tobago and mainland Guyana) imported indentured labourers from South Asia to cultivate the sugar cane that the ex-slaves (not unnaturally) wanted to avoid, and this source of labour lasted until the early years of the 20th century. Among numerous results of these population movements, a system of social stratification developed in the Caribbean which, although much debated, is generally agreed to have been strongly correlated to 'racial' categories. Indeed, during the period in which island states received their political independence, from the early 1960s onwards, issues of race and 'black power' were dominant and sensitive topics in periods of domestic unrest (Smith, 1965; Oxaal, 1971; Lowenthal, 1972). It was in the period of self-government, too, that international tourism on any scale commenced in the Caribbean: white tourists visiting islands whose black populations were still smarting from the ignominy of slavery, servitude and colonialism at the hands of white masters. In short, international tourism to the Caribbean was superimposed on monocrop (or peasant) economies, long incorporated into the world system, where land was (generally) freely available for purchase, and where social inequality was strongly correlated with racial difference.

By contrast, colonialism arrived relatively late in the South Pacific, in the latter half of the 19th century. There were some attempts to establish plantation agriculture in the islands, and in Queensland, Australia, and in the pre-colonial mid-1800s thousands of men were taken from Melanesia as forced labour. In Tahiti, indentured labourers were brought from China, while (as in the Caribbean) indentured Indians were taken to Fiji. However, whereas plantations were established in US-influenced Guam or Hawaii, plantation agriculture in the South Pacific was successful only in Fiji (where the Indians provided the bulk of the labour force), and benign indifference seemed to be the key characteristic of colonial rule. Island populations continued to practise subsistence agriculture, and even at the end of the 20th century a relatively small proportion of the working population was engaged in the formal sector. In some territories, colonial rulers made deliberate attempts to protect indigenous people from the impact of urbanization and modernization. In Fiji, for example, Sir Arthur Gordon, Governor of the islands from 1875 to 1880, followed a totally different policy from the one he previously pursued in Trinidad (Wood, 1968: 265–280) and ensured that native land remained in Fijian hands (Routledge, 1985: 217–219), to the extent that even at the end of the 20th century, more than 80% of it was collectively owned by clans. Elsewhere in the region, the French had fewer scruples (and perhaps more foresight) about taking over native land, with the result that freehold title is widely available in New Caledonia and Tahiti and the Islands, territories still ruled by France.

In short:

1. Land became freely available in the Caribbean and South Pacific islands ruled by France, whereas in the former British colonies of the South Pacific most remained in, or was returned to, collective ownership, where it is the source of continuous problems for investors and landowners in all economic sectors, but most notably the tourism industry (Harrison, 1997: 173–176, 1998: 135–136).
2. Because of the more developed infrastructure of the Caribbean, when compared with the South Pacific, the population is more urbanized, with a smaller proportion in subsistence agriculture and a greater proportion engaged in wage labour (Fairbairn and Worrell, 1996: 16, 75–78; World Bank, 1997: 114–116; UNDP, 1999: 111). As a consequence, the economy has been subjected to a greater level of monetization.
3. Whereas relationships of white colonialists with the former slaves and their descendants in the Caribbean continued to be characterized by resentment, those with Pacific islanders were of a much shorter duration, less based on control of agricultural labour, and were more amicable (albeit no less unequal). As a result, while the hospitality industry in the Caribbean has been stigmatized as entailing black servility to white visitors, in the South Pacific (with some exceptions alleged in Tahiti) local people see no stigma in working in the tourism industry.
4. Nevertheless, the Caribbean as a region is more 'developed' than the South Pacific.

Because of its early incorporation into the world economy, it possesses a better-trained work force and a better infrastructure. It has a longer history of self-government, and benefits from its closeness to North America and the relative ease of access to neighbouring islands (Fairbairn and Worrell, 1996: 98). At the same time, for good or ill, the culture of many South Pacific islands has more continuity with the past than that of the Caribbean (and tends to figure more strongly in promotional material). Economic incorporation does not occur in a cultural vacuum.

The above analysis is hardly comprehensive but does indicate how differential incorporation of LDCs into the world capitalist system influenced levels of commoditization in these societies and, in turn, how these are reflected in the current characteristics of their tourism industries. A similar exercise comparing the experience of former members of the Eastern bloc would be equally instructive, and would demonstrate how their close association with the USSR led to inadequate or partial commoditization, and how it influenced the post-1989 development of tourism in these societies.

A historical approach to the development of capitalism in LDCs would also facilitate a more comprehensive analysis of tourism's role in economic development. This is normally ascertained by examining its contribution to a country's foreign exchange, gross domestic product and employment, by relating tourism earnings to exports, and by comparing tourist income multipliers (e.g. Harrison, 1992a: 13–18). Some of these indicators were discussed earlier in this chapter. However useful such data may be, they provide, in essence, a snapshot of the importance of tourism at a specific time, whereas a more historical analysis would enable comparisons to be made over a longer period and would also facilitate wider regional comparisons.

Butler, in his well-known approach to tourism destination areas, for example, suggested that local residents are likely to be involved in the early stages of tourism development, with outside interests taking over as the development stage gets under way (Butler, 1980: 7–8). However, research in LDCs suggests that this did not occur. Swaziland's

tourism industry, for instance, was developed by white settlers, first for white business visitors and later for white holidaymakers, largely from the Republic of South Africa. Similarly, research in East Africa and the Caribbean reveals a conspicuous lack of indigenous involvement in financing and managing tourism (Harrison, 1992b: 23, 1995: 140, 146–148). In South Pacific islands, too, tourism has been developed by white residents for white visitors, and the indigenous population has been involved primarily as part of the islands' attraction and as lower-level workers in the hospitality industry (Harrison, 1998: 133). In fact, given the available evidence, it has probably been the norm for international tourism to be financed and operated by outsiders in LDCs with a poorly developed infrastructure, whether or not they had a colonial background.

Tourism's critics commonly bewail the lack of local expertise in hospitality management and condemn the tourism industry for employing locals primarily as 'bell boys and chamber maids' – tending to forget that such jobs usually provide more money and better working conditions than agriculture. However, the case for advocating policies to enable locals to progress through the industry is strong, if only because a greater proportion of their earnings is likely to remain in the country. The success of such policies depends on several factors, which critics frequently ignore. First, workers in the tourism industry must have some familiarity with the tourists' cultural background and (more so) with hotel culture. If cultures in the destination area differ greatly from that of the tourists (and this is often part of their attraction in many LDCs), nothing less than a comprehensive socialization of locals into hotel culture and management is required. In so far as this can be achieved (and the effort might well encounter local opposition), it takes time.

Secondly, operating a hotel to international standards requires financial as well as cultural capital, and in many LDCs both are in short supply. In formal terms, the less a country is developed, the less capital is likely to be readily available. It must also be recognized that cultural definitions of the role of entrepreneur may differ. De Burlo's study of a guest-house owner in Vanuatu, in the South Pacific, for instance, demonstrates that entry into the hospitality business may be motivated as much by a desire to increase status in the community as to make a financial profit, and that success may be achieved through the former, even if the project is a financial disaster (de Burlo, 2001). A similar view is put forward by Dahles (1999: 8–15), who noted the importance of social networks in the success or failure of Indonesian entrepreneurs, especially in circumstances where state policy is focused on the bigger players in the tourism industry.

The characteristics of tourism entrepreneurs in LDCs have been discussed in detail elsewhere (Harrison, 1992b: 22–24). These include the predominance of settler capital, the role of 'marginal' ethnic groups (for example, ethnic Chinese in Malaysia) and the importance of returning migrants and retiree tourists, who introduce skills and financial capital accumulated overseas. It was also indicated that, depending on the local context and external circumstances, local (usually small-scale) and metropolitan (usually large-scale) capital may variously compete for tourists at local level and yet join forces to market the destination overseas (Harrison, 1992b: 23).

None of these patterns can be predicted in advance. However, as a general rule, the more developed the society, the more likely it is that entrepreneurs will come from the local population – a situation that can be much assisted by the state. In (South) Cyprus, for instance, which is a mature destination area, a combination of state incentives, local expertise and the availability of finance from overseas has led to a situation where the vast majority of hotels, including some chains, are Cypriot-owned. The influence of international chains has been confined to a few management contracts and lease agreements (Andronikou, 1993: 68–69). Such policies seem also to have succeeded in Tunisia (Bleasdale and Tapsell, 1999: 187). In much of sub-Saharan Africa, though, where levels of economic development are relatively low, evidence suggests that international tourists are more likely to patronize hotels owned or operated by international chains. By contrast, at least in some urban areas, local hoteliers are known to concentrate on the domestic scene, frequently catering for couples wishing to use the facilities for an hour or

so – a niche market that might indeed encourage repeat visits but is unlikely to threaten the Sheraton or Holiday Inn (Harrison, 2000).

Interestingly, Bleasdale and Tapsell (1999: 191) noted that in parts of Tunisia most visited by tourists, 'a trend towards "fixed price" selling has emerged, which could be seen to undermine cultural authenticity'. It is nevertheless a move that many tourists might welcome, as the attention of Tunisian shopkeepers can persist to the point of intimidation (Hogan, 1992). Similar developments have been observed elsewhere. In Jerusalem, for example, it is noticeable that Jewish taxi drivers charge at a fixed rate, whereas Arab drivers negotiate the fare with the passenger. Whether or not such changes are welcomed, they raise another aspect of commoditization and 'authenticity' that would repay careful research. How far does the tourism sector *lead* the process of commoditization? To what extent are the changes welcomed? And if they are not, how can local cultures counter the process?

A historical perspective that directs attention to tourism as a relatively recent feature of capitalist expansion in LDCs enables several important issues, hitherto approached in a somewhat disparate way, to be considered in a more coherent framework. Patterns of commoditization, of material goods and cultural performances, are thus part and parcel of capitalism, and the extent to which local cultures maintain the distinctions between use or symbolic value, on the one hand, and exchange values, on the other, becomes a matter for research – as does the degree to which the quality of 'authenticity' is retained in goods and non-material cultural products in a rapidly changing socio-economic climate. There is nothing automatic about the process. While capitalism involves the transformation of subsistence goods into commodities (Smith and Sender, 1986: 10), even in the most developed countries the process is never complete, while in LDCs (including China and other former communist states) vast areas of social and economic life are still not subjected to strictly economic considerations of profit and loss. At the risk of parodying Marx, the reference here is to tendencies, which can be subjected to countervailing pressures, rather than to predetermined outcomes.

Conceptualizing tourism as an aspect of a dynamic capitalist expansion also situates the debate about the role of transnational corporations in global tourism in a wider perspective, shifting it from a staged and artificial confrontation between (alleged) representatives of good and evil to research on the circumstances in which transnationals come to dominate sectors of the tourism industry in some societies, and the contexts in which they are unable (or unwilling) to dominate in others. Bianchi (2000: 4, 6), for example, recognized that tourism has 'helped overcome some of the more entrenched aspects of peripherality in certain southern European regions', but yet remained uneasy over the increasing (but not dominant) role played by transnational corporations (TNCs) in southern European tourism. One might retort that capitalist development has always been uneven and that in tourism, as in other economic sectors, the overall power of TNCs is overestimated (Hirst and Thompson, 1999: 96). Much is likely to depend on the power of the state and its willingness to enter into joint ventures with overseas capital. China, for instance, has increasingly welcomed direct foreign investment, especially in hotels for international tourists (Lew, 2000: 275), a policy which has yet to counter the dominant influence of the country's many and largely inefficient state-owned enterprises (Anon., 2000a). In some market sectors transnational companies clearly exercise considerable influence, especially in air transport and tour operations in Europe (Williams, 1995), and in the UK there has been increasing concern about the dominant role played by a few outbound tour operators (Monopolies and Mergers Commission, 1997; O'Connor, 2000). Clearly, such dominance has ramifications for the tourism industry in some destination areas (Sinclair et al., 1992). However, as Sinclair and Stabler (1997: 58–94) indicated, tourism markets are more heterogeneous than is often supposed and research carried out by the author in Fiji in 1998 indicated that there, at least, hotels operated by transnational companies paid higher wages and provided better training than those that were locally owned, primarily because the TNCs were all unionized, whereas most locally owned hotels were not. Similar findings emerged from an earlier study of tourism in the

eastern Caribbean (Harrison, 1975: 45). More generally, while a detailed analysis of the role of TNCs in international tourism is not possible in this context, their involvement in LDCs is likely to be greatest when local capital is unavailable, and/or where it lacks the human resources to provide a service of international quality. In any case, the relationships of local and international hotels, inbound and outbound tour operators, and transport providers are best approached as constituent parts of a global system, which nevertheless takes on very different characteristics at local level.

Finally, a focus on tourism within a more comprehensive framework would facilitate a coherent approach to the ebb and flow of destination areas and tourist-sending societies. It was indicated earlier that, along with ease of access and geographical closeness, tourist movement has a correlation with previous colonial relationships. However, one characteristic of capitalist expansion is the creation of new 'centres', and the increased importance of tourism in the East Asia/Pacific region, for example, can be understood only in the context of what has been described as 'the East Asian miracle' (Wade and White, 1984; World Bank, 1993). As Michael Hall indicates in Chapter 8, the Japanese government has used tourism as a form of development assistance, to the extent that Japan is a major supplier of tourists throughout the region, and it is likely that China will also become an important source of tourists. China is one of the most rapidly developing countries in the world, and the experience of Europe, North America and Japan indicates that economic development and tourism are closely linked. In 1997, when overseas travel was still constrained by government policy, the Chinese government reportedly issued 3 million passports. On the assumption that more liberal regimes will develop as economic prosperity spreads across the country, China's government printer would be well advised to take in further supplies.

Tourism and the State

Reference to the role of government in Japan and China highlights the more general importance of the state. Even in developed countries, the formal organization of tourism varies (Pearce, 1992), but the state generally has a vital role to play. Indeed, during the 1980s theorists and practitioners alike were much exercised over its role in promoting 'development', and positions ranged from that which envisaged the state as a kind of prime mover of industrialization, fulfilling the role in LDCs that, in developed societies, had been taken by the bourgeoisie, to advocacy of a minimal state where development was best left to market forces, and the state – at most – acted only to enable the market to operate as freely as possible. These issues have been discussed at length elsewhere (Harrison, 1988: 138–145, 167–169; Henderson, 1994: 265–272; Clancy, 1999: 1–8) and the purpose of this section is less to prescribe the state's role than to illustrate its importance in tourism, especially in LDCs, and the difficulty of generalizing the consequences of state action for those of its subjects who are frequently the tourist 'attractions'.

According to the World Tourism Organization (WTO), the state is involved in tourism in five distinct ways: it establishes a framework within which the private and public sectors can cooperate; it legislates and regulates to protect the environment and cultural heritage; it constructs the infrastructure; it develops training and education for tourism; and it formulates overall policy and plans for tourism development (Raphael, 1993: 1–3). It is a moot point, however, how far most governments in LDCs are able to carry out these functions satisfactorily. By contrast, Jenkins and

Henry (1982) suggested that government participation can vary, as indicated in Table 2.1. They distinguished between 'passive' involvement, which has negative or positive implications for tourism but may not be primarily directed at the industry, and 'active' participation directed specifically at tourism-orientated goals. Within these categories, they further distinguished between passive involvement which is mandatory (essentially legislative) and that which is supportive, and active involvement which is either managerial (including the setting of objectives) or developmental, where government may be directly involved in operating parts of the tourism industry (Jenkins and Henry, 1982: 501–503).

Clearly, there is little chance of finding a society where government involvement in tourism is entirely absent. However, levels of participation of LDC governments in tourism have varied widely. In some, the state has played a vital role in owning and operating key parts of the tourism industry. This was especially so in the former USSR and throughout the Eastern bloc, where the state owned and operated most hotels, tour operations, travel agencies and large-scale means of transport (Hall, 1991; Harrison, 1993: 523–525). In this respect, tourism mirrored the rest of the economy, which was similarly centralized but (like undemocratic states generally) governments wary of Western influence saw additional advantages in their (apparent) ability to concentrate tourists in large complexes and exercise control over their movements. Indeed, it is noteworthy that the economic and social argu-

Table 2.1. Government involvement in tourism in less developed countries.

Passive	Active
Mandatory	Managerial
Usually legislative, e.g. employment of foreign nationals; investment incentives; air service agreements	Sets objectives and gives organizational/ legislative support, e.g. facilitating employment of foreign nationals, investment incentives (via
Supportive	Tourist Development Bank); charter agreements
For example, approval of hotel associations or tourist boards; training courses, e.g. in management	Developmental
	Government directly involved in tourism industry, e.g. for ideological reasons or where private sector unwilling/unable to invest. Government-run training courses in tourism

Source: Jenkins and Henry (1982: 501–504).

ments for and against tourism in communist central and south-east Europe were an exact match of those still put forward on tourism's impacts in other LDCs (Hall, 1998: 425). In the Caribbean, Castro's Cuba was decidedly cold towards international tourists (except those from the Eastern bloc) and, like the USSR, ensured that virtually all tourism was in state hands. The policy was modified in the early 1970s, for the sake of hard currency, and by the 1990s international investment in Cuban tourism was being actively obtained (Hall, 1992: 110–111; Avella and Mills, 1996: 56–59; de Holan and Phillips, 1997: 784). In Africa, Tanzania's experiment with 'African Socialism' commenced with the Arusha Declaration of 1967, when it adopted a policy of 'self-reliance' and, as a consequence, 'tourism became bound up with the growth of the parastatal sector. It was one of the newer forms of parastatal activity, relying largely on domestic funding and control' (Curry, 1990: 137). As Curry noted, most government investment was in new hotels and infrastructure in rural areas where wildlife was found, whereas private investment was 'in less risky town hotels' (Curry, 1990: 139). In Swaziland, too, government involvement in the hotel sector is in areas considered too risky or unattractive by private capital (Harrison, 1995: 143).

Curry indicated, that the Tanzanian government's direct involvement in tourism was not a success. Government hotels had much higher investment costs than the town hotels; there were no foreign partners to assist with the initial costs; projects were relatively small-scale and had to meet stringent conservation criteria; and, finally, the government had no experience of running hotels. Unsurprisingly, the result, which was exacerbated by the closure of the border with Kenya in 1977, was that govenment-owned hotels soon made substantial losses (Curry, 1990: 143–146). By the end of the 1990s, the government had formed the Presidential Parastatal Sector Reform Commission, its privatization agency, and was actively seeking buyers for its hotels and wildlife lodges. In common with other countries in the region, too, it was attempting to transfer other state-owned companies into private ownership (Anon., 2000b).

Tunisia and Jamaica also attempted to follow a self-reliant strategy in tourism. In Tunisia, from the 1960s on, the Bourguiba government directed its efforts to attracting Western package tourists, with a strong state involvement in tourism facilities and strict restriction on the repatriation of profits overseas. The policy was modified in the mid-1980s and attempts were made to encourage foreign investment, with some success (Poirier and Wright, 1993: 150–155), but by the end of the 1990s foreign investment in Tunisian tourism was estimated at only 10% (Saihi, 1989: 14). In Jamaica, government purchase of hotels from expatriate owners in the early 1970s was prompted by socialist principles and the desire to protect hotel employment during a recession (Manley, 1987: 147; Thomas, 1988: 159) but, as noted by Mather and Todd (1993: 100), by the mid-1980s there was 'a general move towards privatisation and the free market. Hotels which were government-owned have now almost all been sold, the majority to Jamaicans'.

Poirier and Wright (1993: 152) noted that the Tunisian government's decision to privatize was 'more a consequence of necessity generated by the failure and inefficiency of state-run enterprises, combined with prodding by external interests and agencies, rather than any strong ideological commitment'. In this respect, Tunisia was not alone. Most available evidence suggests that, once tourism is established, a good service is far more likely to be provided by the private sector. As in Mexico, initial state involvement can prime the pumps for future investment from the private sector (Clancy, 1999: 10), but governments are not usually successful hotel owners, and state employees are not enthusiastic service providers.

Overall, once the ideological attraction of state ownership fell out of favour (Brett, 1987; Dearlove, 1987), economic wastefulness and poor service together persuaded governments to divest themselves of direct ownership, except when the national interest seemed to override economic considerations. These are still considered important in air transport, where the symbolic value of 'flying the flag' has often outweighed the costs of entry, maintenance and state subsidies, but even here privatization is increasing. By 1993, only four state-owned airlines were among the top 25 airlines (ranked in terms of sales), and the trend towards privatization was being accompanied by increased foreign owner- ship and employee participation (Hanlon, 1996: 9).

It was noted earlier that, by actively encouraging its citizens to travel overseas, the Japanese government directly influenced tourism development in other societies, and fiscal policies of developed states can have a significant effect far beyond national bound- aries. Ideological considerations also play their part, as evidenced by the imposition of travel restrictions on citizens of the former USSR and its Eastern bloc partners, on US nationals wishing to visit Cuba, and on Chinese increasingly looking to travel over- seas. Such examples demonstrate the power of governments of powerful states to influence tourism elsewhere. However, the managerial role of government, where the state acts to condition or enable other actors to operate in line with state-defined tourism policies, occurs primarily within state boundaries, which actually serve to circumscribe the extent of its legitimate power, and it is the proper role of government to set objectives and give organizational support so that these policies can be achieved.

Merely formulating objectives does not guarantee success. Many governments offer such incentives as tax holidays and subsidized interest rates to investors, but so do others, within and outside the destination region, and the result can easily be a prolonged auction at which the main beneficiaries are international companies able to play one tour destination against the other and thus obtain the best deal for the longest period. In fact, key decisions for any LDC government include a prior defin- ition of the kind of tourist it can realistically hope to attract and the extent to which it is prepared to work with national and interna- tional capital (in so far as these are available) to develop its tourism industry. When effi- ciently implemented, government policy can undoubtedly affect the nature of the tourism industry. In (South) Cyprus, for example, local capitalists have been encouraged to invest in tourism, loans have been made at favourable interest rates, and incentives provided for duty-free imports. In addition, legislation has prescribed minimum standards in accommo-

dation, and the government has invested heavily in airport facilities. Finally, after the partition of Cyprus that followed the Turkish intervention of 1974, government in the South provided special incentives to refugee hoteliers. The result of such policies was that the vast majority of Cypriot hotels are locally owned – many as family-run establishments (Ioannides, 1992).

Analysis is further complicated once attention is drawn to the various partnerships available to 'the state' in LDCs, because it soon becomes evident that 'the state' itself is, in fact, a highly disparate collection of institu- tions. It is but a short step to ask, with many Marxist commentators of the 1970s and 1980s, whom the state actually 'represents' (Harrison, 1988: 138–145). This is not the place to develop a detailed theoretical response, but it is surely legitimate to ask apparently empirical questions as to whose economic interests are best served by particu- lar categories of tourists (high spenders in five- star hotels, package tourists in three-star hotels, or backpackers in hostels), and how the economic benefits that tourism brings are distributed within a specific society. Clearly, such questions are situated in wider debates about 'development' and 'dependency,' and it is equally appropriate to ask which social groups hold power in any specific society, and how national tourism (and development) strategies are influenced by external agencies – international consultants, other nations, regional blocs, transnational companies, non- governmental organizations, international organizations and so on.

It was suggested above that such questions are 'apparently empirical'. Equally, though, they are theoretically informed, and the data obtained in pursuing them have implications for the further development of theoretical insights. Again, the issues raised are immense, but they can be illustrated, at least, through a single example (Harrison, 1998: 133), which relates to the portrayal of tourism destinations through tourism promotion.

In Fiji, despite the fact that some 44% of the population of the Fiji Islands is of East Indian ori- gin, Indian people and their culture rarely appear in promotional material issued by the Fiji Visitors' Bureau (FVB). Instead, focus is almost entirely on the culture of ethnic Fijians, who are portrayed in 'traditional' dress, drinking the highly valued *kava* root, and living in houses of traditional thatch (which are highly unusual in the main centres of population in the Fiji Islands). Overall, the portrayal is of a colourful and almost mystical people, an exotic 'other', quite specifically designed to attract visitors from Australia, New Zealand, North America and Europe. And in the promotional literature of 1998, the key reference was: 'Fiji Islands: the way the world should be'.

Why is this example relevant to the role of the state in tourism development? First, as in many other countries, the FVB is an arm of government which exists primarily to market the Fiji Islands overseas and which is the major recipient of government funds for tourism promotion. Secondly, its work, and that of the (lesser funded) Department of Tourism, has been considerably influenced by overseas consultants who, over the years, have produced a series of tourism development plans, largely funded by overseas agencies. These include the United Nations Development Programme (UNDP) and the World Bank (Belt, Collins and Associates Ltd, 1973), the UNDP and the WTO (Adhikari, 1988), the Asian Development Bank (Coopers and Lybrand Associates, 1989) and the European Union (Deloitte and Touche, Government of Fiji and Tourism Council of the South Pacific, 1997). Thirdly, much of the promotional material used by the FVB has been selected by overseas consultants. In December 1998, for instance, some 16 months before Fiji's elected (mixed-race) government was overthrown by a coup, consultants recommended the slogan. 'Fiji: the one truly relaxing tropical getaway.' Fourthly, the emphasis on Fijian culture has clearly served the political interest of indigenous Fijians, in whose name the coup of May 2000 was carried out, as were those of May and September, 1987 (Scarr, 1988; Keith Reid, 2000). Indeed, the material used to promote Fiji's tourism directly answers a question raised by a senior Fijian civil servant after the 1987 coups: 'The question is: should Fiji be more Fijian or should it become more Indian? Put another way … should Fiji promote a Fijian image or an Indian image?' (Scarr, 1988: vii).

The image of Fiji portrayed in the brochures is undoubtedly at variance with the experience of many East Indians and of other ethnic groups (including many indigenous Fijians). However, the key point is that there is a wide consensus in government, among international consultants working for outside funding agencies, and among the major actors of the Fiji tourism industry, which is dominated by expatriates who employ indigenous Fijians as front-line staff (Harrison, 1998: 133–134), that the main emphasis of Fijian tourism should be the indigenous Fijian, and that other ethnic groups are to be largely unrepresented. In this context, however idealized the representation of Fijians, their portrayal in the brochures reflects and reinforces their political (but not their economic) supremacy. That said, it is a moot point as to whether or not Australia, New Zealand and the USA, on whom Fiji most relies for its trading links, will allow the transitional government that followed the May 2000 coup to dispense with international standards of 'democracy' and permanently deny civil and political rights to the Indian minority.

In the Fijian example, images in tourism brochures reflect the symbolic dominance of the majority ethnic group, but this is not always the case. Picard (1993), for example, placed the development of Bali as a tourist destination within a wider historical process of colonization and Indonesianization. In this process, some aspects of Balinese culture have undoubtedly been emphasized, to the detriment of others; nevertheless, 'tourism culture has been transformed into the island's main economic resource and by the same token Balinese culture has become a major bargaining point with central government' (Picard, 1993: 86). Put somewhat crudely, the state and the Balinese have used Bali's culture for their own ends.

The Balinese experience is not unique. In Mao's China, when tourism and the movement of tourists were strictly controlled, handicrafts and traditions of ethnic minorities were suppressed. After Mao's death, in 1976, an 'open-door' policy was implemented, increasingly involving foreign capital (Zhang *et al.*, 1999), and religions and traditions of ethnic minorites previously targeted by government, including Tibet, were increasingly portrayed to tourists as examples of the diversity of Chinese culture (Sofield and Li, 1998: 369–376). The role of the Chinese state in the 'commoditizing of ethnicity' was also discussed by Swain (1990: 26), who crucially emphasized how ethnic groups may be differentially placed to take advantage of their newly-discovered importance as tourism attractions (Swain, 1990: 29):

> Whether tourism promotes cultural continuity of touristized ethnic groups or ethnic group assimilation depends on the state's allocation of control in the process of ethnicity commoditization. If the ethnic group, through individual actors, has no control over tourism activity – as seems the case on Hainan island – then it is likely that their participation is exploitative and devalues their culture. If the ethnic group can take control – as the Sani have through their own actions and programs – then ethnic tourism can well give the group economic power to reinforce its identity as it adapts to new definitions and cultural values for ethnic markers. This type of 'indigenous tourism development' validates the power of the autonomy or self-government that the groups – in theory – have from the state.

Swain's remarks can be applied more generally. Like 'race', 'ethnicity' is not a fixed category. Instead, it is subject to continuous negotiation and renegotiation and is thus influenced by changing patterns of power and status. These, in turn, are affected by the development of international tourism, but how they are affected will depend on specific cicumstances. As Wood and Deppen (1994: 6–11) suggested, tourism is often superimposed on existing patterns of inequality, and may lead to acculturation and the subsequent dilution of ethnic distinctiveness or, alternatively, to its reinforcement. As the Fiji example indicates, it might also promote the culture of one ethnic group above another. Wood (1984: 363) noted that if the state is already dominant, it is no more likely to consult people about tourism than any other form of development. Precisely what does happen when the state becomes involved in tourism, and the nature of its impact on ethnic relations, cannot be predicted in advance. There is evidence, though, that community responses to tourism are partly determined by their prior access to local resources, the level of consensus and cohesion in the community,

and the degree to which they are able to work with outside institutions (Harrison and Price, 1996: 14):

> The moral, perhaps, is that we should no longer seek to know how far 'development' is either 'top-down' or 'bottom-up', but rather ask which institutions, local and outside, are involved in tourism, and how they articulate with one another.

This extended discussion of the role of the state, while not comprehensive, illustrates the complexity of its role in tourism development. It has to be emphasized that what the state intends and what it actually achieves may be quite different. Formulating plans for tourism (and development plans generally) is relatively easy, especially if funded by international aid agencies and carried out by overseas consultants, who often use the same template for producing 'Master Plans' for quite different societies, but there is no guarantee that once money is paid and the report presented, the plan will be successfully implemented.

Reasons for the lack of implementation vary. Governments in LDCs often lack the will to implement policies. In particular, consultants and governments often fail to consider the social and cultural implications of their recommendations, leaving such matters, if they are considered at all, to the end of the process. One result is that while lip service is given to the importance of social issues, rhetoric is not matched by state action, which is more directed towards economic objectives. To give but two of many possible examples, prostitution is illegal in Thailand, but police posts are commonly found next door to brothels in Bangkok, Pattaya and Phuket. Public nudity is an offence in Tunisia, but tourist police concentrate on protecting tourists from unwelcome harrassment and ignore obvious contraventions of the law. Ethical considerations are raised in the Afterword of this volume, but strict, consistent and well-publicized treatment of tourists who flout local laws would sharply reduce such tendencies, as those who have tried to import alcoholic drinks into some Islamic states would testify. Clearly, such steps would reduce tourist arrivals, but government reluctance to act perhaps reflects state priorities more than any 'immorality' intrinsic to the international tourism industry.

Secondly, as Butler (1999: 12) noted, plans for tourism should be implemented within a wider development strategy, but this does not always occur. In development strategies generally, old habits die hard. For at least three decades, for example, critics of tourism in Caribbean island states have pointed to the need to develop linkages with agriculture, thus widening the spread of benefits brought by tourism and reducing leakages from the economy, but Caribbean governments have continued to focus on the export of such primary products as sugar, coffee and cocoa, to the detriment of the domestic market (Doxey and Associates, 1971: 87–95; Hope, 1986: 48–50; Deere, 1990: 197; Pattullo, 1996: 43–46).

Thirdly, the state in many LDCs is incapable of implementing an agreed development policy, either because it is inefficient or, in some cases, because it is riddled with corruption (Brett, 1988; Harriss-White and White, 1996); sometimes both characteristics are found. Even in such a relatively mature tourist destination as Cyprus, legislation to protect the environment can soon be overtaken by the sheer momentum of change, especially where it is encouraged by government incentives (Godfrey, 1996: 74). In addition, the work force in many LDCs is characterized by low levels of education and training, with the result that in all sectors of the economy there is a lack of qualified personnel. Without competent business people, administrators, managers and planners, trainers and educationalists, 'development' will inevitably be stunted, just as an efficient tourism industry requires a supply of hotel managers, chefs, front office administrators, accountants and so on. In such circumstances, long check lists of what government should be doing to bring about 'sustainable tourism development', for instance, are simply exercises in wishful thinking (Butler, 1999: 21).

Sometimes the expansion of tourism triggers state action, without prior planning. Mexican villagers whose rowdy and allegedly dangerous and coarse activities were curtailed by the arrival of a policeman (Nunez, 1963) were unlikely to have been pleased that tourism led to more state control, but

incorporation into a wider economy normally results in a loss of local autonomy. However, the process can work in reverse. Not all tourists are content with a staged version of national unity and consensus. By appropriating Buddhism for its own purposes and attempting to restrict tourist access to Burmese nationals, for example, the Burmese government is indeed acting self-interestedly (Philp and Mercer, 1999: 29–37) but, as the former USSR and China discovered, opening up to tourists, even to a limited extent, has unforeseen consequences. With foreign currency come foreign ideas and (arguably) totalitarian governments are no better qualified to control the process of acculturation than those of open societies.

Conclusion

The focus in this chapter has been on three aspects of international tourism: migration, capitalism and the role of the state. Clearly, international tourism is not new. However it is defined, it preceded capitalism but under capitalism, and the wealth and innovations with which it was associated in the West, international tourism became big business. Following the mass domestic tourism that emerged in the second half of the 19th century, international tourism increasingly took on the character of mass travel. In this crucial respect, international tourism, although temporary for individual holidaymakers and business travellers, has its most obviously permanent effect on destination areas. It carries with it the potential to bring about radical changes in their landscape and, indeed, the economic basis of their existence. It is also permanent in other respects. In developed societies, holidays have become a regular part of annual, even seasonal routines. Like birthdays and religious festivals, they help to punctuate the passing of time and, like these other landmark events, reflect changes in the individual and family life cycle. Young clubbers to Ibiza or Agia Napa will soon be taking their young families to more child-centred destinations, perhaps even with their own parents, before the young ones, in turn, seek the independence of adult-free holidays.

Holidays in favoured destinations are often repeated and this, in turn, leads to the development of second homes and, in some cases, retirement and even permanent migration. Such phenomena have long been recognized in domestic tourism and the process is now being replicated at international level. Interspersed in the process, too, is the most popular form of global travel of all – visits to friends and relatives. From tourist to repeat visitor to retiree to migrant: the process is not automatic, but it occurs often enough to warrant further research, as does the extent to which 'permanent' migration itself may set up a pattern of visits between one country and another, involving VFR tourism on a regular basis and, at least in some cases, the return of migrants, temporarily or permanently, to their countries of origin.

It has been argued that while commoditization (or commodification) and the alleged loss of 'authenticity' have often been analysed within the context of tourism, they are really part of a much wider pattern of capitalist expansion. In somewhat dated Marxist terms, capitalism involves the development of markets, a move from use value to exchange value, and the articulation of different social and economic units ('social formations') within a wider and pervasive global capitalist system. In this context, the role of the returned migrant is yet another bridge between different parts of this increasingly coherent and cohesive system. The argument is no longer about the relative merits of capitalism or socialism, but about what kind of capitalism is most appropriate for 'development' and how much political control is required to expedite the process. For many LDCs, tourism – its potentials and its dangers – is at the heart of the debate. Linked as most already were to capitalist 'metropoles', tourism was but one more step in bringing the 'periphery' closer to the centre – a step that, for many LDCs, brought economic prosperity and further incorporation into a global economy.

While patterns can be observed in the relationships of LDCs with tourist-sending societies, the process is subject to considerable regional variation and new centres continually emerge. Peripheries, too, may become centres or, alternatively, lose their earlier appeal. Earlier ties of history and colonialism articulate with differences in economic, social and ethnic structures to ensure that local and regional responses to tourism will vary widely. Critics who bewail the globalization of culture generally, and the evils of tourism specifically, do LDCs no service. While such simplistic notions reflect well-meaning but ultimately patronizing attitudes to LDCs, they are not based on careful analysis of tourism's impacts in LDCs. In particular, they are no substitute for an understanding of the complex linkages of local factors – capital, status, class, religion and ethnicity, for example – with such external agencies as transnational corporations, foreign governments and non-government organizations, as well as a range of international institutions. Perhaps most important of all, there is a clear need to focus on the role of the state in LDCs. Finally, the state (like tourism) is not new. One can argue about 'whom it represents' but it became increasingly powerful in both capitalist and state socialist societies. Indeed, the debate among developmentalists from the 1960s to the 1980s was an attempt to come to terms with its role in developed as much as less developed societies. Nowadays, the state is no longer a central weapon used by ideologues to demolish opponents by the sheer force of their moral fervour and there is a more general readiness to assess the role and nature of states at specific times and places. It is generally accepted, too, that governments are usually inefficient at running businesses – in tourism or other economic sectors – but this is not to advocate a *laissez-faire* alternative. Clearly, the state has a role: to set the scene, to enable markets to operate and to formulate and implement national objectives. It also has to secure its borders and keep its citizens safe from danger, whether from inside its borders or from external agencies. In this context, perceptions of tourism's importance and impacts clearly vary. Does the state want tourism? Does it offer financial incentives for tourism development? To whom? For what kind of tourism? Does the state legislate against specific tourist behaviour and – equally important – is it willing and able to enforce such legislation? Such issues relate to the constitution of the state at local and at national level, to the degree that it 'represents' the population of tourist destination areas, to its stance towards overseas capital, whether of individual entrepreneurs or transnational companies, and to the importance it attaches to economic development generally and to tourism as a tool in achieving such development. These are empirical issues rather than religious dogma.

In many LDCs the state lacks the competence to carry out many policies, however well thought out they may be. Markets are often poorly developed. Infrastructures leave much to be desired. 'Human resources' often lack training and education for management and other roles in tourism. State functionaries, at local and governmental level, may be corrupt. Special interest groups may hold a disproportionate amount of power and exert it for their own benefit. Development policies generally may be unconsidered or ill-considered, and approaches to tourism may be unrelated to wider strategies for change. Where such phenomena are found, in developed or less developed countries, they should be recognized, but they cannot be predicted in advance: levels of state competence in the formulation and implementation of policy and the configuration of forces for and against specific tourism strategies can be ascertained only through specific empirical research and analysis. Just as the initial empirical questions are theoretically informed, so, too, the findings are theoretically relevant.

It was indicated earlier that the choice of these 'key issues' was subjective. Other commentators might focus on different topics: on marketing, advertising and image formation in tourism promotion, for example, or on the role of women (or, better, gender relationships) in tourism development, on place and changing perceptions of landscape, or on what they see as the continued defilement of innocent LDCs by Westernization. It is not suggested here that such matters are unimportant, but in many respects they can be situated within the broad framework suggested in this chapter. Marketing and management are key features of capitalist production and capitalist markets. The image of a destination area is related not only to marketing, but also to the persistence of stereotypes, which may date back hundreds of years to the beginning of colonialism and even earlier forms of culture contact. Stereotypes of gender, race and ethnicity are similarly historically and socially conditioned.

The fascination of tourism as an area of study is that it incorporates all these issues, and more, and enables academics from different backgrounds not only to follow their own leanings but also to learn from the work of scholars in different disciplines. In this respect, as in so many others, tourism inevitably encourages acculturation, if not always in ways of our own choosing.

References

Adhikari, S. (1988) *Brief General Features for Policy Guidelines on Secondary Tourism Development in Fiji.* United Nations Development Programme and World Tourism Organization, Suva, Fiji.

Adler, J. (1985) Youth on the road: reflections on the history of tramping. *Annals of Tourism Research* 12(3), 335–354.

Ahlburg, D.A. and Brown, R.P.C. (1998) Migrants' intentions to return home and capital transfers: a study of Tongans and Samoans in Australia. *Journal of Development Studies* 35(2), 125–151.

Andronikou, A. (1993) The hotel industry in Cyprus: problems and future prospects. *Tourism Management* 14(1), 67–70.

Anon. (2000a) China's state-owned enterprises. *The Economist* 30 September–6 October, pp. 113–116.

Anon. (2000b) New trade protocol to bring community economies in line with the move to free markets. *South African Development Community: Part 1.* Images, Words Ltd pp. 2–3 (issued with *The Observer*, 17 September).

Avella, A.E. and Mills, A.S. (1996) Tourism in Cuba in the 1990s: back to the future? *Tourism Management* 17(1), 55–60.

Belt, Collins and Associates Ltd (1973) *Tourism Development Programme for Fiji.* International Bank for Reconstruction and Development (World Bank), Washington, DC.

Berno, T. (1999) When a guest is a guest: Cook Islanders' view of tourism. *Annals of Tourism Research* 26(3), 656–675.

Bianchi, R. (2000) The regional dynamics of tourism in Southern Europe: exploring the South–South divide. In: *North–South: Contrasts and Connections in Global Tourism.* ATLAS International Conference, 18–21 June 2000, Savonlinna, Finland.

Bianchi, R. (2000) Migrant tourist-workers: exploring the 'Contact Zones' of post-industrial tourism. *Current Issues in Tourism* 3(2), 107–137.

Bielckus, C.L., Rogers, A.W. and Wibberley, G.P. (1972) *Second Homes in England and Wales: a Study of the Distribution and Use of Properties Taken Over as Second Residences.* School of Rural Economics and Related Studies, Wye College, Ashford, Kent, UK.

Bleasdale, S. and Tapsell, S. (1999) Social and cultural impacts of tourism policy in Tunisia. In: Robinson, M. and Boniface, P. (eds) *Tourism and Cultural Conflicts.* CAB International, Wallingford, UK, pp. 181–203.

Boissevain, J. (ed.) (1996) Ritual, tourism and cultural commoditization in Malta: culture by the pound? In: Selwyn, T. (ed.) *The Tourist Image: Myths and Myth Making in Tourism.* John Wiley & Sons, Chichester, UK, pp. 105–120.

Boorstin, D. (1964) *The Image: a Guide to Pseudo-Events in America.* Harper and Row, New York.

Booth, D. (1994) Rethinking social development: an overview. In: Booth, D. (ed.) *Rethinking Social Development: Theory, Research and Practice.* Longman, Harlow, UK, pp. 3–34.

Brett, E.A. (1987) States, markets and private power in the developing world: problems and possibilities. *IDS Bulletin* 18(3), 31–37.

Brett, E.A. (ed.) (1988) Adjustment in the state: problems of administrative reform. *IDS Bulletin* 19(4).

British Hospitality Association (1999) *British Hospitality: Trends and Statistics, 1999.* British Hospitality Association, London.

Butler, R. (1980) The concept of a tourism area cycle of evolution: implication for management of resources. *Canadian Geographer* 24(1), 5–12.

Butler, R. (1999) Sustainable tourism: a state-of-the-art review. *Tourism Geographies* 1(1), 7–21.

Byron, M. (1994) *Post-War Caribbean Migration to Britain: the Unfinished Cycle.* Avebury, Aldershot, UK.

Castles, S. and Miller, M.J. (1998) *The Age of Migration: International Population Movements in the Modern World,* 2nd edn. Macmillan Press, Houndmills, Basingstoke, UK.

Chamberlain, M. (1997) *Narratives of Exile and Return.* Macmillan, London.

Chamberlain, M. (1998) Introduction. In: Chamberlain, M. (ed.) *Caribbean Migration, Globalised Identities.* Routledge, London, pp. 1–17.

Clancy, M. (1999) Tourism and development: evidence from Mexico. *Annals of Tourism Research* 26(1), 1–20.

Cohen, E. (1988) Authenticity and Commoditization in Tourism. *Annals of Tourism Research* 15(3), 371–386.

Cohen, E. (1993) The heterogeneization of a tourist art. *Annals of Tourism Research* 20(1), 138–163.

Cohen, R. and Kennedy, P. (2000) *Global Sociology.* Macmillan Press, Houndmills, Basingstoke, UK.

Coopers and Lybrand Associates (1989) *Government of Fiji Tourism Master Plan,* Vols. I–III. Department of Tourism, Suva, Fiji.

Coppock, J.T. (ed.) (1977) *Second Homes: Curse or Blessing?* Pergamon Press, Oxford, UK.

Crick, M. (1994) *Resplendent Sites, Discordant Voices: Sri Lankans and International Tourism.* Harwood Academic, Chur, Switzerland.

Crocombe, R. (1987) Overview: the pattern of change in Pacific land tenure. In: Crocombe, R. (ed.) *Land Tenure in the Pacific.* University of the South Pacific, Suva, Fiji, pp. 1–24.

Curry, S. (1990) Tourism Development in Tanzania. *Annals of Tourism Research* 17(1), 133–149.

Dahles, H. (1999) Tourism and small entrepreneurs in developing countries: a theoretical perspective. In: Dahles, H. and Bras, K. (eds) *Tourism and Small Entrepreneurs: Development, National Policy and Entrepreneurial Culture: Indonesian Cases.* Cognizant, New York, pp. 1–19.

Daniel, Y. (1996) Tourism dance performances: authenticity and creativity. *Annals of Tourism Research* 23(4), 780–797.

Dann, G. (1996a) *The Language of Tourism.* CAB International, Wallingford, UK.

Dann, G. (1996b) The people of tourist brochures. In: Selwyn, T. (ed.) *The Tourist Image: Myths and Myth Making in Tourism.* John Wiley & Sons, Chichester, UK, pp. 61–81.

Dearlove, J. (1987) Economists on the state. *IDS Bulletin* 18(3), 5–11.

Deere, C.B. (Co-ordinator) (1990) *In the Shadows of the Sun: Caribbean Development Alternatives and US Policy.* Westview Press, Boulder, Colorado.

de Burlo, C. (2001) Tourism, Conservation and the Cultural Environment in Rural Vanuatu. In: Harrison, D. (ed.) *Tourism in the South Pacific*. Cognizant, New York, (in press).

Deloitte and Touche, Government of Fiji and Tourism Council of the South Pacific (1997) *Fiji Tourism Development Plan: 1998–2005*. Ministry of Transport and Tourism, Suva, Fiji.

Downing, P. and Dower, M. (1974) *Second Homes in England and Wales*. Prepared for the Countryside Commission, Dartington Amenity Research Trust, Dartington, UK.

Doxey, G.V. (1975) A causation theory of visitor–resident irritants: methodology and research inferences. In: *The Impact of Tourism*. Proceedings of the Travel Research Association Sixth Annual Conference, San Diego, California, 8–11 September, pp. 195–198.

Doxey, H.V. and Associates (1971) *The Tourist Industry in Barbados: a Socio-economic Assessment*. Dusco Graphics, Kitchener, Ontario.

Economist Intelligence Unit (1991) Vacation homes in South East Asia. *EIU Travel and Tourism Analyst* 5, 24–41.

Fairbairn, T.I.J. and Worrell, D. (1996) *South Pacific and Caribbean Island Economies: a Comparative Study*. The Foundation for Development Corporation, Brisbane, Australia.

Gartner, W.C. (1987) Environmental impacts of recreational home developments. *Annals of Tourism Research* 14(1), 38–57.

Girard, T.C. and Gartner, W.C. (1993) Second home, second view: host community perceptions. *Annals of Tourism Research* 20(4), 685–700.

Godfrey, K.B. (1996) Towards sustainability? Tourism in the Republic of Cyprus. In: Harrison, L.C. and Husbands, W. (eds) *Practicing Responsible Tourism: International Case Studies in Tourism Planning, Policy and Development*. John Wiley & Sons, Chichester, UK, pp. 58–79.

Graburn, N. (1984) The evolution of tourist arts. *Annals of Tourism Research* 11(3), 393–419.

Greenwood, D. (1978) Culture by the pound: an anthropological perspective on tourism as cultural commoditization. In: Smith, V. (ed.) *Hosts and Guests: the Anthropology of Tourism*, 1st edn. Basil Blackwell, Oxford, UK, pp. 129–138.

Hall, D. (1991) Evolutionary pattern of tourism development in Eastern Europe and the Soviet Union. In: Hall, D. (ed.) *Tourism and Economic Development in Eastern Europe and the Soviet Union*. Belhaven Press, London, pp. 78–115.

Hall, D. (1992) Tourism development in Cuba. In: Harrison, D. (ed.) *Tourism and the Less Developed Countries*. John Wiley & Sons, Chichester, UK, 102–120.

Hall, D. (1998) Tourism development and sustainability issues in Central and South-Eastern Europe. *Tourism Management* 19(5), 423–431.

Hanlon, P. (1996) *Global Airlines: Competition in a Transnational Industry*. Butterworth-Heinemann, Oxford, UK.

Harrison, D. (1975) Report on the pilot survey of tourism in St Vincent. Overseas Development Administration, London.

Harrison, D. (1988) *The Sociology of Modernization and Development*. Routledge, London.

Harrison, D. (1992a) International tourism and the less developed countries: the background. In: Harrison, D. (ed.) *Tourism and the Less Developed Countries*. John Wiley & Sons, Chichester, UK, pp. 1–18.

Harrison, D. (1992b) Tourism to Less Developed Countries: the social consequences. In: Harrison, D. (ed.) *Tourism and the Less Developed Countries*. John Wiley & Sons, Chichester, UK, pp. 19–34.

Harrison, D. (1993) Bulgarian tourism: a state of uncertainty. *Annals of Tourism Research* 20(3), 519–534.

Harrison, D. (1994) Tourism, capitalism and development in less developed countries. In: Sklair, L. (ed.) *Capitalism and Development*. Routledge, London, pp. 232–257.

Harrison, D. (1995) Development of tourism in Swaziland. *Annals of Tourism Research* 22(1), 135–156.

Harrison, D. (1997) Globalization and tourism: some themes from Fiji. In: Oppermann, M. (ed.) *Pacific Rim Tourism*. CAB International, Wallingford, UK, pp. 167–183.

Harrison, D. (1998) The world comes to Fiji: who communicates what, and to whom? *Tourism, Culture and Communications* 1(2), 129–138.

Harrison, D. (1999) *A Cultural Audit of Turtle Island, Fiji*. Centre for Leisure and Tourism Studies, University of North London.

Harrison, D. (2000) Tourism in Africa: the social and cultural framework. In: Dieke, P. (ed.) *The Political Economy of Tourism in Africa*. Cognizant, New York.

Harrison, D. and Price, M. (1996) Fragile environments, fragile communities? An introduction. In: Price, M. (ed.) *People and Tourism in Fragile Environments*. John Wiley & Sons, Chichester, UK, pp. 1–18.

Harriss-White, B. and White, G. (eds) (1996) Liberalization and the new corruption. *IDS Bulletin* 27(2).

Hellicar, M. (2000) Repats: we just want to be treated as equals. *Cyprus Mail* 12 September, p. 2

Henderson, J. (1994) Electronic industries and the developing world: uneven contributions and uncertain prospects. In: Sklair, L. (ed.) *Capitalism and Development*. Routledge, London, pp. 258–288.

Henshall, J. (1977) Second homes in the Caribbean. In: Coppock, J.T. (ed.) *Second Homes: Curse or Blessing?* Pergamon Press, Oxford, UK, pp. 75–84.

Hirst, P. and Thompson, G. (1999) *Globalization in Question*, 2nd edn. Polity Press, Cambridge, UK.

Hitchcock, M. (2000) Introduction. In: Hitchcock, M. (ed.) *Souvenirs: the Material Culture of Tourism*. Ashgate, Aldershot, UK, pp. 1–16.

Hogan, P. (1992) Pestered in paradise. *The Observer* 23 August.

Hoivik, T. and Heiberg, T. (1980) Centre-periphery tourism and self-reliance. *International Social Science Journal* 32(1), 69–98.

de Holan, M. and Phillips, N. (1997) Sun, sand and hard currency. *Annals of Tourism Research* 24(4), 777–795.

Hope, K.R. (1986) *Economic Development in the Caribbean*. Praeger, New York.

Hughes, G. (1995) Authenticity in tourism. *Annals of Tourism Research* 22(4), 781–803.

Ioannides, D. (1992) Tourism development agents: the Cypriot resort cycle. *Annals of Tourism Research* 19(4), 711–731.

Jaakson, R. (1986) Second home domestic tourism. *Annals of Tourism Research* 13(3), 367–391.

Jenkins, C.L. and Henry, B.M. (1982) Government involvement in tourism in developing countries. *Annals of Tourism Research* 9(4), 499–521.

Jordan, J.W. (1980) The summer people and the natives: some effects of tourism in a Vermont vacation village. *Annals of Tourism Research* 12(1), 34–55.

Kang, S.K.-M. and Page, S.J. (2000) Tourism, migration and emigration: travel patterns of Korean-New Zealanders in the 1990s. *Tourism Geographies* 2(1), 50–65.

Keith-Reid, R. (2000) Fiji's rocky road. *Islands Business* 26(7), 28–31.

Kenna, M. (1993) Returned migrants and tourism development: an example from the Cyclades. *Journal of Modern Greek Studies* 11(1), 75–95.

King, B. (1994) What is ethnic tourism? An Australian perspective. *Tourism Management* 15(3), 173–176.

King, R., Warnes, A. and Williams, A.M. (1998) International retirement migration in Europe. *International Journal of Population Geography* 4(2), 91–112.

Lew, A.A. (2000) China: a growth engine for Asian tourism. In: Hall, C.M. and Page, S. (eds) *Tourism in South and South-East Asia*. Butterworth-Heinemann, Oxford, UK, pp. 268–285.

Littrell, M.A., Anderson, L.F. and Brown, P.J. (1993) What makes a craft souvenir authentic? *Annals of Tourism Research* 20(1), 197–215.

Lowenthal, D. (1972) *West Indian Societies*. Oxford University Press, Oxford, UK.

MacCannell, D. (1976) *The Tourist: a New Theory of the Leisure Class*. Macmillan, London.

MacCannell, D. (2000) Postmodernism. In: Jafari, J. (ed.) *Encyclopedia of Tourism*. Routledge, London, pp. 457–458.

Manley, M. (1987) *Up the Down Escalator: Development and the International Economy: a Jamaican Case Study*. Howard University Press, Washington, DC.

Martin, A. (1992) May the curse of Peter Mayle be upon you all. *The Guardian* 26 June.

Mather, S. and Todd, G. (1993) *Tourism in the Caribbean*. Special Report No. 455, The Economist Intelligence Unit, London.

Mayle, P. (1989) *A Year in Provence*. Hamish Hamilton, London.

Meller, N. and Horowitz (1987) Hawai'i: themes in land monopoly. In: Crocombe, R. (ed.) *Land Tenure in the Pacific*. University of the South Pacific, Suva, Fiji, pp. 25–44.

Minerbi, L. (1996) Hawai'i. In: Hall, C.M. and Page, S.J. (eds) *Tourism in the Pacific: Issues and Cases*. International Thomson Business Press, London, pp. 190–204.

Monopolies and Mergers Commission (1997) *Foreign Package Holidays: a Report on the Supply in the UK of Tour Operators' Services and Travel Agents' Services in Relation to Foreign Package Holidays*. Stationery Office, London.

Nunez, T. (1963) Tourism, tradition and acculturation: weekendismo in a Mexican village. *Ethnology* II(3), 347–352.

O'Connor, J. (2000) The Big Squeeze. *Tourism in Focus* 36(Summer), 2–3.

O'Reilly, K. (2000) *The British on the Costa del Sol: Transnational Identities and Local Communities*. Routledge, London.

Oppermann, M. (1998) Destination threshold potential and the law of repeat visitation. *Journal of Travel Research* 37(2), 131–137.

Oxaal, I. (1971) *Race and Revolutionary Consciousness: an Existential Report on the 1970 Black Power Revolt in Trinidad.* Schenkmann, Cambridge, Massachusetts.

Patterson, S. (1965) *Dark Strangers: a Study of West Indians in London.* Pelican, Harmondsworth, UK.

Pattullo, P. (1996) *Last Resorts: the Cost of Tourism in the Caribbean.* Cassell, London.

Peake, R. (1989) Tourism and Swahili identity in Malindi Old Town, Kenyan Coast. *Africa* 59(2), 209–220.

Philp, J. and Mercer, D. (1999) Commodification of Buddhism in contemporary Burma. *Annals of Tourism Research* 26(1), 21–54.

Picard, M. (1990) 'Cultural tourism' in Bali: cultural performances as tourist attractions. *Indonesia* 49, 37–74.

Picard, M. (1993) 'Cultural tourism' in Bali: national integration and regional differentiation. In: Hitchcock, M., King, V.T. and Parnwell, M.J.G. (eds) *Tourism in South-East Asia.* Routledge, London, pp. 71–98.

Picard, M. (1996) *Bali: Cultural Tourism and Touristic Culture.* Archipelago Press, Singapore.

Poirier, R.A. and Wright, S. (1993) The political economy of tourism in Tunisia. *Journal of Modern African Studies* 31(1), 149–162.

Popelka, C.A. and Littrell, M.A. (1991) Influence of tourism on handicraft evolution. *Annals of Tourism Research* 18(3), 392–413.

Raphael, M. (1993) Conclusions of the round table on tourism development and the role of the state. In: World Tourism Organization (eds), *Round Table on Tourism Development and the Role of the State.* 10th General Assembly, Bali, Indonesia. WTO, Madrid, pp. 1–3.

RCI Europe (1993) *Timeshare – the New Force in Tourism: Course Notes for Higher Education.* RCI Europe Ltd, Kettering, UK.

Ritzer, G. (1996) *The McDonaldization of Society: an Investigation into the Changing Character of Contemporary Life.* Pine Forge Press, London.

Ritzer, G. (1998) *The McDonaldization Thesis: Explorations and Extensions.* Sage, London.

Routledge, D. (1985) *Matanitu: the Struggle for Power in Early Fiji.* University of the South Pacific, Suva, Fiji.

Ryan, C.A. (1995) Learning about tourists from conversations: the over-55s in Majorca. *Tourism Management* 16(3), 207–215.

Ryan, C.A. and Crofts, J. (1997) Carving and tourism: a Maori perspective. *Annals of Tourism Research* 24(4), 898–918.

Saihi, T. (1989) L'investissement dans le tourisme tunisien. *Information Touristique* 111 (Aout), 13–15.

Scarr, D. (1988) *Fiji: Politics of Illusion – the Military Coups in Fiji.* New South Wales University Press, Kensington, Australia.

Schwartz, R. (1997) *Pleasure Island: Tourism and Temptation in Cuba.* University of Nebraska Press, Lincoln.

Selwyn, T. (1996) Introduction. In: Selwyn, T. (ed.) *The Tourist Image: Myths and Myth-making in Tourism.* John Wiley & Sons, Chichester, UK, pp. 1–32.

Silver, I. (1993) Marketing authenticity in Third World countries. *Annals of Tourism Research* 20(2), 302–318.

Sinclair, M.T. and Stabler, M. (1997) *The Economics of Tourism.* Routledge, London.

Sinclair, M.T., Alizadeh, P. and Onunga, E.A.A. (1992) The structure of international tourism and tourism development in Kenya. In: Harrison, D. (ed.) *Tourism and the Less Developed Countries.* John Wiley & Sons, Chichester, UK, pp. 47–63.

Smith, M.G. (1965) *The Plural Society in the British West Indies.* University of California Press, Berkeley, California.

Smith, S. and Sender, J. (1986) *The Development of Capitalism in Africa.* Methuen, London.

Sofield, T.H.B. and Li, F.M.S. (1998) Tourism development and cultural policies in China. *Annals of Tourism Research* 25(2), 362–392.

Souder, P.B. (1987) Guam: land tenure in a fortress. In: Crocombe, R. (ed.) *Land Tenure in the Pacific.* University of the South Pacific, Suva, Fiji, pp. 211–225.

Sternberg, E. (1997) The iconography of the tourism experience. *Annals of Tourism Research* 24(4), 951–969.

Strapp, J.D. (1988) The resort cycle and second homes. *Annals of Tourism Research* 15(4), 504–516.

Stymeist, D.H. (1996) Transformation of Vilavilairevo in tourism. *Annals of Tourism Research* 23(1), 1–18.

Swain, M.B. (1990) Commoditizing ethnicity in Southwest China. *Cultural Survival Quarterly* 14(1), 26–30.

Thomas, C.Y. (1988) *The Poor and the Powerless: Economic Policy and Change in the Caribbean.* Latin America Bureau, London.

Travis, J.F. (1993) *The Rise of the Devon Seaside Resorts: 1750–1900.* University of Exeter Press, Exeter, UK.

Tsartas, P. (1992) Socioeconomic impacts of tourism on two Greek isles. *Annals of Tourism Research* 19(3), 516–533.

Turner, L. and Ash, J. (1975) *The Golden Hordes: International Tourism and the Pleasure Periphery.* Constable, London.

Tyagi, N. (1991) *Hill Resorts of U.P. Himalaya: a Geographical Study.* Indus Publishing Company, New Delhi.

Underwood, E. (1978) *Brighton.* Batsford, London.

UNDP (1999) *Pacific Human Development Report, 1999: Creating Opportunities.* United Nations Development Programme, Suva, Fiji.

Wade, R. and White, G. (eds) (1984) Developmental states in East Asia: capitalist and socialist. *IDS Bulletin* 15(2).

Waldren, J. (1996) *Insiders and Outsiders: Paradise and Reality in Mallorca.* Berghahn Books, Providence, USA and Oxford, UK.

Waldren, J. (1997) We are not tourists – we live here. In: Abram, S., Waldren, J. and Macleod, D.V.L. (eds) *Tourists and Tourism: Identifying with People and Places.* Berg, Oxford, UK, pp. 51–70.

Williams, A.M. (1995) Capital and the transnationalisation of tourism. In: Montanari, A. and Williams, A.M. (eds) *European Tourism: Spaces and Restructuring.* John Wiley & Sons, Chichester, UK, pp. 163–176.

Williams, A.M. and Hall, C.M. (2000) Tourism and migration: new relationships between production and consumption. *Tourism Geographies* 2(1), 5–27.

Williams, A.M. and Shaw, G. (eds) (1991) *Tourism and Economic Development: Western European Experiences,* 2nd edn. John Wiley & Sons, Chichester, UK.

Williams, A.M., King, R. and Warnes, T. (1997) A place in the sun: international retirement migration from northern to southern Europe. *European Urban and Regional Studies* 4(2), 115–134.

Wood, D. (1968) *Trinidad in Transition: the Years After Slavery.* Oxford University Press, Oxford, UK.

Wood, R.E. (1984) Ethnic tourism: the state and cultural change in Southeast Asia. *Annals of Tourism Research* 11(3), 353–374.

Wood, R. and Deppen, M. (1994) Cultural tourism: ethnic options and constructed otherness. Tourism Working Group No. 5, XIIth World Congress of Sociology, Bielefeld, Germany, 18 July–23 July.

World Bank (1993) *The East Asian Miracle: Economic Growth and Public Policy.* Oxford University Press (for the World Bank), Oxford, UK.

World Bank (1997) *World Development Indicators, 1997.* World Bank, Washington, DC.

WTO (1999) *Yearbook of Tourism Statistics,* Vol. 2, 51st edn. World Tourism Organization, Madrid.

Zhang, H.Q., Chong, K. and Ap, J. (1999) An analysis of tourism policy development in modern China. *Tourism Management* 20(4), 471–485.

3

Tourism Challenges in Developing Nations: Continuity and Change at the Millennium

Linda K. Richter

The collapse of space, time and borders may be creating a global village, but not everyone can be a citizen. The global professional elite faces low borders, but billions of others find borders as high as ever.

(UNDP, 1999: 31)

Introduction

It is perhaps one part fashion and one part naivety to assume that 2000, or for purists 2001, marked a major transformation across the gamut of public policy areas. In fact, most policy sectors will have experienced no sharp discontinuities, least of all developing nations. Poor nations generally suffer from continuous grinding poverty and political decay. Change results too often not in ameliorating poverty but in exacerbated overcrowding and pollution. Even the population time bomb has been blunted, as much by AIDS as by enlightened policy-making.

At the beginning of the 20th century there were far fewer countries than now, and many were administered by a handful of colonial powers. In these developing nations, poverty was then the norm and most tourism was an example of the conspicuous consumption of an elite, with facilities to pamper both the daring explorer and the worldly traveller making

the modern version of the Grand Tour. Except for migration, family travel on an international scale was rare, and single women were characteristically well chaperoned – as with the tours of Thomas Cook (Enloe, 1989: 18).

Nevertheless, the acceleration of international travel in the early 20th century, for health, business, recreation or religious pilgrimage, led governments to issue passports, require visas, and take a generally more proactive stance toward the protection of their citizens abroad. In 1912, within weeks of the sinking of the *Titanic*, international policies required 24 hour monitoring of wireless communication, ocean liners were fitted with enough life jackets and lifeboats for all passengers, and there were international patrols in iceberg-dense sections of the oceans.

Traveller safety continues to be a major feature of public policies surrounding tourism but the complexity of the task has grown enormously. Problems are most acute in developing nations, where government capacity is limited and tourist numbers are increasing. Such nations disproportionately rely on tourism and are therefore most devastated when other countries discourage tourist travel because of fears (justified or otherwise) over safety.

These issues and many more have grown as international tourism arrivals have soared to over 800 million annually. By 2020 that figure is expected to be over 1.6 billion (WTO, 1997). In this chapter, it is possible only to sketch a few policy challenges that the arrival of mass tourism has posed and aggravated for poor nations. However, it is important to stress that, like modernization more generally, the growth in international travel also offers opportunities for many developing societies. In this chapter, five challenges common to developing nations grappling with tourism are explored, obstacles and opportunities involved in meeting these challenges are then discussed in terms of current trends and, finally, the focus is on the range of policy developments at all levels, and on new factors involved in tourism development.

The Continuity of Challenges

The need for redistribution

The policy challenges associated with tourism development are common to most nations, but they are intensified in those that are developing. They are characterized not only by poverty, which heightens the gulf between tourists and the average citizen, but also by the more pervasive inability of governments to act on any policy. Progressive policies may be subject to manipulation or bribery, for example, but governments of developing nations too often lack the power to implement policies of any type.

In extreme cases, central governments have little power beyond the capital city and its environs. Indeed, the international rhetoric of privatization and devolution of power must sound quaint when central power is so limited. Consider efforts in Uganda, Kenya or Egypt to protect tourists from rebels, poachers or the regime's religious opponents, even as tourists venture further from the state control of the centre.

Poor governments may also lack the capacity to adapt or the flexibility to find appropriate alternative approaches or resist political pressures that may cripple development (Huntington, 1968: 12). Such a political environment makes tourism challenges all the more daunting.

Today, more than 125 nations can be considered developing nations, as measured by low per capita income and a modest or low ranking on such human development criteria as literacy, life expectancy and education. That definition can be refined into degrees and types of impoverishment. Thirty-four nations are the poorest of the poor, with life expectancies ranging from 37 to 60 years (UNDP, 1999), and among these are several members of the former USSR and Yugoslavia, which are currently experiencing economic privation and political decay and might even be regarded as failed states.

While per capita income may be the lowest common denominator for categorizing nations, it masks the cruel and often accelerating gap between rich and poor and the redistribution challenge that confronts developed and developing nations. The crisis is at national as well as international levels. In Indonesia, for example, enormous gaps exist between rich and poor individuals, and between Java and less fortunate regions of the country, but there is no consensus about how this can be remedied. The Hindu island of Bali, for instance, resents the fact that it leads the country in tourism receipts but the money is sent to the Indonesian capital (Richter, 1988).

Tourism policies that foster more equitable impacts generally will succeed only if they are designed to reduce disparities and are specifically monitored to ensure competent implementation. This can happen. Groups in Kenya and Madagascar, for instance, try to protect wildlife by giving villagers a stake in employment and income arising from tourism. Scores of such initiatives exist elsewhere, but the conditions that give rise to cooperation and entrepreneurial solutions remain relatively unexamined (Bramwell, 1998).

Nevertheless, it is important that nations use tourism receipts to reduce rather than widen income disparities, and some organizations and mechanisms encourage this possibility. In 1998, for instance, the World Tourism Organization sponsored a conference on excellence and sustainability in Poland; a year later, at its Third Global Conference (held in Glasgow), the International Institute for Peace through Tourism focused on 200 'success stories' of how peace, culture and prosperity had been linked through sustainable tourism. At a more general networking level, McLaren (1998: 133–173) has compiled a particularly helpful set of resources for both critics and supporters of tourism to utilize.

Much remains to be done. Currently, the tourism sector is best understood as a broad pyramid, the base of which consists of low-skilled, poorly paid employees, usually organized along racial or gender lines, and often denied basic benefits or the right to organize collectively. This is especially true in developing nations. Countries with high levels of unemployment are not overly concerned with worker conditions, living wages or gender equity (Enloe, 1989: 33–35; McLaren, 1998: 72–73; Richter, 1995: 75–81, 1998a), but lack of attention to these issues in the tourism sector could lead to sabotage of the industry from within and without (Richter, 1982, 1992, 1999a; Richter and Waugh, 1991).

In theory, the globalization of the tourist industry could promote the spread of more enlightened policies towards the labour force, but many developing countries are in no position to bargain aggressively with foreign investors. Moreover, local elites with capital for joint ventures with international partners may be reluctant role models for the industry. The egalitarian cause receives little assistance from the diffuse and transient travelling public, which is unlikely to prioritize basic human rights, let alone working conditions, at their proposed holiday destinations above 'bargains' in package tours, as illustrated by travel to authoritarian Burma (Myanmar) and China (SLORC'S Burma, 1997). The focus of tourists on their own economic self-interest is captured in a cartoon depicting a couple in a travel office, asking, 'Which country's economic collapse will give us the best bargain for the dollar?' (Anon., 1998).

The challenge of redistribution, then, is likely to persist, especially for poor nations. Policymakers need to keep asking: who gets what, when, and how? (Lasswell, 1936). If such questions are not asked, or are ignored, and the labour force in developing nations – in the tourism sector or among the general public – becomes militant, tourism is jeopardized.

Long-range risk analysis is needed to assess the extent to which threats are external, and how far they can be affected by internal pol-icy decisions. Much of the implementation will be subject to government regulation, but it will succeed only if governments can muster the political will and capacity to foster equity (Richter and Waugh, 1991; Richter, 1999a).

The cultural challenge of tourism

Huntington and others consider the clash of civilizations to be the defining political battle of the future, but often the most savage struggles involve culture clashes within nations (Huntington, 1993). Indeed, the second major challenge for policymakers is managing the cultural clashes over tourism in the face of growing hostility to tourism *per se*.

Over the last 20 years, criticism of tourism has shifted from the financial costs involved in developing this sector to the cultural costs incurred by societies embracing mass international tourism. The critique is especially germane and strident in developing nations, most of which are socially conservative. According to this view, the mix of traditional citizens and non-traditional travellers can often be a recipe for disaster, and 'differences in cultural behaviour can be so great that mutual understanding is replaced by antipathy' (Archer and Cooper, 1998: 71).

In many respects, the cultural crisis (and others to be discussed) reflects the highly unequal distribution of power and influence. When acknowledging the cultural divide, it is important to identify the 'owners' of a country, to ask who controls the interpretation of its heritage (Richter, 1999b), how its indigenous people and other minority groups are portrayed, and who protects, controls or sells culture to the tourist.

Alternatively, cultural features can be considered irrelevant, and the nation marketed instead as a playground of beaches, casinos, and golf courses. In the *Driving Through Malaysia* brochure, for example, tourists are given no hint that they should be interested in anything but their golfing prowess (Anon., 1997). Perhaps the most striking political reaction to such tourism marketing occurred when nationalist Michael Manley, on gaining power in Jamaica in the early 1980s, changed the tourism slogan to 'Jamaica's More than a Beach;

it's a Country'. His administration proceeded to alienate the US Reagan administration, which directed its Caribbean Basin Initiative elsewhere. When Manley was later replaced, the tourism slogan became 'Jamaica's Jamaica Again' (Richter, 1989a).

The trivialization of culture is often self-inflicted, as in the Malaysian brochure or Jamaica's post-Manley promotions. It is particularly harmful and controversial when marketing by the National Tourism Organizations (NTOs) is more suggestive than the culture supports. Two examples suffice. During the dictatorship of President Marcos, the NTO of the Philippines advertised 'a fresh peach on every beach', with illustrations to match the copy, and in the 1980s the United States spent taxpayers' dollars instructing potential tourists to 'TRY A VIRGIN ... island'. The territory was not amused, any more than the Caribbean Council of Churches, which challenged the tacky promotion (Richter, 1989a: 78, 1989b). Such advertising is especially distasteful as poor nations continue to struggle with the disease and crime associated with sex tourism generally and child prostitution in particular (Hall, 1992a, 1994: 174–189; Leheny, 1995; Donnelly, 1998).

Increased numbers of culturally oblivious and insensitive tourists have hardened opposition to tourism, particularly among fundamentalist religious groups in such countries as Iran, Egypt, Turkey and Afghanistan. Government responses have generally fallen into two policy camps, advocating either control or segregation. In the case of the former, government has limited the number of tourists and their behaviour (Bhutan), insisted on modest dress (Iran), monitored entry to sacred places (India) or has distributed cultural advice intended to minimize the disruption caused by tourists (Sri Lanka) (Richter, 1989a: 163, 177, 102).

The second approach has been to develop enclave tourism, which isolates foreigners from the local population. In many such instances, the staff of the beach resorts and casinos, which are off limits to citizens, are low-paid nationals, as in Malaysian and Egyptian casinos or Maldivian and Indonesian resorts. Indonesia exemplifies how even advice and aid from the so-called developed world – in this case the World Bank – can create oases of culturally alien environments in the midst of traditional society, such as those at Nusa Dua on the island of Bali (Richter, 1988).

The consumption gap

The consumption gap, which to some extent exists whenever leisured visitors are pampered by poor employees, is exacerbated by the incredible scarcity that exists in poor nations. Unlike tourists, most of whom are from societies where employees may receive up to 5 weeks of paid vacation a year, workers in the tourist sector in developing nations are unlikely ever to be tourists themselves. That makes the 'Paving of Paradise,' to use McLaren's term, or the excessive luxury of tourism resorts, a stimulus to popular resentment (McLaren, 1998).

Golf courses and enormous pools are an insult to more than 1.3 billion people denied access to clean water (UNDP, 1999: 28). In developing nations, infectious disease and gastrointestinal parasites, a direct result of unclean water, kill millions. Those who use such luxury tourist facilities at home and abroad do not seem to care. The Malaysian Sultan Abdul Azaz Shah Golf Club advertises 'a lifestyle so leisurely and so gracious that thankfully it can be enjoyed only by a select few' (Anon., 1993: 33). In the Public Broadcasting System's *World* television programme, 'Who Pays for Paradise?' (1 June 1978), there was a haunting scene of Gabon women carrying buckets of water on their heads as they walked past a five-star hotel filled with tourists frolicking in a huge pool. More recently, in Kenya a scarce stream was diverted to provide water for tourist resorts (Turco, 1997: 7). In other areas, local people are denied access to now private beaches, or reefs are dynamited to make beaches larger and more sandy. The fishing industry of villages is sacrificed to jet skis and scuba adventures for tourists.

It might be assumed that when tourist facilities are upgraded, host populations will benefit. They do sometimes receive roads, electric power and telecommunications, but scarce foreign exchange is often sacrificed to import luxury items for tourists. Expensive medicines and facilities for wary travellers may consume resources that might otherwise have funded basic immunization programmes and low-tech medical care for tens of thousands; indeed, cost and the location of medical facilities may effectively restrict their use to tourists (Bauer, 1999). As Bushell and Lea have argued, the focus in developing countries needs to shift from travellers' health to more general health care for both the tourist and the host population to prosper (cited in Bauer, 1999: 12).

Terrorism

Terrorism makes tourism a risky strategy to achieve national development. Not so long ago, undemocratic regimes tried to improve their international respectability by attracting tourists, and such attempts have been made by fascist Spain, Marcos-led Philippines and the current regime in Myanmar (Pi-Sunyer, 1979; Richter, 1982, 1999d). The tourism industry has frequently been depressed by war, civil strife and unstable conditions, and tourists have frequently been affected, even to the extent of being caught in the crossfire. However, over the last 20 years tourists have increasingly been targeted by terrorists and used to call attention to the abuses of dictatorial regimes (Richter, 1989a: 9–10, 1992, 1999a). In October 1999, for example, the Myanmar Embassy in Thailand was occupied by a group opposing that brutal regime (Pennington, 1999). The incident was unusual in occurring outside the country at which protests were directed, probably depressing tourism in Myanmar and Thailand. Terrorism is also seen as a way of opposing the perceived cultural costs of tourism, and as a means of sabotaging an industry often presumed to be dominated by outsiders.

Although terrorist attacks worldwide peaked several years ago, their salience to the governments affected and the travelling public has grown with media attention. Moreover, tourists are easily isolated targets for attacks designed to protest against tourism or to destabilize fragile regimes dependent on tourism receipts. Tourist lifestyles are different from those of the general population, particularly in developing nations, and so terrorists risk less of a backlash than if they had targeted local businesses or residential neighbourhoods. In addition, the regime can be made to appear impotent and the publicity and impact are worldwide because victims are from a variety of nations (Richter and Waugh, 1991; Anon., 1999; Bekker, 1999; CNN, 1999a: 1; CNN,1999b: 1).

A recently introduced element in terrorism against tourists is the way in which they are sometimes targeted because of their nationality. The 1999 murders of eight tourists in the Ugandan forests were ostensibly aimed at US and British policies. Similarly, the NATO bombing of Belgrade and other targets in the spring of 1999 led to fears of protests against tourists from NATO countries in Russia (Bekker, 1999). Nor are only Westerners targeted. In March 1999, Kurd leaders attempted to derail Turkish tourism by a series of bombing and arson attacks (Anon., 1999). In late December 1999, predominantly Indian tourists were hijacked on a flight from Kathmandu. The prolonged ordeal was designed to pressure India to release political prisoners involved in the Kashmir conflict. The 6-day crisis ended only after a passenger was killed and several prisoners were released (Anon., 2000).

Sustainability

Ecotourism is big business. It can provide exchange and economic reward for the preservation of natural systems and wildlife. But ecotourism also threatens to destroy the resources on which it depends. … frenzied activity threatens the viability of natural systems. At times we seem to be loving nature to death.

(Berle, 1990)

Sustainability is a fashionable topic, but coordinated and consistent efforts to achieve it in the face of soaring tourism are rare indeed. However, some case studies offer hope that the interest in thoughtful development is more than rhetoric (Hawkins and Khan, 1998). More common, however, are examples of policymakers jettisoning even well-conceived plans and substituting unwise development. Political pressures are particularly hard to resist in developing countries, where seizing the moment to make badly needed profits is more attractive than abstract notions of intergenerational equity. Nations desperate to promote international tourism are not especially susceptible to concepts of tourist carrying capacity, managed growth, or similar environmental niceties (Bramwell, 1998). Even areas where the main attractions are flora and fauna, and where 'ecotourism' is the buzzword, still allow shortcuts in environmentally sensitive development and permit far too many to visit fragile nesting, hatching or other endangered habitats. Ecotourism can make a virtue of small numbers of tourists, but unfortunately pressures to expand the scale and type of tourism grow with the industry's importance to the economy. In the Galapagos Islands, for example, the once pristine environment now hosts more than 300% of the number of visitors originally allowed (McLaren, 1998: 106). Another example is Costa Rica, renowned for its biodiversity and its commitment to make over 20% of its land mass a series of national parks. For years, growth in tourism was slowed by civil wars in neighbouring Central American nations, and promotion rather than control of tourism was the priority. However, since peace developed in neighbouring states, Costa Rican tourism has skyrocketed and the nation has become seduced by the money that tourism has brought. Lavish beach resorts without sewage systems have been developed and harsh and thoughtless logging practices near national parks threaten mudslides (Richter, 1998b).

The Costa Rican government's problems have been twofold: firstly, they had to develop policies to keep pace with the mushrooming growth in tourism and, secondly, it was necessary to enforce the few existing regulations. However, although the country is politically stable and tourism is well-received, the single-term presidencies required by the constitution make leaders 'lame ducks' almost as soon as they are elected. Political leverage evaporates quickly.

In general, most discussions on sustainability focus on natural attractions, but it is also related to the growth, pace and type of tourist and the accompanying infrastructure. None of these factors can be taken for granted in developing nations. In some, accustomed to a high level of contact with outsiders, trading traditions have led to an entrepreneurial lifestyle that easily accommodates tourism, but elsewhere this is not the case and the potential for conflict can be high. Similarly, the adaptability and types of tourists may be an issue.

Thirty years ago, it might have been assumed that former colonial societies would be accustomed to Western visitors and that increasing exposure would lead to a heightened comfort level with international tourism, but this is no longer the case. Because of the rapid increase in tourism, and its expansion to virtually every part of the world, modern tourists are inadequately prepared for visits to areas that seldom if ever saw colonial administrators. As a result, in some countries – notably India, Pakistan, Uganda, Algeria and Guatemala – opposition to tourists in general, and to certain nationalities and religions in particular, has grown. Other governments (for example, Afghanistan, Iran, Iraq and Saudi Arabia) have moved to isolate their people from the allegedly pernicious effects of tourism, especially those emanating from Western women, by restricting or discouraging tourism (Pelton et al., 1998: 46–47, 309–320, 418).

Even in developing countries with highly sophisticated tourism industries, the issue of sustainability is becoming salient, especially as religious conservatives become more influential. As a consequence, some developed countries have discouraged their citizens from travelling to such destinations. At any given time, for example, the US State Department issues advisories on about 40 nations, ranging from simple cautionary statements, to warnings, to 'Don't Go' advisories. These may be based on probable political dangers, but just as often refer to crime and health hazards and, according to some critics, may also reflect political bias (Tidwell, 1998; Watson and Dennis, 1999).

In the context of developing nations, then, sustainability has several facets. Firstly, even in the absence of tourists, a nation must decide how to allocate scarce resources to nurture and sustain the natural and man-made heritage for its own citizens. Borabadur, Anghor Wat, Dubrovnik, the Amazon and the Galapagos Islands also have a value that should be supported by non-citizens as well.

This is why the United Nations Educational, Scientific and Cultural Organization (UNESCO) World Heritage List is critical for reinforcing the political will and helping developing nations to resist development that threatens world treasures (Richter and Richter, 2000). In essence, the allocation of resources to protecting sites, restoring habitats and promoting domestic and international tourism is a political rather than a technical decision. Similarly, the degree to which national culture is exhibited, modified, or influenced by visitors should not be a function of the advertising budgets of tour operators, the venture capital of investors, or the incapacity of government to know its own needs and those of its citizens.

It is a cliché that tourists visit developing nations for sun, sand, sea and sex, and such motivations will continue, and will be facilitated by the Internet's ability to market anything, including child prostitution. But to these 'four Ss' must be added four more: a preoccupation with security, sanitation, safe transport, and the sensible protection of the built and natural heritage.

Opportunities and Obstacles in Current Trends

The growth of international tourism

Several trends complicate the ability of developing nations to handle the problems just discussed, and the first is the sheer growth of international tourism, which will crucially affect developing societies. Over the next two decades, tourism arrivals are estimated to double to over 1.6 billion people (WTO, 1997). Currently, Africa receives only 4% of all international travellers, but as other destinations become saturated, international travel to that continent, and to Asia, Latin America and the Pacific, is expected to soar. Other trends reflect the changing demographic mix of those travelling.

Senior tourism

The political and economic importance of huge numbers of senior travellers has been recognized by the United Nations (UN). It declared 1994 the 'Year of the Elderly' and called on countries to recognize that 'Government must draft and implement active policies for training, employment, leisure, and social integration, which take into account the exponential growth in the number of older people' (Senior Tourism brochure, UN, 1999). In addition, a series of conferences on senior tourism focused on this demographic category of people who have money, time and an increasing proclivity for travel – but who also have special requirements in matters of comfort, health and safety (Richter, 1999c). The US senior travel market is illustrative of a trend that will accelerate as 'baby boomers' (those born in the aftermath of the Second World War) retire. Even now, those over 65 form 25% of the population and, more importantly, control 70% of the nation's wealth (Blazey, 1992: 771). They represent an attractive market for developing nations, but they will also be 'high maintenance' travellers, making special demands on impoverished nations for comfort and health. Just as early tourists travelled on religious pilgrimage, to shrines or to spas to 'take the waters', the tourist at or near retirement age is increasingly coupling tourism with health or spiritual interests (Hall, 1992b: 141–158).

Senior tourism runs the gamut from adventure travel to more sedentary vacations, but increasingly it is older tourists who are eager to move beyond the Grand Tour favoured by earlier generations. Today's seniors may favour precisely those trips that cater to their intellect. Earthwatch, which pairs all ages of tourists with scientists on hundreds of projects, rates its trips by their difficulty rather than by any stereotypical notions about what age or gender can cope. More than half of these trips are in developing nations. The Elder Hostel movement offers low-frills trips to both developed and developing countries with an emphasis on cultural learning and basic accommodation. Such travel is far less costly for host countries and their guests and more culturally benign than many other types of tourism. Begun in 1975, Elder Hostel now has several hundred thousand participants in scores of countries (Kalinowski and Weiler, 1992: 22).

Travel and disabilities

The third trend is the increasing number of disabled people who are travelling. Their needs are only belatedly receiving attention in developed countries, and are all but ignored in most developing societies. As a participant at the 1985 UN Decade for Women Conference in Nairobi, Kenya, it was sobering to discover that some 100 disabled women had to meet on the University of Nairobi lawn because all the conference buildings were inaccessible. Fifteen years later, the disabled have far more resources, but coverage remains uneven. The passage of the Americans with Disabilities Act in 1990 and the Air Carriers Access Act encouraged and in some cases required accessible facilities for travellers. Although the initial impact was on domestic American tourism, the acts also evoked a response from international cruise lines and tour operators abroad. Indeed, the growing affluence and influence of senior and disabled tourists will encourage developing nations to take their needs into account when promoting new destination areas and attractions. If demographics are not enough to encourage such accessible development, legal initiatives by the disabled, including handicapped students, are likely to affect tour operators and programmes in tourist-generating nations, so that their own operations may require accessibility at the destinations. Among the groups focused on improving travel opportunities are Mobility International, Disabled Peoples International and the Society for the Advancement of Travelers with Handicaps (SATH). In January 2000, the 2000 SATH World Congress and Trade Show for Travelers with Disabilities hosted representatives from more than 25 nations, including some from developed countries.

Educational travel

The World is a Book. He who stays at home reads only one page.

(St Augustine)

Increasingly students of all ages consider international travel a facet of their education. This partly reflects the expectation that education should be experiential, interactive and participatory. To ensure that student expectations are met, college campuses are reinventing themselves in the face of on-line competition and the challenge of students from everywhere and of all ages (Plummer, 1989).

For most universities, the presence of international students and the encouragement of reciprocal educational visits by domestic students makes good economic as well as pedagogical sense. Students who have studied abroad not only are presumed to be better prepared for the 21st century in terms of diversity, language and globalization but they also promote the university overseas. Foreign students are also less likely to be subsidized by the host institution, which makes them worth more financially than a domestic or instate student. Hosting short-term educational visits allows universities to make use of university facilities during otherwise slow times, e.g. vacations. Elder Hostel, described earlier, was able to keep its costs down while helping educational institutes make use of facilities during slow times.

Service learning is one of the fastest growing forms of educational travel. For more than 30 years, Dutch work camps and some churches have pioneered experiential travel combined with projects in developing nations. Today, the service model is focused more on student expertise than physical effort to assist communities at home and abroad. Some universities require a period of internship or service, but in recent years that interest has expanded to overseas service in developing nations. One of the first to incorporate a service component into its educational programmes abroad was Kansas State University, which in 1990 pioneered international community service programmes. At the time of writing, these extend to 11 developing nations on three continents (C. Peak, Kansas City University, January 2000, personal communication).

The US Peace Corps has also adopted an internship programme that allows students to explore while working in developing nations, without obliging them to extend their duty abroad. On the non-governmental level, the New York-based Partnership for Service Learning places individuals all over the world

(C. Peak, Kansas City University, January 2000, personal communication).

Students themselves are utilizing university years for travel vacations, overseas study (no longer confined to the junior year of an elite few) and for internships and service-based learning (Eisenberg, 1989; Weiler and Kalinowski, 1990). Are these examples of tourism? They are at least in part, for they expose students, faculty and others to different cultures and traditions. Whether or not students spend money and time in the host society, they can be important assets in national development. They are also valuable to the tourism industry, becoming involved in needs assessments and planning; developing inventories of skills and attractions; teaching hotel and restaurant management and small business development; and engaging in marketing and promotional work. However, if such programmes are to flourish, the safety of those involved is imperative and this has not always been the case. In fact, issues of institutional liability are becoming major concerns at educational institutions worldwide (CIEE, 1999: 218–385).

The information technology revolution

The revolution in information technology is reshaping the tourist industry in ways both positive and negative for developing nations. The Internet allows entrepreneurs opportunities to bypass foreign-owned tour companies and to advertise and take reservations directly from groups and individuals. This can be a tremendous advantage for business in a poor nation. However, tourists may be disappointed to find that developing nations lack the computers, fax machines, satellite dishes and cell phone connections required to maintain contact with home and business. At best, such access is uneven, and apt to be located only in the more expensive destination areas. Even among developing regions, great inequalities exist. In all of Africa, for example, there are fewer cell phones than in Thailand (UNDP, 1999: 135).

The insecurity that accompanies the globalization of technology was much in evidence in fears that there would be massive computer

malfunctions, glitches and power failures when the year 2000 arrived. Such concerns created a virtual depression in some tourist regions – particularly developing countries, which were presumed less prepared for the changeover. The feared breakdowns did not occur, but much of the economic cost did – in the form of decreased travel around the New Year and into the first quarter of 2000.

Political trends

Some trends that shape the tourism problems discussed earlier result not from increased tourist numbers, or changes in demography, but from political developments. Deregulation, privatization, democratization and decentralization, for example, have had a profound impact and have served to highlight the uneven global distribution of resources.

Global health policies, for example, are threatened by the deregulation of transport, lax sanitation requirements, and the overall reduction in health requirements for travellers (Anon, 1995; Hayden, 1999; Richter, 1999c). Such changes occur as travellers increasingly visit more remote environments, often in regions with substandard health care. This is hazardous not only to the health of tourists, but also to that of the host community and tourist-generating societies (McLaren, 1998: 84–87). Although only a small fraction of international tourism arrivals goes to developing countries, tourism remains for many a major source of foreign exchange. As a consequence, when adequate international health standards are not enforced, poor nations are reluctant to report outbreaks of infectious diseases, or indeed any other threat to tourists. Negative publicity inevitably leads to reduced tourism receipts, especially if accompanied by the realization that many developing countries are ill-equipped to remedy such problems.

Also, the World Health Organization (WHO) has been criticized by the Lancet and other medical journals for not doing more to prevent the spread of disease. Member states controlling WHO funding favour the facilitation of tourism over vaccination requirements, health warnings and tough spraying and sanitation regimes for transport. WHO guidelines developed in the 1960s leave nations to cope with diseases such as ebola, the Marburg virus, West Nile fever and even the AIDS epidemic on a country-by-country basis. As a consequence, nations with higher standards are actually violating outdated WHO regulations, which insist on common regulations. Since 1976, over three dozen new infectious diseases have been discovered – mostly in poor countries – and yet WHO has been slow to pressure nations to develop adequate precautions against their spread. Seemingly forgotten are the lessons of 1917/18, when influenza from Fort Riley, Kansas, was responsible for the deaths of 30 million people worldwide (Anon, 1995; Heymann, 1995). Privatization is a mixed blessing. Although it may favour small enterprises, which in other circumstances might have to compete with state-owned facilities, it does nothing to counter the influence of large multinational facilities, which under deregulation and privatization may come to dominate the tourism industry and attract local capital, which could have been invested in smaller, indigenous enterprises (Smith, 1998).

Nevertheless, governments or non-governmental organizations (NGOs) may offer encouragement, loans, management, health and safety training to families, cooperatives and communities, thus allowing them to share in the booming tourist industry. Examples of such programmes include the Community Baboon Sanctuary in Belize, Village Tourism in Senegal, and the Monarch Butterfly Project in Mexico (Hawkins and Khan, 1998: 197–200).

What is Being Done and What is Needed?

The challenges and trends outlined in this chapter are not exhaustive, but they do indicate a daunting policy agenda for developing nations. At the same time, there are grounds for optimism about what tourism can mean for poor nations in the 21st century. In particular, there are numerous ways whereby groups not oriented towards profit and community-based initiatives can reduce the negative effects of tourism and enhance the benefits it brings to developing nations.

One of the first pressure groups to address issues of tourism's negative impacts was the Ecumenical Coalition on Third World Tourism (ECTWT). Formed in the early 1980s, it enlisted the aid of church organizations around the world, developed a useful library and a magazine (Contours, which is highly critical of Third World tourism) and sponsored a series of international conferences. It also produced a widely circulated Code of Ethics for Travellers, especially targeted at tourists going to developing nations (de Sousa, 1993). Following the success of ECTWT, other groups were formed: the Tourism Ecumenical Network in Europe; the Center for Responsible Tourism in the USA; Just Tourism in New Zealand; Equations in India; and the Ecumenical Coalition Against Child Prostitution in Asian Tourism (ECPAT), based in the Philippines.

ECPAT, in particular, has been instrumental in publicizing and confronting the growing problem of child prostitution. Once focused specifically on Asian tourism, its concern has now widened to include tourism's links with such exploitation throughout the world. With other organizations, it has documented the international extent of the problem, and the growing use of the internet in its spread. As a result of ECPAT's campaign for stiff penalties against paedophile tourists in both developed and developing countries, some of the former countries have extended their legal jurisdiction to crimes committed against children by their citizens when overseas (McLaren, 1998: 88–89; Patty, 1999) and some developing nations, including the Philippines and Thailand, have sought to try tourists for sex crimes. This is major progress when one considers the promotion of sex by the Philippine government's NTO in the Marcos era (Richter, 1982; Leheny, 1995).

The global interconnectedness highlighted and accelerated by the technology revolution has linked professionals in poor countries to the rest of the world in increasingly cheap and effective ways. Moreover, cooperative efforts are being forged to assist poor countries in ways that bypass governments entirely. One such example is the Program for Monitoring

Emerging Diseases (PROMED), which links more than 10,000 doctors in 120 countries by Email. They have been monitoring health conditions throughout the world. Coverage is uneven, particularly in the poorest tropical countries, where outbreaks are most likely to occur, but such responses to health threats are the basis for a future system of health and security surveillance. Such activism has also spurred the WHO to launch WHONET, which links microbiology laboratories to a central database (Pirages and Runci, 2000: 189).

Developing countries are also working on strategies to address other problems associated with tourism. In 1996, for example, Costa Rica introduced the Certificate for Sustainable Tourism (CST) to encourage hotels, cruise ships and others involved in tourism to compete with one another to adopt environmentally friendly practices. The achievements of successful companies were rewarded with publicity and other incentives (Richter, 1998a). In its first 2 years, so many hotels and resorts requested evaluation along CST standards that plans were made to include other sectors of the industry. Costa Rica also persuaded all other Central American nations to agree in principle to the future development of similar programmes (Richter, 1998a). Although at the time of writing it is unclear whether or not future Costa Rican governments will continue to make the CST a priority in its sustainability efforts, the Costa Rican initiative is a model that can be adapted by other nations interested in the issue.

At the international level, several branches of the UN now take tourism seriously. These include the WHO, the World Tourism Organization, the World Heritage programmes of the UNESCO, and the United Nations Development Programme. Among their activities is help for developing nations in protecting their environment, their heritage and their health. In one instance, after decades of organizational lethargy, WHO, through WHONET, is accelerating its efforts to detect and prevent the spread of drug-resistant microbes (Pirages and Runci, 2000: 189). However, member nations still need to utilize WHO as an enforcement mechanism for meaningful health regulations – a function that will become increasingly critical as international tourism increases.

Another positive example is UNESCO's impressive efforts to assist the recovery of Dubrovnik during and after the war in Croatia. When war broke out in 1991, Dubrovnik, already on the list of World Heritage Sites, was reclassified as a Heritage Site in Danger. Even during hostilities, a recovery plan was adapted from an earthquake recovery document compiled 12 years earlier, and repair and restoration plans were under way even before the war ended (Jemo, 1996). Arguably, UNESCO's high-profile involvement prevented the ancient city from being destroyed (Woodward, 1996; Richter and Richter, 2000).

This chapter began with an exploration of the challenges associated with tourism. They will undoubtedly test policymakers at all levels, but they also represent opportunities for making tourism a more constructive force for development. From initiatives now being promoted at international conferences, and in the burgeoning literature on tourism, it is evident that many groups and nations consider tourism a tool to improve host societies. Clearly, it is necessary to be concerned about the negative impacts of international tourism, and to be aware of trends that are likely to impact developing nations, but there are also grounds for optimism as we anticipate tourism in the 21st century.

References

Anon. (1993) Congratulations and thanks to the IOC. *Contours* 6(1), 33–34.
Anon. (1995) Fortress WHO: breaking the ramparts for health's sake. *Lancet* 28 January, 345(8944), 203–204.
Anon. (1997) *Driving Through Malaysia*. Government of Malaysia brochure.
Anon. (1998) *Travel Weekly* 29 January, as reproduced in *Contours* 8(1) 1998, 9.
Anon. (1999) Kurds plan tourism attack. *Kansas City Star* 16 March, p. A12.

Anon. (2000) Hostages released! *Kansas City Star* 1 January, p. 1.

Archer, B. and Cooper, C. (1998) The positive and negative impacts of tourism. In: Theobald, W.F. (ed.) *Global Tourism: the Second Decade*, 2nd edn. Butterworth-Heinemann, Oxford, pp. 63–81.

Bauer, I. (1999) The impact of tourism in developing countries on the health of the local host communities. *Journal of Tourism Studies* 10(1), 2–17.

Bekker, V. (1999) 'Are terrorists targeting St Pete? *St Petersburg Times* 17 September, p. 1.

Berle, P. (1990) Two faces of eco-tourism. *Audubon* 92(2), 6.

Blazey, M. (1992) Travel and retirement Status. *Annals of Tourism Research* 19(4), 771–783.

Bramwell, B. (1998) Selecting policy instruments for sustainable tourism. In: Theobald, W.F. (ed.) *Global Tourism: the Second Decade*, 2nd edn. Butterworth-Heinemann, Oxford, UK, pp. 361–379.

CIEE (1999) *Safety and Responsibility in Education Abroad*. Workshop Manual, CIEE, New York.

CNN (1999a) South Africa plans crackdown on urban bombers. *World:News* 9 February, p. 1.

CNN (1999b) Busload of US tourists robbed in South African township. *World:News* 12 February, p. 1.

de Sousa, Fr.D. (1993) The original vision and the evolving strategy of ECTWT. *Contours* 6(1), 4–12.

Donnelly, D. (1998) Where have all the children gone? In: McLaren, D. (ed.) *Rethinking Tourism and Ecotourism*. Kumarian Press, West Hartford, Connecticut, pp. 88–89.

Eisenberg, G. (1989) Learning vacations. In: *Peterson's Guide*, 6th edn. Peterson Publishers, Princeton, New Jersey, p. ix.

Enloe, C. (1989) *Bananas, Beaches and Bases: Making Feminist Sense of International Politics*. University of California Press, Berkeley, California.

Hall, C.M. (1992a) Sex tourism in South-East Asia. In: Harrison, D. (ed.) *Tourism in the Less Developed Countries*. Belhaven, London, pp. 64–74.

Hall, C.M. (1992b) Adventure, sport and health tourism. In: Weiler, B. and Hall, C.M. (eds) *Special Interest Tourism*. Belhaven, London, pp. 141–158.

Hall, C.M. (1994) *Tourism and Politics*. John Wiley & Sons, Chichester, UK.

Hawkins, D. and Khan, M. (1998) Ecotourism opportunities for developing countries. In: Theobald, W.F. (ed.) *Global Tourism: the Second Decade*. Butterworth-Heinemann, Oxford, UK, pp. 191–204.

Hayden, T. (1999) Tuberculosis is making a comeback. *Newsweek* 8 November, p. 77.

Heymann, D. (1995) Emerging infectious diseases. *World Health* 50(1), 4.

Huntington, S.L. (1968) *Political Order in Changing Societies*. Yale University Press, New Haven, Connecticut.

Huntington, S.L. (1993) The clash of civilizations. *Foreign Affairs* 12(3), 22–49.

Jemo, I. (1996) *Experiences in the Postwar Reconstruction of the Historical Core of Dubrovnik*. Paper prepared for International Conference on Settlement Revitalization in Postwar Reconstruction, Zagreb, April 26–27.

Kalinowski, K. and Weiler, B. (1992) Review educational travel. In: Weiler, B. and Hall, C.M. (eds) *Special Interest Tourism*. Halsted Press, New York, pp. 15–26.

Lasswell, H. (1936) *Politics: Who Gets What, When and How*. McGraw Hill, New York.

Leheny, D. (1995) A political economy of Asian sex tourism. *Annals of Tourism Research* 22(2), 367–384.

McLaren, D. (1998) *Rethinking Tourism and Ecotravel*. Kumarian Press, West Hartford, Connecticut.

Patty, A. (1999) Australian sex tourists find their laws back home don't take a vacation. *The World Paper* January–February, p. 16.

Pelton, R.Y., Aral, C. and Dulles, W. (1998) *Fielding's The World's Most Dangerous Places*, 3rd edn. Fielding, Inc., Redondo Beach, California.

Pennington, M. (1999) Talks pause with dissidents holding Myanmar Embassy. *Kansas City Star* 2 October, p. A17.

Pirages, D. and Runci, P. (2000) Ecological interdependence and the spread of infectious disease. In: Cusimano, M.K. (ed.) *Beyond Sovereignty*. Bedford/St Martin's Press, New York, pp. 176–194.

Pi-Sunyer, O. (1979) The politics of tourism in Catalonia. *Mediterranean Studies* 1(2), 46–69.

Plummer, J.T. (1989) Changing values. *The Futurist* 23(1), 8–13.

Richter, L.K. (1982) *Land Reform and Tourism Development: Policy Making in the Philippines*. Schenkman, Cambridge, Massachusetts.

Richter, L.K. (1988) Indonesian tourism: the good, the bad and the ugly. *Contours* 14(1), 29–30.

Richter, L.K. (1989a) *The Politics of Tourism in Asia*. University of Hawaii Press, Honolulu.

Richter, L.K. (1989b) Action alert. *Contours* 4(4), 4.

Richter, L.K. (1992) Political instability and tourism in the Third World. In: Harrison, D. (ed.) *Tourism in the Less Developed Nations*. Belhaven, London, pp. 35–46.

Richter, L.K. (1995) Gender and race: neglected variables in tourism research. In: Butler, R. and Douglas, P. (eds) *Change in Tourism.* Routledge, London, pp. 71–91.

Richter, L.K. (1998a) Exploring the role of gender in tourism research. In: Theobald, W.F. (ed.) *Global Tourism: the Second Decade,* 2nd edn. Butterworth-Heinemann, Oxford, UK, pp. 390–404.

Richter, L.K. (1998b) *Public–Private International Tourism Cooperation: Strategies for Excellence and Sustainability in Croatia and Costa Rica.* Paper presented at the WTO Conference in Krakow, Poland, 8–10 October.

Richter, L.K. (1999a) After political turmoil: the lessons of rebuilding tourism in three Asian countries. *Journal of Travel Research* 38, 41–45.

Richter, L.K. (1999b) The politics of heritage tourism development. In: Pearce, D.G. and Butler, R.W. (eds) *Contemporary Issues in Tourism Development.* Routledge, London, pp. 108–126.

Richter, L.K. (1999c) *Health Issues in International Tourism: Policy Prescriptions for the Twenty-first Century.* Paper presented at the International Academy for the Study of Tourism conference in Zagreb, Croatia, June.

Richter, L.K. (1999d) Myanmar. In: *Encyclopedia Americana Yearbook.* Grolier Press, Danbury, Connecticut, p. 375.

Richter, L.K. and Richter, W.L. (2000) Back from the edge: recovering a public tradition in Dubrovnik. In: Nagel, S. (ed.) *Handbook of Global Social Policy.* Marcel Dekker, New York.

Richter, L.K. and Waugh, W.L. (1991) Tourism and terrorism as logical companions. *Tourism Management* 7(4), 318–327.

SLORC's Burma (1997). *Contours* 7(11–12), 20.

Smith, V. (1998) Privatization in the Third World: small-scale tourism enterprises. In: Theobald, W.F. (ed.) *Global Tourism: the Second Decade,* 2nd edn. Butterworth-Heinemann, Oxford, UK, pp. 205–215.

Tidwell, M. (1998) Who can you trust? *Travel Holiday* 5 May, 46, 49–51.

Turco, M. (1997) The greed behind the green in tourism. *Contours* 7(11–12), 6–7.

UNDP (1999) *Human Development Report.* Oxford University Press, Oxford, UK.

Watson, R. and Dennis, M. (1999) Be careful out there. *US News and World Report* 22 February, pp. 64–65.

Weiler, B. and Kalinowski, K. (1990) Participants of educational travel: a Canadian case study. *Journal of Tourism Studies* 1(2), 43–50.

Woodward, C. (1996) Morning in Dubrovnik. *Bulletin of the Atomic Scientists* 52(6), 11.

WTO (1997) *WTO News* No. 1, 1.

4

Human Resources in Tourism Development: African Perspectives

Peter U.C. Dieke

Introduction

Perhaps the main constraint on continuing tourism development [in African countries] is the lack of trained people available to work in the industry. The problem is well recognised and has attracted much financial support from the international funding agencies to help overcome this bottleneck. Much more needs to be done not only to train entrant-level workers but also to develop the middle [indigenous] managers who will eventually become the senior managers ... [and thus] provide opportunities for nationals. [One key objective in all this is to] attract quality staff to meet the increasingly globalised service standards.

There is a major role for government in achieving this objective. However, like so many other aspects of the tourism sector, policies will have to be formulated in consultation with the private sector, and with the continuing support of the specialist international agencies.

(Jenkins, 1997: 16)

Human resources can be described as the pool of human capital under an organization's control in a direct employment relationship. They have two distinct features, of which the first is the knowledge, skills and abilities inherent in individuals who make up the organization. According to the World Bank (1980: 32), human resources development encom-passes education and training, better health and nutrition, and fertility reduction. The second feature is the manner by which individual characteristics are utilized in the performance of roles of employees, broadly defined.

The purpose of this chapter is to discuss the role of human resources (HR) in tourism development planning in Africa. It is suggested that human resources are an important source of sustained competitive advantage in the international tourism industry, and the wide range of elements which constitute HR and the consequent problems associated with their interaction are identified. Finally, implications for tourism destinations in general are discussed, and parameters for a human resource strategy for the tourism sector suggested.

For many people, the need to focus on HR is self-evident. 'Given the importance of the quality aspect of the tourism product and its labour intensity, the pool of human resources available for tourism in a given country is a fundamental factor in the successful development of this industry' (UNCTAD, 1998: 10). One can therefore argue that HR development is needed to take into account the wide range of jobs which constitute the tourism 'product'. This is particularly important, because tourism has the capacity to create more jobs than any other sector of the economy. It is also recognized that one aim of development is human development, which involves the complex interaction of people and institutions within the tourism development process.

According to the United Nations Economic Commission for Africa (ECA, 1996: 202; see also ECA, 1988a,b, 1989, 1991; UNDP, 1995: 9):

> one of the basic elements of the long-term development strategy is the crucial role assigned to human resources and other forms of indigenous capital in spearheading the process of economic transformation. The internationalisation of the factors of production is the backbone of such a strategy.

It is further argued that 'policies that seem pertinent to the attainment of the projected growth in tourism in Africa include ... the training of the different personnel of the tourism sector' (ECA, 1996: 94–95).

ECA's comments on human resources in tourism stem from several considerations, not least the realization that the increasing labour force in the tourism sector in many African countries creates dependency and other problems, often because workers come from outside the region (WTO, 1984). It is unfortunate if this view is accepted without questioning. Firstly, dependency is an emotive word which can be differently interpreted depending on one's viewpoint. In essence, the word underscores the gap between the developed and less developed worlds in terms of the availability of human resource expertise for tourism development. Secondly, Africa lacks the required expertise to progress tourism, a problem which it might overcome by recourse to overseas assistance – for example, from the World Tourism Organization (WTO) or the International Labour Organization (ILO). Thirdly, unless Africa takes concrete steps to develop its own 'home-grown' personnel, it will be increasingly forced to continue to rely on international help to support its tourism development efforts – a situation surely against the broad principles of self-reliance and self-sustainability and the view that Africa's future should be in Africa's hands.

Principles of self-reliance were enshrined by the Organization of African Unity (OAU), first in the Lagos Plan of Action, subsequently in the Final Act of Lagos, and then in the 1991 Abuja Treaty (which became operational in 1994).

They were also emphasized more recently, in September 1999, when the Sirte Declaration was adopted at the OAU Extraordinary Summit on African Union in Libya, and in the Cairo Declaration and Cairo Plan of Action, adopted at the first Africa–Europe Summit, held in April 2000 under the aegis of the OAU and the European Union in Cairo (OAU, 1981, 1991; UNCTAD, 2000).

Human Resources in Tourism Development

In recent years, human resources have taken 'centre stage' in tourism development and management in many countries. There are several reasons for this, including changing trends in international tourism, and the competitive environment within which tourism operates. Taken together, these factors underline the need for a strategy for human resources for the tourism sector. Before examining each factor in turn, however, it is useful to examine the role of human resources in tourism development, focusing on employment and related policy issues.

As noted in the introduction, tourism is usually considered a labour-intensive activity. This implies that tourism creates more jobs per capital unit invested relative to investment in other sectors of an economy (the 'cost per job' in one sector compared with another). Human resources in tourism can therefore be examined from a number of angles. While economists might regard cost-effectiveness as being of prime importance, tourism planners focus on the number and quality of human resources available in the sector. At the operational level, the concern of tourism managers is likely to be the extent to which trained and effective personnel are available to provide the required quality of service for tourists, be they high spenders or low spenders. However, irrespective of one's viewpoint, there is a consensus on several aspects of the present enquiry.

It is generally accepted that the role of human resources in the development of tourism is crucial. In broad terms, the traditional view is that human resources involves recruiting and selecting staff, training them for particular roles, assessing their performance and remunerating them accordingly (Fombrun *et al.*, 1984). Within the service sector, key emphasis is given to coordinating staff contributions to service quality, to overcome the five gaps of service-quality shortfalls, namely: (i) between customer expectations and management perceptions; (ii) between management perceptions and specifications of service quality; (iii) between specifications of service quality and the actual delivery of the services; (iv) between the delivery of the service and external communications; and (v) between customers' expectations and their perceptions of the quality of the service (McClleland, 1993).

At a general level, these gaps highlight the importance of effective communication between those who give and receive the service. Customers constantly expect the best service and only when this is received and their satisfaction demonstrated, through feedback or repeat business, can a hotel's performance be measured. If such gaps are not bridged, customer satisfaction (and thus success in tourism) will not be achieved. However, where gaps continue to exist, they may raise more questions than answers, particularly over such characteristics of tourism employment as low skill levels, seasonal demand and the problems and opportunities they pose to tourism human resources.

There is much merit in moves made in recent years to indigenize labour in the tourism industry, especially in developing economies, thus giving indigenous people a voice in the ownership and management of the tourism sector. The development of indigenous business ownership will lessen the perception of tourism as a foreign-dominated and foreign-controlled sector. However, it then becomes even more incumbent on tourism policy-makers to ensure that there are well-trained personnel to perform these tasks at a satisfactory level of competence.

Human resource managers in tourism face numerous challenges, including the nature of tourism employment (which is often unskilled, seasonal, part-time or casual), the low pay and little training workers receive. Coupled with a lack of employer commitment, these may all result in high labour turnover. As a consequence, 'the industry is (anecdotally) viewed as an industry lacking a firm career structure, being an employer of temporary staff, who tend to be working there while looking for a "real" job' (Davies *et al.*, 1999: 203).

Such a depiction may not apply universally, but the nature of tourism demand, remuneration, skill levels and training are important policy areas for consideration. However, tourism is perhaps not different from other sectors of the economy, for it is widely accepted that all economic sectors have a hierarchy of jobs and that entry thresholds are generally low. One practical problem that must be addressed is how to move people up the employment ladder, and this is also a legitimate policy issue. That said, if successful policies are to be developed, and training programmes designed and implemented, data shedding light on job profiles are required. If these are not produced, foreign expertise will continue to be needed, with wide implications for the local economy (for example, exacerbating leakages), possibly leading to social and political unrest.

Referring specifically to human resources policies in the tourism sector, Doswell (1994, unpublished; see also Doswell, 1997, 265–286) has sought to expand the debate, pointing to the need to:

> offer competitive employment conditions and career opportunities to ensure the adequate recruitment of all levels of personnel. To provide educational and training opportunities for all occupations and specialisations, at general and specified levels of skills, in all necessary parts of the country.

It is further suggested that such sectoral policies have to be seen against the broader national human resources framework. Subject to a country's stage of development, other general objectives might include a flexible and adaptive labour market, less inequality of income and education, and improved education and training delivery systems. Studies have also identified specific objectives relevant to tourism, including indigenization of the labour force, the development of inter-sectoral linkages, and reduced dependency on foreign inputs and community involvement (Othman, 1998; Tosun, 1998). In essence, these ideas underscore widespread recognition of the need to address the relative exploitation in the tourism sector by foreigners. By pursuing such objectives, it is expected that local people will be empowered and become part of the owner-ship structure. As an example, switching pur-chases to local suppliers can assist in the development of local entrepreneurs.

Again, as Doswell (1994, unpublished) noted:

> The country-specific background to employment in the tourism sector will depend on a number of influences. For example, the size, structure, characteristics of the tourism sector, its image as an employer, current labour market conditions, the structure and characteristics of the educa-tional system, employer attitudes to staffing, recruitment, selection, and training and, of course, government policies.

From the outset, governments should relate tourism to economic and social development in general, identify what is expected from the sector and set out the development parame-ters accordingly. Once these have been articu-lated, HR development should focus on how trained personnel are to be produced in the right numbers, in the needed specializations and occupations, and at the right levels of skill. It is important that such decisions are not made in a national vacuum, but in the context of changing trends in international tourism and in an increasingly competitive interna-tional environment.

International tourism trends

The first of these is the growing importance of tourism as a major international economic activity, globally and regionally, with con-sequent impacts on tourism numbers, receipts and employment. Estimates from the WTO have shown that in 1998 international tourism accounted for approximately 1.5% of world gross national product, 8% of world merchan-dise exports by value and 35% of the world exports of services (WTO, 1999). It is further estimated that 625 million tourists trips took place across international boundaries in 1998, generating about US$445 billion and 11.3 mil-lion jobs. Projections to the year 2020 envisage a rise in tourism arrivals and earnings to about 1.6 billion and US$2 trillion, respectively. Although these predictions must be interpreted cautiously, and may well be underestimates, the trends have considerable implications for human resources for the tourism sector.

The competitive environment

The second factor of major relevance to national decisions over HR development is the market structure of international tourism. Competitiveness in tourism arises from several sources, not least of which is the discretionary nature of tourism demand. It is discretionary because, unlike business tourists and those visiting friends and relatives, leisure tourists are under no obligation to take a holiday, either at home or abroad. We thus confront a key feature of international tourism – the pos-sibility of destination substitution, which high-lights the negative consequences of poor and inadequate service levels at destination areas.

A synthesis

The human resources challenge that substitu-tion evokes is understandable. Arguably, tourists choose specific destinations as part of a total 'value for money' experience, which includes the quantity and quality of the tourism 'product' (that is, attractions, ameni-ties and access) and the human element avail-able at a destination. The latter is important in the delivery of support services (for example, food, accommodation and hygiene) and the manner of their delivery. The tourist makes demands upon the country's HR by asking for acceptable standards of service and behav-iour. In fact, tourism is both a human activity and a dynamic sector. The first is based on human contacts and endeavours, and the sec-tor's most valuable contribution can be made from HR. However, this requires resources to be developed. At the same time, because tourism is a dynamic sector, hosts are faced with apparently endless needs and wants of tourists, who might be characterized as the Oliver Twists of the travel scene.

At the same time, it is also arguable that people first choose the type of holiday they want, calculate how much they can afford, and only then choose a destination. At this point, of course, issues of image, health and safety come to mind, with the service reputedly on offer much lower on the list of priorities.

HR in the Tourism Sector in Africa

In this section, discussion first focuses on Africa's place in international and regional tourism markets and the evolution of its hotel capacity, and then moves to an analysis of the role played by HR and employment in the region. It then raises general considerations concerning the determination of HR requirements, identifies constraints on the development of HR in tourism, and presents elements of a strategy to deal with these areas of concern.

Africa in the world tourism economy

The extent and impact of international tourism in 1998 have been noted. According to the

WTO (1999), in 1998 Africa received approximately 8% of international tourist trips (25 million arrivals), an increase over the 1997 level of 6.1% (23 million tourists). Similar increases in receipts were recorded, and the region's share rose from 3.3% (US$9 million) in 1997 to 5.9% (US$10 million) in 1998. Within Africa, the Northern sub-region had the highest share of traffic (34.6%) and revenue (33%), followed in descending order by South Africa, East Africa, West Africa, and Central Africa, as indicated in Table 4.1.

In 1998, almost 40% of all visits to Africa originated in the region, with Europe accounting for about 36% of total arrivals (WTO, 1999). The most visited destination is South Africa (as indicated in Table 4.2), which took 24% of total traffic, followed by two northern countries, Tunisia (18%) and Morocco (13%), and two eastern countries, Zimbabwe (6.4%) and Kenya (4.3%). The pattern of receipts is similar (as indicated in Table 4.3), with South Africa the leading earner (24.8%), followed by Tunisia and Morocco. However, although Zimbabwe and Kenya attracted considerable numbers of tourists, Mauritius and Tanzania were able to earn more from tourism.

Table 4.1. Tourism trends in Africa by sub-regions, 1995–1998.

Sub-regions[a]	Tourist arrivals (000s) 1998	Change over 1997 (%)	Market share of total Africa (%) 1995	Market share of total Africa (%) 1998	Tourist receipts (US$ million) 1998	Change over 1997 (%)	Market share of total Africa (%) 1995	Market share of total Africa (%) 1998
East	5,761	7.7	21.7	23.1	2,426	5.75	23.4	25.4
Central	483	7.81	1.4	1.9	82	5.13	1.7	0.9
North	8,623	7.79	38.7	34.6	3,176	9.90	38.1	33.3
South	7,671	7.94	29.9	30.8	2,950	2.54	28.1	30.9
West	2,365	4.97	8.3	9.5	917	4.23	8.5	9.6
Total Africa	24,903	7.5	100.0	100.0	9,551	5.9	100.0	100.0

[a]Countries of the sub-regions:
East: Burundi, The Comoros, Djibouti, Ethiopia, Kenya, Madagascar, Malawi, Mauritius, Mozambique, Réunion, Seychelles, Somalia, Tanzania, Uganda, Zambia, Zimbabwe.
Central: Angola, Cameroon, Central Africa Republic, Chad, Congo (Brazzaville), Democratic Republic of Congo (Kinshasa), Equitorial Guinea, Gabon, Sao Tomé and Principé.
North: Algeria, Morocco, Sudan, Tunisia.
South: Botswana, Lesotho, Namibia, South Africa, Swaziland.
West: Benin, Burkina Faso, Cape Verde, Côte d'Ivoire, The Gambia, Ghana, Guinea, Guinea Bissau, Liberia, Mauritania, Niger, Nigeria, Senegal, Sierra Leone, Togo.
Source: WTO (1999: 14–29).

Table 4.2. Top five destinations in Africa, 1998.

Rank	Country	Tourist arrivals (000s)	Change over 1997 (%)	Market share of total Africa (%)
1	South Africa	5981	10.0	24.0
2	Tunisia	4718	10.7	18.9
3	Morocco	3243	5.6	13.0
4	Zimbabwe	1600	7.0	6.4
5	Kenya	951	−5.0	4.3

Source: WTO (1999: 31).

Accommodation capacity

According to the UN ECA (1987), between 1980 and 1984 the annual increase in hotels in Africa was 5.8%, a rate which put the continent ahead of America (4.6%) and Europe (2.3%) but behind the Middle East (12.8%) and Asia (10.5%). At the beginning of this period, there were nearly 182,000 hotel rooms (346,366 beds), and by 1984 there were 216,000 (407,131 beds). This capacity was distributed among the Northern subregion (52.7%), West Africa (21.1%), East Africa (19.1%), Central Africa (5.9%) and South Africa (1.2%). In 1984 Africa accounted for 2.1% of all hotels in the world – more than South Asia (0.9%) and the Middle East (0.6%) but less than Europe (52.2%), America (37.8%) and East Asia and the Pacific (6.4%).

After 1984, the growth rate of hotels in Africa slowed down, primarily because many hotels had been under-equipped. By 1997, the situation was as indicated in Table 4.4. Africa had less than 3% of all hotel beds in the world – more than the Middle East and South Asia but considerably less than Europe, the Americas and East Asia/Pacific.

This brief background illustrates the nature and scope of international tourism in Africa and the significance of tourism in some countries, which is clearly influenced by the wider nature of economic development. For the purposes of this chapter, this profile provides a framework within which to examine the scope of human resources in the tourism sector.

HR and employment

Several efforts have been made to examine human resources and employment in Africa (ECA, 1987, 1992, 1993; WTO, 1999: 13) and to highlight the main constraints to the region's tourism. Although there are clear differences across the continent, some general conclusions can be reached.

First, the problems in Africa's tourism are closely related to structural imbalances in its overall development pattern. There are no clear strategies for development in general or for tourism in particular, and tourism has not been integrated with other economic sectors. As a consequence, whereas tourism development in some countries has been insufficient

Table 4.3. Top five tourism earners in Africa, 1998.

Rank	Country	Tourist receipts (US$ million)	Change over 1997 (%)	Market share of total Africa (%)
1	South Africa	2366	3.0	24.8
2	Morocco	1600	10.9	16.8
3	Tunisia	1550	8.9	16.2
4	Mauritius	503	3.7	5.3
5	Tanzania	431	9.9	4.5

Source: WTO (1999: 33).

(as in Cameroon), in others (for example, Kenya) it has been uncontrolled and excessive. Organization of the tourism sector has been inadequate, which has contributed to a lack of profitability in many operations, and promotion prospects are poor, with massive reliance on expatriate staff. Above all, the major setback is inadequate training.

Secondly, tourism embraces many component activities: for example, the travel trade (tour operations and travel agencies), transport and the hotel sub-sector. The emphasis in this chapter is on accommodation, although such a focus may lead to an underestimate of the full requirements of human resources. In 1997, tourism in Africa employed over 500,000 workers – over 80% in the hotel area and the rest in travel agencies and related services. Compared with other regions of the world, and with the world average, this indicates a great imbalance, with a proliferation of travel agencies, tourism offices and various transport companies. Although limited in scope, it is instructive to examine the employee/room ratio, which allows comparison, in particular, with other developing countries.

The employee/room ratio is higher in Africa than all other regions except South Asia, a level of overemployment which itself has numerous interconnected causes. These include structural imbalances at all levels of the work force. In general, for example, administration, accounting services and, by extension, management represent a very low proportion of workers in an average African hotel of 50 employees. Typically, first-level supervision is provided by two to three

people, which helps to explain the poor quality of reception or services. This means that training reception staff is a key priority, which would raise the standard of service on offer without requiring the deployment of more supervisory staff. Recruitment generally is haphazard; the floors, laundry-room, bar and kitchen are often overstaffed; productivity is low; there is a lack of proper equipment; and maintenance, in particular, is much neglected in African hotels. All of this is exacerbated by a climate that is often harsh and for which there are special requirements for installing air-conditioning units, refrigerators, or generators. Indeed, the acquisition of ill-adapted equipment is the most frequent cause and effect of inadequate maintenance – and qualified maintenance staff are in short supply.

The situation is hardly helped by a general lack of managerial staff throughout Africa and the relatively low qualifications held by those who do occupy positions of responsibility. As a consequence, the management of many African hotels is impaired, with little attempt to assess profitability or control costs, and with a distinct lack of suitably trained managers for commercial operations, technical matters, or personnel. In fact, managerial and administrative personnel constitute only 1.4% of all staff, with all others occupying unskilled jobs. The result is a lack of supervision. Catering and the kitchen are maintained at a low level by mainly unskilled staff, the maintenance service lacks technicians, and there is overemployment among the unskilled.

Although the hotel trade undoubtedly requires many unskilled personnel – to work,

Table 4.4. Hotels and similar establishments – accommodation capacity.

Region	Bed-places (000s)			Market share (%)		
	1980	1985	1997	1980	1985	1997
Europe	8,542	8,637	11,731	52.5	47.3	40.0
Americas	6,436	6,933	9,345	39.5	38.0	31.8
East Asia/Pacific	763	1,694	6,725	4.7	9.3	22.9
Africa	269	525	834	1.7	2.9	2.8
Middle East	141	254	400	0.9	1.4	1.4
South Asia	126	198	310	0.8	1.1	1.1
Total	16,277	18,241	29,344	100.0	100.0	100.0

Source: WTO (1999: 13).

for example, in restaurants and small hotels – hotels also need supervisors and managers. By contrast, analysis of staff required by travel agencies, airlines and tour operators indicates that the need in these sub-sectors is almost entirely for people who are qualified. In short, in its lack of managerial and administrative staff, Africa is far behind other regions of the world.

It should be emphasized that such deficiencies are not typical of all African countries; but many are widespread, especially in countries that accord tourism a low priority in their national development plans.

Determining HR requirements for tourism in Africa

On the basis of the above prognosis, the ECA (1987, 1992) estimated HR requirements, recognizing the diverse tourism structures and the lack of statistics that make such forecasts a relatively problematic exercise. Its focus was thus on overall trends, with the definition of needs predicated upon an in-depth knowledge of specific countries, as well as an awareness of the sector's growth forecast, state by state and project by project. The broad outlines of the trends it identified were as follows.

- The tourism sector is increasing.
- New forms of accommodation, catering and recreation focus less on 'class' service and more on efficiency and rapidity in work.
- These phenomena will first apply to countries with a developed tourism sector and the big cities.
- Tourism is becoming increasingly internationalized as a result of a growing international clientele.
- National and intra-regional tourism are increasing.
- The economic crisis is affecting employment. While the employee/room ratio is falling because of management constraints, the number of jobs is increasing as the accommodation sector expands. In addition, HR requirements are influenced by amalgamations and restructuring, the search for employee loyalty and participa-

tion, and by privatization of the hotel sector.

- Hotel categories are being transformed, and while four-star accommodation continues to be important, more two- and three-star units are required. There is also a need to create 'para-hotel' units – for example, camping facilities and home-stay operations.
- The economic crisis and the need to provide more employment compels governments to speed up the replacement of expatriate senior staff by nationals.
- International chains of hotels also want to replace their senior expatriate staff.
- There are vast possibilities for employment in the hotel sector, which is no longer limited to the kitchen, service and reception areas.
- The mobility and versatility of staff members are increasingly important, as is the development of skills related to recreation activities.

With these trends in mind, it was estimated that if Africa's needs were to be met, over the 3-year period 1986 to 1989 it would need to train about 3000 managerial staff, 15,000 senior technicians, 28,000 intermediate technicians, 51,000 low-level technicians and 64,000 apprentices and other staff. In short, more than 160,000 employees were required, at a rate of 53,000 a year, eventually increasing the number of employees in African tourism by almost a third. Importantly, whereas in-service training could be used to develop apprentices and other staff, the remaining 100,000 could be trained only in institutions especially geared for the purpose.

In fact, in contrast to these estimated needs of African tourism, those trained by the end of 1990 were 600 managerial staff, 1600 senior staff, 4500 intermediate technicians, 9200 low-level technicians and 1500 apprentices and other workers – a total of 17,500 employees.

In retrospect, it has to be noted that in Africa, especially, there is a dearth of reliable statistical and other data, and that many African countries are committing resources to tourism. Mention should also be made of the increasingly significant role of the private sector in developing the African tourism product.

This tendency will strengthen competition between operators, and professionalism will have to take precedence over bureaucratic amateurism. Nevertheless, the message from the above analysis is obvious. There is an urgent need for action to prepare African countries for the development of tourism and to satisfy the increasing needs of the African people in terms of leisure and travel.

The distribution of training centres and programmes in Africa

Table 4.5 indicates the distribution (according to the ECA 1992 study) of selected national training institutions (all of which are in the public sector) and their tourism and hotel programmes in Africa. Their geographical distribution is skewed: 20 centres are found in only three countries in North Africa; and while Morocco alone has 11, some other sub-regional countries (for example, Côte d'Ivoire, Ethiopia and Zimbabwe) have only one. There is similar variation in the levels at which training is provided: while over 20 centres train middle management and junior staff, only seven (two in Algeria and others in Ethiopia, Morocco, Mozambique, Senegal and Zimbabwe) train staff at university for senior management, whereas 30 centres train to secondary level. While some centres provide hotel training, others combine hotel management and tourism training.

In French-speaking countries the Brevet d'É-tudes du Premier Cycles, or its equivalent in English-speaking countries, is the basic entry requirement for centres of the secondary school level, but in addition a competitive entrance examination is usually organized for admission. Higher institutions require at least a high school certificate, with the baccalauréat and a hotel school ordinary diploma or work experience. Only one centre (Seychelles Polytechnic) admits foreign students on the basis that their parents are resident expatriates on contract in the country (ECA, 1992: 62) and the others are generally open to nationals of other African countries, provided the host society has diplomatic relations with the student's country of origin. However, some institutions admit foreigners on the presentation of a dossier if, for political reasons, admission is in 'government interests', a tendency that must undermine teaching standards and damage the image of the establishment concerned.

In general, courses last from 2 to 3 years, but some institutions train people for a year or less. Instruction is in either French or English, or even Arabic, depending on the language commonly used in the country concerned, but knowledge of a second or third language is always required for those who deal directly with tourists.

Most establishments provide training for work in the hotel sector, and some also offer courses in 'tourism' and 'travel'. However, the diplomas awarded are national diplomas; courses vary in title and range; and training for the hotel sector, and tourism generally, is often inadequate, especially in countries lacking specialized tourism institutions. The availability and level of training is invariably linked to the extent to which a country has developed its tourism industry. Where relatively adequate and suitable levels of training have been maintained (as, for example, at Kenya Utalii College and in North Africa), it is often because local staff have benefited from international expertise, supplied through bilateral assistance or, in many cases, by the ILO. In fact, a few centres have sought to match their qualifications with partners elsewhere, tending to associate with reputable Western institutions rather than African partners. However, there is a clear need to establish much more equivalence of qualifications at certificate and diploma level, with non-African and, perhaps especially, with African institutions. This would facilitate course sharing and staff exchange, which do not currently occur. It should also be noted that large airlines have their own training facilities, where the pooling of training facilities is possible. In-flight services, catering, ticketing, reservation and reception all involve transferable skills of value and relevance to other sectors of the travel and tourism industries.

Elements of a Strategy for Africa's Tourism Industry

HR development in tourism is aimed at reducing dependence on imported personnel and

Table 4.5. Selected national training/tertiary centres and programmes in Africa in 1992.

Sub-region[a] and country	Training centre		Teaching language	Training level	Training offered	Training duration (months)	Qualifications awarded
	Name of centre						
Eastern							
Ethiopia	Catering and Training Institute (CTTI)[b]		E	University	Mixed (tourism and hotel)	6–24	Certificates, Diplomas
Kenya	Kenya Utalii College[b]		E	Secondary	Mixed (hotel and tourism)	12–48	Diplomas, Associate Diplomas, Diplomas
Mozambique	Hotel Escola Andalucia[b]		P, E	Postgraduate vocational training	Reception, catering, cooking	4–12	Certificates
Seychelles	Seychelles Polytechnic		F, E, K	Secondary	Mixed (hotel and tourism)	12–24	Certificates, Diplomas
Zambia	Evelyn Hone College of Applied Arts and Commerce[b]		E	Secondary	Mixed (hotel and tourism)	12–60	Certificates, Diplomas
Zimbabwe	Bulawayo Technical School of Hotel and Catering[b]		E	University	Mixed (hotel and tourism)	6–36	Certificates, Diplomas: Ordinary, Higher and Postgraduate Diploma
Northern							
Algeria	Institut supérieur d'hôtellerie et du tourisme d'Alger (ISHT)[b]		F, A	University	Mixed (hotel and tourism)	24	Certificates, Diplomas
	Institut des techniques hôtelières et touristiques de Tizi-Ouzou (ITHUT)[b]		F, A	University	Mixed (hotel and tourism)	15–24	Certificates, Diplomas
	Institut des techniques hôtelières de Bou-Saada (ITH)[b]		F, A	Secondary	Hotel	24	Certificates, Diplomas
Morocco	Centre de formation professionnelle hôtelière de Benslimane (CFPH)[b]		A, F, E	Secondary	Hotel	24	Certificates, Diplomas
	Centre de formation professionnelle hôtelière de Casablanca (CFPH)[b]		A, F, E	Secondary	Hotel	24	Certificates, Diplomas
	Centre de formation en restaurant traditionnelle de Rabat (CFRT)[b]		A, F, E	Secondary	Hotel, restaurant	24	Certificates, Diplomas

Country	Institution	Teaching languages	Level	Type	Months	Qualification
	Ecole hôtelière de Ouarzazate (EHO)[b]	F	Secondary	Hotel	36	Certificates, Diplomas
	Ecole hôtelière de Fes (EHF)[b]	F	Secondary	Hotel	36	Certificates, Diplomas
	Ecole hôtelière d'El Jadida[b]	F	Secondary	Hotel	36	Certificates, Diplomas
	Ecole hôtelière d'Agadir (EHA)[b]	F	Secondary	Hotel	24–36	Certificates, Diplomas
	Ecole hôtelière de Rabat (EHR)[b]	F	Secondary	Hotel	24–36	Certificates, Diplomas
	Ecole hôtelière de jeunes filles de Tanger (EHJF)[b]	F	Secondary	Hotel	24–36	Certificates, Diplomas
	Ecole hôtelière de Marrakech (EHM)[b]	F	Secondary	Hotel	24–36	Certificates, Diplomas
	Institut supérieur international du tourisme de Tanger (ISITT)[b]	F, E, A, S, I	University	Mixed (hotel and tourism)	24	Certificates
Tunisia	Institut Supérieur d'hôtellerie et de tourisme de Sidi Bou-Said (ISHT)[b]	F, E	University	Mixed (hotel and tourism)	24	Certificates, Diplomas
	Ecole hôtelière de Nabeul (EHN)[b]	F, E	Secondary	Hotel	12	Certificates
	Ecole hôtelière de Sousse (EHS)[b]	F, E	Secondary	Hotel	12	Certificates
	Ecole hôtelière de Monastir (EHM)[b]	F, E	Secondary	Hotel	12	Certificates
	Ecole hôtelière de Hammanet (EHH)[b]	F, E	Secondary	Hotel	12	Certificates
	Ecole hôtelière de Jerba (EHJ)[b]	F, E	Secondary	Hotel	12	Certificates
Western Ivory Coast	Lycée professionel hôtelier[b]	F, E	Secondary	Reception, restaurant operations	12	Certificates
The Gambia	Gambia Hotel School[b]	E	Secondary	Hotel operations, catering	24	Certificates
Senegal	Ecole nationale de formation hôtelière et touristique de Dakar (ENFHTD)[b]	F, E	University	Mixed (hotel & tourism)	24	Certificates
Togo	Centre de formation de perfectionnement hôtelier (CFPH)*	F, E	Secondary	Hotel	18	Certificates

[a]Sub-regions as in Table 4.1, based on WTO classification of countries.
[b]Status = public.
Teaching languages: A, Arabic; E, English; F, French; I, Italian; K, Kreole; P, Portuguese; S, Spanish.
Source: ECA (1992).

replacing them with workers from local areas. This requires an understanding of the market for labour in the tourism industry, and an awareness of the quantitative and qualitative requirements of the industry. The following section presents elements of a strategy to deal with the HR problems that currently beset African tourism.

Intra-African cooperation in HR for tourism development

Cooperation in developing tourism in African countries is advocated not to achieve self-sufficiency but to promote dialogue and international trade, and the structures proposed below would supplement (and interact with) such organizations as the Southern African Development Community and Economic Community of West African States that also exist for further cooperation within Africa.

In African tourism, cooperation is especially urgent in education and training. Reference has already been made to a shortfall of thousands of tourism managers, instructors and administrators, and it is impossible for most African countries to bear all the costs of training them. It is therefore suggested that, in collaboration with the ILO, the OAU should establish an appropriate structure and institutions to oversee the development of African tourism, the first task of which would be to develop a tourism plan for the continent, focusing on hotels and related sectors. As a matter of urgency, this would involve the collection and compilation of tourism statistics, the articulation of an overall strategy for Africa's tourism and specific objectives for tourism in the region, and the formation of structures necessary for these to be achieved and consistently and regularly evaluated. Such a plan would incorporate regional sub-plans, define the modes and scope of intra-regional and international exchanges, and establish the syllabuses and profiles of Africa's tourism training institutions. The joint involvement of the OAU and ILO in the project would help to ensure progress and enable the voices of the smallest African states to be heard.

The creation of an Association of African Training Centres for Hotel Tourism (AATCHT) would provide such a structure. It would facilitate the exchange of teachers and information, further the development of training programmes, link individual centres to one another through a central organization, disseminate technical information and assistance, and promote interaction and cooperation with international hotel chains. Once operational, it could make a major contribution to training and the subsequent professionalization of the hotel sector.

Like other economic sectors, tourism in Africa suffers a continuous 'drain' of senior staff. It is therefore proposed that an African Tourism Experts Association (ATEA) is formed, similar to the Association of Scientific Experts on Tourism. It would be a 'think tank' and meeting-point for experts with the diverse skills required in tourism, allowing geographers, architects, engineers, research departments and social scientists, for example, to work closely with specialists in management, training and land development. As part of its activities, the Association should establish research programmes and consultancies.

If mandated by the Conference of African Ministers of Tourism, the OAU (in collaboration with other interested parties) could quickly establish this association, and ensure that it received sufficient financial and other resources. Once this has been done, the regional representatives of the OAU, working with the ILO, could monitor the association's progress and ensure that it functions smoothly. As part of this continuing review, it would be necessary to ensure that the list of African tourism experts remained up to date and available to all involved in Africa's tourism industry.

The formation of these two associations and their supporting structures would enable increased cooperation within Africa, and with the rest of the world. Indeed, as part of their remits, both would be required to seek and develop cooperation in the international arena. Clearly, once formed, it would take time for the AATCHT and the ATEA to become established, and their initial activities would be relatively small in scale. However, with the support of the OAU and ILO, they could develop concrete proposals, suggest realistic solutions, and become a major force for change in African tourism.

Creating an enabling environment

African governments have a role to play in formulating appropriate policies and strategies for human resource development in tourism. Support for continental and regional structures are part of this, but it is also necessary to encourage private initiatives and, in particular, African entrepreneurs. Properly conceived, government intervention in the tourism sector can play an important catalytic role. It is important, for example, to create institutional mechanisms that bring together governments and private entrepreneurs, thus avoiding damage that may be caused if they work at cross purposes.

Education and training

It is important to emphasize, again, the importance of training in a wide range of skills, including management and information technology. This should not be confined to the formal education system. While formal training is obviously important, it may often be more beneficial and more cost-effective, in practice, to focus on informal training, either on the job or through programmes carefully tailored to meet defined objectives and targeted at specific types of individuals.

If financial leakages arising from the employment of foreign nationals, especially by transnational corporations (TNCs), are to be minimized, governments and the private sector should collaborate in the formulation of policies and strategies to develop indigenous capabilities (Dieke, 1992). If appropriate incentives are provided by governments, for example, TNCs could develop training programmes for their African staff abroad, or organize in-service training for them.

Conclusions

The importance of developing HR in African tourism cannot be overemphasized. The argument presented in this chapter is that in African countries with a strong tourism sector, growth has been almost entirely demand-led. Late starters have been forced to invest heavily in accommodation and there is an urgent need for staff with technical expertise. Under these circumstances, a tendency has developed to employ expatriates, import the required technology, and even promote local staff who lack the necessary qualifications. However, although untrained workers are abundant and available, observation and practice are an inadequate basis for the acquisition of technical skills, which can be obtained only through planned and effective professional training. Furthermore, it is not simply a matter of initial training. Once trained, individuals must then keep pace with new developments and technical advances.

In such circumstances, then, there is often a shortage of skilled labour. Remuneration is correspondingly low, and the result is a general fall in the quality of service provided. The reputation of the country is tarnished, and the tourism industry turns to foreign partners to improve their tourism product.

In countries where the 'finished tourism product' is still undeveloped, the successful formulation and implementation of a tourism development policy is predicated upon the mobilization of human resources. These resources spearhead any tourism policy, for they ensure the identification of the tourism product, organize its marketing, and are responsible for the overall control of the sector and its integration into the national economy. If they are inadequate, tourism plans will not succeed. As a consequence, it is increasingly necessary to estimate and plan the 'human resource' component, integrate it in the sector's general development plan, and consider it not as a consequence of a chosen policy, but a prior condition for the attainment of set objectives. The human factor is especially vital where the notion of 'service' is found. The quality of a hotel, for example, hinges upon its equipment and the quality of services provided, with a high degree of complementarity between the two. Mediocre service can completely undermine first-rate structures. Alternatively, good service can upgrade modest premises and sites.

Tourism planning leads to the development of HR through training, and its objective is to ensure a better balance between workers and structures. Clearly, plans for hotel and tourism training reflect analysis of present and future market conditions, and require abundant and reliable statistical data (which are not always available). However, it is generally accepted that account should be taken of the following elements.

- Analysis of tourism development objectives as defined by the nation's policy.
- Translation of these objectives into structured employment terms.
- Systematic analysis of the present employment structure.
- Consideration of the present and future system of education, which provides potential candidates for vocational training.
- Determination of possibilities to adopt existing training resources to future quantitative and qualitative needs.
- The integration of sub-regional and regional considerations into national plans.
- Analysis of systems of cooperation and exchanges.

In essence, development in Africa would greatly benefit from a sustained programme of HR development for tourism, and it has been argued that a lack of attention to the issue has been a major barrier to upgrading service standards in the region's tourism sector. As a consequence, the continent has been unable to compete in the international tourism marketplace.

Suggestions have been made as to how some of these difficulties might be overcome, and particular reference has been made to the need for intra-African cooperation to benefit from economies of scale. Alternatively, to do nothing would simply mean that in the new millennium Africa will continue to lag behind in a highly competitive tourism industry. If any single idea could guide tourism policy-makers in Africa, it should be that 'Africans are their brothers' keepers'.

References

Davies, D., Savory, L. and Taylor, R. (1999) Human resources management procedures in variety of tourism accommodation in Western Australia. In: Heung, V.C.S., Ap, J. and Wong, K.K.F. (eds) *Proceedings of Asia Pacific Tourism Association 5th Annual Conference, Tourism 2000 – Asia Pacific's Role in the New Millennium*, Vol. 1. Asia Pacific Tourism Association and Hong Kong Polytechnic University, Hong Kong SAR, China, pp. 202–210.

Dieke, P.U.C. (1992) Tourism development policies in Kenya. *Annals of Tourism Research* 19(3), 558–561.

Doswell, R. (1997) *Tourism: How Effective Management Makes the Difference.* Butterworth-Heinemann, Oxford, UK.

ECA (1987) *Human Resources Requirements and Training of Qualified Personnel for the Tourism Profession in Africa* (Transcom/Tru/CMT.1/3). Economic Commission for Africa, Addis Ababa, Ethiopia.

ECA (1988a) *The Development and Utilization of Human Resources: the Case of the African Least Developed Countries.* (E/ECA/LDCs/ EXP.7/4). Economic Commission for Africa, Addis Ababa, Ethiopia.

ECA (1988b) *The Khartoum Declaration.* International Conference on the Human Dimension of Africa's Economic Recovery and Development, Khartoum, The Sudan (5–8 March).

ECA (1989) *Handbook for Manpower Planning in Africa.* ECA/PHSD/HRP/89/26(6.1(iii)(a). Economic Commission for Africa, Addis Ababa, Ethiopia.

ECA (1991) *Africa's Human Resources Agenda for the 1990s and Beyond.* E/ECA/PHSD/ MC/91/6(6.3(ii)(a)) Economic Commission for Africa, Addis Ababa, Ethiopia.

ECA (1992) *Directory of Vocational Training Facilities in Tourism in Africa.* (Transcom/ 91/1500 Rev. 1. Economic Commission for Africa, Addis Ababa, Ethiopia.

ECA (1993) *Human Resources Development Programme for Tourism in Africa.* Trans/Tru/93/Mad.11. Economic Commission for Africa, Addis Ababa, Ethiopia.

ECA (1996) *Africa in the 1990s and Beyond: ECA-Revised Long-term Development Perspective Study* (ECA/SERPD/TP/96/3). Economic Commission for Africa, Addis Ababa, Ethiopia.

ECA (1998) *Economic Report on Africa 1998.* Economic Commission for Africa, Addis Ababa, Ethiopia.

Fombrun, C., Tichy, N. and Devanna, M. (1984) *Strategic Human Resources Management.* John Wiley & Sons, New York.

Jenkins, C.L. (1997) Social impacts of tourism – background paper. *World Tourism Leaders' Meeting on Social Impacts of Tourism*, Manila, Philippines, 22–23 May.

McClleland, D.C. (1993) The concept of competence. In: Spencer, L.M. and Spencer, S.M. (eds) *Competence at Work*. John Wiley & Sons, New York.

OAU (1981) *Lagos Plan of Action for the Economic Development of Africa: 1980–2000*. International Institute for Labour Studies, Geneva.

OAU (1991) *Treaty Establishing the Africa Economic Community*. Organization of African Unity, Abuja, Nigeria.

Othman, I. (1998) Entrepreneurial opportunities for small and medium scale companies related to tourism development: the case of Langkawi, Malaysia. Unpublished PhD thesis, The Scottish Hotel School, University of Strathclyde, Glasgow, UK.

Tosun, C. (1998) Local community participation in the tourism development process: the case of Urgup in Turkey. Unpublished PhD Thesis, The Scottish Hotel School, University of Strathclyde, Glasgow, UK.

UNCTAD (1998) *Report of the Expert Meeting on Strengthening the Capacity Focus on Tour Operators, Travel Agencies and other Suppliers* (TD/B/COM.1/17, TD/B/COM.1/EM.6/3). United Nations Centre on Trade and Development, Geneva.

UNCTAD (2000) *Cairo Declaration* and *Cairo Plan of Action*. Trade and Development Board (TD/B/EX[24]/2, May), United Nations Centre on Trade and Development, Geneva.

UNDP (1995) *Human Development in Africa 1995 Report*. United Nations Development Programme, New York.

World Bank (1980) *World Development Report*. The World Bank, Washington, DC.

WTO (1984) *The Development of Human Resources for Tourism Employment* (CRCLAT/84/9). World Tourism Organization, Madrid.

WTO (1999) *Tourism Market Trends 1999 – Africa*. World Tourism Organization, Madrid.

5

Tourism in the Southern Common Market: MERCOSUL

Guilherme Santana

Introduction

While tourism development in Asia and Africa has attracted the attention of scholars and other professionals, South America has been largely overlooked. This chapter examines tourism in South America, more specifically in the *Mercado Comum do Cone Sul* (in Portuguese, or MERCOSUL), the Southern Common Market, which involves Brazil, Argentina, Paraguay and Uruguay as full members, and Chile and Bolivia as Associate Members (Fig. 5.1). The chapter commences with a brief description of MERCOSUL and the role reserved for tourism within the overall structure in this early stage of its development. Following this, South American tourism, with special emphasis on MERCOSUL, is described and specific issues influencing and shaping the tourism industry in MERCOSUL are highlighted. Constant political change, economic instability, increasing social problems, and safety and security are all important issues that influence tourism development in the region. At the end of the chapter, the future of tourism in the region, and the challenges it faces are summarized.

Institutional and statistical data on tourism in MERCOSUL are scarce. Although the standardization of the region's tourism statistics was an early priority after the formation of MERCOSUL, and in December 1992 all member states signed a letter of intent to this effect, it has not yet been achieved (Borba, 1993; Guimarães, 1993; Senra *et al.*, 1993). The lack of such statistics is a major limitation to any review of the region's tourism.

Fig. 5.1. MERCOSUL.

International Tourism and South America

According to the World Tourism Organization (WTO), international tourist arrivals in 1996 increased by 5.6% from 1995 and tourism receipts increased by 8.2% (excluding international transport) (WTO, 1998). Revised data for 1997 revealed a decline in the growth rate of tourism activities worldwide, which has been attributed largely to the stagnation of international tourism in East Asia and the Pacific in 1997. Data for 1997 showed an increase in tourist arrivals of 2.8% to 612 million and receipts increasing by 2.2% to US$443 billion (excluding international transport), though the latter figure is more a reflection of the fluctuation of the US dollar than a real decrease in tourism spending. However, despite the devastating economic crises experienced in many regions of the world over the period 1997–1998, tourism continued to increase. WTO data for 1998 reveal that receipts from international tourism, excluding airfares, reached US$445 billion and international tourist arrivals improved to 625 million (WTO, 1999), indicating that tourism can thrive even when economic conditions fluctuate.

Considering other recent major international events in this decade – for example, high unemployment rates in major tourism-generating countries, continuous conflicts in the Balkans and the Middle East, as well as the economic crisis in Asia in 1997 – it is interesting to observe that international tourism still increased by 4.3% between 1993 and 1997, a clear indication of resilience in the face of adversity. This fact is further confirmed by data provided by the International Civil Aviation Organization on international air traffic for 1997, which revealed that 447 million passengers travelled internationally using air services, an increase of 8% over 1996 (WTO, 1998).

An analysis of tourism results over a 10-year period for 1988–1997 reveals that international tourist arrivals grew at an annual average rate of 5% while international tourism receipts (excluding international transport) experienced a 9% annual increase over the 10-year period. Tourism receipts in 1997 represented over 8% of world exports of goods

and almost 35% of the total world exports of services (WTO, 1998).

Although tourism is not new in South America, its economic impact started to be felt only after the Second World War. However, the growth and expansion of tourism was limited by distance from the main generating markets and the chronic economic difficulties of most South American countries. Moreover, the lack of disposable income was reflected in both regional and intra-regional travel.

The great tourism boom of the 1960s and cheaper airfares, coupled with the social status of taking holidays abroad, allowed many destinations, especially in the Mediterranean, to develop, but South America still attracted little interest from the international market. This was not without reason. Throughout the 1970s, almost the entire region was characterized by serious social and political disputes, and armed conflict, guerrilla warfare, military coups, social inequality and domestic tension, terrorism, natural disasters and health-related issues all helped to create a reputation which, for many in tourism-generating countries, remains to this day. As a consequence, all of South America, and not just the southern 'continent,' is thus seen as a politically and economically unstable region where all travellers are unsafe.

In the 1980s, international news on South America centred, with great suspicion, on democratization in some countries and on economic developments. Hyper-inflation was experienced in such major South American players as Brazil and Argentina, and economic fragility and political and social uncertainties continued to keep both tourism investment and tourists out of the region. Nevertheless, the tourism industry survived. In the late 1980s and early 1990s, democracy was consolidated in many countries and some economies also improved dramatically.

Tourism in Latin America, then, has changed considerably. The World Travel and Tourism Council (WTTC) estimated that, in 1998, travel and tourism in Latin America would generate US$155 billion of economic activity (supply/demand) and 9.9 million jobs (WTTC, 1998: 2) and by 2010 would produce US$347.1 billion of economic activity and 15.3 million jobs. For the purposes of this estimate, the WTTC considered Latin America as comprising the following countries: Argentina, Belize, Bolivia, Brazil, Chile, Colombia, Costa Rica, Ecuador, El Salvador, Guatemala, Guyana, Honduras, Nicaragua, Panama, Paraguay, Peru, Surinam, Uruguay and Venezuela.

The Formation and Purpose of MERCOSUL

In line with the global tendency to form economic blocks, Brazil, Argentina, Paraguay and Uruguay established MERCOSUL in 1995. The process commenced in March 1991, with the Treaty of Assuncion, and was extended until December 1994. During this transition period, the focus was on two basic issues: the removal of tariffs and negotiations over common trade policies. Agreements on these topics facilitated the constitution of the common bloc and led to a further period of consolidation. The organization was subsequently extended in 1996 and 1997, when MERCOSUL was joined first by Chile and then by Bolivia, with both countries becoming 'Associate Members'. They are expected to join the free trade zone by 2007. Thus, over a relatively short time scale, MERCOSUL was transformed from a simple project into a fully functional and complex organization.

The economy incorporated into MERCOSUL involves a territorial area of over 12,000,000 km², a potential market of 204 million inhabitants, and a gross domestic product (GDP) (in 1997) of over US$1 trillion. It is the fourth largest economy in the world,

Table 5.1. MERCOSUL's gross domestic product (GDP) compared with other world economies (1997).

Economic bloc	GDP (US$ billion)
NAFTA	8822
EU	8093
Japan	4223
MERCOSUL	1230
China	910
Asia	629
CER	460
Russia	327

Source: O MERCOSUL Hoje (1998).

Table 5.2. Average gross domestic product (GDP) growth in MERCOSUL, 1990–1997, compared with other world economies.

Economic bloc	GDP growth 1990–1997 (%)
China	11.2
Asia	6.4
MERCOSUL	3.9
CER	2.9
NAFTA	2.2
EU	1.7
Japan	1.6
Russia	−6.4

Source: O MERCOSUL Hoje (1998).

behind only North American Free Trade Agreement, the European Union and Japan (as indicated in Table 5.1). It is also one of the most dynamic economies in the world. As Table 5.2 shows, average growth for the period 1990–1997 was 3.9%, well above the world average, and the regional trade among its members prompted by the organization grew by 312% from 1991 until 1997, reaching US$20 billion by the end of 1997 (O MERCOSUL Hoje, 1998).

The share of world direct foreign investment of full member countries of MERCOSUL grew from 1.4% between 1984 and 1989 to 2.6% between 1990 and 1996, and 4% in 1998. Brazil alone received over US$14 billion in direct investment in 1998, a 108% increase over 1996. Bilateral trade between Brazil and Argentina, the two main players in MERCOSUL, increased by 600% between 1991 and 1997. In 1997 alone, trade between the two countries reached US$15 billion (Associação Brasileira de Normas Técnicas, 1998: 26).

MERCOSUL has six clear objectives:

1. The free circulation of goods and elimination of trade barriers.
2. The adoption of a common external tariff.
3. The coordination of macroeconomic policies.
4. Free commerce in services.
5. The free circulation of labour.
6. Free circulation of capital.

Not all were achieved by 1 January 1995, and many are being revised, with others still to be discussed and implemented. Services alone are responsible for more than half of MERCOSUL's GDP but progress in the region's tourism industry has been particularly slow. Indeed, according to Silva (1995: 92), services are a focus of international trade negotiations, and delays in this sector are compromising further integration. Given that international tourism is a highly competitive business, MERCOSUL thus finds itself in a distinctly uncomfortable situation.

Tourism and MERCOSUL

Cooperation in tourism in the Southern Cone pre-dated the establishment of MERCOSUL. The *Comissão Latino-Americana para o Turismo* (Latin American Commission for Tourism), which operates within the Latin American Commission for Integration, decided to create the first experimental sub-commission for tourism, *Comissão de Turismo da America do Sul* (COTASUL: South American Tourism Commission). Every South American country was represented on this commission through their official tourism bodies. The main objective of the Commission was to create mechanisms for integration (Silva, 1995: 95–96).

One of the first indications of integrated tourism policies took place in Montevidéu, Uruguay, in July 1991, when representatives of official bodies of tourism in MERCOSUL met to formalize joint actions (Schlüter and Winter, 1993). Their proposals included the following:

- A promotional 'air pass' for all four countries, and journeys linking them.
- A common body, *Mercado Comum do Turismo* (Tourism Common Market: MERCOTUR) for joint policies in tourism development.
- Joint action to promote the sub-region as a single tourism destination at international tourism trade fairs.
- Tourism to be included as a special commission within MERCOSUL.
- Tourism to be on the agenda of country members as a force of integration and economic development for each country and for the region as a whole.
- Encouragement of the private sector to participate in creating and executing promotional plans.

In particular, official carriers of the member states were provided with a series of challenges:

- To include the MERCOSUL air pass in their tariffs.
- To revise their internal and external tariffs, which were prohibitively high.
- To allow passengers to disembark in different countries without incurring additional costs.
- To reduce or eliminate restrictions on promotional tickets.
- To form an airline pool which would increase the number of routes and/or the frequency of flights in the region.
- To have specific and distinctive counters at airports to cater for air pass holders.
- To increase the weight allowance for air pass holders.

The importance of tourism for national and regional development was further emphasized when it gained a distinct and independent position within the main organizational framework of MERCOSUL. This is made up of 'specialized meeting groups', best described as Working Groups, notably Tourism, Science and Technology, and Communications. They come under the auspices of the Common Market Group, within which they function as advisory bodies. More specifically, the aim of the Tourism Working Group is to develop a common policy for tourism development in the region and to harmonize economic policies relevant to tourism development in individual countries.

The Tourism Working Group brings together representatives from the official tourism bodies of member states and defines and proposes joint policies for tourism development in the MERCOSUL region. In 1994, at an early meeting held during the transition period, in San Juan, Argentina, discussion centred on legislation, air transport and marketing. Among the results were, first, an agreement on personal identification documentation and its validity for inter-state travel, and on the proposal from the Marketing Commission for joint marketing policies (Silva, 1995: 97).

Despite the heterogeneity of member states, and the difficulty in harmonizing macroeconomic policies, the 1994 meeting achieved some positive results, specifically on institutional and legal structures, which were to serve as the basis for future arrangements in the imminent economic bloc. They were in place when MERCOSUL was formalized on 1 January 1995.

Later discussions concentrated on more strategic aspects for tourism development, as indicated by proposals that emanated from four Tourism Working Group Meetings in 1998 (MERCOSUL 1998a,b,c,d). They can be summarized as follows:

- A project to encourage intra-regional tourism development within MERCOSUL (PROMERCOTUR, *Projeto MERCOSUL para o Turismo*, or MERCOSUL Tourism Project). Financial support for the project was sought from the Inter-American Development Bank (IDB). The objective was to develop public and private investment in infrastructure to facilitate tourism flows across member states. As part of the project, Chile (an Associate Member of MERCOSUL) applied for and was granted participation in PROMERCOTUR.
- A subregional Air Transport Treaty, to develop new east–west routes and provide services to airports not served by major airlines.
- Agreement among member states and Chile to joint participation in international trade fairs and exhibitions, promoting the MERCOSUL region as a destination.
- The free circulation of privately owned and rented cars within the member states.
- The creation of a Guide for Tourists. This would provide them with information on customs procedures, health, and other relevant matters concerning travel in MERCOSUL, as well as rules and regulations, and more general information (for example, about the police and hospitals) on driving in specific countries.
- The creation of regional tours across member states, which would focus on culture, landscape and heritage, thus generating employment and further tourism development in selected areas. One such project is the Jesuit Mission Project, involving Brazil, Argentina and Uruguay.
- The development of free health assistance

for tourists throughout the MERCOSUL region. At the time of writing, such arrangements are restricted to Brazil's bilateral agreements with Argentina and Uruguay.
- An agreement with Australia and New Zealand ('Closer Economic Relations Countries') to facilitate the issue of visas involving residents of MERCOSUL and CER.
- A proposal to encourage tourism development in MERCOSUL.

Many proposals concerning tourism put forward in 1991 have not yet materialized and are still on the 2001 agenda. This might reflect the difficulties encountered, or the lack of political will to implement practical measures for tourism development in the region. More generally, although it seems that much progress has been achieved in the short time that the Tourism Working Groups of MERCOSUL have been functioning, the main advances have been in the legal and institutional arena. Tourism and tourists have not yet seen the benefits of a functional extra-state tourism body and, in fact, there is considerable scepticism about the effectiveness of such an organization. Much criticism also comes from the private sector, as the Working Group is a bureaucracy within a structure that clearly has other major priorities. However, the question is not so much over the necessity of such an organization (for it is indeed desirable if destinations are to be marketed as clusters) but rather whether or not it can be flexible enough to address pressing local and regional demands and to compete in a highly competitive global environment.

At an even wider level, the effectiveness of the Tourism Working Group may be restricted by more urgent issues. The serious economic crisis in Brazil (the power house of MERCOSUL) during 1998 and 1999 had a domino effect throughout the region and made it unlikely that political attention would be focused on tourism. Past experience indicates that, in hard times, attention is focused on such traditional sectors as manufacturing and agriculture, and the furore caused by the troubled Brazilian economy in the region called into question MERCOSUL's very existence. Argentina and Paraguay resented the way that Brazil handled the crisis, and Argentina even threatened to seek compensation for being drawn into the crisis. In addition, continuous political uncertainties in Uruguay and the political crisis in Paraguay after the assassination of the Vice-President in March 1999 have also put question marks on the success of the economic bloc. The combination of all these factors suggests a real fragility in the integration process.

When it is also recognized that individual governments are attracted by the prospects of developing their own tourism industries, generally mirroring the Spanish success of the 1950s and 1960s, it is evident that the Tourism Working Groups of MERCOSUL must operate in a complex and difficult environment.

The Evolution of Tourism in the MERCOSUL Region: a Review

The economic importance of tourism

In 1995, MERCOSUL had nearly 200 million inhabitants and a GDP of US$433.63 billion. At that time, tourism activities in the economic bloc represented 7.1% of GDP, 7.2% of consumption, 6.1% of total investment and 3.6% of government expenditure and, although below the world average, tourism was already a major employer. One in every 16 workers was employed in the tourism industry. EMBRATUR (the Brazilian Tourist Board) (1995/96: 118) estimated that, by 2005, investment in MERCOSUL tourism would total some US$24.6 billion and would be creating 745 jobs a day – the equivalent of 2.7 million jobs – or 36% of new working positions, over the period 1995–2005.

The above trends are to some extent countered by less optimistic indications in the econ-

omy. Between 1988 and 1996, South America as a whole moved from a positive tourism balance of payments of US$623 million in 1988 to an overall deficit of US$770 million in 1996. Within MERCOSUL over the same period, there was a decline in the relative contribution of tourism to the economy, and the tourism balance (the difference between receipts received from inbound tourism and expenditure of nationals on outbound tourism) declined from a positive balance of US$1087 million in 1988 to one of only US$13 million in 1996 (WTO, 1998: 4–5).

While not as important as in other regions of the Americas (for example, the Caribbean), the importance of tourism in MERCOSUL should not be underestimated. In 1996, it represented 63.3% of total receipts in services and the share of tourism receipts in merchandising exports was 11.45% (WTO, 1998: 8).

In 1996, apart from Paraguay, tourism receipts as a percentage of the GDP of MERCOSUL's members remained much the same as in 1992, as indicated in Table 5.3. In Brazil, especially, it continued to make a relatively small contribution to GDP – less than 0.5%.

In 1997, despite the geographical concentration of tourist arrivals in a few countries of the Americas (the USA, Canada and Mexico received almost 72% of total arrivals in the region), three MERCOSUL countries were among the top seven in the ranking of the top 20 tourism destinations in the Americas. Argentina was fourth, Brazil (ninth in 1990) was sixth, and Uruguay seventh. Paraguay, which received 387,000 tourists in 1997, was not among the top 20 (WTO, 1998: 28–29) (Tables 5.4 and 5.5). At the time of writing, both arrivals and receipts in MERCOSUL seem

Table 5.3. Tourism in the economy of MERCOSUL countries, 1996.

Country	Receipts per capita (US$)	Receipts per arrival (US$)	Receipts as % of GDP	
			1992	1996
Argentina	130	1067	1.4	1.5
Brazil	15	926	0.3	0.3
Paraguay	168	1955	2.4	8.7
Uruguay	224	333	3.4	3.8

GDP, gross domestic product.
Derived from WTO (1994a, 1998).

to be increasing; compared with 1996, for example, total arrivals in 1997 were up by 7.4%, and receipts by 7% over the same period. (WTO, 1998: 15). Brazil alone saw an increase in arrivals of 12.3%, reaching almost 3 million (WTO, 1998: 29), but its tourism receipts over the period increased by only 5.4%.

The importance of intra-regional tourism

Distance from the main generating markets, which are between seven and 17 h to Europe and the USA, and well over 24 h to Asia, is a major limiting factor for the region in the long-haul market of international tourism. As a consequence, intra-regional travel represents by far the greatest proportion of international arrivals. There is a corresponding need, then, to focus and invest in intra-regional travel, which is where the immediate growth potential lies. It is also the present reality, for in 1997 three-quarters of all tourism arrivals in the Americas (87 million visits) were from within the region. According to the WTO (1998: 34–35), intra-regional tourism grew at an average of 4.1% in the decade up to 1997, and it is estimated this rate will continue up to the year 2000, bringing intra-regional arrivals to 105 million.

A closer examination of MERCOSUL countries illustrates the general trend. In 1997, South America was the main destination for Argentinian travellers and, within South America, Uruguay the most favoured. By the same token, 98% of Uruguay's outbound travel is within the Americas, the vast majority (95%) to South America. Much the same is found for Brazil, and while Brazilian outbound tourism increased by 9.8% a year

between 1988 and 1996, tourism to the Americas during the same period increased by 11.9%, with Southern and Northern sub-regions as preferred destinations for Brazilians. Both received 29% of outbound tourists from Brazil in 1996. However, it is also noteworthy that between 1988 and 1996, while the market share in North America has increased by 7%, the Southern American share increased by only 1% in the same period (WTO, 1988).

Issues in MERCOSUL Tourism

Infrastructural development in Brazil and Argentina

Tourism relies on many services provided or controlled by the public sector, including public utilities and sometimes transport and financial services. This is especially so for most developing countries and tourism infrastructure within MERCOSUL varies dramatically among the bloc's members. The lack of basic infrastructure is serious and has hampered international tourism to the region, especially long-haul tourism from North America, Europe and Asia, and information gathered by Brazil and Argentina – the only two countries for which data are available – regularly confirms a wide range of inadequacies that compromise tourist satisfaction and spending in the region.

The most common complaints relate to a lack of telecommunication facilities (and the high cost of those that do exist), poor airport facilities, the cost of air tickets and lack of route alternatives, poor hygiene in accommodation facilities and restaurants, the lack of general information for tourists, unsafe roads,

Table 5.4. Tourist arrivals for MERCOSUL for 1992 and 1997.

Country	1992 arrivals (000s)	Share (%)	1997 arrivals (000s)	Share (%)
Argentina	3,031	45.64	4,540	43.72
Brazil	1,475	22.20	2,995	28.84
Paraguay	334	5.03	387	3.73
Uruguay	1,802	27.13	2,462	23.71
MERCOSUL	6,642	100.00	10,384	100.00

WTO (1994a,b, 1998).

Table 5.5. Tourism receipts for MERCOSUL, 1992 and 1997.

Country	Receipts 1992 (US$ million)	Share (%)	Receipts, 1997 (US$ million)	Share (%)
Argentina	3090	62.66	5069	55.16
Brazil	1307	26.51	2602	28.32
Paraguay	153	3.10	759	8.26
Uruguay	381	7.73	759	8.26
MERCOSUL	4931	100.00	9189	100.00

WTO (1994a , 1998).

traffic congestion, noise and pollution, over-charging of foreign tourists by taxi drivers, restaurants and souvenir shops, the lack of public toilets (and poor hygiene in those that do exist), inadequate signs, the low standard of public transport, and the general lack of safety for tourists. However, improvements have been made, especially in Brazil and Argentina, where privatization has had a beneficial effect on telecommunications, and where road and air networks have been notably extended and upgraded, often as a consequence of deregulation.

The case of Brazil, especially, is instructive in demonstrating how changes in the tourism industry are linked to wider economic and political developments. During 21 years of military rule (1964–1985), widespread corruption and decades of 'unwise' economic policies, Brazilian tourism remained in obscurity. In the 1990s the situation began to change dramatically: the economy was opened up, economic management improved, the inflation of a decade (which had once reached 80% a month) was reduced, and the real was introduced and pegged in value to the US dollar. Past trends were completely reversed and, supported by a strong currency, travel by Brazilians surged. In 1997, over 4 million Brazilians travelled abroad, against 2.9 million international arrivals. The result was a huge deficit that destabilized the country's balance of payments (Anon., 1998: 4).

Other variables also contributed to the travel deficit. According to the US Department of Commerce (Pinheiro, 1998: 33), in 1997 Brazilians spent US$2373, on average, while visiting the USA – considerably more than the average Japanese or German tourist. This contrasts with an average expenditure of about US$1840 by US visitors to Brazil. In fact, both

nationals and foreign visitors found Brazil expensive. Interest rates were high, reaching 49% in 1999. It was thus cheaper to travel abroad than to take a holiday in Brazil, and a trip overseas could be financed through overseas institutions at a rate of 1% a month, against 7% at Brazilian rates. The result was an increase in outbound tourism to neighbouring countries and to other continents. Of all international trips abroad in 1995 and 1996, for example, 36% were to the USA, 23% to Europe, and 15% to Argentina (Folha de São Paulo, 1996).

The collapse of East Asian economies in 1997, and of Russia's in 1998, also had ramifications in Brazil, which early in 1999 suffered a serious decline. The sharp devaluation of the real against the US dollar was immediately reflected in tourism figures: the country suddenly became attractive to foreign travellers, while the domestic market experienced an unprecedented boom.

Another factor contributing to the increase in domestic tourism was the long-awaited deregulation of air transport. In 1998 alone, the number of air passengers increased by 25%, and in that year 17% of all passengers had never before travelled by air (Breitinger, 1999: 54). In the same year, 38.2 million Brazilians (almost a quarter of the entire population) travelled within the country, an increase of 43% from the previous year. According to Carvalho (1999), package tours alone increased by 26% in 1998. Along with the deregulation of air travel, Brazilian airports were modernized and new ones were under construction, to serve international and domestic demand and meet the need for higher standards. At the time of writing, in the north-east alone, eight airports were being upgraded, at a cost of over US$250 million.

The process of tourism development is being accompanied by financial incentives from federal, state and regional authorities. In the north-east, PRODETUR (*Projecto para o Desenvolvimento do Turismo*: the Tourism Development Project), involving nine states, is changing the face of tourism in the region. Massive investment, financed by national and international institutions, is designed to improve existing tourism facilities and expand infrastructure, as well as provide basic infrastructure for development in areas of tourism potential. The IBD has contributed US$670 million for this programme in its first phase, and will contribute a further US$600 million for the next phase, which is due to start in 1999 (Schneider, 1999). In the modernization of the airports IBD is providing 50%, with local governments and other parties meeting the remaining 50%. Overall, direct investment in the Northeast is expected to reach US$8 billion by 2003 (Carvalho, 1999).

There are indications that these trends will continue. In 1998, over 5.5 million international tourists visited Brazil, bringing with them US$3.6 billion (WTO, 1999: 18) and it is expected, with the devaluation of the real in February 1999, that this figure will increase by 20% in 1999 (FADE-EMBRATUR, 1998: 4). Despite the economic crises, domestic tourism is also expected to rise. A study conducted by the Fundação Instituto de Pesquisas Econômicas (FIPE) envisaged an increase of 10–12% in 1999, with receipts up to US$32 billion (FIPE, 1998).

The response of EMBRATUR, the government tourism agency, to all these developments has varied over time. In the 1980s, when Brazil's international image reflected its internal economic and political situation, marketing budgets were cut and, as a result, tourist receipts fell (FADE-EMBRATUR, 1998: 6–7). In the 1990s, however, the importance of tourism was recognized and marketing budgets were substantially increased. In addition, efforts were made to encourage domestic tourism, with the slogan, 'Enjoy your country: Wherever you go, you will be at home.' EMBRATUR also engaged in a campaign to make people aware of the importance of tourism to the nation and to communities, focusing especially on cleanliness of destination areas: 'Trash or Tourists?'

The most visible changes have been in the accommodation sector. In 1997, according to FADE-EMBRATUR (1998: 97), total investment in the Brazilian hotel industry reached US$76 billion. There were over 18,000 hotel establishments in the country, with an average of 59 rooms, and investment in accommodation was at record levels. National hotel groups as well as individual and institutional investors also significantly increased their level of investment. In 1998, for example, more than 200 hotels were added to the country's stock of accommodation, and the city of São Paulo alone was boosted by the addition of 10,000 new rooms. Furthermore, in 1999 the Accor Group was scheduled to build more than 60 new hotels. Because of economic stability and the significant increase in both domestic and international tourism, hotel occupancy in Brazil increased from 47% in 1993 to 59% in 1996 and 67% in 1997 (FADE-EMBRATUR, 1998: 64; Horwath Consulting/Soteconti, 1998: 3). Accommodation facilities expanded across the range, from the deluxe to economy hotels (with the involvement of most major hotel chains) and over a similarly diversified price range.

Crucially, EMBRATUR decided to abolish the old hotel classification and grading system. At the time of writing, the new classification system had not been finalized and there was much confusion surrounding the issue. Nevertheless, this drastic decision was much welcomed by some sectors within the tourism industry and by consumers. The hotel industry in Brazil is characterized by diversity and fragmentation, with considerable variation across geographical regions and within categories. A hotel allocated three stars in the South, for example, might receive five stars in the north-east. This diversity was a key factor in EMBRATUR's decision to discard the old system. By mid-1999, however, only a few hotels had been reclassified and regions were still very divided as to what course of action to take. The official position is that the industry cannot, or should not, be allowed to control or regulate itself.

There is a strong concentration of hotels in the south-east, the most developed region, which accounts for 48% of all hotels. By contrast, the southern region has 25% and the north-east 18%, with the remaining 9% divided between the centre-west (5%) and the northern (4%) (FADE-EMBRATUR, 1998: 21). Two-star hotels (using the old classification system) account for 43% of the total, while those with four or five stars account for only 14% and 4%, respectively. The vast majority of hotels (84%) are privately owned, but the largest of these, with over 70 rooms, tend to be managed by professionals. The remaining hotels fall under a variety of social and institutional arrangements. Hotel chains account for less then 20% of the accommodation supply in the country and are mostly concentrated in the South, usually in medium and large cities (FADE-EMBRATUR, 1998: 28).

In 1997, there was an average of 31 employees per hotel. As a consequence, 18,000 hotels provided jobs to over 500,000 people, the equivalent to 0.8% of the total Brazilian workforce (FADE-EMBRATUR, 1998: 47). Stimulated by government incentives, the sector is booming, but service quality remains a problem. The lack of investment by public and private sectors in training and education has contributed to inefficiency and customer dissatisfaction. Most hotel tasks are performed by lower-class employees with little or no formal education, most of whom are contracted on a part-time basis. As the great majority of hotels in Brazil are operated by individual proprietors, often employing family members, little training (if any) is provided. Moreover, hotel employees are poorly paid: the average monthly salary is only about US$130. There are, of course, many variations according to region, job levels, hotel categories and employers, but wages are generally low by Brazilian standards. The problem is that the lowest-paid employees are those in the front line; few hotel employees, for example, can speak another language.

The hotel industry in Argentina also experienced a boom and the number of hotel rooms increased by more than 27% from 89,800 in 1992 to 114,500 in 1996. At the beginning of the 1990s, though, the industry suffered a decline as a result of the process of adjustment and economic stabilisation following the effects of the Mexican economic crisis. Budget hotels were the most damaged, suffering a reduction in total room capacity from 108,812 in 1990 to 68,330 in 1991. After this turbulent period, and with the economy in better shape, growth in the hotel industry was driven mainly by expansion of and large investment in luxury and mid-range categories, led mostly by international hotel companies. The so-called tequila effect of the Mexican financial crisis had a stronger impact on Argentina than on Brazil, as during that period Argentina was implementing its 'Convertibility Plan' which put a heavy burden on overheads at a time of relatively stable price variations. As a consequence, many hotels were forced to close, especially small and budget hotels (Euromonitor, 1998: 216).

Argentina now boasts the largest number of rooms in luxury hotels in South America. Between 1992 and 1996, room capacity in this category increased by 75% to nearly 8400. It should be noted that, in Argentina, upmarket hotels are largely concentrated in Buenos Aires, whereas mid-range hotels are more widely spread across the country. The growth related to this category, in the same period, has also been extensive, and capacity increased by nearly 37%, accounting for 49,500 rooms. The market share of budget hotels, however, which are concentrated in the capital, was reduced, and fell from 54% in 1992 to 49% in 1996 (Euromonitor, 1998: 218).

As in Brazil, new market conditions in Argentina have attracted international hotel chains and investors. The Sheraton recently added another unit to its presence in Buenos Aires and had planned to open six more units, the first two opening in Córdoba and Mar del Plata. Other international hotel chains present (and expanding) in Argentina include Inter-Continental, Marriott, Westin, Kempinsk, Claridge, Holiday Inn, Hyatt, Sol-Melia, Best Western and Accor. According to the WTO (1998: 70), 214 establishments were constructed over the period 1996–1997, involving an investment of nearly half a billion US dollars.

Safety and Security

Irrespective of why people travel, safety is a primary requirement (Santana, 1998) or, rather, the *perception* of safety is necessary. As Cassedy (1992) has shown, in studying reactions to events in Hong Kong, Fiji and San Francisco, a perceived crisis can quickly cripple the travel industry. Similarly, the tourist industry in Florida went into decline following a series of crimes against tourists, even if the media overestimated the risks posed to visitors (Crystal, 1993; Brayshaw, 1995).

Terrorism, especially when directed at tourists, is particularly damaging to the industry. Attacks on tourists in Egypt during the early 1990s are estimated to have cost the country more than US$2 billion in tourist revenues (Associated Press, 1993), and in Cuba in 1997 a series of bomb attacks on hotels led to thousands of holiday cancellations – a devastating blow to a country hungry for foreign currency. It is estimated that every time a bomb scare occurs in London, the tourism industry loses a few million pounds. Armed conflicts have a similar effect, irrespective of where they occur. In Europe, the Irish Republican Army (IRA) and Spanish separatists (ETA) have had a negative influence on the British and Spanish tourism industries, while in South America such notorious groups as the *Sendero Luminoso* (Shining Path) of Peru have actively targeted tourists and tourist facilities (Wahab, 1996: 177). In 1999, several examples of terrorism and armed conflict made headline news: in Yemen, for example, 16 tourists were kidnapped, and four subsequently killed in a rescue attempt; three months later eight Western tourists were murdered by Rwandan Hutu rebels in Uganda. Importantly, the effects of all these violent incidents reverberate on neighbouring countries, as international travellers tend to associate violence with the wider region, rather than the country, in which it occurs.

South America does not enjoy the best of images as a tourist destination. Tourists have been kidnapped in Venezuela, Peru and Colombia, street crime has surged in Brazil; armed conflict and hostage taking has occurred in Peru, as when hundreds were held at the Japanese ambassador's residence in 1996; and drug-related crimes are common in Colombia, Peru, Bolivia and Brazil. A closer look at the recent history of the region easily identifies long-established, brutal military regimes, human rights abuses, and enduring economic, political, and social problems. Terrorism, cholera, malaria, natural disasters and social and political upheaval are often associated with the region.

Although many tourist destinations in Brazil have created specially trained 'Tourist Police Forces', to protect tourists, this has not convinced tour operators and tourists to return. Negative images are more persistent than objective 'knowledge' of the reality may suggest and governments must do more than 'assure' tourists and investors about safety and security in media campaigns. It is urgently necessary to develop and maintain a genuine dialogue with tour operators and to convince the travelling public of the realities of the situation.

Tourism and Development in MERCOSUL: the Future

Tourism development usually reflects the economic model that a country adopts and national development strategies have long been the topic of heated debate. In particular, considerable interest has focused on the 'Asian Tigers' (fast developing countries in the Asian-Pacific region), which achieved remarkable economic growth and income distribution by adopting export-oriented policies.

The story from South America, especially the countries of MERCOSUL, is different. They have pursued inward-oriented strategies and the results have been inefficiency in all productive sectors, corruption, an increase in international debts to the point of near-bankruptcy, excessive bureaucracy and a widening social gap between rich and the poor. This analysis may be rather simplistic, but it does enable links to be drawn between the development process and tourism. Because of the above factors, South American countries became known for high rates of inflation and unemployment, economic and political instability, military coups, and the expanded production and consumption of narcotics. All those factors, along with negative international headlines which discouraged international travellers and investors, exercised a negative influence on the development of tourism within the region. This legacy, coupled with unclear and vacillating development strategies, helps to explain the present state of tourism in the region.

As indicated earlier, in the mid-1980s the picture started to change, and there is no doubt that tourism presents considerable development potential for the region. It clearly makes a valuable contribution to employment, the GDP and foreign exchange, and can also help to balance trade in the region. However, the economic dimension is not the only one, and tourism does have other implications and benefits (Tooman, 1997: 33). The impacts of tourism on welfare programmes, labour force participation, and environmental protection and enhancement are also important, even if they are more difficult to measure than standard economic variables.

The benefits of tourism can be obtained only if the most appropriate policies are followed, and a range of possibilities should be explored by governments of MERCOSUL countries. It is suggested here that they should invest in the infrastructure and superstructure, encourage privatization, private initiative, innovation and individual entrepreneurial activity, and promote education and research in tourism. Centralization and bureaucratic control should be reduced, and governments should promote a sectorial shift from secondary to tertiary activities to counter the impact of globalization on the industrial base of the region. Flexible production technologies at destination areas should be encouraged and issues of safety and security should be addressed. Finally, the region should be marketed, with special attention paid to niche specialization and sector segmentation.

The MERCOSUL region undoubtedly has a competitive advantage in nature-based tourism and vast areas of unspoilt nature lead naturally to the development of tourism in this direction. Attractions include the Amazon Forest, the Andes, the Brazilian Pantanal (the largest wetland in the world), thousands of kilometres of unspoilt beaches, the Pampas in Argentina, Paraguay and Uruguay, diverse and unique cultures, the richest biodiversity in the world and thousands of unique species of plants and animals. All could contribute to a highly competitive MERCOSUL tourism product. However, by themselves, these attributes are not enough. They require commitment and action on the part of the private sector and government. They also require considerable caution, for apart from large cities such as Buenos Aires, Rio de Janeiro, and Mar del Plata, and some highly specialized tourism products such as ecotourism in the Amazon Forest or in the Brazilian Pantanal, MERCOSUL is not yet ready to compete in world tourism on a large scale.

The policies outlined above would help to foster a process of growth and development in tourism, and in other sectors, throughout the region. If it is to compete on a global or regional scale, MERCOSUL also needs to invest in a tourism culture which would both create and maintain its sustainable competitive advantages. This has to be done in an increasingly volatile and uncertain political, social and economic environment – circumstances that may be especially noticeable now but have long characterized the region.

Since the 1970s, international tourism has become increasingly global. In the 1970s, Europe and the USA accounted for almost 94% of international arrivals, but by 1995 their share of the market was reduced to 79%. Over the same period, the share of the market of Asia and the Pacific increased by 12%, and Africa, Latin America and the Middle East have also shown signs of increasing their market share (WTO, 1995; Oppermann and Chon, 1997).

The influence of globalization can be seen on both the supply and demand sides of the tourism market. On the demand side, change in demographic characteristics and lifestyles, increased incomes, more complex motivations for travel, the increased demand for multi-activity destinations and for more specialized products at destinations, especially for a closer affinity with 'nature', have been highly significant. As far as supply is concerned, the impact of technology – mainly information and reservation systems – has made it possible for suppliers to act on a global basis. Global Distribution Systems allow hotel chains, tour operators and airlines to cater for virtually all aspects of international tourist demand. Expansion strategies such as joint ventures, franchising and strategic alliances also make the world for tourism suppliers a truly small place, and the process is exacerbated by the rapid growth of new and emerging destinations all over the world.

Conclusion

Tourism in MERCOSUL will continue to grow regionally well into the 21st century but long-haul tourism might take a long time to realize, as it requires major changes in structure and organization as well as in investment patterns. MERCOSUL's biggest challenge, however, must be to consolidate its Working Groups as an effective entity and to move from rhetoric into action. Tourism competes with many other priorities and many governmental officials still regard it as important only for obtaining foreign exchange, and valuable only in projecting an image and gaining international recognition. Moreover, financial resources are scarce and innovative ways and approaches must be found to carry out development.

Apart from infrastructural development, partnerships with tourism suppliers and other international institutions might bring benefits and could also be considered a solution for the short and medium term. Perhaps the most urgent requirement is a 'tourism culture'. This demands time and investment, but it is necessary if current problems are to be solved and the region's tourism is to compete effectively in the international arena.

Further tourism development may also be delayed by the inability of authorities to provide security and safety for tourists and the local population. The countries of MERCOSUL have been democratized and their economies are now stable, but more than cosmetic action is required if tourists and potential tourists are to be convinced that it is now safe to visit the region. It not only has to be safe, but has to be perceived to be safe.

Acknowledgement

The author would like to thank Mr Humberto Figueiredo, EMBRATUR's Multilateral Project and Treaty Supervisor, for his kind collaboration in permitting access to reports and other unpublished material relating to meetings of MERCOSUL's Tourism Working Groups.

References

Anon. (1998) Turismo, prioridade definitiva para Fernando Henrique Cardoso. *Brasilturis Jornal* 18(396), October, p. 4.

Associação Brasileira de Normas Técnicas (ABNT) (1998) Os Desafios do MERCOSUL. *Revista Oficial da Associação Brasileira de Normas Técnicas* 3(6), 24–28.

Associated Press (1993) Tourism falls prey of terrorism. *Gainsville Sun* 6 May, p. 2A.

Borba, E.A. (1993) *MERCOSUL: Sinopse Estatística*, 1. Instituto Brasileiro de Geografia e Estatística (IBGE), Rio de Janeiro, pp. 207–209.

Brayshaw, D. (1995) Negative publicity about tourism destinations – a Florida case study. *Travel and Tourism Analyst* 5, 62–71.

Breitinger, J. (1999) A guerra dos Cola. *Exame* (Edição 680), 32(2), 52–54.

Carvalho, C. (1999) Turismo: a idade da razão. *Brasilturis Jornal* 8(402), January, p. 5.

Cassedy, K. (1992) Preparedness in the face of crisis: an examination of crises management planning in the travel and tourism industry. *World Travel and Tourism Review* 2, 169–174.

Crystal, S. (1993) Welcome to Downtown. *USA Meetings and Conventions* 28(3), 42–59.

EMBRATUR (1995/96) *A Indústria do Turismo no Brasil – Perfil e Tendências*, EMBRATUR (Brazilian Tourist Board), Brazília, Brazil.

Euromonitor (1998) Argentina. *Market Research International*, 209–258.

FADE-EMBRATUR (1998) *Estudo Econômico-Financeiro dos Meios de Hospedagem e Parques Temáticos no Brasil*. EMBRATUR, Brazília, Brazil.

FIPE (1998) *Caracteristicas e Dimensionamento de Mercado Doméstico de Turismo no Brasil*. Fundação Instituto de Pesquisas Econômicas, São Paulo, Brazil.

Folha de Sao Paulo (1996) Brasil – turismo. *Caderno Dinheiro* 28 October.

Guimarães, E.A. (1993) *MERCOSUL: Sinopse Estatística*, 1, Rio de Janeiro. Instituto Brasileiro de Geografia e Estatística (IBGE), Rio de Janeiro, pp. 255–258.

Horwath Consulting – Soteconti Auditores Independentes S/C (1998) *The Brazilian Hotel Industry*. São Paulo, Brazil.

MERCOSUL (1998a) *Report of the XXV Tourism Working Group Meeting, Common Market Group*. MERCOSUL, Ministérios das Relaçoes Exteriores, Brasília, Brazil.

MERCOSUL (1998b) *Report of the XXVI Tourism Working Group Meeting, Common Market Group*. MERCOSUL, Ministérios das Relaçoes Exteriores, Brasília, Brazil.

MERCOSUL (1998c) *Report of the XXVII Tourism Working Group Meeting, Common Market Group*. MERCOSUL, Ministérios das Relaçoes Exteriores, Brasília, Brazil.

MERCOSUL (1998d) *Report of the XXVIII Tourism Working Group Meeting, Common Market Group*. MERCOSUL, Ministérios das Relaçoes Exteriores, Brasília, Brazil.

O MERCOSUL Hoje (1998) *Resultados da Presidência Pro Tempore Brasileira*. Ministério das Relações Exteriores, Brasília, Brazil.

Oppermann, M. and Chon, K. (1997) *Tourism in Developing Countries*. International Thomson Business Press, London.

Pinheiro, F. (1998) O Brasil que viaja. *Veja* 30 September.

Santana, G. (1998) Sports tourism and crisis management: beyond contingency planning. *Sports Tourism Journal* 4(4). http://www.mcb.co.uk/ journals/jst/issue.htm (15 April, 1999).

Schlüter, R. and Winter, G. (1993) *El Fenomeno Turístico: Reflexiones Desde Una Perspectiva Integradora*. Docencia, Buenos Aires.

Schneider, S. (1999) *EMBRATUR Calcula mais de 5 milhões de Emprego*. (Pesquisa). *Diario Catarinense*, Caderno de Economia, 6 July, p. 13.

Senra, N.C., Pereira, R.S. and Silva, W.M. (1993) *MERCUSOL: Sinopse Estatística* 1. Instituto Brasileiro de Geografia e Estatística (IBGE), Rio de Janeiro, pp. 55–57.

Silva, J.A. (1995) Turismo diante das tendências de globalização e integração regional: Mercosul (1988–1993). *Turismo em Análise* 6(1), 89–117.

Tooman, L. (1997) Tourism and development. *Journal of Travel Research* 35(3), 33–40.

Wahab, S. (1996) Tourism and terrorism: synthesis of the problem with emphasis on Egypt. In: Pizam, A. and Mansfeld, Y. (eds) *Tourism, Crime and International Security Issues*. John Wiley & Sons, New York, pp. 175–186.

WTO (1994a) *Yearbook of Tourism Statistics*, Vol. 1. World Tourism Organization, Madrid.

WTO (1994b) *Turismo Internacional en las Americas: 1970–1993*. World Tourism Organization, Madrid.

WTO (1995) *Yearbook of Tourism Statistics*, 47th edn. World Tourism Organization, Madrid.

WTO (1996) *Yearbook of Tourism Statistics*, Vol. 1. World Tourism Organization, Madrid.

WTO (1998) *Tourism Market Trends, Americas 1988–1997*. Thirty-second Meeting, Guayaquil (Ecuador), 28–29 May. World Tourism Organization Commission for the Americas, Madrid.

WTO (1999) *Tourism Highlights 1999*. World Tourism Organization, Madrid.

WTTC (1998) *The Travel and Tourism Satellite Account: Latin America Economic Impact*, April, 1998. World Travel and Tourism Council.

6

Tourism and Development in Communist and Post-communist Societies

Derek R. Hall

This chapter evaluates the nature and role of tourism in the development processes of communist and post-communist societies. In so doing, it seeks three objectives: (i) to review briefly the role of tourism under communism; (ii) to undertake an evaluation of post-communist tourism development processes; and (iii) to articulate briefly post-communist relationships of tourism and development through issues of heritage and identity. The chapter is organized into four major parts that mirror these three objectives, together with a final concluding section. The societies considered in this chapter (Tables 6.1. and 6.2) make up the former Soviet bloc countries of central and eastern Europe (CEE: central Europe, south-eastern Europe and the former Soviet Union) and Mongolia, together with Cuba, Vietnam and North Korea, which continue to be dominated by communist parties and centrally directed development policies. Reference will also be made to China, although the particular circumstances and especially the diversity of that country render generalizations inevitably more speculative.

Although de Kadt (1979: 19) drew attention to the dearth of studies on tourism development under state socialism, a response from the academic literature was slow in emerging. This was for a number of reasons: logistical problems of empirical research, the relatively low priority given to and poor documentation of tourism development in most state socialist societies, and the relatively small number of academics holding an appropriate convergence of interests. The English-language literature on tourism development processes in post-communist societies has been more bountiful (e.g. Harrison, 1993; Mazaraki and Voronova, 1993; Balaz, 1994, 1995, 1996a,b; Hall, 1995, 1998a,b, 2000b; Johnson, 1995; Aun, 1996; Unwin, 1996; Bachvarov, 1997), but there persists a lack of conceptual and theoretical strength informing much of this work.

Hanson (1998) argued that the lack of conceptual attention paid to accommodating 'transitions' from communism to post-communism within the comparative political economy literature results from an inability to accommodate adequately the particular dynamics of formation and decline of 'the Stalinist socio-economic system'. None of the three dominant frameworks of political economy – modernization, world-systems and rational choice – is able to account sufficiently for the diversity of post-communist economic and social dynamism, although each can relate to a limited range of post-communist experience. Thus modernization theory appears consistent with processes taking place in central Europe. World-systems theory is consonant

Table 6.1. Communist and post-communist societies: international tourist arrivals (in millions).

	1988	1990	1992	1994	1996
Central Europe					
Czechoslovakia	6.89	8.10			
Czech Republic		(7.29)	10.90	17.00	17.00
Hungary	10.56	20.51	20.19	21.43	20.67
Poland	2.50	3.40	16.26	18.83	19.41
Slovakia		(0.82)	0.57	0.90	0.95
South-eastern Europe					
Former Yugoslavia	9.02	7.88			
Albania	nd	0.03	0.03	0.03	0.06
Bosnia-Herzegovina			< 0.01	0.01	0.10
Bulgaria	3.97	4.50	1.32	3.90	2.80
Croatia			1.27	2.29	2.65
FYR Macedonia			0.22	0.19	0.14
Romania	5.51	3.01	3.80	2.80	2.83
Serbia-Montenegro			0.16	0.25	0.30
Slovenia			0.62	0.75	0.83
Former Soviet Union	6.01	7.20			
Armenia			nd	nd	nd
Azerbaijan			0.21	0.32	0.15
Belarus			nd	0.18	0.23
Estonia			0.37	0.55	0.60
Georgia			nd	nd	0.12
Kyrgyzstan			0.01	0.01	0.01
Latvia			0.04	0.09	0.10
Lithuania			0.33	0.22	0.26
Moldova			0.23	0.02	0.03
Russia			3.01	5.82	14.59
Tadjikistan			nd	nd	nd
Turkmenistan			nd	0.06	0.22
Ukraine			0.58	0.77	0.81
Uzbekistan			nd	nd	nd
Other Asia					
China (excluding Hong Kong)	12.36	10.48	16.51	19.15	22.77
Mongolia	0.24	0.15	0.13	0.12	0.07
North Korea	nd	0.12	0.12	0.13	0.13
Vietnam	0.15	0.25	0.44	1.02	1.61
Cuba	0.30	0.33	0.46	0.62	1.00

Source: WTO (1994, Vol. 1, pp. 58, 82, 106; 1996b, Vol. 1, pp. 48, 72, 96; 1998b, Vol. 1, pp. 52, 78, 103).

with the type of 'dependency' emerging in regions such as central Asia and the Caucasus. Rational choice analysis informs the 'devolution' of state structures in countries where the *nomenklatura* (political and bureaucratic élite) still control, directly or indirectly, most of the national wealth. It is within this broader conceptual dilemma that frameworks for the evaluation of tourism in post-communist processes are explored later in this chapter.

Tourism under Communism

The adoption of a communist-inspired model of political, economic and social development cut short previous development paths and introduced new roles and patterns for recreational activity. In relation to international tourism development, there appeared to be a number of 'socialist' objectives that appropriate inbound tourism could support. These

Table 6.2. Communist and post-communist societies: international tourist receipts (US$ millions).

	1988	1990	1992	1994	1996
Central Europe					
Czechoslovakia	608	470			
Czech Republic			1,126	2,230	4,075
Hungary	758	824	1,231	1,428	2,246
Poland	206	358	4,100	6,150	8,400
Slovakia			213	568	673
South-eastern Europe					
Former Yugoslavia	2,024	2,774			
Albania			9	5	11
Bosnia-Herzegovina			nd	nd	16
Bulgaria	484	320	215	362	388
Croatia			543	1,801	2,014
FYR Macedonia			11	29	21
Romania	171	106	262	414	529
Serbia-Montenegro			88	31	43
Slovenia			671	959	1,230
Former Soviet Union	216	2,752			
Armenia			nd	nd	12
Azerbaijan			42	64	158
Belarus			nd	39	48
Estonia			27	92	470
Georgia			nd	nd	nd
Kyrgyzstan			2	3	4
Latvia			7	18	182
Lithuania			103	82	345
Moldova			4	8	33
Russia			752	2,412	6,875
Tadjikistan			nd	nd	nd
Turkmenistan			nd	nd	7
Ukraine			173	175	202
Uzbekistan			nd	nd	nd
Other Asia					
China (excluding Hong Kong)	2,247	2,218	3,948	7,323	10,200
Mongolia	nd	5	3	7	21
North Korea	nd	nd	nd	nd	nd
Vietnam	35	85	80	85	87
Cuba	189	243	443	763	1,231

Source: WTO (1994, Vol. 1, pp. 64, 88, 112; 1996b, Vol. 1, pp. 54, 78, 102; 1998b, Vol. 1, pp. 58, 84, 109).

included a redistribution of employment opportunities, the promotion of positive regional and national images, and thus a means of convincing visitors of the superiority of the communist system (Hall, 1984, 1991). Tourism was often viewed as an instrument of foreign policy, and in China, for example, was employed very explicitly as a propaganda tool (Qiao, 1995). But the very structural characteristics of state socialism – centralized bureaucratic organization, inflexibility and antipathy towards individualism and entrepreneurialism, resulting in constraints on mobility and a low priority given to service industries, coupled with cold war attitudes (including an alleged fear of Western ideological contagion and social corruption) – were the very antithesis of the flexibility, responsiveness and market orientation required to develop international tourism attractive to non-socialist markets. This appeared to suggest that a centralized 'command economy' and successful international tourism development were incompatible. Indeed, this was reinforced by the outstanding success of the only decentralized 'socialist market economy', Yugoslavia, which by the end of the 1980s was generating international tourism receipts equivalent to the total for the rest of CEE (Table 6.2).

Domestic recreation was subsidized to provide cheap accommodation and transport for (usually urban industrial) workers and their families. But this trade union- and enterprise-supported activity tended to exclude a substantial element of the rural population, rendering them unsubsidized and relatively immobile. Despite the human rights clauses of the 1975 Helsinki agreement, few citizens were permitted to travel to the capitalist world. Currency inconvertibility, restricted access to hard currency and stringent vetting and exit visa policies proscribed most forms of extra-bloc tourism. Thus outbound tourism was socially and spatially distorted, being dominated by exchanges of 'friendship groups' between severely prescribed like-minded countries. Until 1989, it was easier for, say, Czechs and Slovaks to travel several thousand kilometres to holiday in Cuba or Vietnam than to cross the Czechoslovakian border into West Germany. Members of the *nomenklatura* with access to convertible currency, however, were able to travel to the capitalist world and to profit from the patronage and privileges flowing from such access. There were clearly several layers of tourist and recreation underclass as a consequence of prevailing social, economic and political relations: those unable to afford or gain access to domestic recreation because of their structural and/or spatial positions within the economy (essentially the rural peasantry); those workers denied access to overseas vacations within the socialist bloc because of their structural position, lack of access to hard currency or record of non-compliance; and those denied access to non-bloc overseas visits because of their lack of ideological or bureaucratic status and connections, which was usually most of the population.

Subsequent political change reordered priorities. Although a residual of collective provision remained in the early years of post-communism to provide low-cost holidays (Williams and Balaz, 2001), ability to pay became the major criterion in access to domestic tourism. This was severely influenced by national and local inflation, unemployment, privatization (in its various forms), subsidy withdrawal, and the imposition of sometimes high rates of value added tax. New constraints modified pathways of outbound tourism. The 'Iron Curtain' was replaced by a 'dollar curtain' lowered by potential Western host countries out of fear of a flood of Eastern migrants. The need to secure exit visas from home countries was largely removed but, despite bilateral and European Union (EU) wide agreements, the requirement for hard currency entry visas, often costing more than a month's income, was imposed by Western governments for citizens of several post-communist and all remaining state socialist countries.

An Evolutionary Framework

Despite common ideological inspiration, the outcome of decades of state socialism produced far from monolithic developmental patterns and processes, reflecting differences in pre-existing levels of development, relative resource bases, cultural histories and orientations, and the adoption and adaptation of ideology to complement or buttress national aspirations. Nonetheless, a loose evolutionary framework advanced previously (Hall, 1991: 79–115) provides an analytical starting point from which to view the broad systemic characteristics of tourism within state socialist economic and social development programmes. This framework implicitly recognizes the differing paths, speeds and attitudes taken towards tourism development and the overlapping nature of 'evolutionary' elements of development: the timing and gradients between them varied both within and between societies.

Pre-socialism

Reflecting relatively early stages of economic development and hierarchical social structures, the pre-socialism period is generally characterized by limited tourism from without, with outbound and to some extent domestic tourism restricted largely to the countries' economic, social and political elites. A major exception was Cuba, which was only drawn into the Soviet bloc from 1960, and which in the early decades of the 20th century had been a major recreational attraction for North Americans, for whom the island was easily accessible, with a winter climate widely considered to be healthy. In 1915 there were over 70 hotels on the island (Sims, 1916) and tourism became the country's third most important 'export' commodity after sugar and tobacco. At the outbreak of the First World War, Cuba was host to more than a third of all tourists visiting the Caribbean (Momsen, 1985), and the country remained the region's tourist hub well into the 1950s. The demonstration effect of the US-dominated industry saw the Cuban elite seeking North American lifestyles. This reinforced a colonial dependency relationship by stimulating the import of goods to meet such aspirations. A high degree of outbound tourism to the USA was also sustained (Hall, 1989), as a consequence of which the annual balance of the tourism account only moved into the black in 1956. In the next year visitor numbers reached their peak when almost 356,000 foreign tourists and excursionists visited the country, 87% of whom were from the US. Most activity was concentrated in and around the capital, Havana, with a secondary concentration at the purpose-built north coast resort of Varadero, exacerbating spatial and structural inequalities within the country's economy. This merely emphasized the dependency relationships – both internal and external – which characterized tourism's role, alongside sugar and tobacco, as a structural centrepiece of Cuba's semi-colonial status. It was such relationships that the Cuban revolution – with a little help from the subsequent US embargo – severed in 1959 (Hall, 1992b: 109–111).

Early socialism

This phase typifies the Soviet Union from the 1920s to the 1950s, the early post-war period in eastern Europe (although in Albania it lasted to the mid-1980s), Mongolia from the 1920s to the 1970s, (North) Vietnam in the 1970s and North Korea from the late 1940s to the present. This may be termed the 'Stalinist' period in that its basic characteristics and dogmas arose from Stalin's leadership and echoed a number of the dimensions of 'Stalinist' economic policy, notably rapid economic growth based upon heavy industrialization. Service industries had a minor role, foreigners were regarded with suspicion and centralized state control characterized economic life. Under these circumstances, international tourism was severely constrained, with economic development placed on a virtual war footing. In China, for example, 'Maoism' carried forward Stalinist ideology to the late 1970s and rejected tourism as an appropriate form of economic activity (Sofield and Li, 1998: 369). In the 25 years from 1954, a mere 125,000 visitors were hosted by the Chinese state travel organization (Richter, 1989).

The social dimension of state socialism emphasized the well-being of the working population and its economically productive capacities, and the need to inculcate a sense of collective responsibility among young people within the context of healthy outdoor environments (and implicitly away from their parents). To this end, facilities were developed for domestic, group-orientated tourism and recreation in coastal resorts, upland areas, mountains and rural spas, sponsored by economic enterprises, trade unions and youth organizations. This represented an important component of the cycle of production and reproduction (Hall, 1991: 84). The 'collective consumption' of tourism and recreation thus particularly characterized the early socialism period.

Middle socialism

From the mid-1950s, following the hiatus after Stalin's death in 1953, dogmas began to be relaxed in most countries. Living standards gradually rose and the need to emphasize the 'benefits' of international socialism, if only for propagandist reasons, saw a growing development of international tourism. Paralleling the growth of international economic aid and cooperation within the Soviet bloc, this phase tended to be characterized by the more developed societies generating most tourist outflows, although the statistics of the period are not well documented. Yugoslavia largely bypassed this stage, since, having been expelled from the Soviet sphere in 1948, tourism exchanges with bloc countries were initially embargoed. Low living standards and other structural constraints in Vietnam, Cuba and Mongolia largely precluded outbound tourism, while for Albania (Hall, 1984, 1990) and North Korea (Hall, 1986, 1990) this was reinforced by an isolationist ideological outlook. The overall emphasis of this period, therefore, was the development of intra-bloc international tourism – albeit qualified by the 1961 Sino-Soviet rift – together with the consolidation and expansion of domestic tourism.

Later socialism

The economic circumstances of the late 1960s and the 1970s brought increasing convertible-currency debt to the Soviet bloc. One response was to embark on enhanced programmes of attracting hard currency tourists. This was despite often inadequate and inappropriate infrastructural and management systems, coupled to considerable ideological hesitancy towards permitting access to particular parts of state territories. Indeed, until 1991 substantial parts of the Soviet Union, Mongolia and Albania remained proscribed to foreigners; much of North Korea and parts of China are still 'closed'.

Domestic tourism became more sophisticated, with rising levels of car and second-home ownership in the more advanced economies. Opportunities to organize individualized vacations grew considerably. Intra-bloc international flows also became more complex, relating not only to recognized tourist areas but also to increasing amounts of 'ethnic diaspora tourism'. This resulted from decreasing constraints on minorities wishing to visit kith and kin located on the other side of international boundaries, together with influences from emigrant communities in North America, Australasia and other diaspora regions.

Post-Soviet state socialism

In the case of those countries where the communist party is still in power in an essentially one-party state, adaptation to relative ideological isolation has been required, although in the case of China notions of isolation are almost academic given the size and relative self-sufficiency of the country and its international ideological stance since 1961. For both Vietnam and Cuba, continuing communism in the post-Soviet era required readjustment from semi-colonial client state status (in relation to the Soviet Union) to an independent status exposed to the rigours of the (capitalist) global economy, of which international tourism is clearly an integral element. In Vietnam, of the four communist development stages recognised by Wu and Sun (1998) – independent socialism (1975–1977), orthodox socialism (1978–1985), glasnost (opening up of economy, society) socialism (1986–1990) and market socialism since 1991 – the 'orthodox' and glasnost phases were the direct result of Hanoi's dependency relationship with Moscow. Wu and Sun (1998) argue that, since the lifting of such hegemony, Vietnam's latitude for domestic and international policy-making, including tourism development, increased significantly. The cultural heritage of the country, from ancient to colonial times, is substantial (e.g. Parenteau et al., 1995) but the economic and social liberalization process doi moi (economic reform, Vietnam) has been heavily concentrated on the two main cities of Hanoi and Ho Chi Minh City (Drakakis-Smith and Dixon, 1997). The spatial and structural inequalities in the country's development processes emerging from this, including those of tourism, have raised serious questions about the sustainability of national development policy and have highlighted the need to address urgently a range of social and environmental problems (Bolay et al., 1997).

As a country substantially dependent upon a single primary product (sugar) and without major fuel and energy resources of its own, Cuba had relied heavily upon the Soviet Union as a ready market with a guaranteed price for much of its sugar crop and as a supplier of cut-price shipments of oil (a proportion of which was routinely sold on at a profit). With the break up of the Soviet empire between 1989 and 1991, and Fidel Castro's outright rejection of perestroika (economic reform, Soviet Union) as a guiding philosophy,

Cuba needed to create new internal and external strategies in order to survive, economically and politically (Berrios, 1997). Economic decline here in the early 1990s was more dramatic than for the post-communist states undergoing 'shock therapy' in CEE, as output shrank to just 60% of 1989 levels (Pickel, 1998). As a consequence, the Cuban system of centralized economic planning and management was dismantled. Cuba did not adopt rapid, panic, shock therapy but employed elements or variants of the Chinese and Vietnamese models, decentralizing economic activity while maintaining a tight rein on political structures. All three countries have managed to demonstrate that neither shock therapy nor multi-party democracy are necessary ingredients for relatively successful economic change (Naughton, 1996). Cuba's Latin American and Caribbean cultural identity has been reinforced by the continuing uncompromising US embargo policy, which has imposed the additional constraint on Cuba of an inability to access investment funds from the World Bank and the International Monetary Fund (Leogrande, 1997). However, Cuba does receive approximately US$500 million per annum in remittances and fees from Cuban-Americans (Avella and Mills, 1996).

Three stages of restructuring were pursued in Cuba between 1989 and 1995 (Everleny Perez, 1995), the first of which was crisis management, with economic adjustment to address major distortions. The 'special period in times of peace', 1989–1993, sought to reduce imports and increase efficiency in strategic sectors including tourism (Simon, 1995). Since 1993, key reform measures have included a new law on foreign investment, decriminalization of the use of hard currency and the authorization of self-employment in 150 private occupations – often clearly contradictory to previously declared policies and principles (Berrios, 1997). Private rented accommodation and restaurants were legalized in 1995, and joint ventures with overseas interests (Spanish, Canadian, German, Mexican) have grown to a greater extent in tourism than in any other sector. The emerging dual economy, however, has seen a widening gap between the traditional socialist sector using the Cuban peso and a dynamic internationalized sector, most notably tourism, operating in US dollars (Mesa-Lago, 1998). At the same time tourist numbers and spending have increased (Tables 6.1 and 6.2). Although by the turn of the century some 1.5 million tourists are visiting Cuba annually, such numbers could probably be trebled without the US embargo and consequent exclusion of the country from access to both the US market and the Caribbean cruise industry.

Sex tourism – anathema to Castro's puritan concept of a Cuban nation and a target for eradication by the revolution – has returned (Davidson, 1996; Segre et al., 1997: 266) as a concomitant of an economic policy that places emphasis on international mass tourism growth while retaining low domestic incomes and restricted mobility, thereby inducing relative deprivation (Seaton, 1996, 1997) and demonstration effects. If we accept the contested argument of Ryan and Kinder (1996) (compared with e.g. Jeffreys, 1999) that visiting a prostitute is fully consistent with the motivation of some tourists, the (gendered?) socio-political paradox of international tourism promotion within a domestically proscriptive communist society is manifest in contemporary Cuba.

By contrast, international tourism policy in North Korea appears to have shifted little from the centralized Stalinist model of severe prescription long pursued (Hall, 1990). Sea access from South Korea has been initiated, but plans for transport coordination between the two halves of the peninsula (Pak and Kim, 1996) have not been realized. Emulating China's Shenzhen and other special economic zones, North Korea has established a free zone in the border area with Russia and China, with a $160 million casino, bank and hotel complex built by Hong Kong interests, at Rajin-Sonbong (Foster-Carter, 1998). Recent arguments by Kimura (1999) have challenged the notion that a collectivist political economy in North Korea after 1945 was a discontinuity with the past. Such a critique implicitly suggests that in any post-communist North Korea which retains its separate identity from the South, a collectivist culture might persist, perhaps to generate a variant of the Chinese, Vietnamese and Cuban 'Third Way'. The German model of post-communist (re-)unification and North Korea's apparently deepening economic crisis (Eberstadt, 1997; Intriligator, 1998), might suggest that this is unlikely.

In China, tourism has emerged as a vehicle for mediating between some of the tensions of modernization resulting from the interplay of a rigid application of state socialism, the conservatism of tradition, and the demands of economic development. In this way, by contributing to the modernization process, promoting heritage for product development, and apparently meeting a number of socialist objectives, tourism has been viewed as exerting a centripetal influence in China (Sofield and Li, 1998). However, it has been predicted that by 2020 China will be the world's most important tourist destination, with 137.1 million international arrivals, representing 8.6% of global market share and an annual growth rate over 1995–2020 of 8.0% (WTO, 1997). This compares with nearly 22.8 million arrivals in 1996 (Table 6.1) and suggests social and political impacts that can barely be foreseen. Further, China's domestic tourism has rapidly expanded in the 1990s, from 240 million domestic arrivals in 1989 to 640 million in 1996 (Wen, 1997), and Chinese tourism to Hong Kong increased considerably in the later 1980s and 1990s before that territory was reincorporated in 1997 (Zhang and Qu, 1996).

Post-communist Tourism Development

Three dynamic contexts have been recognized as important in moulding the evolving post-communist tourism industry (Johnson, 1997). These involve changes in: (i) the political economies of individual countries; (ii) a country's pattern of external relationships, including tourism patterns; and (iii) the global tourism industry itself. As an integral part of post-communist regional economic restructuring, tourism is a concomitant and often prime example of: (i) growth, privatization and 'flexibilization' of service industries; (ii) reduction of centralization, subsidy and bureaucratic control; (iii) deregulation and price liberalization; (iv) emphasis upon private initiative and

individual entrepreneurial activity, not least in the encouragement of small- or medium-sized enterprises; (v) enhancement, through comparative advantage, of niche specialization and sector segmentation; (vi) sectoral shift from secondary to tertiary activities, from manufacturing to services; (vii) exposure of enterprises to national and international market forces; (viii) market penetration and foreign direct investment of transnational corporations; and (ix) changing circumstances for personal mobility.

Tourism's multifaceted role in economic restructuring can be summarized by reference to the following features (Hall, 1991, 1992a; Jaakson, 1996):

1. As a means of improving balance of payments. Post-communist economic programmes, whether of the 'shock therapy' or more gradual (and uncertain) variety, have needed to respond to a range of previously unknown economic circumstances: a loss of eastern markets, high levels of industrial closure and unemployment, price inflation and diminishing living standards. In attempting to combat these circumstances, improving the trade balance has been a vital governmental objective, although the acknowledgement of tourism's role in this process has varied considerably between countries. Indeed, states that lacked entrepreneurial experience did not always readily acknowledge the fact that the economic and employment significance of tourism became heightened as a result of primary and secondary industrial sectors being significantly reduced through rationalization of production and employment in the face of subsidy loss, privatization and international competition. As a result, early policy statements tended not to be accompanied by appropriate state investment in tourism nor by the securing of international funding.
2. As a means of gaining convertible currency. Achievement of currency convertibility has become one symbol of the fiscal maturity of post-communist states and of their integration into the global economy. While some central European states have achieved convertibility, the currencies of other post-communist societies remain inconvertible and thus a pejorative indicator of economic status.

3. Encouraging greater and closer interaction between formerly restricted host populations and the outside world. Both inbound and outbound tourism may be seen as a catalyst of change: as a positive educational force stimulating a thirst for knowledge of the outside world, encouraging entrepreneurial activity, providing supplementary incomes, generating new forms of employment, creating new patterns of travel, or in setting up potentially negative demonstration and relative deprivation effects, modifying cultures and generating major economic leakages through transnational involvement.

4. Encouraging investment in and upgrading of tourism services. At the end of state socialism, the quality of tourist services was variable but generally low by accepted international standards (Hunt, 1993; Lennon, 1996). Accommodation, catering, utilities, transport and telecommunications had suffered from decades of neglect. Belatedly, adaptation of existing economic mechanisms took place in the waning years of the command economies to ameliorate the more centralized and inflexible aspects of the Soviet model, but this was very uneven. Thus the opening of private guesthouses to foreigners was only possible in Czechoslovakia after 1989, and in the Soviet Union, Mongolia and Albania from 1991. Subsequent foreign direct investment has been most prevalent in the hotel sector (Lennon, 1995; Bartl, 1997), with international chains supporting new construction and buying into existing capacity. Initial investment tended to reinforce a bias towards the higher end of the market; only from the mid-1990s did the gap in middle-range accommodation availability begin to be filled by such groups as Accor and Holiday Inn (Simpson, 1997).

5. Developing new employment skills and standards of service provision (Baum, 1995), bringing with them new employment conditions and considerations of employee welfare (e.g. Hall and Brown, 1996). The requirement for staff training in hotel management, catering, travel agencies, and in such areas as computing, telecommunications and foreign languages, was recognized in multilateral projects emphasizing training and skills enhancement, including EU PHARE (Poland/Hungary Assistance for Economic Reconstruction,

extended to most of Central and Eastern Europe) and TACIS (assistance programme for the Newly Independent States of the former Soviet Union and Mongolia) programmes (Airey, 1994, 1999; Burns, 1995; Richards, 1996). Multinational companies introduced their own training programmes, either *in situ* or in Western institutions. Entrenched attitudes to service, or rather the absence of a service mentality in older generations, encouraged foreign direct investors to select front-line catering (Vikhanski and Puffer, 1993) and hotel staff on the basis of specifically having no prior employment experience and thus no inappropriate work practices (Chaieb, 1994).

6. Encouraging the improvement of local and regional infrastructures, notably transport and telecommunications, although tourism's specific contribution is variable and not necessarily readily apparent in relation to other development stimuli. Major road, airport and other regional and international transport infrastructures continue to be upgraded as part of a wider process of improved access from, and closer integration with, global markets (Hall, 1993a,b; Lijewski, 1996; Taylor, 1998).

7. Thereby helping to integrate post-communist states into the global economy and in particular to assist preparation for possible accession of individual countries to the EU – a prime foreign policy driving force of the more advanced economies of central Europe.

8. As a symbol of post-communist 'freedoms', opening up the potential for travel both within and from each country.

Jaakson (1996: 631) and others have observed that there exists a paucity of conventional models to serve as explanatory frameworks for post-communist tourism development. This is reinforced by: (i) the increasingly complex patterns of tourism activity and other mobility processes experienced in and from post-communist states; and (ii) the range of players and roles within global tourism development.

For example, regional cross-border mobility is a significant by-product of post-communist restructuring. It reflects forces of both integration (tourism, labour migration, shopping) and disintegration, or at least dislocation – refugee flight and the need for informal petty trading and exchange. Indicative of an intricate web of linkages and networks on both sides of borders, such mobility experiences have expanded dramatically (Konstantinov, 1996), raising new questions for regional integration (Kratke, 1998). For example, while the Russian–Finnish border crossing checkpoint of Nuijamaa recorded 200,000 crossings in 1990, in 1996 the figure was 1.16 million – predominantly Russians on shopping expeditions (Barber, 1997). Of Bulgaria's 6.8 million visitor arrivals at frontiers in 1996 (WTO, 1998b: 239–240), over 4 million were day visitors and only about 25% of the total were actually holiday tourists (WTO, 1998a: 73). That 84% of Bulgaria's visitors are from neighbouring countries suggests significant local cross-border activity (Hall, 2000a). Despite its importance, however, there has been relatively little systematic detailed research on such mobility processes (but see Böröcz, 1996; Wallace *et al.*, 1996; Iglicka, 1998).

Such 'tourists' tend to be low spending and relatively short stayers. This is reinforced by the mode of their mobility: the vast majority of CEE's international arrivals cross borders by road, a significant number are visiting friends and relatives, and many others are likely to be circuit tourists, although few data exist on these latter two phenomena. Partly as a consequence of these structural characteristics, while in 1997 CEE was host to 23.2% of all international tourist arrivals in Europe, only 12.9% of the continent's receipts were generated here. The sector's financial performance thus appears to be only around half of what might be expected, given the level of arrivals. This has clear regional economic significance and reflects the relative role of cross-border activity in the wider context of what is understood to be global tourism.

Heritage and Identity: Tourism, Development and the Post-communist Condition

One of the more salient elements of the convergence of the post-communist search for identity and a global shift from mass towards niche tourism has been the adoption of 'heritage' as both a leisure resource and a cultural symbol. The irony of employing the past as an element of restructuring for the future, particularly for newly independent states drawing on their pre-communist semi-colonial heritage, has been long debated (e.g. Hewison, 1987).

'Heritage' is clearly far from being a value-free concept: economic power and politics influence what is preserved and how it is interpreted (Chance, 1994; Lowenthal, 1997). Promotion of heritage and a recognition of the importance of cultural history was a significant feature of the communist period. Open-air village museums such as Bucharest's (Focsa, 1970), Albania's 'museum cities' (Hall, 1994) and the large-scale refurbishment of central Kraków (Dawson, 1991) exemplify this. Yet such heritage promotion tended not to be primarily for international tourism purposes, but rather to promote a sense of (implicitly national) identity and solidarity. This was most notably seen in the priority given to the faithful reconstruction of Warsaw's Old Town after Second World War destruction.

Places of pilgrimage, such as the Roman Catholic shrine to the Black Madonna at Czestochowa in southern Poland and the Herzegovinian village of Medjugorje, site of the now somewhat discredited recurrent apparition of the Virgin (Vukonic, 1992, 1996), were often irritants to the authorities. Many actual religious buildings – such as the early Croatian churches on Adriatic islands and externally painted Moldavian Orthodox churches and monasteries – intertwine tourist appeal and national cultural sentiment. Yet organized religion itself has needed to re-evaluate its role in post-communist circumstances (Bria, 1998; Tomka, 1998). Further, the resurgence of nationalist expression alongside a (re-)creation of new state systems has encouraged some countries to employ the heritage industry as a means of reinforcing national or particular ethnic identity (Hall, 1996, 1999; Burns, 1998).

The relationship between heritage, tourism and identity is clearly a crucial one in many post-communist societies, but particularly in south-eastern Europe (Carter *et al.*, 1995; Hall and Danta, 1996), in terms of: (i) the need for national image building, especially for newly independent states; (ii) the requirement to emphasize a Europeanness (as defined by Brussels?) with aspirations for EU membership and recognition as a legitimate resident of the 'common European home'; (iii) disassociation from the Yugoslav and communist past; (iv) disassociation from current regional instability; and (v) meeting the needs of differentiated tourist markets – Western niche and rejuvenated domestic/regional/international mass coastal demands.

As one of the favoured CEE states for early accession to the EU (Hall and Danta, 2000), Slovenia has employed tourism as an important ingredient in its post-independence economic and political strategy. The country's promoters have gone to some length to emphasize its central rather than south-east European credentials – a Habsburg heritage, Alpine associations, and contiguity with Austria and Italy. This is highlighted in the promotion of the country's lakes and mountains when the prospective visitor is enticed with 'delightful villages and warm and hospitable people, whose lives are still steeped in the traditions of centuries of Austrian rule' (Anon., 1998b: 70). Croatia, exploiting its previous coastal attractions for the UK and other West European markets, is promoted as 'an old friend with a new name', anchoring the country firmly within the familiarity of the European Mediterranean tourism product and culture. 'So many aspects of Croatia will remind you of Italy, Spain and France, where strong family values remain and churches are always full on Sundays' (Anon., 1998a: 4).

For some governments of south-eastern Europe, the post-communist reinvigoration of a sense of historical perspective and a heightened awareness of nationality has encouraged the use of the rapidly growing heritage industry to reinforce an exclusive national or particular ethnic identity. Traditional representations of the people in this region are heavily featured in tourist brochures (Morgan and Pritchard, 1998: 233–234). This is not unique to the semiotic ethnography (Dann, 1996) of post-communism, but was a practice of state socialist times to reinforce the images, myths and language of rural idyll and pastoral tranquillity. However, the practice in some parts

of the 'new' Europe of promoting ethnic exclusivity as part of the national image-building process, for tourism consumption, is a dangerous path. It implicitly compromises and ideologically challenges the tourist, resurrecting an arena of ethical conflict that was encountered by tourists to much of the communist world (although usually not in Yugoslavia), and indeed other totalitarian regimes, in terms of general human rights abuses, and more specifically the marginalization of minorities. For example, in the tourism promotion brochure *Serbia: Landscape Painted from the Heart* (Popesku and Milojevic, 1996), 'landscape' is interpreted as both natural and cultural. In terms of heritage, however, the cultural 'landscape' portrayed reveals an exclusive concentration on Serbian/Orthodox tradition. Although one third of the total population of Serbia is (or at least was in 1996) not Serbian, there is no representation of minority ethnic Hungarian or Albanian (or Romanian, Slovak, Croat or Turkish) Catholic or Muslim heritage. The minority groups have been erased from this particular cultural landscape. Exclusion of the Islamic 'Other', sadly, has not been confined to tourism.

The negative synergy between nationalism and heritage (and implicitly tourism) was further illustrated with the Yugoslav attack on the medieval walled city of Dubrovnik on the Dalmatian coast. Bombardment of the former icon of the Yugoslavian tourism product by Serbs and Montenegrins was aimed specifically at damaging newly independent Croatia's tourism economy (Oberreit, 1996). Four-fifths of recorded Yugoslav tourism earnings had been previously generated in Croatia, mostly from the long Dalmatian coast and offshore islands. Dubrovnik, as a United Nations Economic, Social and Cultural Organization World Heritage Site and the most visited place in Yugoslavia, claimed 3.5 million annual visitors in the later 1980s (Letcher, 1989: 82).

Unfortunately, Western responses to the plight of Dubrovnik appeared to place a higher priority on the need to protect the heritage value of Dubrovnik's *built* environment, rather than being concerned to stop the *human* suffering wrought by the conflict. This appeared to confound ideals of sustainable urban and heritage tourism through the active involvement in, and benefit for, local communities, from processes of protection and promotion (e.g. Richards and Hall, 2000). Indeed, a form of tourism that is far from realizing collective local support or benefit but which has arisen out of such hostilities in post-communist regions is the growth of 'morbid', 'dark' or *thana* tourism, whereby visitors follow trails through sites of destruction, to gaze on the physical remnants of human suffering (O'Reilly, 1996; Foley and Lennon, 1999).

Summary, Conclusions and Questions

This chapter has attempted to evaluate some of the more significant aspects of the nature and role of tourism in the development processes of communist and post-communist societies. It reviewed tourism under conditions of state socialism, employing a loose evolutionary framework to discern dynamic structural relationships within a slowly unravelling ideological environment. A summary discussion of contemporary state socialist tourism and development processes raised questions relating to both the paradox of international tourism development within command economies, and the possibility of discerning a 'Third Way' in the political economy of tourism development.

The evaluation of theoretical frameworks for understanding post-communist tourism and development addressed four approaches, none of which were able to embrace holistically the interrelationships between tourism, development and restructuring processes. Social inheritances of state socialism were examined in a brief discussion of sustainability questions relating to tourism development. These illuminated some of the problems associated with niche tourism development and questions of social inclusion in less favoured areas. Finally, post-communist relationships between tourism and development were articulated, with particular reference to issues of heritage and national identity.

Most forms of international tourism appear best suited to market economy conditions. The paradox of its pursuit under conditions of state socialism, particularly in 'Stalinist' circumstances, and its role in the economies of contemporary state socialist societies is of importance to development theory. Is international tourism an anomaly and ideological Trojan horse set to undermine state socialism, or a vital plank of gradualist economic restructuring and an indicator of a realistic 'Third Way'? What can both the post-communist relatively developed world and the non-communist less developed countries learn from the recent experience of Cuba, Vietnam and China (e.g. Harrison, 1994)?

Where tourism has flourished in post-communist CEE, it may be despite rather than because of government action. The late socialism phase saw governments viewing tourism not just as an instrument of reproduction of the labour force but also as an export industry. However, with the post-communist reduction of the role of the state, despite various incentives and policy statements, most state governments have shown an unwillingness or inability to invest significantly in the tourism industry or to secure significant international funding for it. Yet, the relative flexibility and proactive stance of a number of parastatal bodies, sometimes in partnership, has stimulated initiatives in relation to the development of particular niche tourism products and value-added services. Rural and nature tourism, for example, have received promotion in recent years from local government (e.g. Bognar, 1996) and non-governmental organizations (e.g. Ruukel, 1996) as well as from the private sector and international agencies. Nonetheless, the relationship between such niche market developments responding to evolving 'Western' tastes, and the ever-growing domestic and post-communist regional demand for mass tourism, will need to be planned and managed very carefully, not least in respect to longer-term cultural and environmental sustainability. This might suggest combining the role of central government at a strategic level with local and regionally based partnership schemes.

Tourism has the potential to exacerbate uneven regional development through the differentiated integration of particular territories into changing domestic and global markets and networks of international capital. This has tended to result in a reinforcement of the economic dominance of metropolitan regions, and differentiation amongst poorer regions: urban-industrial rust belts, peripheral and certain rural areas. Spatial and structural distortions in both communist (e.g. Vietnam) and post-communist (e.g. Hungary) economies have tended to focus activity on major urban areas in favoured regions, not least in tourism. One characteristic of post-communist tourism in the 1990s was the transformation of urban tourism – notably in Prague and Budapest – from a niche to a mass activity, exacerbating congestion and infrastructural problems as well as distorting territorial development. Several other central European urban 'cultural' destinations have positioned themselves through marketing programmes within the almost paradoxical context of 'European' heritage and progress (e.g. Goluza, 1996; Blonski, 1998).

Tourism also has the potential to ameliorate such distortions through niche development and opportunities which may be focused, for example, on rural and nature-based attractions acting as a resource that can be organized and sustained through locally owned small enterprises. Such a resource can act as a vehicle for integrated rural development to raise incomes, stabilize populations, sustain cultures and redistribute economic roles within rural households. Poland, for example, has moved to promoting itself as a 'natural' destination, with tourism literature becoming notably niche-orientated (e.g. Gordon and Wolfram, 1995; Witak and Lewandowska, 1996) and emphasizing a spatially redistributive dimension. Mongolia has a distinctive rural product based upon a nomadic herding culture and employing the traditional yurt (or more accurately *ger*) – round felt tent – for accommodation. In 1995 the Romanian Ministry of Tourism identified rural tourism as a major growth area (Light and Andone, 1996), raising the question of the extent to which social and cultural inequalities can be addressed and ameliorated through the inclusion of ethnic and other minorities (e.g. Kinnaird and Hall, 1996). Earlier advocates of tourism as a strategy for development viewed tourism employment as a positive means of integrating socially excluded groups into the formal economy. Such policies may be close to echoing stereotyped racist (and sexist) social ideologies, however, acting to reinforce existing social stratification systems (de Kadt, 1979). They can also create overt ethnic and gender divisions of labour within the tourism industry (Britton, 1991).

Finally, the need for more research is considerable and growing. Conceptualization of tourism and development in the societies discussed in this chapter is still weak. Flowing from that are many questions, some alluded to above, regarding the relationships between mass and niche tourism, the role of mass tourism in evolving societies, the search for a 'Third Way', questions of inclusion and exclusion relating to ethnicity, gender and location, the role of tourism as a refuge employment sector, differential impacts and uneven development, the roles of *nomenklatura* and successor networks and, by contrast, the ability of community participation to influence tourism and development decision-making processes.

Tourism embodies a range of important development-related issues. Yet it continues to be treated superficially by many governments and development analysts, such as economic geographers, who often cannot see beyond the next manufacturing plant (Debbage and Daniels, 1998).

References

Airey, D. (1994) Education for tourism in Poland: the PHARE programme. *Tourism Management* 15(6), 467–471.

Airey, D. (1999) Education for tourism: East meets West. *International Journal of Tourism and Hospitality Research* 1(1), 7–18.

Anon. (1998a) *Dalmatian Riviera and Islands*. Holiday Options, Burgess Hill, UK.

Anon. (1998b) *Transun's Croatia*. Transun, Oxford, UK.

Aun, C. (1996) Economic development and tourism opportunities in Estonia. *Journal of Baltic Studies* 27(2), 95–132.

Avella, A.E. and Mills, A.S. (1996) Tourism in Cuba in the 1990s: back to the future? *Tourism Management* 17(1), 55–60.

Bachvarov, M. (1997) End of the model? Tourism in post-communist Bulgaria. *Tourism Management* 18(1), 43–50.

Balaz, V. (1994) Tourism and regional development problems in the Slovak Republic. *European Urban and Regional Studies* 1(2), 171–177.

Balaz, V. (1995) Five years of the economic transition in the Slovak tourism, successes and shortcomings. *Tourism Management* 16(2), 143–150.

Balaz, V. (1996a) *International Tourism in the Economies of Central European Countries.* Tourism Research Group, University of Exeter, Exeter, UK.

Balaz, V. (1996b) *Regional Tourism Management in the Slovak Republic.* Tourism Research Group, University of Exeter, Exeter, UK.

Barber, T. (1997) Russian bogey turns into gold mine for Finns. *The Independent* 19 April.

Bartl, H. (1997) The hotel market in the former Eastern Bloc – an overview. *Journal of Vacation Marketing* 3(4), 343–353.

Baum, T. (1995) *Managing Human Resources in the European Tourism and Hospitality Industry. A Strategic Approach.* Chapman & Hall, London.

Berrios, R. (1997) Cuba's economic restructuring, 1990–1995. *Communist Economies and Economic Transformation* 9(1), 117–130.

Blonski, K. (1998) *Krakow 2000: European City of Culture.* City and Voivodship of Krakow, Krakow.

Bognar, A. (1996) *Budapest's Protected Natural Heritage.* Municipality of the City of Budapest, Budapest.

Bolay, J.C., Cartoux, S., Cunha, A., Du, T.T.N. and Bassand, M.T.I. (1997) Sustainable development and urban growth: precarious habitat and water management in Ho Chi Minh City, Vietnam. *Habitat International* 21(2), 185–197.

Böröcz, J. (1996) *Leisure Migration.* Pergamon Press, Oxford, UK.

Bria, I. (1998) The Orthodox Church in post-Communist Eastern Europe. *Ecumenical Review* 50(2), 157–163.

Britton, S. (1991) Tourism, capital and place: towards a critical geography. *Environment and Planning D: Society and Space* 9, 451–478.

Burns, P.M. (1995) Hotel management training in Eastern Europe: challenges for Romania. *Progress in Tourism and Hospitality Research* 1(1), 53–62.

Burns, P.M. (1998) Tourism in Russia. *Tourism Management* 19(6), 555–565.

Carter, F.W., Hall, D.R., Turnock, D., Williams, A.M., Stevenson, I. and Lowman, G. (1995) *Interpreting the Balkans.* Royal Geographical Society, London.

Chaieb, K. (1994) Untitled presentation to the Proceedings of the EuroCHRIE Conference Hospitality Schools East–West, Vienna, April.

Chance, S. (1994) The politics of restoration: the tension between conservation and tourism in Samarkand and Bukhara. *Architectural Review* 196(1172), 80–83.

Dann, G. (1996) The people of tourist brochures. In: Selwyn, T. (ed.) *The Tourist Image: Myths and Myth Making in Tourism.* John Wiley & Sons, Chichester, UK, pp. 61–81.

Davidson, J.O. (1996) Sex tourism in Cuba. *Race and Class* 38(1), 39–48.

Dawson, A.H. (1991) Poland. In: Hall, D.R. (ed.) *Tourism and Economic Development in Eastern Europe and the Soviet Union.* Belhaven Press, London, pp. 190–202.

de Kadt, E. (1979) *Tourism: Passport to Development.* Oxford University Press, Oxford, UK.

Debbage, K. and Daniels, P. (1998) The tourist industry and economic geography: missed opportunities. In: Ioannides, D. and Debbage, K.G. (eds) *The Economic Geography of the Tourist Industry.* Routledge, London, pp. 17–30.

Drakakis-Smith, D. and Dixon, C. (1997) Sustainable urbanization in Vietnam. *Geoforum* 28(1), 21–38.

Eberstadt, N. (1997) North Korea as an economy under multiple severe stresses: analogies and lessons from past and recent historical experience. *Communist Economies and Economic Transformation* 9(2), 233–255.

Everleny Perez, O. (1995) *Las Reformas Economicas en Cuba: un Analisis Critico.* Centro de Estudios de la Economia Cubana, Havana.

Focsa, G. (1970) *Muzeul Satului din Bucuresti.* Meridiane, Bucharest.

Foley, M. and Lennon, J. (1999) *Dark Tourism.* Cassell, London.

Foster-Carter, A. (1998) Asia's deadly enigma. *The Times* 4 September.

Goluza, M. (1996) *Zagreb: the New European Metropolis.* Tourist Association of the City of Zagreb, Zagreb.

Gordon, A. and Wolfram, K. (1995) *Wonders of Nature in Poland*. National Tourist Promotion Agency, Warsaw.

Hall, D.R. (1984) Foreign tourism under socialism: the Albanian 'Stalinist' model. *Annals of Tourism Research* 11(4), 539–555.

Hall, D.R. (1986) A last resort: North Korea opens to tourism. *Inside Asia* 9, 21–23.

Hall, D.R. (1989) Cuba. In: Potter, R.B. (ed.) *Urbanization, Planning and Development in the Caribbean*. Mansell, London, pp. 77–113.

Hall, D.R. (1990) Stalinism and tourism: a study of Albania and North Korea. *Annals of Tourism Research* 17(1), 36–54.

Hall, D.R. (ed.) (1991) *Tourism and Economic Development in Eastern Europe and the Soviet Union*. Belhaven Press and Halsted Press, London and New York.

Hall, D.R. (1992a) The challenge of international tourism in Eastern Europe. *Tourism Management* 13(2), 41–44.

Hall, D.R. (1992b) Tourism development in Cuba. In: Harrison, D. (ed.) *Tourism and the Less Developed Countries*. Belhaven Press, London, pp. 102–120.

Hall, D.R. (1993a) Impacts of economic and political transition on the transport geography of Central and Eastern Europe. *Journal of Transport Geography* 1(1), 20–35.

Hall, D.R. (ed.) (1993b) *Transport and Economic Development in the New Central and Eastern Europe*. Belhaven Press, London.

Hall, D.R. (1994) *Albania and the Albanians*. Frances Pinter, London.

Hall, D.R. (1995) Tourism change in Central and Eastern Europe. In: Montanari, A. and Williams, A.M. (eds) *European Tourism: Regions, Spaces and Restructuring*. John Wiley & Sons, Chichester, UK, pp. 221–244.

Hall, D.R. (1996) Resources for sustainable tourism: cultural landscapes. In: Turnock, D. (ed.) *Frameworks for Understanding Post-socialist Processes*. Leicester University Geography Department Occasional Paper 36, Leicester, UK, pp. 17–20.

Hall, D.R. (1998a) Central and eastern Europe. In: Williams, A.M. and Shaw, G. (eds) *Tourism and Economic Development in Europe*. John Wiley & Sons, Chichester, UK, pp. 345–373.

Hall, D.R. (1998b) Tourism development and sustainability issues in central and south-eastern Europe. *Tourism Management* 19(5), 423–431.

Hall, D.R. (1999) Destination branding, niche marketing and national image projection in Central and Eastern Europe. *Journal of Vacation Marketing* 5(3), 227–237.

Hall, D.R. (2000a) Cross-border movement and the dynamics of 'transition' processes in South-eastern Europe. *GeoJournal* 50(2–3), 249–253.

Hall, D.R. (2000b) Tourism as sustainable development? The Albanian experience of 'transition'. *International Journal of Tourism Research* 2(1), 31–46.

Hall, D. and Brown, F. (1996) Towards a welfare focus for tourism research. *Progress in Tourism and Hospitality Research* 2(1), 41–57.

Hall, D. and Danta, D. (eds) (1996) *Reconstructing the Balkans*. John Wiley & Sons, Chichester.

Hall, D. and Danta, D. (eds) (2000) *Europe Goes East: EU Enlargement, Diversity and Uncertainty*. The Stationery Office, London.

Hanson, S.E. (1998) Development, dependency, and devolution: the anomalous political economy of communist and post-communist societies. *Environment and Planning C: Government and Policy* 16(2), 225–246.

Harrison, D. (1993) Bulgarian tourism: a state of uncertainty. *Annals of Tourism Research* 20, 519–534.

Harrison, D. (1994) Learning from the Old South by the New South? The case of tourism. *Third World Quarterly* 15(4), 707–721.

Hewison, R. (1987) *The Heritage Industry: Britain in a Climate of Decline*. Methuen, London.

Hunt, J. (1993) Foreign investment in Eastern Europe travel industry. In: *Travel and Tourism Analyst* 3. Economist Intelligence Unit, London, pp. 65–85.

Iglicka, K. (1998) The economics of petty trade on the Eastern Polish border. In: Iglicka, K. and Sword, K. (eds) *Stemming the Flood: the Challenges of East–West Migration for Poland*. Macmillan, London.

Intriligator, M.D. (1998) Democracy in reforming collapsed communist economies: blessing or curse? *Contemporary Economic Policy* 16(2), 241–246.

Jaakson, R. (1996) Tourism in transition in post-Soviet Estonia. *Annals of Tourism Research* 23(3), 617–634.

Jeffreys, S. (1999) Globalizing sexual exploitation: sex tourism and the traffic in women. *Leisure Studies* 18(3), 179–196.

Johnson, M. (1995) Czech and Slovak tourism, patterns, problems and prospects. *Tourism Management* 16(1), 21–28.

Johnson, M. (1997) Hungary's hotel industry in transition, 1960–1996. *Tourism Management* 18(7), 441–452.

Kimura, M. (1999) From fascism to communism: continuity and development of collectivist economic policy in North Korea. *Economic History Review* 52(1), 69–87.

Kinnaird, V. and Hall, D. (1996) Understanding tourism processes: a gender-aware framework. *Tourism Management* 19(2), 95–102.

Konstantinov, Y. (1996) Patterns of reinterpretation: trader-tourism in the Balkans (Bulgaria) as a picaresque metaphorical enactment of post-totalitarianism. *American Ethnologist* 23(4), 762–782.

Kratke, S. (1998) Problems of cross-border regional integration: the case of the German–Polish border area. *European Urban and Regional Studies* 5(3), 248–262.

Lennon, J.J. (1995) Hotel privatisation in Central and Eastern Europe: progress and process. In: Leslie, D. (ed.) *Tourism and Leisure: Culture, Heritage and Participation.* Leisure Studies Association, Eastbourne, UK, pp. 45–58.

Lennon, J.J. (1996) Tourism marketing in Eastern Europe. In: Seaton, A.V. and Bennett, M.M. (eds) *Marketing Tourism Products.* International Thomson Business Press, London, pp. 237–274.

Leogrande, W.M. (1997) Enemies evermore: US policy towards Cuba after Helms-Burton. *Journal of Latin American Studies* 29, 211–221.

Letcher, P. (1989) *Yugoslavia: Mountain Walks and Historical Sites.* Bradt, Chalfont St Peter, UK.

Light, D. and Andone, D. (1996) The changing geography of Romanian tourism. *Geography* 81(3), 193–203.

Lijewski, T. (1996) The impact of political changes on transport in Central and Eastern Europe. *Transport Reviews* 16, 37–53.

Lowenthal, D. (1997) *The Heritage Crusade.* Viking, London.

Mazaraki, A. and Voronova, E. (1993) Prospects for tourism in Ukraine. *Tourism Management* 14(4), 316–317.

Mesa-Lago, C. (1998) Assessing economic and social performance in the Cuban transition of the 1990s. *World Development* 26(5), 857–876.

Momsen, J. (1985) Tourism and development in the Caribbean. *Mainzer Geographische Studien* 26, 25–36.

Morgan, N. and Pritchard, A. (1998) *Tourism, Promotion and Power: Creating Images, Creating Identities.* John Wiley & Sons, Chichester.

Naughton, B. (1996) The distinctive features of economic reform in Vietnam and China. In: McMillan, J. and Naughton, B. (eds) *Reforming Asian Socialism: the Growth of Market Institutions.* The University of Michigan Press, Ann Arbor, Michigan, pp. 273–296.

Oberreit, J. (1996) Destruction and reconstruction: the case of Dubrovnik. In: Hall, D. and Danta, D. (eds) *Reconstructing the Balkans.* John Wiley & Sons, Chichester, UK, pp. 67–77.

O'Reilly, D. (1996) Massacre trail lures sightseers. *The European* 14 November.

Pak, M.S. and Kim, T.Y. (1996) A plan for cooperation in transport between South and North Korea. *Transport Reviews* 16(3), 225–241.

Parenteau, R., Charbonneau, F., Toan, P.K., Dang, N.B., Hung, T., Nguyen, H.M., Hang, V.T., Hung, H.N., Binh, Q.A.T. and Hanh, N.H. (1995) Impact of restoration in Hanoi French colonial quarter. *Cities* 12(3), 163–173.

Pickel, A. (1998) Is Cuba different? Regime stability, social change, and the problem of reform strategy. *Communist and Postcommunist Studies* 31(1), 75–90.

Popesku, J. and Milojevic, L. (1996) *Serbia: Landscape Painted from the Heart.* National Tourism Organization of Serbia, Belgrade.

Qiao, Y. (1995) Domestic tourism in China: politics and development. In: Lew, A.A. and Yu, L. (eds) *Tourism in China: Geographical, Political and Economic Perspectives.* Westview Press, Boulder, Colorado, pp. 121–130.

Richards, G. (ed.) (1996) *Tourism in Central and Eastern Europe: Educating for Quality.* Tilburg University Press, Tilburg, The Netherlands.

Richards, G. and Hall, D. (eds) (2000) *Tourism and Sustainable Community Development.* Routledge, London.

Richter, L.K. (1989) *The Politics of Tourism in Asia.* University of Hawaii Press, Honolulu.

Ruukel, A. (ed.) (1996) *Estonia – the Natural Way.* Kodukant Ecotourism Association of Estonia, Pärnu.

Ryan, C. and Kinder, R. (1996) Sex, tourism and sex tourism. *Tourism Management* 17(7), 507–518.

Seaton, A.V. (1996) Tourism and relative deprivation: the counter-revolutionary pressures of tourism in Cuba. In: Robinson, M., Evans, N. and Callaghan, P. (eds) *Tourism and Culture: Image, Identity and Marketing.* Business Education Publishers, Sunderland, UK, pp. 197–216.

Seaton, A.V. (1997) Demonstration effects or relative deprivation? The counter-revolutionary pressures of tourism in Cuba. *Progress in Tourism and Hospitality Research* 3, 307–320.

Segre, R., Coyula, M. and Scarpaci, J.L. (1997) *Havana: Two Faces of the Antillean Metropolis.* John Wiley & Sons, Chichester.

Simon, F.L. (1995) Tourism development in transition economies – the Cuba case. *Columbia Journal of World Business* 30(1), 26–40.

Simpson, P. (1997) Polish hotels: rooms vacant. *Business Central Europe* 5(39), 32.

Sims, G.A. (1916) *The Republic of Cuba.* Banker's Loan and Securities Co., New Orleans, Louisiana.

Sofield, T.H.B. and Li, F.M.S. (1998) Tourism development and cultural policies in China. *Annals of Tourism Research* 25(2), 362–392.

Taylor, Z. (1998) Polish transport policy: an evaluation of the 1994/5 White Paper. *Journal of Transport Geography* 6(3), 227–236.

Tomka, M. (1998) Coping with persecution – religious change in communism and in post-communist reconstruction in Central Europe. *International Sociology* 13(2), 229–248.

Unwin, T. (1996) Tourist development in Estonia: images, sustainability, and integrated rural development. *Tourism Management* 17(4), 265–276.

Vikhanski, O. and Puffer, S. (1993) Management education and employee training at Moscow McDonald's. *European Management Journal* 11(1), 102–107.

Vukonic, B. (1992) Medjugorje's religion and tourism connection. *Annals of Tourism Research* 19(1), 79–91.

Vukonic, B. (1996) *Tourism and Religion.* Pergamon Press, Oxford, UK.

Wallace, C., Chmouliar, O. and Sidorenko, E. (1996) The eastern frontier of western Europe: mobility in the buffer zone. *New Community* 22(2), 259–286.

Wen, Z. (1997) China's domestic tourism: impetus, development and trends. *Tourism Management* 18(8), 565–571.

Williams, A.M. and Balaz, V. (2001) Domestic tourism in a transition society: from collective provision to commodification. *Annals of Tourism Research* 27.

Witak, A. and Lewandowska, U. (eds) (1996) *Poland: the Natural Choice.* Sport i Turystyka, Warsaw.

WTO (1994) *Yearbook of Tourism Statistics*, 46th edn, 2 vols. World Tourism Organization, Madrid.

WTO (1996a) *Compendium of Tourism Statistics 1990–1994*, 16th edn. World Tourism Organization, Madrid.

WTO (1996b) *Yearbook of Tourism Statistics*, 48th edn, 2 vols. World Tourism Organization, Madrid.

WTO (1997) *The World's Most Important Tourist Destinations in 2020.* World Tourism Organization, Madrid. http://www.world-tourism.org/calen.htm

WTO (1998a) *Tourism Market Trends: Europe.* World Tourism Organization, Madrid.

WTO (1998b) *Yearbook of Tourism Statistics*, 50th edn, 2 vols. World Tourism Organization, Madrid.

Wu, Y.S. and Sun, T.W. (1998) Four faces of Vietnamese communism: small countries' institutional choice under hegemony. *Communist and Post-Communist Studies* 31(4), 381–399.

Zhang, H.Q. and Qu, H. (1996) The trends of China's outbound travel to Hong Kong and their implications. *Journal of Vacation Marketing* 2(4), 373–381.

7

Tourism Development in China: the Dilemma of Bureaucratic Decentralization and Economic Liberalization

Alan A. Lew

Introduction

China is the third largest country in the world in land area (slightly larger than the USA) and the largest in total population (close to 1.3 billion by 1999). The five stars on China's flag stand for the country's five historically important ethnic groups: Han Chinese, Manchurian, Mongolian, Tibetan and Uyghur. The country contains 51 additional government-recognized ethnic groups, ranging in size from the Zhuang, with 14 million people in the Guangxi region of Southwest China, to the Lhoba, with only 2312 people on the Tibet–Nepal border (Embassy of the PRC, 1999). China's landscapes range from densely crowded urban and rural communities along its eastern coast and riverways, to the desolation of the Taklamakan Desert and the wonders of the Himalayas.

China is the world's oldest continuous civilization and during the 20th century it underwent major socio-economic transitions, moving from imperial rule through world and civil wars to impassioned communism, before arriving at 'socialist capitalism'. To generalize about the development of tourism across such a vast array of people, places and events is challenging, for China is distinct from other developing countries in many respects, most of which

influence its tourism development in one way or another. As indicated above, the sheer size and diversity of its land and people set it apart from many other societies. In addition, the country has a long history of highly centralized bureaucracy which, more than in many other countries, has exercised a high degree of economic and social control and has taken a major role in national policy-making. Despite this, it has an equally long history of periodic disorder and disunity, and its far-flung provinces demonstrate varying degrees of independence. Governmental involvement has been especially marked in economic development projects and industry, with governmental organizations owning and operating hotels, travel agencies, transportation companies and other tourism-related business activities. Nevertheless, despite China's major importance in the international marketplace, its currency, even in 1999, was not fully convertible, and major regulatory limitations were still imposed on outbound leisure travel for its peoples – a policy only a few small and isolated countries continue to apply to their citizens. Finally, compared with developing economies that have long been exposed to the global economy, China's international tourism started only in the early 1980s. Domestic tourism, which started seriously in the 1990s, is even more recent.

© CAB *International* 2001. *Tourism and the Less Developed World: Issues and Case Studies* (ed. D. Harrison)

Notwithstanding the enormous economic advances made in the 1980s and 1990s, China shares problems of tourism development with many other developing countries. Neither its transportation infrastructure nor its accommodation and other tourism facilities have kept pace with tourism demand, and there is a poor market mix, with considerable reliance on foreign investment for high quality international facilities. This reliance on foreigners extends to tourism management, and human resource development in tourism is generally inadequate, prompting considerable client dissatisfaction. The overall situation is not helped by corruption within the tourism industry and among government regulators, which leads to high costs and poor quality in products and services. Finally, the great disparity in wealth between coastal urban and interior rural populations, combined with increasing domestic tourism, results in overcrowding and social tension at major domestic tourist destinations.

Rather than attempt a cursory review of the breadth of tourism issues in China, this chapter focuses on the impact of China's bureaucracy and administration on the development of Chinese tourism. Historically, bureaucratic influence has been pervasive throughout the country, and this is also true for the period since 1949, when the communist revolution took place. In particular, since 1978, when economic reforms were first introduced, there have been evident tensions between centralization and decentralization, on the one hand, and social control, economic liberalization and individual freedom, on the other. Whereas the natural tendency of the Chinese bureaucracy has been toward centralization and control, the social trend, as seen in the behaviour and aspirations of the Chinese people, has been toward economic and social decentralization and greater freedom.

Maintaining social stability in the face of these opposing forces has been the major objective of China's central government since the passing of Mao Zedong in 1976. Tensions were at their height in the spring of 1989, when pro-democracy student protestors occupied Tiananmen Square in Beijing, calling for greater freedom and decentralization of political power (Roehl, 1995). The Chinese government responded on 4 June 1989 by brutally using the People's Liberation Army to crush the protests – with major consequences for China's tourism industry and its international image ever since.

In the discussion below, international tourism to and from China is examined within the context of societal control, while decentralization is considered within the setting of domestic tourism. All societies have some form of bureaucracy, and centralization and decentralization, societal control and freedom, are debated throughout the world. Simply because the Chinese experience is so distinctive, it may offer new perspectives and contribute valuable insight into tourism development in other developing economies.

Tourism Development in China

For most of this century, China has been of great interest to many, yet visited by few. Soon after the communist victory in 1949, the 'Bamboo Curtain' was drawn, and China's internal ideological and development struggles isolated it from the rest of the world. Modern tourism to China began in the late 1970s, after the death of Mao Zedong, when Deng Xiaoping became the country's leader. In 1978, he announced that China was opening its doors so that its economy could be brought rapidly into the global marketplace. International tourism was to be an important part of this strategy. Since 1979, and the institutionalization of the 'Four Modernizations', China has undergone nothing short of an economic and social transformation. Buoyed by high annual economic growth rates, which during the 1980s and 1990s sometimes exceeded 10%, it has become one of the world's largest economies. In the process, many (but clearly not all) of China's citizens have moved from poverty to varying levels of prosperity. In addition, during the 1997–1998 Asian economic crisis, China was a major force in trying to bring financial stability to other parts of Asia.

From the start of the economic reforms, tourism was targeted by the government's planners for major investment and development (Zhang, 1995). However, in the early 1980s, tourism development was approached cautiously. From an ideological standpoint, it was considered a source of corrupting foreign values, and numerous nationwide campaigns were initiated to try to limit this influence by minimizing contacts of Chinese citizens with foreign tourists and tourism facilities (Lew, 1987). Domestic tourism was not permitted at all, partly through a fear that it would over-whelm the transport system and place too much pressure on the existing accommodation. There was still only one airline in China, mostly using Russian-made planes with questionable safety standards, and only a few hotels were of 'international' quality. As a consequence, investment in upmarket, international hotels, both in buildings and human resources, was a major feature of joint venture investment in the early years of tourism development in China.

In addition, China was still a highly central-ized society; its bureaucracy was barely able to meet the growing demand of international visitors and far less able to permit domestic leisure travel. International demand to visit China in the early years was so enormous that tourism very quickly became an important source of hard currency. From 1979 until the Tiananmen Square crackdown in 1989,

China's average annual growth in tourist arrivals was 36.4% (Table 7.1), while receipts grew at an average 25.0%, far surpassing the average world growth of 5.5% (Johnson and Xu, 1996). That said, it must be noted that China's arrival figures include both overnight visitors and excursionists (day visitors), thus differing from statistics produced by the World Tourism Organization (WTO) and by most other countries. Thus the WTO ranked China as the sixth most visited country in the world in 1997 with 23.7 million international arrivals, as opposed to the 57.6 million arrivals claimed by China. Most of the arrivals were from Hong Kong, Taiwan and Macau and only 10–15% were 'foreigners' from elsewhere.

In the 1980s, Europe was the major source of foreign visitors to China, while arrivals from China's Asian neighbours were comparatively modest. A significant decline in international arrivals occurred in 1989, as a reaction to events in Tiananmen Square, but this was soon reversed. European arrivals, had already begun to flatten prior to 1989 and most of the growth during and since the Tiananmen

Table 7.1. International visitor arrivals to China, 1978–1998.

Year	Total		Foreigners		Compatriots[a]	
	(000)	Growth (%)	(000)	Growth (%)	(000)	Growth (%)
1978	180.9		229.6		1,561.5	
1979	4,203.9	132.4	362.4	57.8	3,820.6	144.7
1980	5,702.5	35.6	529.1	46.0	5,139.0	34.5
1981	7,767.1	36.2	675.2	27.6	7,053.1	37.2
1982	7,924.3	2.0	764.5	13.2	7,117.0	0.9
1983	9,477.0	19.6	872.5	14.1	8,564.1	20.3
1984	12,852.2	35.6	1,134.3	30.0	11,670.4	36.3
1985	17,833.1	38.8	1,370.5	20.8	16,377.8	40.3
1986	22,819.5	28.0	1,482.3	8.2	21,269.0	29.9
1987	26,902.3	17.9	1,727.8	16.6	25,087.4	18.0
1988	31,694.8	39.7	1,842.2	6.6	29,773.3	18.7
1989	24,501.4	−22.7	1,461.0	−20.7	22,971.9	−22.8
1990	27,461.8	12.1	1,747.3	19.6	25,623.4	11.5
1991	33,349.8	21.4	2,710.1	55.1	30,506.2	19.1
1992	38,114.9	14.3	4,006.4	47.8	33,943.4	11.3
1993	41,526.9	9.0	4,565.9	14.0	36,704.9	8.1
1994	43,684.5	5.2	5,182.1	13.5	38,387.2	4.6
1995	46,386.5	6.2	5,886.7	13.6	40,384.0	5.2
1996	51,127.5	10.2	6,744.3	14.6	44,228.6	9.5
1997	57,587.9	12.6	7,428.0	10.1	50,060.9	13.2
1998	63,478.4	10.2	7107.7	−4.3	56,250.0	12.4

[a]Compatriots are citizens of Hong Kong, Taiwan and Macau.
Source: CNTA (1999).

Square incident has been in arrivals from Asian countries (Table 7.2). In addition, business travel to China has increased at a far faster rate since the late 1980s than leisure tourist arrivals, reflecting Asia's improving diplomatic and economic ties with China (Roehl, 1995; Lew, 2000). For example, after diplomatic talks between the Chinese and South Korean governments in 1993, and the subsequent action in 1994 of South Korea in lifting the ban on its citizens visiting China, the number of visitors from South Korea soared. Scheduled flights now operate between Seoul and major northern Chinese cities, including Beijing, Tianjin, Shenyang, and Dalian. In the 1990s, China's land borders also became more open, with large numbers of visitors crossing from Vietnam, central Asia and Russia, which shares the world's longest land border with China and was the second largest source of visitors since 1996. Indeed, until the Asian economic crisis started in mid-1997, the growth in travel from Asia and the former USSR was the most important market change to take place in the 1990s. During the 1990s, Chinese citizens benefited from the country's economic success and domestic tourism exploded. By 1998, there were an estimated 694 million domestic trips in China, an increase from around 300 million in the late 1980s (Qiao, 1994; Sun, 1995;

CNTA, 1999), and this figure is expected to reach 1 billion early in the 21st century. In addition, Chinese citizens have begun to travel overseas (Table 7.3) and 'official' travellers can now visit most countries on business trips, combining their professional activities with a large degree of leisure. At the time of writing, private travellers were limited to Hong Kong and Macau, along with designated 'Tourism liberalizing countries,' which, in 1999, included Singapore, Malaysia and Thailand (all designated in 1990), the Philippines (1992), Australia (1997), and South Korea and New Zealand (both designated in 1998) (Brady, 1998; Lew, 2000).

Bureaucratic Control and International Travel

When Mao Zedong was its leader (1949–1976), China was one of the most centrally controlled societies on earth. Through its various organizations, all answerable to a higher level, the Chinese Communist Party (CCP) controlled both daily and long-term social and economic activities, from the neighbourhood upwards. No one departed from or returned to their birthplace, or started or ended a job, without CCP approval. Such

Table 7.2. China's leading foreign visitor markets, 1993 and 1998.

	1993		1998	
	(000)	Change from 1992 (%)	(000)	Change from 1997 (%)
Countries				
Japan	912.0	15.2	1572.1	−0.6
USSR/Russia[a]	928.2	3.7	692.0	−15.0
USA	399.7	15.4	677.3	9.9
South Korea	189.9	68.9	632.8	−19.0
Mongolia	230.5	106.1	364.8	6.4
Singapore	200.9	23.9	316.4	−0.1
Regions				
Asia	2333.1	26.3	4139.5	−6.2
Europe[b]	1592.0	4.8	1734.4	−8.2
Americas	564.1	13.9	947.9	9.3
Oceania and Africa	154.6	16.9	273.1	12.6

[a]USSR figures are for 1993; Russia only figures are for 1998.
[b]Europe figures include most of the former USSR.
Sources: Sun (1995); CNTA (1999).

Table 7.3. China outbound travel, selected years 1985–1998.

Year	Number of trips
1985	529,900
1990	980,000
1992	2,800,000
1993	4,082,504
1994	4,045,468
1995	4,864,340
1996	5,060,000
1997	5,300,000
1998	8,400,000

Sources: WTO (1997); Brady (1998); Chen (1998); Xinhua (1999).

an extreme of control was a reaction to a century of internal chaos and humiliation at the hands of European imperialists. Maoist communism was seen as a way of modernizing China as quickly as possible, which, in the process, also required a fundamental transformation of Chinese society. Thus, absolute control was necessary to eradicate old and 'backward' ways of thought.

Except for official administrative and government purposes, domestic travel was considered a potential threat to societal control and was thus almost non-existent. Similar official attitudes were extended to inbound international tourism, which was seen as a 'diplomatic' rather than an economic activity (Zhang, 1995). International outbound travel was limited solely to Chinese government officials, and inbound tourism to diplomats and professional organizations touring China for the purposes of 'education' and 'friendship'. Only compatriot Chinese from Hong Kong and Macau were given relatively free entry into China.

During the 1970s and early 1980s, international tourism was seen as a means of promoting the benefits of Maoist communism in the outside world, and as such was administered under China's Ministry of Foreign Affairs. From 1971 to 1977, for example, only 15,000 visas were issued to US citizens out of more than 200,000 applications (Lew, 1987); from 1974 to 1978, foreign visitors to China are estimated to have been between 25,000 and 35,000 a year. Before this, they had numbered

about 2000 a year, whereas arrivals of compatriot Chinese, mostly from Hong Kong, were between 1 and 2 million a year prior to 1979, and about half that number in the 1950s and 1960s.

Elements of xenophobia continued into the early 1980s, and Maoist elements in the Chinese leadership were still suspicious of 'bourgeois' tourism (Tan, 1986). Foreign visitors to China could visit only officially designated 'open' sites and cities, which grew from about 40 in 1979 to 257 by 1986 (Kaplan, et al., 1986). However, facilities in fewer than half of these were capable of serving foreign visitors. Travel was almost exclusively in organized groups, which allowed considerable control over where visitors went, whom they met and what they were told. While compatriot and overseas Chinese had long been permitted independent travel, it was extended to foreigners in only the mid-1980s, and even then was constrained by language barriers, limited transport and accommodation in open cities, especially during the high tourist season, and by high costs. Nevertheless, by the 1990s, much of eastern China was open to visitors and independent travel became easier, though structural barriers still existed. Most of the remaining restricted areas were in more remote central and western China, including most of Tibet (Xizang) and Xinjiang provinces, where separatist movements were a problem. Language difficulties, the lack of an adequate travel reservation system and poor banking facilities still keep many foreign visitors away from many areas outside major tourist destinations.

Since 1978, major reforms instituted in China have included the rationalization and decentralization of administrative and economic decision-making. During the 1980s, especially, tourism became increasingly conditioned by economic rather than diplomatic considerations, and by the 1990s economic imperatives were the fundamental basis for most decisions on tourism development. The decentralization of bureaucratic decision-making that occurred over this time period has been less than successful. A major part of the problem has been the difficulty of building adequate provincial and local structures to replace the highly centralized administrative organs that previously existed (Leaf, 1998). Corruption, inefficiency, mismanagement and legal confusion have been major stumbling blocks, slowing the process considerably.

For the average Chinese citizen, the decentralization in authority and the economic turn in policy have contributed to travel bans being progressively lifted over the past 20 years. Private international outbound travel, for example, was prohibited until 1990, whereas travel for business and education has been allowed since the economic reforms of 1978. The change has been accompanied by much confusion over who can travel and how they can travel. The necessary passports and exit visas have been extremely difficult to obtain, even when all other forms and papers were properly filed, and although this situation has gradually been relaxed over the years, it remained the single biggest complaint of Chinese travellers throughout the 1990s (Muqbil, 1996b).

China issues two types of passport: business travel passports, valid for 2 years, and private travel passports, valid for 6 years. Exit visas must also be obtained. In 1990, a 'Travel Abroad' campaign was initiated, to encourage international travel as a form of professional development and to enhance the expertise of China's professionals and government officials. Since then, business travel has been less stringently regulated than leisure travel, and many Chinese have used business travel to justify leisure trips, using company funds to finance them. Because many larger companies in China are government-owned, this form of outbound travel had an impact on the nation's currency reserves. In 1993, when a major central government crackdown on nominal business travel took place, it accounted for 61% of all international outbound travel (Liu, 1995). The result was a modest decline in outbound travel in 1994 (Table 7.3), while the proportion of business trips fell to 56%.

Once a passport is obtained for private travel, the easiest way to obtain an exit visa is to join a package tour group. At the time of writing, such tours were limited to Hong Kong, Macau and the seven designated Tourism Liberalizing Countries (all in the Asia-Pacific), even though the USA and Europe were the preferred destinations of most Chinese (Muqbil, 1996a). Clearly, the Chinese government is not yet ready to give free rein to its citizens to roam the world. Part of this is a result of corruption within the system, with some poorly paid government officials seeking special compensation in return for not hindering the process. However, the policy also curtails unnecessary currency leakages to other countries. This aim is common to many developing countries, where hard currency is needed for economic development, but where others may encourage their citizens to travel at home rather than overseas during economic hard times, for the 'good of the country,' China's central government resorts more to administrative and regulatory restrictions, opening itself to criticism within and from outside of the country.

For over a thousand years, outbound travel from China has generally been small in scale and illegal. An exception occurred as a result of the Opium Wars of the late 19th century, when the British forced imperial China to allow its citizens to emigrate to plantations in South Asia and South-East Asia (Lew, 1995). This resulted in a great Chinese diaspora, which lasted until 1949, and many Chinatowns and Chinese communities were subsequently formed throughout the world. More recent figures, if accurate, suggest that the mainland government's centralized control may have been relaxed, and from 1997 to 1998 (Table 7.3) there was a 58.5% increase in outbound travel. This could herald the start of a great boom in Chinese arrivals, long anticipated throughout the Asia-Pacific region (Chen, 1998).

In terms of inbound international travel, China's tourism development has been sacrificed in an effort to maintain central control through the suppression of political dissent against the CCP's single-party rule over the country. The 1989 Tiananmen Square incident resulted in a dramatic and instantaneous reduction in the number of visitors (Table 7.1), and reports of the Chinese government's suppression of human rights and pro-democracy and religious groups continuously trickle into the global news media. In 1997, for example, the US State Department condemned China for having a 'national campaign to suppress unauthorized religious groups and social organizations' through 'threats, demolition of property, extortion of "fines", interrogation, detention, and reform ... through ... education sentences' (Palmer, 1997: 1). Such oppression has been particularly severe when directed at Tibetans desiring independence and at unauthorized political parties. Such reports dissuade some segments of the international community from travelling to China. However, from the CCP's perspective, reduced tourism revenue is a small price to pay for ensuring continued rule and political stability. The Party also counts on the short memories that most tourists have of past transgressions, and on the knowledge that tourists prefer to visit places that are relatively stable and economically advancing, even if political activism is suppressed. Indeed, some travellers might consider such suppression a necessary price of development in less developed economies or an inherent feature of Asian culture. Many political leaders throughout Asia justify their heavy-handed rule in this manner.

Decentralization and Domestic Travel

In general, the process of centralization that enabled the Chinese government to move China through the enormous social and political shifts it has undergone since 1949 has been highly resistant to its own need for institutional change. Deng Xiaoping and his successors made repeated efforts to devolve administrative power from the central government to provincial and local authorities, but with mixed success. This also applies specifically to tourism. Three years after the 1978 reforms, responsibility for tourism was taken from the Ministry of Foreign Affairs and allocated to the National Tourism Administration of the People's Republic of China (the China National Tourism Administration, or CNTA), which has since been the principal central government agency responsible for all aspects of tourism development and administration (Zhang, 1995). In the early 1980s, one of the first steps taken by the CNTA to decentralize was the separation of its three travel

agencies: the China International Travel Service (for non-Chinese foreign visitors), the China Travel Services (for overseas ethnic-Chinese visitors) and the China Youth Travel Service (for international youth exchanges). This change was made to enable their many local branches spread throughout the country and overseas to function as business entities without excessive political interference. Many of these branch travel agencies had historically served as official local travel bureaux, working closely with provincial and local government authorities. In 1985, separate provincial tourism bureaux were formed, with authority to enter contracts with foreign tour operators and issue visas to foreign tourists. This was extended in 1988 to municipalities, when both municipalities and provinces were also permitted to establish local travel agencies in direct competition with agencies operated by the CNTA. At the same time, private and collective travel agencies were also authorized, most of which served domestic tourists.

'Collectives' (danwei, or 'work units'), are a distinctly Chinese form of administration and business activity. They consist of branches of government working as integrated units (for example, an army unit or a public works agency) and in rural areas typically take the form of agricultural communes. This system, first introduced in the 1950s and expanded and modified over the years, is a major relic of the Maoist era, affecting all aspects of Chinese urban and rural life, and served the needs of a cash-strapped central government quite well when China was closed to much of the world. Collectives were designed to be largely self-supporting, and are responsible for housing, educating and employing household members. As government agencies, collectives receive favourable treatment in the allocation of land and, at the time of writing, continued to maintain a high degree of independence from local authorities.

Collectives are important in tourism because they have been major owners and operators of China's hotels, even to the extent of operating joint ventures with overseas companies. In order to reduce its budget in the 1980s, for example, the People's Liberation Army began to participate in many commercial business ventures (Anon., 1991), while the three-star Lantian (Blue Sky) Hotel in Shanghai was built, owned and managed by the local air force unit and has often been booked by international travel services (Yu, 1995). Of 2130 hotels officially recorded in China for 1991, 71% were developed by government collectives.

Unfortunately, the largely independent, collective-owned travel and tourism businesses complicate provincial and local regulation and require strong central administration. Decentralizing administrative functions to local collectives lacking adequate authority and human resources has led to corruption, mismanagement and general confusion (Leaf, 1998). At the same time, China's market-orientated economic reforms have so encouraged development of entrepreneurial skills and ingenuity – factors greatly contributing to the success of overseas Chinese – that the result has been rampant entrepreneurism. The rapid growth in business activity has often outstripped the ability of decentralized government administrative agencies to regulate them, and most large cities in China are growing faster than local governments can efficiently serve and manage.

Development at the local level has been especially important for the country's domestic tourism which grew 231% over the 10-year period from 1988 (300 million trips) to 1998 (694 million). Huge amounts of capital have been invested in transport to meet the needs of an increasing number of domestic travellers, and the number of travel agencies has grown exponentially. Both areas have had their growing pains, which have often resulted in problems for China's domestic travellers.

In the 1990s, domestic tourism rapidly increased as discretionary income and free time became available. Many urban residents, for example, obtained two work-free days on alternate weekends. Domestic tourism is lucrative, with 10 to 20 times more domestic trips than inbound trips, but domestic travellers spend about a fifth as much per trip compared with international visitors (US$43.41 compared with US$198.49). Wealthier residents of China's metropolitan east coast take twice as many trips and spend three times as much as does China's majority rural population (Table 7.4). Increased prosperity in the Chinese countryside is expected to unleash an even greater flood of domestic travellers over the coming decade. As with international outbound travel, business travel predominates, but since restrictions on the improper use of business funds for leisure travel were imposed, family holidays have increased dramatically in eastern coastal China (Shen, 1993).

Despite government calls for its limitation, China's domestic tourism has grown spontaneously. Until the early 1990s, the general consensus among central government decision-makers was that because it produced no foreign exchange, and might interfere with international tourism, it should not be promoted. But with increasing prosperity the Chinese were soon able to enjoy luxuries hitherto afforded only by foreigners. Urban and coastal residents have participated in domestic tourism at higher rates because they have experienced the fastest income growth, with per capita gross national product in Shanghai, Beijing and Guangdong Province several times higher than the national average. However, because of the central government's attitude, China's tourism industry was un-

Table 7.4. China's domestic travel, 1998.

	Total population (million)	Trips made (million)	Trip propensity (trips as % of population)	Mean expenditure per person[a]	
				RMB¥	$US
Urban	280	250	89	607.00	72.84
Rural	945	444	47	197.10	23.65
Total	1225	694	57	344.50	41.34

[a]RMB¥, renminbi yuan (People's yuan); RMB¥ 1.00 = approximately US$0.12, UK£0.076 (based on 1999 rates).
Source: CNTA (1999).

prepared to meet the challenge posed by domestic tourism in the early 1990s. Tourism professionals were confused about how to handle domestic tour arrangements and received little assistance from government administrators. As a result, transport was placed under severe pressure by rapidly increasing numbers of domestic tourists and considerable environmental degradation occurred as virtually every popular destination in eastern China was regularly overrun with tourists (Gormsen, 1995).

In the late 1980s, recognizing their economic potential, travel agencies and other travel services targeted domestic travellers and rapidly flourished. In popular destinations, for example, local residents added guest rooms to their houses, supplementing their income and, as Xu (1999) has shown, contributing to the local economy in a more sustainable manner than large, international hotels with very high leakage rates. By the end of 1992, the number of travel agencies officially authorized to service only domestic travellers had grown to 1506 (Li, 1995: 40), and most larger and more experienced international travel agencies were also starting to cater for domestic tourists. By 1996, China had almost 4000 travel agencies serving the domestic tourist market (Anon., 1996).

Many of the newer travel agencies were poorly managed and lacked trained personnel. As a result of administrative decentralization, most were inadequately monitored and some operated without a legitimate business licence. The quality of service was frequently substandard and considerable confusion in the early years of domestic travel, led to unnecessary losses for travellers and damage to the industry's reputation. In 1994, by way of a response, the CNTA conducted a nationwide audit of agencies serving domestic travellers, reprimanding many and forcing the closure of about 140 (Liu, 1995: 61). Decentralization continued, however, and in February 1999 the government allowed domestic travel agents to establish joint ventures with overseas partners for the first time, on a pilot basis (ChinaOnline, 1999). The goals were to encourage foreign investment as well as to strengthen and enhance the service quality of China's travel agencies. This will also further integrate China's tourism industry into the global business community. More serious – even life-threatening – problems accompanied the end of China's state airline monopoly and the deregulation of domestic and international air travel (Yu and Lew, 1997). Like the CNTA, the Civil Aviation Administration of China (CAAC) was originally both a regulatory body and the operator of the country's only airline. Like CNTA, its administration changed in 1980 from China's Military Commission to the country's central administration, and independent regional and provincial airlines were then allowed. Between 1984 and 1988, CAAC separated its regulatory and business activities and broke up the single state-owned airline into regional airlines. Air China continued as the country's primary flag carrier for international flights, operating out of the CAAC Beijing Branch, but other former branch offices of CAAC became independent carriers, including China Southwest (Chengdu Branch), China Northwest (Xian Branch), China Southern (Guangzhou Branch), China Eastern (Shanghai Branch) and China Northern (Shenyang Branch). Some have since developed their own international routes.

Most new airlines were not originally affiliated with CAAC and have sometimes been referred to as 'rogue airlines' (Baily, 1993). Shanghai Airlines, for example, was founded in 1985 by the Shanghai municipal government and is widely recognized in China for its high quality of service. It was the first Chinese airline to take reservations by telephone and to deliver tickets to customers (Barnathan and Yang, 1993). By contrast, China United Airlines, the aviation arm of the People's Liberation Army, is able to use military airfields and plays an important role as a charter service for international tourists during the peak season. The airline industry in China has thus been dramatically transformed from a single, government-owned airline to an estimated 40 regional, provincial and local airlines.

The rapid development of new airlines and destinations created major problems for China's airline industry and its regulators, and dangers for passengers. Aircraft and ground facilities were becoming antiquated, safety standards were poorly enforced, and there were acute shortages of trained and qualified staff. Such problems were often cited as causes of a series of passenger airline disasters that plagued China in the early to mid-1990s (Yu and Lew, 1997), most notoriously from July to November, 1992, when 310 people died in five crashes. Although not conclusively documented, China's poor flight safety record over this period probably discouraged a considerable number of international tourists. Airline hijacking also occurred regularly (there were three in 1993), with Taiwan as the most preferred destination, and in 1990 an attempt to end a hijacking resulted in a crash landing that killed 132 passengers. Fortunately, by the late 1990s, hijacking was far less frequent and the rate of airline crashes much closer to international norms.

In the 1990s, institutional structures in China could not cope with the prevailing levels of economic activity, and the problem is likely to continue well into the next decade. During the rule of Mao Zedong, central authorities managed local development on a regular basis, but by the late 1990s economic liberalization had become the fundamental basis of government policy, and had indeed materially improved the lives of most Chinese. As a result, the central government can intervene only periodically, to take corrective action. However, while decentralization has undoubtedly occurred in China's travel and tourism industry, as in other sectors, it has not necessarily led to flexibility and efficiency in the marketplace. The power of central authorities has been reduced, but adequate regulatory mechanisms have not yet been created at the local level, where decentralization has been complicated by both a lack of experience and the presence of collectives, which continue as fundamentally independent players on the local scene. So far, decentralization in China has been easier to espouse than to practise.

Conclusions

This chapter has focused on the relationship of international and domestic tourism to major societal conflicts and stresses in China at the end of the 20th century. These involve continuing tension between centralization and decentralization of authority, including the issue of how far the Chinese are to be subjected to centralized control, and problems that arise when efficient management institutions at local levels do not exist. Other problems arise from uncontrolled growth.

Although China is geographically, historically and socially distinct from most other countries, such problems are widespread, especially in less developed countries. During the 1990s, for example, many countries lowered trade barriers and encouraged foreign investment far beyond that allowed by the Chinese government. Some of these economies, notably in Asia, were far more damaged by the 1997 Asian economic crisis than China, which was active in preventing an even worse economic collapse throughout Asia. It may be that a relatively protected and centralized economy, like that of China, is more appropriate for a developing country. However, an overbearing bureaucracy can be one of the greatest frustrations that citizens of any country can experience, as many prospective Chinese travellers can verify.

China also demonstrates the need for regulatory mechanisms appropriate to a country's particular social structure when a process of decentralization is initiated. As China's travel industry shows, it is not enough to borrow institutional structures from more developed countries. They must be adapted to local circumstances and needs, which often entail a series of trials and errors until an appropriate mechanism evolves. Also, as both developed and developing countries have experienced, growth must be managed, though not stifled.

China aims to be the leading tourist destination in the world by the year 2002 (Xinhua, 1999). Whether or not such a goal is reasonable, or even desirable, is open to question. However, if it is to be achieved, fundamental shifts in China's travel and tourism policies, and in the way they are managed by national and local bureaucracies, will be necessary. That such changes may already be taking place is indicated by the dramatic increase in international outbound travel by Chinese citizens in 1998 (Table 7.3). Some leading Chinese political dissidents have also observed significant recent changes in government policies (Guo, 1999). At the same time, as the millennium approached, social tensions seemed to be on the rise. In 1999, labour unrest, terrorist bombings, and dissident protests all increased (e.g. *Time*, 1999).

Just as centralized bureaucratic control has long influenced China in general, and travel in and to China in particular, so have periods of unrest and instability. Future tourism development in China will continue to be closely related to wider social changes. In some respects, China is still trying to redefine itself as a modern country, after its shock encounter with superior European war power over 100 years ago. Oakes (1998) has pointed out that tourism is an integral part of that redefinition, as the Chinese central government seeks to both modernize and integrate this vast land through the development of tourism. Just as was the case during the Cultural Revolution, state policy encourages the standardization and controlled image of China for international consumption (i.e. tourism marketing), resulting in a restricted and simplified experience of China by mass foreign tourists. The desired image is of a country that is modern, yet respectful of its historical heritage. Much of the 'real' China, though, remains closed to foreign tourists, as the vast majority of those who do come are confined to group tours, due to the difficulties of language and dealing with Chinese bureaucracy.

Domestically, the gradual but steady increase in travel opportunities for China's citizens has similarly evolved in a largely controlled manner, at least most of the time. The nature of Chinese society, with its many governmental bodies involved in private sector ventures, means that no tourist destination development occurs without some form of central government authorization and influence (Oakes, 1998). Even when this involvement is minimal, the current move toward modernity, which was started in 1977 by Den Xiaoping, is so pervasive that almost all domestic tourism reflects local attempts to emulate an international mass tourism product. This centralized effort to create a new and modern China often appears contrived and unauthentic, because the theme is too narrow for such a vast country. The decentralization of tourism in China is slowly allowing for greater regional and local diversity but, as with the country's human rights record, this is still open to considerable criticism from a Western perspective. How tourism is further decentralized in China, especially how it is used and managed by the state and how well it comes to reflect the country's great diversity, will be a good index of how Chinese society is changing to meet the challenges of the 21st century.

References

Anon. (1991) China: the army that makes money. *The Economist* 5 October, p. 38.

Anon. (1996) Domestic tourism soars. *Beijing Review* 39, 5–11. http://sun.ihep.ac.cn/ins/BOOK/bjreview/February/96–6–16.html

Baily, M. (1993) China's airline boom. *Interavia Aerospace World* 48(3), 52–55.

Barnathan, J. and Yang, D.J. (1993) Look up in the sky: a swarm of Chinese airlines. *Business Week* 17 May, p. 60.

Brady, S. (1998) China's outwardly mobile. *Time* (Asia edition) 21 September, p. 10.

Chen, C. (1998) Rising Chinese overseas travel market and potential for the United States. In: Chon, K. (ed.) *Advances in Hospitality and Tourism*, Vol. III. Proceedings of Third Annual Graduate Education and Graduate Students Research Conference in Hospitality and Tourism, January 8–10, 1998, University of Houston Hilton Hotel. http://www.hotel–online.com/Neo/Trends/AdvancesInHospitalityResearch/ChineseTravelMarket998.html (accessed 18 June, 1999).

China National Tourism Administration (CNTA) (1999) Outline of China tourism statistics. http://www.cnta.com/HTMLE/news/shuju.htm (accessed 17 June, 1999).

ChinaOnline (1999) China opens travel agencies to foreign participation. *ChinaOnline* 2 February. www.chinaonline.com/top_stories/today_b2_99020321.html (accessed 25 May, 1999).

Embassy of the PRC (1999) China ABCs: fifty-six ethnic groups. www.chinese-embassy.org.uk/China/china.pl-D3.htm (accessed 16 June, 1999).

Gormsen, E. (1995) Travel behavior and the impacts of domestic tourism in China. In: Lew, A.A. and Yu, L. (eds) *Tourism in China: Geographical, Political, and Economic Perspectives*. Westview Press, Boulder, Colorado, pp. 131–140.

Guo, Fang (1999) China is changing fast. *Time*, http://cgi.pathfinder.com/time/asia/magazine/1999/990607/guo1.html (accessed 20 June, 1999). http://www.cnd.org/CND–Global/CND–Global.96–04–18.html

Johnson, A. and Xu, Mingyang (1996) News summary. *China News Digest*, 14 April.

Kaplan, F., Sobin, J. and de Keijzer, A. (1986). *The China Guidebook*. Eurasia Press, Teaneck, New Jersey.

Leaf, M. (1998) Urban planning and urban reality under Chinese economic reforms. *Journal of Planning Education and Research* 18(2), 145–153.

Lew, A.A. (1987) The history, policies and social impact of international tourism in the People's Republic of China. *Asian Profile* 15(2), 117–128.

Lew, A.A. (1995) Overseas Chinese and compatriots in China's tourism development. In: Lew, A.A. and Yu, L. (eds) *Tourism in China: Geographical, Political, and Economic Perspectives*. Westview Press, Boulder, Colorado, pp. 155–175.

Lew, A.A. (2000) China: a growth engine for Asian tourism. In: Hall, C.M. and Page, S. (eds) *Tourism in South and South East Asia: Issues and Cases*. Butterworth-Heinemann, Oxford, UK, pp. 268–285.

Li, Jun (1995) Domestic tourism. In: Liu, Yi (ed.) *The Yearbook of China Tourism, 1995*. National Tourism Administration of the People's Republic of China, Beijing, pp. 11–15.

Liu, Yi (ed.) (1995) *The Yearbook of China Tourism, 1995*. National Tourism Administration of the People's Republic of China, Beijing.

Muqbil, I. (1996a) China travelers seek clean and pleasant lands. *TravelNews Asia*, 20 May. http://web3.asia1.com.sg/timesnet/data/tna/docs/tna3249.html

Muqbil, I. (1996b) Profile of a traveler. *TravelNews Asia*, 20 May. http://web3.asia1.com.sg/timesnet/data/tna/docs/tna3250.html

Oakes, T. (1998) *Tourism and Modernity in China*. Routledge, London.

Palmer, B. (1997) Caesar vs. Christ in China: millions worship with and without the blessings of the state. *US News Online*, 4 August. www.usnews.com/usnews/issue/4chur.htm (accessed 19 June, 1999).

Qiao, Yuxia (1994) On China's domestic tourism. In: Cai, X., Yan, B. and Wu, H. (eds) *Domestic Tourism: Theory and Practice*. Li Jiang Press, Beijing, pp. 56–64. (In Chinese.)

Roehl, W.S. (1995) The June 4, 1989, Tiananmen Square incident and Chinese tourism. In: Lew, A.A. and Yu, L. (eds) *Tourism in China: Geographical, Political, and Economic Perspectives*. Westview Press, Boulder, Colorado, pp. 19–39.

Shen, Tong (1993) The warming up of China's domestic tourism. In: Sun, D. and Fan, J.J. (eds) *Hainan Province: Tourism Planning and Development*. Hainan International Press Center, Hainan, pp. 230–240.

Sun, Gang (ed.) (1995) *The Yearbook of China Tourism Statistics*. National Tourism Administration of the People's Republic of China, Beijing.

Tan, M. (1986) China tourism: big growth, immediate problems. *China Reconstructs* 35(6), 8–10.

Time (1999) Human rights. *Time*. http://cgi.pathfinder.com/time/daily/special/newschina/human.html (accessed 20 June, 1999).

WTO (1997) *Tourism Market Trends: East Asia and the Pacific, 1986–1996* and *Tourism Market Trends: South Asia, 1986–1996*. World Tourism Organization, Madrid.

Xinhua (1999) Tourism boom results in lack of guides in China. Xinhua, 18 June. http://customnews.cnn.com/cnews/pna.show_story?p_art_id=3870306

Xu, Gang (1999) Socio-economic impacts of domestic tourism in China: case studies in Guilin, Suzhou and Beidaihe. *Tourism Geographies* 1(2), 204–218.

Yu, L. (1995) China's hotel landscape: a marker of economic development and social change. In: Lew, A.A. and Yu, L. (eds) *Tourism in China: Geographical, Political, and Economic Perspectives*. Westview Press, Boulder, Colorado, pp. 89–105.

Yu, L. and Lew, A.A. (1997) Airline liberalization and development in China. *Pacific Tourism Review* 1(2), 129–136.

Zhang, Guangrui (1995) China's tourism development since 1978: policies, experiences, and lessons learned. In: Lew, A.A. and Yu, L. (eds) *Tourism in China: Geographical, Political, and Economic Perspectives*. Westview Press, Boulder, Colorado, pp. 3–17.

8

Japan and Tourism in the Pacific Rim: Locating a Sphere of Influence in the Global Economy

C. Michael Hall

Japan is undoubtedly one of the most significant players in the development of contemporary tourism in East Asia and typically is one of the top three international tourist generating countries for nearly all nations in the Asia–Pacific region. However, its market dominance is a relatively recent phenomenon, and dates from the spectacular growth in outbound travel from Japan during the 1980s, which continued relatively unabated until the 1997 Asian financial crisis. This cast a pall over not only the economies of East Asia but also over Japan, which entered into its most serious period of recession in the post-Second World War era.

Despite the Asian crisis, tourism is still extremely important to the region. Indeed, at a time of relatively high unemployment and low economic growth, tourism provides East Asian economies with an opportunity to gain needed foreign exchange and encourage renewed economic development. However, only a limited amount of research has focused on the Japanese tourism production system and its integration within the economy of the Pacific Rim (Yamamoto, 1998). Most research on Japanese tourism has been strongly orientated towards marketing, often focusing on the socio-cultural attributes of Japanese tourists and comparing them with other international market segments (e.g. Woodside and Jacobs, 1985; Yuan and McDonald, 1990; Pizam and Sussmann, 1995).

Ahmed and Krohn (1992), for example, listed ten distinctive cultural characteristics of Japanese tourists: belongingness, family influence, empathy, dependency, hierarchal acknowledgement, propensity to save, the concept of *kinen* (commemoration or souvenir), tourist photography, passivity and risk avoidance. By arguing that Japanese tourists might be unique, they perhaps reinforced stereotypes of the Japanese package tourist. By contrast, Cha *et al.* (1995) demonstrated substantial variations in Japanese travel motivations and identified three distinctive groups of Japanese outbound tourists: sports seekers, novelty seekers, and family/relaxation seekers. Similar indications of the heterogeneity of Japanese tourists come from regular reports of the Japan Travel Bureau (1991, 1996) and Nozawa's (1992) review of major shifts in Japanese outbound tourism in the late 1980s and 1990s, which revealed a decline in average travel expense, increased repeat travel, increased popularity of cheaper holidays, greater diversity in destination choice and an increase in independent tourism.

The shifts in Japanese society and the increased significance of consumerism have contributed significantly to changes in govern-ment policy. However, broader changes in the Japanese tourism production system and their relationship to government policy have received only marginal consideration (Yamamoto, 1998). This chapter examines the development of Japanese policy towards tourism in the Asia-Pacific and, in particular, to South-East Asia. It is argued that the undoubted importance of Japanese tourism in the region is best understood in the wider context of Japanese policies towards eco-nomic, foreign and (increasingly) social goals, and that this helps to explain not only the influence that Japan has had on the region's tourism, but also the role that tourism is likely to play in future Japanese policy towards the region.

Historical Development

Japanese outbound travel has been one of the most spectacular examples of outbound tourist growth in the modern era. Since the Tokyo Summer Olympics of 1964, when restrictions on outbound travel were lifted, Japanese travel overseas has shown consis-tently high growth, except for 1973–1974 (the first oil crisis), 1980 (the second oil crisis), 1991 (the Gulf War and recession) and 1998–1999 (the Asian crisis and domestic recession) (Tamao, 1980; Inoue, 1991; Morris, 1997; Oppermann, 1997).

In fact, Japanese tourism policies are pro-foundly different from those of other countries in the Asia-Pacific, with the possible exception of Taiwan (Republic of China), in that Japan seeks to encourage outbound tourism (Hitchcock et al., 1993; Go and Jenkins, 1997; Hall, 1997; Hall and Page, 1999). Travel-related expenditures are the third largest import category in Japan, behind min-eral fuels and machinery and equipment. In 1990 the number of Japanese travelling abroad reached 10.997 million travellers, ensuring that the plan to increase overseas travel known as the 'Ten Million Programme', launched in 1987, reached its target a year ahead of schedule. In 1989 Japan had the highest deficit travel account balance in the world, ahead of Germany (Japan Travel

Bureau, 1991), and in 1990 the travel trade balance of payments (balance of total travel and passenger fares) was in deficit by US$21.34 billion, a figure equivalent to one-third of the total trade surplus (US$63.5 bil-lion). By 1996 the travel deficit was almost US$33 billion and payments from tourism were almost 10 times those of the receipts, although there has been a subsequent lessen-ing in the travel trade gap in 1997 and 1998 (Table 8.1). Such figures may seem surprising for a nation that has had an export-led eco-nomic development strategy for most of the post-war period. However, it is precisely because of the aggressive export orientation of Japanese industry that tourism has become a significant tool of Japan's trade policy.

How Japan integrates itself with the Asian and world economies has been an important matter for the Japanese economy and Japanese policy-making since the 1950s (MITI, 1999a). Since the late 1970s and early 1980s, the trade imbalance of Japan with many countries has widened substantially, giving rise to trade disputes that involved not simply individual categories of goods and services but the wider economic and trading structure that produced such an imbalance. As the Ministry of International Trade and Industry (MITI) observed (MITI, 1998a), 'to defuse such trade friction and facilitate a smooth development of export has been an important job of [Japanese] trade policy'. Since the mid-1970s, the task of Japanese trade policy-makers was, in the short term, to assert that Japanese exporters did not engage in such unfair trade practices as dumping, and to limit exports to certain countries by taking the political and industrial conditions and market trends of recipient countries into con-sideration. In the longer term, Japan aimed to develop an export structure based on higher value-added goods, diversifying its export markets and maintaining a multifaceted inter-national trade system in the face of growing protectionist pressures. In particular, it aimed to recycle funds from its major trading part-ners, especially the USA, Europe and East Asia, by importing more goods and services from them. It is in the context of this last strat-egy that tourism has become particularly important (Hall, 1997; Morris, 1997).

Table 8.1. Japan's balance of trade in goods and services (US$ million).

	1991	1992	1993	1994	1995	1996	1997	1998
Balance of trade in goods and services	54,336	80,738	96,509	96,354	74,698	21,185	47,318	73,112
Balance of trade in goods	96,188	124,706	139,597	144,422	132,144	83,420	101,474	122,521
Balance of trade in services	−41,852	−43,968	−43,088	−48,068	−57,446	−62,235	−54,156	−49,409
Transport	−8,882	−8,685	−9,971	−11,383	−13,428	−12,025	−9,288	−7,102
Travel	−20,555	−23,249	−23,303	−27,238	−33,565	−32,965	−28,716	−25,036
Other private-sector services[a]	−12,411	−12,032	−9,811	−9,446	−10,448	−17,251	−16,147	−17,274

[a]Telecoms; Construction; Insurance; Finance; Information; Licence fees from patents; Other commercial services; Culture and entertainment.
Note: Dollar trade figures were calculated by JETRO using the dollar exchange rate (monthly average market rate) determined in accordance with the Ordinance on Foreign Exchange Transactions.
Source: prepared by JETRO from Balance of Payments Monthly (Bank of Japan) in JETRO (1999).

Over the period 1960 to 1999, only once (in 1962) has tourism been a net income earner for Japan. Throughout most of the 1960s Japan, like most other nations in the region, used inbound tourism as a source of foreign exchange and to fund economic development. However, as its export economy and the strength of the yen grew, so the economic potential of tourism was regarded as secondary to that based on the production of manufactured goods, in which Japan was regarded as having a stronger competitive advantage. Nevertheless, tourism was still seen as a relatively significant policy area, and outbound tourism was encouraged by government as a way of reducing trade imbalances with other nations in the region and of serving broader cultural, educative, diplomatic and policy goals, particularly at a time of significant stress in trade relationships.

A good example of the changed significance of tourism in Japanese government thinking was the shift in roles for the Japan National Tourist Organization (JNTO). Originally established in 1959 as the marketing organization responsible for attracting foreign tourists to Japan and promoting domestic tourism, since 1979 the JNTO has also been charged with facilitating the travel of Japanese overseas. The JNTO is clearly unusual in terms of the role of national tourist organizations on a global scale and highlights a significant departure from the tourism policies of most countries (Hall and Jenkins, 1995).

The changed functions of the national tourism organization have been accompanied by the development of a range of incentives to encourage travel overseas. Of these, the most significant was the 'Ten Million Programme' developed by the Department of Tourism in the Transport Policy Bureau of the Ministry of Transport and launched in September 1987. Aimed at doubling the annual number of Japanese tourists going abroad from 5.52 million in 1986 to 10 million in 1991, the Programme was designed to reduce Japan's large trade surplus (Table 8.2) and thus avoid potential conflicts with such major trading partners as the US and the European Community (Mak and White, 1992). It was also designed to contribute to the economic growth of countries in the Asia-Pacific which had started to become significant tourism destinations following Japanese aid and investment in the 1980s. Moreover, the Programme signalled the rapid development of a new phase of outbound tourism which sought to extend outbound travel from the first wave of outbound destinations in North-east Asia (e.g. Korea, Hong Kong, Taiwan and China) and North America (the US) to South-East Asia, especially to member countries of the Association of South-East Asian Nations (ASEAN) and Oceania (Australia, New Zealand and some of the Pacific Islands). The number of Japanese outbound tourists exceeded 10 million in 1990, and so the programme reached its target a year ahead of schedule (OECD, 1992).

Table 8.2. Trends in Japanese trade (US$ million, ¥ billion).

	1990	1991	1992	1993	1994	1995	1996	1997	1998	1999[a]
Exports										
Dollar basis	286,947	314,525	339,650	360,911	395,600	442,937	412,433	422,881	386,271	160,966
Change on previous year (%)	4.3	9.6	8.0	6.3	9.6	12.0	-6.9	2.5	-8.7	-0.4
Yen basis	41,457	42,360	43,012	40,202	40,498	41,531	44,731	50,938	50,645	18,936
Change on previous year (%)	9.6	2.2	1.5	-6.5	0.7	2.6	7.7	13.9	-0.6	-9.5
Imports										
Dollar basis	234,799	236,737	233,021	240,670	274,742	336,094	350,654	340,408	279,316	119,504
Change on previous year (%)	11.4	0.8	-1.6	3.3	14.2	22.3	4.3	-2.9	-17.9	-0.6
Yen basis	33,855	31,900	29,527	26,826	28,104	31,549	37,993	40,956	36,654	14,057
Change on previous year (%)	16.8	-5.8	-7.4	-9.1	4.8	12.3	20.4	7.8	-10.5	-9.7
Balance										
Dollar basis	52,149	77,789	106,628	120,241	120,858	106,843	61,779	82,474	106,955	41,462
Change on previous year (%)	-18.9	49.2	37.1	12.8	0.5	-11.6	-42.2	33.5	29.7	0.1
Yen basis	7,602	10,460	13,485	13,376	12,393	9,982	6,738	9,982	13,991	4,879
Change on previous year (%)	-14.0	37.6	28.9	-0.8	-7.3	-19.5	-32.5	48.1	40.2	-9.1

[a] January–May 1999.

Note: As Japan has only released trade statistics in yen since April 1998, dollar trade figures were calculated by JETRO based on rates announced by the Customs and Tariff Bureau.

Source: prepared by JETRO from Trade Statistics (Ministry of Finance, Japan) in JETRO (1999).

Although the Japanese government focused on the economic, foreign and trade policy benefits of the Ten Million Programme, the development of Japanese outbound tourism was considered more than economic in scope. For example, it was argued (Japan Travel Bureau, 1991: 68):

> The significance of promoting overseas travel goes beyond the simple attempt to reduce Japan's surplus in the international balance of trade. It must essentially be seen in the wider context of globalization, and in this sense, it is an important factor for Japan to adopt a more independent position in international society. Overseas travel lets the tourist experience the 'richness of leisure' and gain a hands-on contact with a different, foreign culture, thus acquiring an empirical knowledge which alone creates the breadth of mind that is capable of making cross-cultural and cross-human contacts.

Japanese travel overseas was undoubtedly seen to have significant cultural benefits. However, the economic contribution of Japanese outbound tourism to its Asian trading partners, in particular, enabled them, in turn, to purchase Japanese goods and thus furthered Japan's importance in Asian and world affairs. Moreover, the availability of overseas travel opportunities was an important component in the desire of many Japanese for a higher quality of life, which included increased leisure opportunities (Japan Travel Bureau, 1991, 1996; Harada, 1994). Authors such as Burns (1996) have questioned the real effect of the programme on outbound tourism numbers, but it can be noted that the Ten Million Programme was one of a range of government measures aimed to promote Japanese overseas travel. Such measures included the increased deregulation of the Japanese aviation industry, increased tax breaks for duty-free shopping, increased bilateral visa waiver arrangements, and more development funds for Japanese tourist destinations in South-East Asia and the South Pacific (Nozawa, 1992; Rimmer, 1994; Cha et al., 1995; Leheny, 1995).

Increased Flow of Japanese Tourists into South-East Asia

One of the most significant aspects of Japanese outbound tourism in the 1980s was the increased flow of Japanese tourists into South-East Asia. This occurred for several different but converging reasons: (i) increased attempts by the Japanese to improve diplomatic relations in the area following the Second World War and the subsequent role of development aid as a foreign policy tool; (ii) recognition that low labour and resource costs in the region provided opportunities for Japanese companies to locate plant offshore in order to maintain profits; (iii) a broader economic strategy which recognized the increased interdependency of the economies of the Asia-Pacific region as critical to the long-term growth of the export-based Japanese economy and therefore led to substantial foreign aid and investment; (iv) the need to use tourism as a means of balancing trade between the countries of the region and Japan; and (v) increased demand within Japan for leisure tourism and a greater variety of travel options.

Since 1985, Japanese firms have established a rapidly growing presence in the Asia-Pacific countries through direct investments (Table 8.3), becoming significant owners of tourism-orientated properties in numerous destinations in the region (Forsyth and Dwyer, 1996). In the late 1980s, these investments were often a means of firm diversification rather than a strategic development of Japanese overseas tourism by firms already operating in the domestic leisure and tourism field (Yamamoto, 1998), though such strategic developments have became more commonplace in the 1990s (Hall and Page, 1996, 1999; Hall, 1997). However, the Japanese government recognized that Japanese firms investing in other countries 'sometimes encounter various difficulties and get entangled in problems in their host countries' (MITI, 1998a). Throughout the Asia-Pacific region there was opposition to the increased Japanese investment in real estate, which included hotels and resort and golf complexes (Kuji, 1991; Edgington, 1994, 1995, 1996; Rimmer, 1994; Hall, 1997). The level of Japanese foreign investment in Australia, for example, was a major political issue in the late 1980s and again in the late 1990s. In the late 1980s, Japanese investment in the Australian tourism industry was around nine times as great as the next highest country. It accounted for almost 70% of all expected overseas investment in tourism, and over 90% of it was in Queensland (69%) and New South Wales (23%) (Dwyer *et al.*, 1990). The extent of Japanese investment led to protest meetings against Japanese and Asian investment in the resort areas of Queensland and northern New South Wales in 1989 and 1990 and, more recently, in 1998 and 1999, and contributed to the strength of the vote of the One Australia Party in State and Federal elections in Queensland and New South Wales. Indeed, it was for these very reasons that the MITI White Paper on International Trade (MITI, 1998a) emphasized that:

Japanese firms making direct investment in other countries must strive to win the acceptance of their host countries and their local communities as 'a good corporate citizen' so that their direct investments can contribute to long-term eco-

nomic development of their host countries by promoting locals to positions of responsibility, by fostering the development of related suppliers, and by mixing with members of the local communities.

Opposition to Japanese investment was not simply a legacy of the Second World War, nor was it prompted entirely by the fear of losing 'control' overseas. Attitudes towards Japanese tourism were substantially influenced by sex tourism and by changes in land use.

According to one estimate from the mid-1980s, 'between 70 and 80 per cent of male tourists who travel from Japan, the United States, Australia, and Western Europe to Asia do so solely for the purpose of sexual entertainment' (Gay, 1985: 34). This figure may be an exaggeration, and the true extent of Japanese sex tourism in the region is difficult to assess, but there was undoubtedly substantial demand for sexual services from Japanese

Table 8.3. Japanese direct investment in ASEAN 1989–1997 (¥ hundred million).

Country	Fiscal year								
	1989	1990	1991	1992	1993	1994	1995	1996	1997
Brunei Darussalam									
No. of cases	–	–	–	–	–	–	–	–	–
Value	–	–	–	–	–	15	15	–	–
Indonesia									
No. of cases	140	155	148	122	115	116	168	160	170
Value	631	1,105	1,193	1,676	952	1,808	1,548	2,720	3,085
Malaysia									
No. of cases	159	169	136	111	92	51	57	69	82
Value	673	725	880	704	892	772	555	644	971
Philippines									
No. of cases	87	58	42	45	56	75	100	75	64
Value	202	258	203	160	236	683	692	630	642
Singapore									
No. of cases	181	139	103	100	97	69	94	102	96
Value	1,902	840	613	670	735	1,101	1,143	1,256	2,238
Thailand									
No. of cases	403	377	258	130	127	126	147	196	154
Value	1,276	1,154	807	657	680	749	1,196	1,581	2,291
Vietnam									
No. of cases	–	–	–	8	12	25	54	65	45
Value	–	–	–	10	52	177	192	359	381
ASEAN									
No. of cases	970	898	687	516	499	462	620	667	611
Value	4,684	4,082	3,696	3,877	3,547	5,290	5,326	7,190	9,608
WORLD									
No. of cases	6,589	5,863	4,564	3,741	3,488	2,478	2,863	2,501	2,489
Value	67,540	56,911	41,584	34,138	41,513	42,809	49,568	54,094	66 229

Source: Ministry of Finance, Japan, in ASEAN Centre (1998, 1999).

men travelling in the region on business or on holiday. Such countries as Korea, Taiwan and Thailand catered for the Japanese sex tourism market, often with the support of governments that valued foreign exchange obtained from sex tourism as vital in furthering economic development (Hall, 1992; Leheny, 1995). It is also possible to interpret the provision of sexual service to the Japanese as an attempt to conform to what was considered a 'normal' part of doing business with Japanese (men) – that is, to satisfy what was considered to be Japanese cultural mores (Bishop and Robinson, 1998). For whatever reason, Japanese sex tourism was undoubtedly a significant component of Asian tourism in the 1970s and early 1980s. However, in the mid-1980s women's and human rights groups began vigorous campaigns against sex tourists, focusing especially on visits by Japanese government ministers and officials. According to Matsui (1987: 32), one result of these demonstrations was that 'after the joint campaign against sex tours by Japanese and Filipina women, the number of Japanese tourists to Manila decreased and the proportion of Filipina women coming to Japan increased!'.

The campaign against Japanese sex tourism had a major effect on the nature of Japanese tourist arrivals in the region (Richter, 1989) but demographic shifts in Japanese outbound tourism have also had a substantial impact on the Japanese market in the region. Since 1985, the proportions of travellers in the under-20s category, especially children, and of women in their 30s and 40s, have increased. In 1990, for example, the largest percentage of travellers were women in their 20s (15.8% of the market). By 1994 this figure had risen to 17.5% and women in this category made up almost 40% of all outbound women travellers (Japan Tourist Board, 1996). Indeed, it is only in the age categories of 30 and over that men dominate outbound travel. Reasons for this pattern appear to lie within Japanese social structure and the imperatives of gaining appropriate employment. At the same time, it is likely that over the longer term an increasing proportion of older women will travel overseas, as Western consumer patterns become enmeshed within Japanese society (Hall, 1997).

Other significant elements in Japanese tourism in the Asia-Pacific have been Japanese involvement in ski resorts and, more importantly, in what Kuji (1991) described as the 'political economy of golf'. Golf-related tourism throughout the Pacific Rim occurred for several reasons. Firstly, the popularity of the game in Japan and its growth as a leisure activity and status symbol has created demand for golfing holidays. Secondly, with far lower land and construction costs, clubs in South-East Asia and the Pacific have substantially lower membership fees than in Japan (Inoue, 1991). 'As a consequence, even with air fares and accommodation costs, it may still be cheaper to play golf in Malaysia or the Philippines than an élite club in Japan' (Mackie, 1992: 79). Thirdly, golf courses in Japan are increasingly opposed on environmental grounds, primarily because of pesticide use and negative impacts on the environment, and the construction of golf courses in developing countries may be a means of avoiding government regulation (Hall, 1997). At the same time, similar environmentalist objections are being voiced in South-East Asia, along with concern over the loss of agricultural land.

Despite such opposition to Japanese investment, the Japanese government recognized that Japan's long-term economic security was linked to an improved balance of trade with trading partners and that 'it behoved Japan, as a country running the world's largest trade surpluses, to increase imports and steadily recycle funds to needy countries' (MITI, 1998a). Indeed, since the late 1980s, in an effort to improve the terms of trade and retain company profit levels, foreign direct investment (FDI) by Japanese companies has rapidly increased. FDI outward stock increased fivefold between 1988 and 1998. A large portion of FDI by Japanese companies was directed toward Asia, which in the first half of 1997 accounted for 30% of the total Japanese FDI, as indicated in Tables 8.3 and 8.4 (MITI, 1999b). Significantly, despite the collapse of the 'bubble economy' in the early 1990s, Japanese FDI in East and South-East Asia has continued to grow relative to FDI in North America and Europe. Japanese FDI flows to North America and the European Union were reduced from 49% and 23% of the total, respectively, to 41% and 10% in 1996. By comparison, Japanese FDI flows to Asia increased from 11% of the total in 1993 to 36% in 1996. As Dicken and Yeung (1999: 113) observed, 'Most Japanese firms continue to extend their linkages and production networks into East and Southeast Asia, creating extremely complex intra-regional production chains and networks. As such, they provide perhaps the most important force for economic integration in Asia'.

Parallel to the growth in Japanese direct investment has been the provision of aid to the region, and Japan is the leading overseas development assistance (ODA) donor to 17 countries in Asia. In particular, East Asia is a special focus for Japanese ODA, and Japan accounted for nearly 60% of the total bilateral aid to this region during the 5-year period beginning in 1992 (MOFA, 1999a). Although exact figures are hard to ascertain, tourism-related projects appear to have taken up an increasing proportion of Japanese investment and aid to the Asia-Pacific, including the development of transport infrastructure such as airports (Muqbil, 1995). Tourism's links with wider trade and economic initiatives have also been noted, and it has been suggested that 'Japan sees regional tourism growth as being a major contributor to economic development, thereby making the Asia-Pacific countries more promising markets for Japanese goods and services' (Muqbil, 1995: 55).

The importance of Japan in the region's tourism is indicated in Tables 8.5 and 8.6. Between 1989 and 1996, Japanese outbound tourism to ASEAN countries increased by 82%, compared with an overall rate of outbound growth of 73% (Table 8.5). It is also significant that in 1997 and 1998 the decline in Japanese outbound tourism to the ASEAN region was greater than the overall decline in all Japanese outbound tourism. Despite this, Japanese tourism to ASEAN still remains extremely important and Japan remains the major non-ASEAN market for the majority of countries in the region (Table 8.6). However, Tables 8.5 and 8.6 also illustrate the extent to which tourism to the region and outbound tourism from Japan has been affected by the Asian financial crisis and by the Japanese economic recession of the late 1990s, and it is to the Japanese reaction to this crisis that this chapter now turns.

Table 8.4. Japan's overseas direct investment, by region.

Region	Fiscal year						Cumulative total	
	1995		1996		1997		1951–1997	
	No. of cases	Value (100m ¥)	No. of cases	Value (100m ¥)	No. of cases	Value (100m ¥)	No. of cases	Value (100m ¥)
North America	551	22,394	638	25,933	611	26,247	30,484	277,264
Central and South America	300	3,741	257	5,008	303	7,775	9,284	71,672
Asia	1,629	11,921	1,233	13,083	1,151	14,948	27,976	116,168
ASEAN	620	5,341	667	7,190	611	9,608	13,404	65,550
Brunei Darussalam	–	15	–	–	–	–	32	139
Indonesia	168	1,548	160	2,720	170	3,085	2,872	24,316
Malaysia	57	555	69	644	82	971	2,107	8,527
Philippines	100	692	75	630	64	642	1,307	4,781
Singapore	94	1,143	102	1,256	96	2,238	3,220	14,172
Thailand	147	1,196	196	1,581	154	2,291	3,603	12,252
Vietnam	54	192	65	359	45	381	263	1,363
Middle East	3	148	10	268	6	578	413	5,778
Europe	260	8,281	241	8,305	250	13,749	10,311	121,761
Africa	37	367	41	485	26	407	1,748	9,068
Oceania	83	2,716	81	1,011	142	2,525	5,144	33,817
Total	2,863	49,568	2,501	54,093	2,489	66,229	85,360	635,528

Source: Ministry of Finance, Japan, in MITI (1999b).

Table 8.5. Japanese travellers to ASEAN, 1990–1998.

	1990	1992	1994	1996	1998
Total overseas	10,997,431	11,790,699	13,578,934	16,694,769	15,806,218
Total ASEAN	2,581,007	2,441,701	2,905,526	3,654,275	3,054,169
Brunei Darussalam	2,521	3,013	3,511	–	6,639
Cambodia	–	–	–	33,039	5,646[a]
Indonesia	267,970	400,615	476,456	665,711	469,409
Laos	–	–	–	6,672	12,936
Malaysia	501,342	247,671	271,916	353,204	252,178
Myanmar	–	–	4,223	15,002	20,525
Philippines	201,982	221,578	277,825	350,242	361,631
Singapore	971,637	1,000,775	1,109,350	1,171,899	843,683
Thailand	635,555	568,049	694,649	940,196	986,264
Vietnam	–	–	67,596	118,310	92,258

[a]Figure from January to April.
Source: Statistics on Legal Migrants (Ministry of Justice, Japan); Respective National Tourist Offices;
Ministry of Finance, Negara, Brunei Darussalam, in ASEAN Centre (1998, 1999).

The Asian Financial Crisis and Japan's Response

The criticism that Japan triggered the Asian economic crisis is unfounded, but it is true that, after the outbreak of the economic crisis, Japan could not contribute to the recovery because its own economy was stagnating. East Asian countries had been highly dependent on exports to Japan, and Japan's imports from the region are more responsive to Japan's economic growth than to price fluctuations. East Asian economic recovery is therefore intimately tied to economic recovery in Japan, which, it is hoped, will be speedy and lead to ongoing economic growth (JETRO, 1999: 26).

The cause of the Asian financial crisis was primarily the collapse of property prices in Thailand in 1997, which led foreign creditors to call in loans to Thai financial institutions and, in turn, to a need for hard currency and the subsequent devaluation of the Thai baht. As a consequence, there was a loss of economic confidence throughout the wider region. However, other factors were also relevant, especially the poor state of the Japanese economy, which is a major importer of goods and services from the region (ESCAP, 1997; JETRO, 1999). Indeed, one of the key lessons of the Asian financial crisis was the high degree of economic interdependency in the region.

Economic interdependence between Japan and Asia developed steadily from the mid-1980s, when Japanese companies began to establish offshore operations and Japanese imports from the region showed marked increases, providing new markets for Asian economies. As the economies of the ASEAN nations and China grew at unprecedented rates, Japan and the newly industrializing economies (NIEs) continued to increase their consumption of imports and their industries continued to move offshore. As a result, Asia now has an extremely high degree of intraregional trade and investment interdependence (JETRO, 1999). The NIEs have been the major investors in ASEAN and China, followed by Japan. Trade interdependence within the region – including Japan and the nine East Asian countries (the four NIEs, four major ASEAN economies and China) – has risen as high as 52%. This is almost level with intraregional interdependence in the European Union (which is 61%), and exceeds that of North American Free Trade Agreement, at 48% (Arai, 1998). Around 40% of Japan's trade is now with Asia, which is also the destination for some 30% of Japanese total investment (Yosano, 1998).

As Kaoru Yosano (1998), the Japanese Minister of International Trade and Industry, noted:

Given this close economic relationship, rebuilding the Japanese economy will obviously have a

Table 8.6. Tourist arrivals and markets in ASEAN countries, 1996–1998.

ASEAN Country	Source of tourists	1996 Number	1996 %	1997 Number	1997 %	1998 Number	1998 %
Brunei Darussalam	ASEAN	581,199	93.4	569,967	88.6	861,712	89.4
	UK	8,137	1.3	23,420	3.6	31,500	3.3
	Australia	4,659	0.7	6,406	1.0	10,484	1.1
	Total	622,354	100.0	643,215	100.0	964,080	100.0
Cambodia[a]	France	–	–	–	–	7,049	10.2
	Taiwan	–	–	28,116	12.8	6,807	9.9
	Japan	–	–	25,362	11.6	–	–
	USA	–	–	20,291	9.3	6,323	9.2
	Total	260,489	100.0	218,843	100.0	68,783	100.0
Indonesia	ASEAN	1,832,548	36.4	2,066,857	39.9	2,101,671	45.6
	Japan	638,287	12.7	661,214	12.8	469,409	10.2
	Australia	361,234	7.2	458,733	8.8	394,543	8.6
	Total	5,034,472	100.0	5,185,243	100.0	4,606,416	100.0
Laos	ASEAN	301,450	74.8	353,266	76.3	364,227	72.8
	India	17,238	4.3	–	–	–	–
	China	16,707	4.1	17,661	3.8	–	–
	USA	–	–	14,442	3.1	20,174	4.0
	France	–	–	–	–	17,863	3.6
	Total	403,000	100.0	463,200	100.0	500,200	100.0
Malaysia	ASEAN	5,206,348	72.9	4,440,532	71.5	3,835,735	69.1
	Japan	353,204	4.9	308,902	5.0	252,178	4.5
	Taiwan	236,601	3.3	207,776	3.3	159,447	2.9
	Total	7,138,452	100.0	6,210,921	100.0	5,550,748	100.0
Myanmar	Japan	–	–	24,014	9.1	20,525	7.5
	Taiwan	–	–	23,722	8.9	28,190	10.3
	France	–	–	12,222	4.6	11,680	4.3
	Total	–	–	265,122	100.0	273,858	100.0
Philippines	USA	373,953	18.2	427,431	19.2	468,808	21.8
	Japan	350,242	17.1	376,714	16.9	361,631	16.8
	Taiwan	206,708	10.1	246,370	11.1	185,869	8.6
	Total	2,049,367	100.0	2,222,523	100.0	2,149,357	100.0
Singapore	ASEAN	2,255,948	30.9	2,343,969	32.6	1,878,628	30.1
	Japan	1,171,899	16.1	1,094,040	15.2	843,683	13.5
	Taiwan	528,485	7.2	499,782	6.9	–	–
	Australia	–	–	–	–	427,216	6.8
	Total	7,292,521	100.0	7,197,963	100.0	6,240,984	100.0
Thailand	Malaysia	1,046,169	14.5	1,029,107	14.3	918,071	11.7
	Japan	940,196	13.1	972,056	13.5	986,264	12.6
	S. Korea	506,868	7.0	–	–	–	–
	China	–	–	452,510	6.3	–	–
	Singapore	–	–	–	–	586,113	7.5
	Total	7,192,145	100.0	7,221,345	100.0	7,842,760	100.0
Vietnam	China	377,555	23.5	405,279	23.6	420,743	27.7
	Taiwan	175,486	10.9	154,566	9.0	138,529	9.1
	USA	–	–	–	–	176,578	11.6
	Japan	118,810	7.4	122,083	7.1	–	–
	Total	1,607,155	100.0	1,715,637	100.0	1,520,128	100.0

[a]Figures for first quarter. Estimated total for 1998 was 177,500.
Sources: Economic Planning Unit, Ministry of Finance, Brunei Darussalam; Ministry of Interior, Cambodia; Directorate General of Tourism, Department of Tourism, Arts and Culture, Indonesia; Ministry of National Planning and Economic Development, Myanmar; National Tourism Authority of Laos PDR; Malaysia Tourism Promotion Board; Department of Tourism, Philippines; Singapore Tourist Promotion Board; Tourism Authority of Thailand; Vietnam National Administration of Tourism.

direct bearing on Asian economic recovery by stimulating Japanese trade and investment with Asia. Similarly, rebuilding the Asian economy will have a substantial positive impact on the Japanese economy.

Undoubtedly, Japan's economic links with East Asia enable it to wield considerable influence in the region. However, because of interdependence within the region, individual countries in East Asia and such groupings as ASEAN can, in turn, exert influence on Japanese trade policy. It is for this reason that Japan so emphasizes rules for maintaining and developing multilateral trading systems for goods and services, and the role of the World Trade Organization is pivotal, as are such regional initiatives as Asia-Pacific Economic Cooperation (APEC) and the ASEAN Free Trade Area (Arai, 1998; MITI, 1999a,b,c,e; Yosano, 1999). Over the long term, multilateral trade agreements will substantially affect tourism, especially within APEC, where tourism is considered 'a means of generating benefits for all member economies' with an 'important role' in fostering regional economic development and cooperation (APEC, 1993). However, in the short and mid-term, Japan's influence will continue to be crucial.

Since the Second World War, Japan has implemented numerous economic measures to stimulate economic recovery (MITI, 1998b, 1999e). It is restoring and restructuring its financial system and promoting a series of economic structural reforms, especially supporting new, small businesses in the private sector and assisting in the creation of new industries (MITI, 1999e). In April 1998, the largest-ever package of emergency economic measures (16 trillion yen, or US$119 billion) was adopted, with a supplementary budget passed in June of that year. These measures, with implementation of the budget for the 1998 financial year, were underpinned by new corporate and income tax cuts worth well over 6 trillion yen, or US$44 billion. In addition, a second supplementary budget of more than 10 trillion yen (US$74 billion) was formulated in an effort to revive domestic demand. According to Minister Yosano (1998), 'this domestic demand-led economic recovery will help to restore the Asian economy by providing Asian economies with the stable mar-

ket indispensable for Asian economic growth'. In addition to these ostensibly domestic measures, Japan has also undertaken a number of direct assistance measures for Asia valued at approximately US$44billion as of November 1998 (MOFA, 1999c). These measures included: (i) bilateral cooperation in the context of the International Monetary Fund (IMF)-led assistance package; (ii) assistance for private investment activities; (iii) facilitation of trade financing; (iv) assistance to the socially vulnerable; (v) assistance for economic structural reforms; and (vi) assistance for human resources development.

Japan has also designed a programme to improve the business environment and create new industries. Known as the 'Program for the 15 New and Growing Fields' (MITI, 1999d), it is designed to develop a business environment through deregulation, strengthened technological development and human resource development. The focus is on 15 sectors selected for their high growth potential, including biotechnology, business support, energy, environment, housing, internationalization, marine industries, medicine and welfare, new production technologies and the urban environment. The Japanese government predicts that employment in these sectors will expand from approximately 10.6 million people in 1995 to about 18 million in 2010, and the market scale from about 200 trillion yen in 1995 to about 500 trillion yen in 2010, with as many as 100,000 businesses starting during this period (Yosano, 1998; MITI, 1999d,e).

Tourism expansion is explicitly envisaged within the field entitled 'culture and living' and there is a call for 'the development of sophistication of leisure-related industries such as tourism' (MITI, 1999d). This is to occur on the domestic front, but will also be integrated with international tourism services through the growth of international airport hubs and the deregulation of the domestic aviation market (MITI, 1999d). Increased leisure opportunities are considered integral to a more favourable quality of life in Japan (Economic Planning Agency, 1999). In addition, the Ministry of Foreign Affairs specifically recommended the promotion of two-way interaction between people in Japan and Asian countries and called for the formulation and implementation of 'long-term, large-scale programs for human exchange' through relaxing the constraints on human exchange, particularly through improved international air links and international airport hub development, and 'simplification and acceleration of immigration, quarantine, and customs procedures' (MOFA, 1999b).

At the domestic level, then, tourism is an important component of economic and social policy, and its expansion also furthers the goals of foreign policy, especially in boosting the economies of Asian trading partners. Domestic measures are thus linked to Asian economic stability, while direct assistance to Asian countries is also intended to assist Japanese companies operating in Asia. Japanese companies in ASEAN, for example, account for almost 20% of ASEAN gross domestic product (Yosano, 1998). At the same time, Japanese overseas aid also serves to integrate further the Asian and the Japanese economies.

Ironically, as a consequence of the Asian economic crisis, the balance of trade between Japan and East Asia has shown substantial improvement (Table 8.7). The simultaneous fall in imports and exports between Japan and East Asia and the decline in the export value of services (Table 8.8) were largely due to a

Table 8.7. Japan's trade balance, by region (US$ million).

	1992	1993	1994	1995	1996	1997	1998	1999[a]
World	106,628	120,241	120,858	106,843	61,779	82,474	106,955	41,462
USA	43,563	50,169	54,901	45,451	32,553	41,617	51,069	21,624
EU	31,194	26,263	22,000	21,479	13,645	20,621	32,257	13,420
East Asia	41,942	53,988	62,205	71,026	51,527	53,324	30,589	10,770
Asian NIEs	46,470	53,536	62,443	69,818	60,786	66,203	49,327	18,929
ASEAN4	476	3,744	8,646	15,200	9,402	7,402	−1,864	−895
China	−5,004	−3,292	−8,884	−13,991	−18,660	−20,281	−16,874	−7,264
Middle East	−14,999	−15,181	17,929	−22,901	−25,626	−27,901	−13,057	−6,013
Latin America	7,120	8,556	9,150	7,772	6,452	9,687	11,613	3,996
Russia, Central and Eastern Europe	−1,173	−1,152	2,166	−3,478	−2,691	−2,635	−1,374	−805
Africa	3,130	3,568	2,842	2,800	801	619	1,960	774

[a]1999 figures are for January–May, year-on-year change.
Source: prepared by JETRO from Trade Statistics (Ministry of Finance, Japan) in JETRO (1999).

Table 8.8. Trends in value of exports of services, 1995–1998 (US$ billion).

	1995	1996	1997	1998	Change (%)	Share
World	1193	1274	1318	1290	−2.1	100.0
Japan	64	66	68	61	−10.8	4.7
East Asia[a]	160	178	188	151	−19.6	11.7
Asian NIEs	101	107	111	93	−16.6	7.2
Republic of Korea	22	23	25	24	−7.4	1.8
Taiwan	15	16	17	17	−2.3	1.3
Hong Kong	34	38	38	34	−10.5	2.6
Singapore	30	30	30	18	−40.0	1.4
ASEAN4	41	50	52	35	−32.4	2.7
Malaysia	11	14	15	11	−26.8	0.8
Thailand	15	17	16	13	−18.0	1.0
Philippines	–	9	13	158	−49.6	0.6
Indonesia	–	5	6	74	−39.6	0.3
China	18	21	25	23	−6.0	1.8

[a]Figures for East Asia are totals for the nine economies of the Asian NIEs, ASEAN4 and China.
Source: after JETRO (1999).

Table 8.9. ASEAN and Japan balance of international tourist receipts and expenditures, 1989–1997 (US$ million).

Country	1989	1990	1991	1992	1993	1994	1995	1996	1997
Cambodia									
Receipts	–	–	–	50	48	34	53	82	69
Payments	–	–	–	–	4	8	8	15	13
Balance	–	–	–	–	44	26	45	67	56
Indonesia									
Receipts	1,628	2,153	2,515	3,051	3,651	4,575	5,229	6,184	6,648
Payments	722	836	969	1,166	1,539	1,900	2,172	2,399	2,411
Balance	906	1,317	1,546	1,885	2,112	2,675	3,057	3,785	4,237
Laos									
Receipts	–	3	8	18	34	43	51	62	54
Payments	–	–	6	10	11	18	30	22	21
Balance	–	3	2	8	23	25	21	40	33
Malaysia									
Receipts	1,036	1,684	1,783	2,028	2,190	3,367	3,969	4,477	3,741
Payments	1,365	1,450	1,584	1,770	1,838	1,994	2,314	2,575	2,478
Balance	–329	234	199	258	352	1,373	1,655	1,902	1,263
Myanmar									
Receipts	–	20	11	91	–	–	–	–	–
Payments	–	16	24	16	–	–	–	–	–
Balance	–	4	–13	75	–	–	–	–	–
Philippines									
Receipts	469	466	570	944	1,178	973	1,136	1,546	2,341
Payments	77	111	61	102	130	196	422	1,266	1,935
Balance	392	355	509	842	1,048	777	714	280	406
Singapore									
Receipts	3,359	4,650	4,616	5,730	6,392	6,781	7,747	7,483	6,359
Payments	1,334	1,803	1,843	2,521	3,145	3,898	5,066	5,800	6,137
Balance	2,025	2,847	2,773	3,209	3,247	2,883	2,681	1,683	222
Thailand									
Receipts	3,754	4,325	4,537	5,092	5,638	6,063	8,035	9,089	7,660
Payments	746	1,432	1,900	2,461	3,040	4,065	4,271	4,286	3,416
Balance	3,008	2,893	2,637	2,631	2,598	1,998	3,764	4,803	4,244
Japan									
Receipts	3,150	3,590	3,434	3,591	3 552	3,478	3,224	4,083	4,330
Payments	22,500	24,930	23,949	26,824	26 846	30,703	36,764	37,050	33,010
Balance	–19,350	–21,340	–20,515	–23,233	–23 294	–27,225	–33,540	–32,967	–28,680

Source: Balance of Payments Statistics Yearbook 1998 (IMF) in ASEAN Centre (1998, 1999).

decline in the value of tourism exports over the period 1989 to 1997, as indicated in Table 8.9. Governments in the region therefore face substantial policy issues in attempting to address the problems posed by the Asian economic crisis. While the improved balance of trade between East Asian countries and Japan would normally be regarded as a positive indicator of economic development, the fall in exports places additional pressures on the domestic economies and the desire to increase levels of employment and fulfil social and environmental goals. In this situation,

tourism will remain an important industry, because many Asian countries have competitive advantages in the provision of resort infrastructure and labour costs and enjoy favourable exchange rates.

The Japanese government continues to utilize travel and tourism as a form of development assistance, and tourism offsets Japanese exports to the region and meets domestic demand for increased leisure opportunities. Given Japan's economic importance in the region, and its role as a major provider of tourists, Japanese government policy will continue to influence tourism in Asia for the fore-seeable future. More generally, this chapter has also indicated the extent to which the government of a major tourist-generating country can influence tourism development, and this raises substantial questions over the degree to which minimizing trade barriers in the global economy may reinforce the influence of certain generating nations on the political economy of tourism.

References

Ahmed, Z.U. and Krohn, F.B. (1992) Understanding the unique consumer behavior of Japanese tourists. *Journal of Travel and Tourism Marketing* 1(3), 73–86.

APEC (1993) *Ministerial Statement.* Asia-Pacific Economic Cooperation Working Group on Tourism, Seattle, 19 November, 1993. http://apec-tourism.org/ministerial-statement/

Arai, H. (1998) *A Scenario for Dynamic Recovery from the Asian Economic Crisis.* Thai-Japanese Association and JETRO Bangkok, Bangkok, Thailand, 21 August, 1998. (Hisamitsu Arai, Vice-Minister for International Affairs, MITI, Tokyo.)

ASEAN Centre (1998) *Statistics.* ASEAN Promotion Centre on Trade, Investment and Tourism, Chuo-ku, Tokyo. http://www.asean.or.jp/e_st/est.html

ASEAN Centre (1999) *Statistics.* ASEAN Promotion Centre on Trade, Investment and Tourism, Chuo-ku, Tokyo. http://www.asean.or.jp/e_st/est.html

Bishop, R. and Robinson, L.S. (1998) *Night Market: Sexual Cultures and the Thai Economic Miracle.* Routledge, New York.

Burns, P.M. (1996) Japan's Ten Million Programme: the paradox of statistical success. *Progress in Tourism and Hospitality* 2(2), 181–192.

Cha, S., McCleary, K.W. and Uysal, M. (1995) Travel motivations of Japanese overseas travellers: a factor-cluster segmentation approach. *Journal of Travel Research* 34(Summer), 33–39.

Dicken, P. and Yeung, H.W. (1999) Investing in the future: East and South-East Asian firms in the global economy. In: Olds, K., Dicken, P., Kelly, P.F., Kong, L. and Yeung, H.W. (eds) *Globalisation and the Asia-Pacific: Contested Territories.* Routledge, London, pp. 107–128.

Dwyer, L., Forsyth, P. and Findlay, C. (1990) Japanese investment in the Australian tourism industry: rationales and consequences. *Asian Studies Association of Australia 8th Annual Conference,* Griffith University, Nathan, July.

Economic Planning Agency (1999) *White Paper on the National Lifestyle (Fiscal Year 1999): Toward a Society of Higher Quality of Life with Flexible Job Opportunities for People to Choose – Main Points,* December 1999. Economic Planning Agency, Government of Japan, Tokyo.

Edgington, D.W. (1994) The new wave: patterns of Japanese direct foreign investment in Canada during the 1980s. *The Canadian Geographer* 38(1), 28–36.

Edgington, D.W. (1995) The search for paradise: Japanese property investments in North America. *Journal of Property Research* 12, 240–261.

Edgington, D.W. (1996) Japanese real estate investment in Canadian cities and regions, 1985–1993. *The Canadian Geographer* 40(4), 292–305.

ESCAP (1997). *Asia and the Pacific into the Twenty-first Century: Opportunities and Challenges for the ESCAP Region.* Economic and Social Commission for Asia and the Pacific, Bangkok.

Forsyth, P. and Dwyer, L. (1996) Tourism in the Asia-Pacific region. *Asia-Pacific Economic Literature* 10(1), 13–21.

Gay, J. (1985) The patriotic prostitute. *The Progressive* 49(3), 34–36.

Go, F. and Jenkins, C. (eds) (1997) *Tourism and Economic Development in Asia and Australasia.* Cassell, London.

Hall, C.M. (1992) Sex tourism in South-East Asia. In: Harrison, D. (ed.) *Tourism and the Less Developed Countries.* Belhaven Press, London, pp. 64–74.

Hall, C.M. (1997) *Tourism in the Pacific Rim,* 2nd edn. Addison Wesley Longman, South Melbourne, Australia.

Hall, C.M. and Jenkins, J. (1995) *Tourism and Public Policy.* Routledge, London.

Hall, C.M. and Page, S. (eds) (1996) *Tourism in the Pacific: Issues and Cases.* Routledge, London.

Hall, C.M. and Page, S. (eds) (1999) *Tourism in South and Southeast Asia.* Butterworth-Heinemann, Oxford, UK.

Harada, M. (1994) Towards a renaissance of leisure in Japan. *Leisure Studies* 13(4), 277–287.

Hitchcock, M., King, V. and Parnwell, M. (eds) (1993) *Tourism in South East Asia.* Routledge, London.

Inoue, R. (1991) An army of Japanese tourists. AMPO, *Japan-Asia Quarterly Review* 22(4), 2–10.

Japan Travel Bureau (1991) *JTB Report '91: All About Japanese Overseas Travellers.* Japan Travel Bureau, Tokyo.

Japan Travel Bureau (1996) *JTB Report '96: All About Japanese Overseas Travellers.* Japan Travel Bureau, Tokyo.

JETRO (1999) *JETRO White paper on International Trade Fall in Prices Causes Slowdown in World Trade* (Summary). Japan External Trade Organization, Tokyo.

Kuji, T. (1991) The political economy of golf. AMPO, *Japan-Asia Quarterly Review* 22(4), 47–54.

Leheny, D. (1995) A political economy of Asian sex tourism. *Annals of Tourism Research* 22(2), 367–384.

Mackie, V. (1992) Japan and South-East Asia: the international division of labour and leisure. In: Harrison, D. (ed.) *Tourism and the Less Developed Countries.* Belhaven Press, London, pp. 75–84.

Mak, J. and White, K. (1992) Comparative tourism development in Asia and the Pacific. *Journal of Travel Research* (summer), 14–23.

Matsui, Y. (1987) The prostitution areas in Asia: an experience. *Women in a Changing World* 24 (November), 27–32.

MITI (1998a) *White Paper on International Trade 1998.* Ministry of International Trade and Industry, Tokyo.

MITI (1998b) *Emergency Measures for the Economic Stabilization of South-East Asia (Provisional Translation by MITI,* Cabinet Decision, 20 February 1998. Ministry of International Trade and Industry, Tokyo.

MITI (1999a) *White Paper on International Trade 1999.* Ministry of International Trade and Industry, Tokyo.

MITI (1999b) *Summary of Interim Report Sub-Committee on Trade and Investment, WTO Committee, Industrial Structure Council,* 16 February, 1999. Ministry of International Trade and Industry, Tokyo.

MITI (1999c) *Summary of Interim Report Sub-Committee on Service Trade WTO Committee Industrial Structure Council,* 16 February, 1999. Ministry of International Trade and Industry, Tokyo.

MITI (1999d) *Strategy for Revitalizing Industry,* 29 January, 1999. Ministry of International Trade and Industry, Tokyo.

MITI (1999e) *Fiscal 2000 Priority Trade and Industry Policies,* 1 August, 1999. Ministry of International Trade and Industry, Tokyo.

MOFA (1999a) *Japan's Medium-Term Policy on Official Development Assistance (ODA),* 10 August, 1999. Ministry of Foreign Affairs, Tokyo.

MOFA (1999b) *Report of the Mission for Revitalization of Asian Economy: Living in Harmony with Asia in the Twenty-first Century,* November 1999. Ministry of Foreign Affairs, Tokyo.

MOFA (1999c) *Asian Economic Crisis and Japan's Contribution,* November 1999. Ministry of Foreign Affairs, Tokyo.

Morris, S. (1997) Japan: the characteristics of the inbound and outbound markets. In: Go, F.M. and Jenkins, C.L. (eds) *Tourism and Economic Development in Asia and Australasia.* Cassell, London, pp. 150–175.

Muqbil, I. (1995) Japanese aid and investment assistance for Asia-Pacific tourism. *Travel and Tourism Analyst* 3, 54–65.

Nozawa, H. (1992) A marketing analysis of Japanese outbound travel. *Tourism Management* 13(2), 226–234.

OECD (1992) *International Tourism Policies of OECD Members.* Organization for Economic Cooperation and Development, Paris.

Oppermann, M. (1997) The outbound tourism cycle and the Asian tourism tigers. In: Oppermann, M. (ed.) *Pacific Rim Tourism.* CAB International, Wallingford, UK, pp. 60–81.

Pizam, A. and Sussmann, S. (1995) Does nationality affect tourist behaviour? *Annals of Tourism Research* 22(4), 901–917.

Richter, L.K. (1989) *The Politics of Tourism in Asia.* University of Hawaii Press, Honolulu, Hawaii.

Rimmer, P.J. (1994) Japanese investment in golf course development: Australia–Japan links. *International Journal of Urban and Regional Research* 18(2), 234–255.

Saludo, R. and Shameen, A. (1998) How much longer? *AsiaWeek* 17 July.

Tamao, T. (1980) Tourism within, from and to Japan. *International Social Science Journal* 32(1), 128–150.

Woodside, A.G. and Jacobs, L.W. (1985) Step two in benefit segmentation: learning the benefits realized by major travel markets. *Journal of Travel Research* 24(1), 7–13.

Yamamoto, D. (1998) The Japanese tourism production system: a case study of Whistler, British Columbia. Unpublished Masters thesis, Simon Fraser University, Burnaby, Colorado.

Yosano, K. (1998) *Revitalizing Japanese and ASEAN Economies.* Speech by Kaoru Yosano, Minister of International Trade and Industry, 23 September, 1998, Singapore. Ministry of International Trade and Industry, Tokyo.

Yosano, K. (1999) Remarks by Kaoru Yosano, Minister of International Trade and Industry, Japan, at the APEC CEO Summit, 11 September, 1999, Auckland, New Zealand. Ministry of International Trade and Industry, Tokyo.

Yuan, S. and McDonald, C. (1990) Motivational determinates of international pleasure time. *Journal of Travel Research* 24(1), 42–44.

9

Indian Tourism: Policy, Performance and Pitfalls

Shalini Singh

Introduction

India is often referred to as a legendary country and a mysterious destination for potential visitors, particularly from distant parts of the globe. It presents a diversity of rare natural and cultural endowments, scattered abundantly across its length and breadth, and the quality of its resources rank from the most bizarre to the familiar assets of the Asian region. The reactions of first-time visitors to India are similarly varied: it can be shocking, mysterious, exciting, breath-taking and traditional.

Politically, India is in a strategic position. The Indian Ocean is to the south; to the north is the Asian mainland, with borders to Pakistan, China, Tibet, Nepal, Bhutan, Burma and Bangladesh. As a consequence, India's policies must be finely tuned in order to maintain balance and cooperation in the region.

Geologically and geographically, too, India is a land of great diversity. In the north, tectonic activities produced the extra-peninsular mountainous region of the Himalayas, while to the south are the rich volcanic fluvial deposits of the Gondwanalands of peninsular India. The Himalayas cordon off the subcontinent from mainland Asia and probably constitute the single greatest influence on the life, culture and history of the subcontinent (Pal, 1989).

The forbidding Greater Himalayas pose the greatest challenge to the most adventurous mountaineers. Still lower, in the Middle Himalayas, deep cutting rivers spring out, in sheer defiance of the tough terrain, affording ample scope for river adventures. Within the middle and the lesser Himalayan tracts, summer resorts and spectacular wildlife sanctuaries and parks can be found. Most resorts have British origins and are the favourite hill destinations for tourists from India as well as from overseas.

The Himalayas thus offer many forms of tourism activities. Singh (1989: 231) identified four distinct typologies of tourism in this region: pilgrimage; climate resorts; mass tourism; and, wanderlust, wildlife and wilderness tourism.

Bordering the North-West Frontier is the Thar desert, its flat rocky areas dominated by still larger areas of sand dunes in the west while its north-eastern edge is contained by the oldest mountain ranges of the Aravallis. The desert is largely in Rajasthan, where the Rajputs once held sole sovereignty, bequeathing to the region their distinctive culture and history. Today, much of the Thar desert is designated as the Thar Desert National Park (3000 km^2) and is highly suitable for desert and heritage tourism.

India's southern boundary is defined by the Indian Ocean. The peninsula's coastline, including the islands of Andaman and Nicobar, measures some 7500 km. In the southern parts the eastern seaboard is known as the Coromandel, while the western half is the Malabar, where Kerala's backwaters are the major attraction. North of the Malabar coast-line, in the state of Goa, is the Konkan stretch that harbours some of the world's best beaches, offering tourists the charms of sea, sand and sun. The eastern end of the coastline fades into the huge Gangetic delta, a complex mesh of distributaries interspersed with rich deltaic soil. This triangular patch roughly forms the Sundarbans region of marshy and swampy wet-land enriched with flora and fauna. The western extremity of the coast blends into the heavily dissected cliffs of the western ghats, in the Rann of Kutch (Gujarat), forming a unique ecosystem.

Enclosed within these natural boundaries, the interior of the Indian subcontinent com-prises the fertile plains in the northern parts, the Deccan Plateau in the centre and undulating topography in the southernmost patches. Most of these areas are repositories of rich diverse bio-species. The northern Indo-Gangetic plains, formed by the twin sacred rivers the Ganga and the Yamuna, are largely agricultural, but they also have a high concentration of religious cen-tres that continue to dot the Himalayan foothills and spread further upwards into the higher Himalayas. In fact, religion and religious activities dominate the cultural kaleidoscope of India and shrines drawing national and interna-tional believers of practically all faiths are prominent on its cultural map.

History, too, has been generous in its endowment of living cultures and antiquities. The result is a unique and vibrant mosaic that includes pre-Vedic archaeological ruins of the Indus Valley civilization in the west and north-west quadrant, the vestiges of the Vedic period (still alive in every sphere of Indian lifestyle and ideals), the temple art of the Hindu maharajas, the tangible and intangible her-itage of Buddhist and Jain cults, the forts, *mahals* and *havelis* of the chivalrous Rajputana clan, the architectural genres of Muslim and Mughal dynasties, and the rela-tively recent heritage of the British Raj, espe-cially in the hill region.

Indian Tourism

If travel and tourism are ways of enlightening the spirit and broadening the mind, they have been practised for centuries in India, whose peoples have long expressed a common sense of community in organized religion. That said, the purpose was less to gain liberation from work and more to liberate the soul (Kaur, 1985). *Tirth Yatras* (pilgrimages) have a long history (Bharadwaj, 1973; Sherring, 1975; Jha, 1985, 1991) and have been taken by people of all ages, especially the elderly. In particular, a distinct expression of senior tourism is found in the pursuit of *nirvana* (salvation).

As Tyagi (1991: 9) made clear, the British were not the first in India to escape the sum-mer heat by retreating to the hills, but they certainly did much to develop hill resorts (Singh, 1975; Sen, 1989). However, it was not until the mid-1940s, the fading years of the Raj, that the colonial government started to consider tourism seriously as a source of rev-enue. Under the chairmanship of Sir John Sargent, a committee was formed to discuss the matter. A year later, it was concluded that tourism could be a veritable money-spinner and a separate organization was formed to promote tourism. In 1948, the newly indepen-dent government formed an ad hoc Tourist Traffic Committee and in 1949 a separate Tourist Traffic branch was set up in the Ministry of Transport. Since then, successive governments have attempted to promote both domestic and international tourism. However, in those early years, government officials had little awareness of the need for proper product development and management in tourist desti-nations, and this ignorance and indifference towards the needs of the tourism industry con-tinues to this day.

The Asian context

In global terms, India's tourism industry is barely visible. Nevertheless, in the South Asian context it accounts for about 50% of arrivals and 70% of receipts. This has been so for about a decade, but the rate of increase in arrivals is low. From 1996 to 1997, for exam-ple, it was only 3.8%, compared with 21.2%

in Sri Lanka (Table 9.1). Western tourists began to discover cheaper destinations in Asia, where prices have been much reduced in response to the financial crisis (WTO, 1998a: 7).

Despite this trend, the impact on tourist arrivals has been relatively slight. Asia has a strong intra-regional market and, in any case, the Asian crisis can hardly be responsible for the sluggish performance of India's tourism industry, as a major proportion of its market lies in the West. More generally, although the future of the region's tourism, and that of India in particular, looks rather hazy, there are grounds for optimism. The headquarters of the Pacific Asia Travel Association has recently been moved to Bangkok and there is an increasing interest in the relatively unexplored 'exotic' destinations of the East.

Domestic tourism

In some respects, India might be considered a forerunner in the development of religious tourism. More than 94% of its domestic tourists are religious travellers, and traditional religion is clearly the mainstay of the country's domestic tourism. In general, tour operators are in the private sector and there are about 120 reputable, established companies in the country, with many others of more questionable standards. In 1997, the Indian operation of Resorts Condominiums International reported a healthy growth, with over 100,000 members in India and 59 affiliated resorts in just 4.5 years of its operation (*Indian Express*, 30 March, 1997).

The railways provide easy and cheap travel for the masses, who have a considerable range of accommodation from which to choose.

Several options are available for domestic tourists. *Janata* hotels provide budget accommodation for middle-income groups, and *Yatri Niwas* (literally, 'travellers stay-home') is the mid-priced hotel category budget accommodation offered by the Indian Tourism Development Corporation (ITDC). By contrast, *Dharamshalas*, established by religious groups for pilgrims, are generally located at religious centres and are used not only by pilgrims but also by scholars, merchants and adventure tourists. They are a valuable feature of Indian culture. *Yatrikas* are more secular inns, but may also be located in and around religious centres. Other accommodation is found in bungalows and the residences of friends and relatives.

Increases in income are being reflected in different forms of tourism. As prosperity filters down the social scale, business tourism, adventure tourism, visits to friends and other forms of domestic leisure tourism are increasing (Table 9.2).

In recent years, therapeutic/health tourism and ecotourism have gained in importance. The state of Kerala has taken a lead in establishing centres where traditional medicine is used to treat patients with curable and incurable diseases. This South Indian state also attracts the major share of ecotourists to its natural and cultural attractions. Elsewhere, the princely state of Rajasthan has created an ecotourism niche by offering camel safaris (Shackley, 1998). The Himalayan states cooperated in promoting ecotourism as early as the 1980s and, as a result of their experience of this kind of tourism, they developed a voluntary consultative mechanism, later known as the Himalayan Tourism Advisory Board, which later graduated into a policy-making organization (Ravendran, 1998: 139).

Table 9.1. Top five tourism destinations in South Asia.

Country	Arrivals 1997 (000)	Change: 1996–1997 (%)	Percentage of 1997 total for South Asia
India	2374	3.8	51.1
Iran	580	2.3	12.5
Nepal	418	6.1	9.0
Sri Lanka	366	21.2	7.9
Maldives	366	8.0	7.9
Total	4104	41.4	88.4
Total South Asia	4648	4.8	100.0

Source: WTO (1998c: 25).

Table 9.2. Domestic tourism in India: 1990–1999.

Year	Tourist visits	Percentage change 1990–1999
1990	63,970,024	26.4
1991	66,670,303	4.2
1992	81,293,841	21.9
1993	86,312,554	6.2
1994	123,371,730	42.9
1995	139,129,130	12.8
1996	141,170,657	1.5
1997	131,000,000	7.2
1998	144,000,000	9.9

Source: Department of Tourism (1996); FHRAI Magazine and Newsletter 2000, Vol. 2, 1 March: 12.

The government has played its part in developing domestic (or 'social') tourism by providing an optional allowance for travel during leave, which it has offered its employees and their families. Such benefits are usually taken up during summer vacations (which last almost 2 months) and *Dusshera* holidays (which last for a week), when schools close and children can accompany their parents. During these periods, it is common for railways to announce 'Summer Specials' and 'Puja Specials' to meet passenger demand for popular destinations, and at these peak seasons travel and accommodation have to be booked well in advance.

Leisure tourism for purposes other than pilgrimage would seem to be a relatively recent development. However, there has been a distinct spurt in time-share investments over the last few years (Business Inc., 1997). Although the scarcity of available statistical data seems to suggest that domestic tourism is non-existent, it would be naive to conclude that Indian life styles are devoid of secular travel. The Indian masses may not be able to afford extravagant holiday spending, but visits to friends and relatives are common and there is an urgent need for research on the travel habits of the Indian middle class.

International tourism

Inbound tourism

For centuries, India has played host to numerous types of travellers, traders, crusaders, and seekers after truth. Travelogues, gazettes and other accounts of these globe-trotters conjure up vivid mental images of the country and its people. For some travellers, the images are eternal, while for others the picture has changed, in part or absolutely. However, over the years, despite exceptional and sporadic political strife, civil unrest, fears of epidemics and negative media propaganda, the number of tourists visiting India has increased.

Globally, India has a minute 0.4% share in international arrivals. Nevertheless, despite declining rates of tourist growth, tourist arrivals usually manage to exceed those of the previous year. In 1997, for example, there were 2.4 million, compared with 2.3 million in 1996 (Table 9.3). Singh and Singh (1996: v) attributed such growth to the country's grandiose character, rather than to any intrinsic merits of its tourism industry. This miniature accomplishment is transformed in the context of South Asia, where India holds pride of place (WTO, 1998c: 35), and where it 'emerges like colossus' (Singh and Singh, 2000).

India's overseas tourist market is primarily the West (Table 9.4). In 1997, Europe provided one-third of its international tourist arrivals, with 370,000 from the UK and 408,492 from the rest of Europe. In addition, there were 322,000 from the USA and Canada (WTO, 1998c: 35). From 1995 to 1996, there was significant growth in tourism from Australia, Austria and Japan, but this was not sustained over the following year. In 1997, numbers of tourists from Sri Lanka and Malaysia were substantially increased.

Table 9.3. International tourist arrivals and receipts in India: 1988–1997.

Year	Arrivals (000)	Receipts (US$)
1988	1591	1500
1989	1736	1535
1990	1707	1513
1991	1678	1757
1992	1868	2120
1993	1765	2001
1994	1886	2265
1995	2124	2609
1996	2288	2963
1997	2374	3152

Source: WTO (1998c: 34).

Table 9.4. World tourist arrivals in India: main markets, 1995–1997.

Origin	Number of arrivals			Change (%)	
	1995	1996	1997	1995–1996	1996–1997
UK	334,827	360,686	370,567	7.7	2.7
Bangladesh	318,474	322,355	355,371	1.2	10.2
USA	203,343	228,829	244,239	12.5	6.7
Sri Lanka	114,157	107,351	122,080	−6.0	13.7
Germany	89,040	99,853	104,953	12.1	5.1
Japan	76,042	99,018	99,729	30.2	0.7
France	82,349	93,325	92,449	13.3	−0.9
Canada	63,821	74,031	78,570	16.0	6.1
Malaysia	50,039	53,370	60,401	6.7	13.2
Italy	53,015	49,910	53,854	−5.9	7.9
Singapore	48,632	47,136	52,004	−3.1	10.3
Australia	36,150	48,755	50,647	34.9	3.9
Pakistan	42,981	41,810	45,076	−2.7	7.8
Netherlands	40,147	40,246	45,843	−0.2	11.4
Nepal	34,562	–	43,155	–	–
Switzerland	29,388	34,989	31,717	19.1	−9.4
Spain	24,411	24,419	22,903	0.0	−6.2
South Africa	18,750	19,328	22,218	3.1	15.0
Belgium	18,732	22,160	21,532	18.3	−2.8
Israel	14,806	18,387	20,162	24.2	9.7
UAR	19,749	21,401	19,828	8.4	−7.4
Sweden	19,013	21,192	19,772	11.5	−6.7
Kenya	17,389	19,248	18,993	10.7	−1.3
Russia Federation	–	–	18,243	–	–
Thailand	14,462	16,188	16,494	11.9	1.9
Austria	13,114	17,084	16,369	30.3	−4.2
Oman	17,060	17,020	16,185	−0.2	−4.9
Rest of world	329,230	389,769	311,740	18.4	−20.0
Total	2,123,683	2,287,860	2,374,094	7.7	3.8

Source: WTO (1998c: 35).

Where India really gains is in the duration of these visits. In fact, visitors tend to stay longer in India than in virtually any other part of the world – an average of 27 days (Sengupta, 1997: 16). This is perhaps a reflection of the endowments of India, which compares with Europe in size and diversity as an all-season, multi-destination tourist region. Arguably, the preponderance of European travellers is due to the cultural climate and their fascination for coasts and mountain landscapes. In addition, many British tourists visit friends and relatives in India.

There are few statistics on the movements of tourists to India but as New Delhi is the major entry port, a large proportion visit the 'golden triangle', i.e. Delhi, Agra and Jaipur. The Himalayan states of Uttar Pradesh, Himachal Pradesh and Jammu and Kashmir are equally popular, though at the time of writing the escalation in terrorism in Jammu and Kashmir has diverted many tourists to the southern states of Tamil Nadu, Kerala, Karnataka and Andhra Pradesh.

Outbound tourism

The motivations of outbound tourists are similar to those of domestic tourists, though with a stronger emphasis on visiting friends and relatives (VFR), followed by the business traveller. Economic liberalization and globalization policies have given an impetus to the existing (but small) overseas market for outbound tourists from India.

While there has been no formal study of outbound travel from the Indian region, in 1995 the market was estimated at between 2 and 4 million. Departures by air were said to be segmented into business (20%), VFR (20%), leisure (25%) and labour and others (35%). Current trends are towards a decline in group travel, with a corresponding increase in those travelling independently or in small family groups. Average age is between 35 and 40, and there is a considerable expenditure on shopping (Gill, 1995: 1).

Liberalization, in particular, has generated a breed of business travellers, which is on the rise, but the relationship between inbound and outbound tourism has varied. As indicated in Table 9.5, inbound tourism in 1991 amounted to 73% of outbound tourism. By 1994, this had declined to 56%, increasing again to 66% in 1997. It is worth noting that America is an attractive destination for Indians, particularly those from the states in south India. There were 4 million Indian nationals travelling overseas in 1994 and outbound travel was predicted to exceed 5 million by the year 2000, based on 8% growth per annum (Gill, 1995: 1). This could be exceeded, for the rapidly expanding Indian middle class, the largest in the world, is increasingly able to invest in travel and is equally rapidly developing a taste for it, especially to such distant destinations as Europe and the USA.

The economic impacts of tourism

The economic outcome of tourism activity in India is unclear and press releases, which provide some information, are few and far between. Reports from the Department of Tourism (DoT) and the Government of India (GOI) are intended for bureaucrats and are rarely made public. Even if access can be gained to them, the data are questionable, primarily because of inconsistencies in the gathering and processing stages. Such reports suffer from a near absence of appropriate methodologies and are far from being comprehensive. An accurate system of data collection, tabulation and calculation has yet to be developed for Indian tourism, so as to cover both the formal and the informal sectors.

Like tourist arrivals, revenues from tourism have increased gradually over the years. In 1997, against an approximate investment of Rs 160 crores, India earned about Rs 11,054.3 crores, while in the previous year an investment of Rs 100 crores yielded some Rs 10,052 crores (Khurana, 1998). (1 crore = 10 million. At the time of writing, US$1.00 = approximately Rs 43; and Rs 1 crore = US$232,560.)

The contribution of tourism to employment in India is considerable, as indicated in table 9.6. It is estimated that tourism has generated 47.5 jobs per million rupees of investment – a ratio considered within the country to be higher than any other sector. Employment figures of 1996–1997 suggest that 9.1 million people were directly employed in tourism and a further 21.4 million were indirectly employed in tourism and related industries (Bezbaruah, 1998).

It is often suggested that tourism is the third largest earner of foreign exchange in India, after gems/jewellery and ready-made garments. At the time of writing, the garments industry is reportedly threatened by competitive prices from Bangladesh and, as a result, tourism could change positions with the garments industry and acquire second place, which can hardly be seen as resulting from improved performance by India's tourism industry.

Table 9.5. Inbound and outbound tourism in India: selected years.

Year	Outbounds (million)	Inbound (million)
1997	3.5	2.3
1994	3.4	1.89
1991	2.3	1.68

Sources: Gill (1995: 1, 5, 6); WTO (1998c: 34).

Table 9.6. Tourism-induced employment generation in India: 1990–1995.

Year	Total employment (million)
1990–1991	6.391
1991–1992	6.573
1992–1993	6.960
1993–1994	7.400
1994–1995	7.800

Source: ESCAP (1994).

The administration of tourism

In 1958, the Indian government created a separate tourism department. At the time of writing, the DoT is attached to the Ministry of Civil Aviation and headed by the Director-General (DG) of Tourism. The DG is assisted by a Joint Secretary, a Deputy Secretary and a set of five deputies. The Department is essentially a policy-making executive organization that corresponds directly with other ministries and departments of the central (Federal) and state governments.

There is a neat though quixotic division of responsibility between central and the State Tourism Development Corporations (STDCs). The activities of central government are concentrated on the needs of foreign tourists, while the states focus on domestic tourists. Within guidelines provided by central government, they must develop their own policies, products and strategies, and do so under seven categories: Planning and Programming; Publicity and Conferences; Travel Trade and Hospitality; Accommodation; Supplementary Accommodation and Wildlife; Market Research; and Administration.

Despite having so many officials and an apparently clear allocation of functions, the GOI Tourism Department has been accused of 'lacking a sense of urgency' (Richter, 1989: 120), at least until 1984. It has undoubtedly grown fairly rapidly, throughout the country as well as overseas. In the latter case, the DoT is currently bearing the expense of about 17 overseas tourist offices in its major tourist-generating countries, and only recently have officials realized the inefficiency of these outlets (Pradhan, 1998). What was supposed to be capital investment turned out to be prodigal investment.

Tourism policy-making

India's tourism policy, which is 50 years behind the times, is a peculiar blend of ideals about traditional hospitality and ideas of contemporary capitalist development. Set in a 'democratic' framework, it is the outcome of several revisions and modifications. Despite a long process of learning through trial and error, the current national tourism policy is, at best, relatively undeveloped.

The planning process

Tourism plans in India are designed to fit within the 5-year time frame commonly designated for national planning and policy activities. Plans for tourism commenced as early as 1951, when the first Five Year Plan (FYP), for 1951–1955, was initiated. (The FYPs are not published or made available to the public; information about them has to be gleaned from reports and news releases.) Little came out of this period and the second FYP was similarly unproductive. The only noteworthy benchmark in the history of Indian tourism planning occurred in 1966, the last year of the third FYP, when the ITDC was established. The intention was that it should play a crucial, strategic and catalytic role in the development of tourism by setting up an elaborate infrastructure for tourist services in accommodation, travel, conferences and even shopping.

The Fourth and Fifth FYPs (for 1967–1971 and 1972–1976) are usually examined together. Except for differences in fund allocation, they share much the same objectives and overall framework and both focus on the expansion of existing facilities. Towards the end of the period covered by the Fifth FYP, the concept of 'Resort Tourism' began to dawn upon developers, especially in the states of Kerala, Jammu and Kashmir, Goa and Himachal Pradesh, where tourism was more consistently incorporated into state plans. These states were later to be models for tourism development and are now potential fields of study in integrated tourism development.

In subsequent FYP periods, the planning process would have trudged along at the same pace and on the same path but for the delirium of Asiad '82 (the Asian Games of 1982), a mega sports event hosted by India. Putting aside all the controversy arising before and after the event, it actually prompted tourism development, at least in Delhi, by spurring the city to prepare for visitors – their transport, accommodation and other facilities. The result was the formulation of an annual policy that finally culminated in an action plan, albeit one that was initially restricted to Delhi, the venue for the Games.

The 1982 policy, which was the first tourism policy for India, also specified development objectives and provided an action plan based on tourism circuits, deftly interweaving the concept of integrated planning into the country's tourism policy by identifying and developing centres of single or multiple attractions. The concept of tourism circuits was readily absorbed by the STDCs, which immediately identified centres with similar levels of resources under the broad categories of wildlife, history, religion, culture, adventure and nature. In most cases, the circuits were sited within a state; in exceptional cases a circuit was shared by two or more states, as with the much-publicized 'golden triangle' connecting Agra, Jaipur and Delhi. This cultural circuit is spread over the three states of Uttar Pradesh, Rajasthan and the union territory of Delhi. In like manner, the Buddhist circuit penetrates the states of Uttar Pradesh, Bihar and Madhya Pradesh. This inter-state dependence for the development of a tourism circuit currently awaits stronger cohesiveness, in terms of infrastructure and communication, necessary if this fine idea is to be a success.

The dust of controversy over Asiad has yet to settle. With the seventh FYP imminent, planners were compelled to utilize the infrastructure that had been built. With much flurry and enthusiasm, an ambitious 'watershed plan' was produced and the seventh FYP became the apex of India's planning history. Tourism was promoted as a key objective and accorded industry status, a national committee to evaluate its socio-economic implications was formed; and the Tourism Finance Corporation of India was established. The eighth FYP, for 1992–1997, was presented in more sanguine tones, introducing a series of fresh ideas that were well received. For the first time, planners recognized the importance of domestic tourism. Apart from thematic tourist circuits, the plan proposed intensive development of all-inclusive Special Tourist Areas within this period. In addition, a 'tourism synergy programme' was prepared in 1993, subsequently modified and presented in 1996 as the 'National Strategy for the Development of Tourism' for consideration by the private sector and state governments, and discussed at a conference of state governments in 1997.

In recent years, the India of the past has undergone pangs of transformation on both economic and political fronts, and these changes have been vividly reflected in all government affairs. In addition, global competition and worldwide trends have captured the attention of Indian planners, and such fashionable terms as ecology and the environment, impact assessment, sustainable development, super-highways and participation and partnership are finding their way into plans and policy statements. This provided the context, in June 1997, for the redefinition of India's tourism policy of 1982, apparently through the inclusion of contemporary and more 'fashionable' terminology. The Draft National Tourism Policy of 1997 focused on the role of government in tourism, and on the introduction of regulatory measures to facilitate social, cultural and environmental sustainability. Ironically, while tourism businesses elsewhere were challenging the realities of ecotourism practices, India framed its ecotourism policy in an austere bid to circumvent all the ills of tourism.

Little by way of formal research has been carried out on the negative consequences of tourism in India. However, news reports, observation and hearsay evidence indicate damage to beaches, mountains and the ecosystems of environmentally sensitive regions, along with harm to the built environment – for example, the vandalizing of archaeological monuments and the clandestine sales of antiques. There is also some evidence that traditions have been improvised to cater for tourist demand.

At the time of writing, a central tourism policy is still in the making, but states such as Orissa, West Bengal and Kerala are already implementing ecotourism programmes, where the following priorities are emphasized:

- Coordination of central and state governments in the development of sustainable tourism and ecotourism.
- The encouragement of only ecotourism and eco-friendly growth in environmentally fragile areas.
- The incorporation of carrying capacity and environmental considerations in the planning process.
- Attempts to ensure that benefits of tourism percolate into destination communities.
- Increasing tourist awareness of the destination's attributes.

- Integrated guidelines for development policies.
- The desirability of non-governmental organizations and local support for activities aimed at ecological preservation.
- The need to make local communities aware of the socio-economic benefits of tourism.

The 1997 policy emphasizes the vitality of domestic tourism, the value of international tourism as a global force for peace, and the need to obtain a balance of inbound and outbound tourism. With the explicit intention of making tourism a national priority, policymakers have included it in the concurrent list, thus defining tourism as an area requiring appropriate legislation at both central and state government levels. There is also a proposal to create private tourism development funds and land banks for hotel construction. In addition, the Ministry for Tourism and Civil Aviation has recently granted tourism an Export House status, which entails some relaxation on import duties for identified equipment. How far these announcements and measures will provide impetus to the otherwise neglected tourism industry remains to be seen. What is clear is that the 1997 policy, which has yet to be worked out and is even further from being implemented, will only succeed if serious efforts are made to put it into practice.

Partnerships

Just as tourism administration should strongly 'project' government policies, the industry also bears the stamp of the private sector (Bala, 1990: 60):

> One of the major achievements of the government in the field of tourism has been the involvement of the private sector in the thinking and planning process in the Ministry of Tourism. This has resulted in a close collaboration between the two ... resulting in mutual understanding and pragmatic planning.

At the time of writing, the accommodation sector in India is a mixture of public, private and transnational involvement. In the public sector, the ITDC is the only chain that pro-

vides a range of accommodation, including five-star, de luxe, budget, motel and airport hotels, and resorts. In the private sector, local and regional companies are represented, while transnational companies include the Sheraton, Radisson, Meridian, Holiday Inn and Best Western. Accommodation for specifically religious tourism (for example, *Dharamshalas*, *Yatri Niwas* and *Serais*) is provided by various non-secular organizations.

Governments in Asia have been accused of operating double standards over their collaboration with the private sector, allegedly giving it a free hand in tourism development while simultaneously being 'unhelpful or even hostile to private sector tourism development' (Centre for Transnational Corporations, 1982: 63). However, in India there is evidence throughout the tourism industry that the private sector is dominant (Misra, 1998: 8). Sometimes this much-vaunted 'collaboration' has fostered a degree of connivance and alleged 'foul play,' which has been reported by such pressure groups as the Ecumenical Coalition of Third World Tourism, Jagrut Goankarachi Fauz and the Ladakh Ecological Development Group, which operate locally, regionally and internationally. Discontent has centred especially on tourism development in Goa, Kerala, Tamil Nadu, Orissa and Gujarat, along with a few secluded locations in the Himalayan tracts.

By contrast, states such as Haryana and Rajasthan present examples of successful tourism partnership and are worth emulating. Haryana, for instance, is dotted with small and medium-sized ponds and lakes that serve to dissuade major development projects, and has a primarily rural population which earns its living in agriculture and livestock production. In order to facilitate the movement of goods from Haryana to neighbouring states, and even further, the state government invested heavily in developing state highway systems and encouraged the establishment of safe and indigenous motels and *dhabas* (eating places) at regular intervals. Ponds and lakes were landscaped and made attractive, too, for the traveller to take a short break, and these changes had a definite and positive impact on the economy. Previously desolate locations were improved, and local people obtained part-time employment, supplementing their income by finding markets for surplus farm produce. The lakes became natural winter asylums for migratory birds, which thus became an added attraction in the area. Such tourism development has linked farming and non-farming occupations, given an impetus to a 'multi-crop' economy, and has strengthened the primary occupations of farming and transport.

Similar developments have occurred in Rajasthan, particularly in the arid and semi-arid peripheries where the local people eke out a living from frugal resources of ground water, for drinking and livestock (chiefly camels) and where sporadic rains enable the cultivation of especially hardy grains. Until recently, historical palaces and *havelis* (forts) were largely abandoned, their owners having migrated to urban centres, leaving their properties to be looked after by locals, who were paid in cash or kind for their services. With a little promotion by the government, the exotic desert landscapes, local culture and built environments attracted tourists to these areas, all the year round. As a consequence, abandoned *havelis* and *mahals* (mansions) were soon converted into hotels, motels, restaurants and even museums. With visitors enthusiastically wanting to experience the traditional hospitality of the locals, the region became well known for its natural and cultural heritage and is now part of the 'golden triangle'. Tourism has restored activity and life to this state.

Private-sector involvement in tourism began only in the 1970s. Since then, it has taken an increasingly active role, especially in the development of hotels and other accommodation. It has also become involved in travel agencies and tour operations, airlines, vehicle rentals, consultancies and even human resource development. Public–private partnerships are also found in the development of tourist complexes, golf courses, theatres, other forms of entertainment and shopping plazas, and there has been prominent private-sector involvement in railways, most notably trains in the 'heritage' category – for example, the *Royal Orient, Palace on Wheels, Ferry Queen* and small trains operating in the hills.

As the private sector has become more involved, tourism industry lobbies have reportedly become increasingly vocal and assertive (Misra, 1998: 8). Realizing that privatization of tourism is a key for the future, national and state governments are exploring a number of new partnership ideas. The ITDC, a major public-sector tourism corporation, offers expertise to smaller private-sector hoteliers in setting up and managing properties, through its recently developed consultancy wing. Some of the most commendable outcomes of this inter-sectoral exchange occur in the realm of heritage, ecological and cultural preservation, and in quality control. A notable example is the concept of Heritage hotels, whereby owners of *havelis* and *mahals* (forts and mansions) that are partially or wholly abandoned have the option of converting them into hotels for tourists. Although in public use, the properties remain the possession of their owners, who may or may not hire professional managers to assist in their operation. For its part, the government provides subsidies, promotional and licensing benefits to such units. Operations of this kind have gathered momentum in the states of Rajasthan, Madhya Pradesh and Gujarat, which currently account for a total of 47 properties. Tourist visits to other private homes are being encouraged on similar patterns. However, in the case of home-stays, most owners prefer an entirely private enterprise, while a few others have good reasons to oppose such policies strongly, on the grounds that host–guest interaction may contravene norms of class and caste (Babu, 1998).

Government has also collaborated with agencies outside India. One example is the development of ecotourism in the Andaman and Nicobar Islands, which has involved cooperation with the World Tourism Organization (WTO) and the United Nations Development Programme. Similarly, at the time of writing, the state of Andhra Pradesh was cooperating with the WTO to assist this Indian state in 'producing its own tourism development plans' with a particular focus on the disadvantaged and the threatened, including women, ethnic minorities, and on the natural and cultural environment (WTO, 1998b). India is also an active participant in the WTO's Silk Route project and the South Asia Integrated Tourism Human Resource

Development Project, a Human Resource Programme (Bagri, 1998). Regionally, too, India has affirmed its commitment to countries in the South Asian Association for Regional Cooperation in developing a viable tourism industry for the benefit of all its member nations.

It may be that all such partnerships, with internal and external organizations, are needed if Indian tourism is to survive in a buyers' market, where the experienced tourist is able to exercise choice over the 'product' and, if dissatisfied, to go elsewhere.

Concluding Remarks

Up to this point, the discussion has summarized the processes and practices adopted by the Indian government in formulating its policy on tourism development. It has not been exhaustive, but does afford some scope for analysing tourism development in India.

To begin with, it may be appropriate to ask why, at the time of writing, as in 1989, 'no one [in India] is satisfied with Indian tourism policy' (Richter, 1989: 102). Almost all Indians have their own reasons to discredit the government for its policies. Most of these reasons relate to 'being left out' (Bezbaruah, 1998). As in many other developing countries, the participation of the people in policy-making is almost negligible, and this is despite the fact that India has a huge domestic base for the development of its tourism industry. Rather, it seems that domestic tourism has been taken for granted and, because of the strength of religious motivation in India, has been considered to be self-sustaining. Furthermore, it has been undervalued because it does not generate foreign exchange. It has taken almost five decades of planning for policy-makers to accept that Indian masses are tourists of economic significance, at least in the regional context.

This shoddy treatment was further exacerbated when the Federal government hived off responsibility for domestic tourists while keeping international tourism under the wings of the central government. This is indeed absurd, since the destinations visited by foreign tourists are inevitably under state jurisdiction and tourists are usually provided for by the people of the host state. Also all tourists, foreign or domestic, are the collective responsibility of all Indians. By so dividing responsibility for foreign and domestic tourists, central government has fostered its own role in economic development strategies and has burdened the local state with new economic duties, thereby forcing it into an entreprenurial role.

In India, public sector enterprises (PSEs) are currently in a deplorable condition. According to Carvalho and Bansal (1998), Indian Airlines (IA), the domestic airline, and Air India, India's international airline, both public sector undertakings, incur heavy losses in their operations, with IA ranked the sixth largest loss-making PSE in the country. Problems include periodic fare-hikes, shrinking passenger numbers, ageing aircraft, poor aircraft utilization, unstable routes, high employee–aircraft ratio, heavy borrowings, depleting reserves and, above all, a tense and uneasy relationship of management with the labour force. The ITDCs 21 accommodation units are also criticized and there seems to be a perpetual shortage of available guest rooms. More generally, the organized sector has approximately 63,000 hotel rooms, amounting to half the demand. Interestingly, as a method of coping with their problems, airlines and hotels rashly impose frequent tariff rises, thus making destinations unjustifiably more expensive for their visitors.

Managers of these enterprises point to the arbitrary appointment to positions of responsibility of inexperienced bureaucrats (Carvalho and Bansal, 1998), who usually entertain preconceived tactics of marketing which, when implemented, leave the organization in financial difficulties. PSEs that generate consistent revenues are often unable to account for the scarcity of funds and an oft-posed query is 'Where has the money gone?' (Carvalho and Bansal, 1998). No one seems to take responsibility for financial decisions and accountability is almost nil. At this juncture, it is pertinent to note that tourism promotion by government suffers from the same problems. It might be better for government to take an active role in infrastructural development and in monitoring developments, rather than channelling all its resources into marketing and promotion.

Public policy on tourism is severely afflicted by the serious lack of a research base, which thus reduces the exercise to mere desk work, with undue reliance on imagination and 'guesstimates.' This, in turn, prompts a series of associated problems – for example, ad hocism, a top-down approach and poorly integrated activities. Reflections on such ills are evident in the environmental hazards often reported in newspapers. Such unmonitored developments include: poaching in wildlife sanctuaries; damage to Khajuraho architectural sites by aircraft vibration; disturbances to the coastal ecology of Goan beaches, the Sundarbans and the Rann of Kutch (coastal regions in the east and west with highly distinctive ecosystems); and damage to the Taj Mahal by smoke from an oil refinery. The government could also be charged with failing to monitor the growth of tourism, especially in the highly fragile ecosystems of the coast, the mangroves and the Himalayas. A report in the *Times of India* (Anon., 1998) asserted that Leh, in Laddakh, was being 'robbed' of its beauty and culture by tourism, and Singh and Kaur (1985, 1989) have repeatedly published accounts of ecocultural degradation in the Himalayan ecosystems.

Mention also has to be made of human resource problems. Indian tourism faces an acute shortage of appropriately and adequately trained skilled workers, and levels of professionalism must be seriously addressed. India's primary tourism training body, the Indian Institute of Travel and Tourism Management has assumed the role of an educating and training centre, in response to the industry's needs. Essentially a bureaucratic enterprise, with its headquarters in Gwalior and regional chapters in Delhi, Lucknow, Trivandrum and Bhubneshwar, the Institute offers short- and long-term courses for people aspiring to join the industry as well as those within it, either as industry professionals or as educators. Drawing expertise from the country and even internationally, the Institute encourages optimism for the future (Singh, 1997: 301) and has 20 hotel management and 13 food craft institutions, all in the public sector, which concentrate on a curriculum largely devoted to hands-on skills. Clearly, this is an essential requirement, but there is also a sizeable lacuna in the managerial

workforce. The private sector, particularly such multinational hotel chains as the Taj and the Oberoi, offers programmes for various levels of education and training but, again, the supply of managerial manpower remains a small proportion of the entire demand.

It is not government policies towards tourism that are the major problem. At a theoretical level, Indian tourism policy deserves much appreciation. Rather, the machinery that implements these policies must be examined for its many shortcomings. This is where the political will is needed. Unfeasible economic strategies (high tariffs, excessive taxation and indebtedness, and unwanted investments), debilitating political instability (indecisiveness and developmental priorities that alter with every change in government) and irrational social conservatism are the real leviathans threatening the tourism industry. Most importantly, the one element that overrides all others, and which is almost ubiquitous, not only in India but throughout Asia, is the unreasonable imposition of red-tapism. In voicing its concern over this issue, the WTO (1998d) has pleaded with Asian countries to eradicate this problem to help to ensure healthy and vibrant tourism development. In conclusion, Richter's earlier observation that no one in India is satisfied with India's tourism industry remains accurate. The potential is there to develop tourism, and India has a massive middle-income group whose leisure and recreation needs are relatively unostentatious. It should not be difficult to meet these needs. With this group in mind, it is important not to see the generation of foreign exchange as tourism's major priority, or to allow the tourism industry to monopolize the national or regional assets. Tourism plans should indeed reflect the industry's potential aspirations, but they should also reflect the legitimate claims that tourism has on the country's limited economic resources.

Acknowledgement

The author acknowledges the constructive suggestions and perspectives of Dr Tej Vir Singh, Director of the Centre for Tourism Research and Development, which have proved very useful in writing this chapter.

References

Anon. (1998) Tourism brings money to Leh, but robs its beauty. *Times of India* (Lucknow edn) 9 November.

Babu, Hari (1998) Keralam Diary. *ANLetter, Third World Tourism – Critique and Response* 6(2), August, p. 6.

Bagri, S.C. (1998) Tourism Manpower Development Programmes in India. *Journal of Tourism* 3, 31–50.

Bala, U. (1990) *Tourism in India: Policy and Perspective*. Arushi Prakashan, New Delhi.

Bezbaruah, M.P. (1998) The untapped potential. *The Sunday Pioneer on Holiday* (Lucknow edn) 27 September, p. 2.

Bharadwaj, S.M. (1973) *Hindu Places of Pilgrimage in India*. Thomson Press, New Delhi.

Business Inc. (1997) Dream holidays which remain a dream. *Indian Express* 30 March.

Carvalho, B. and Bansal, S. (1998) Punctured Plans. *Business World* 22 February, pp. 28–35.

Centre for Transnational Corporations (1982) *Transnational Corporations in International Tourism*. United Nations, New York.

Department of Tourism (1996) *Report of Working Group on Tourism for the Ninth Five Year Plan, 1997–2002*. Government of India, New Delhi.

ESCAP (1994) *Tourism Newsletter* 4, 4 August. United Nations Economic and Social Commission for Asia and the Pacific, Bangkok.

Gill, K. (1995). India outbound – on the fast track. *Travel Review* 18(8), 1–6.

Jha, M. (1985) *Dimensions of Pilgrimage: an Anthropological Appraisal*. Inter-India Publications, New Delhi.

Jha, M. (ed.) (1991) *Social Anthropology of Pilgrimage*. Inter-India Publications, New Delhi.

Kaur, J. (1985) *Himalayan Pilgrimages and the New Tourism*. Himalayan Books, New Delhi.

Khurana, M.L. (1998) We'll have to work harder. *The Sunday Pioneer on Holiday* 27 September, p. 2.

Misra, S.K. (1998) Public–private partnerships: new ways of managing tourism in India. *Journal of Tourism* 3, 5–12.

Pal, B.K. (1989) Foreword. In: Singh, T.V. and Kaur, J. (eds) *Studies in Himalayan Ecology*, revised edn. Himalayan Books, New Delhi, p. xii.

Pradhan, A. (1998) Indian Tourism – glorious legacy. *The Sunday Pioneer on Holiday* 27 September, p. 2.

Ravendran, G. (1998) Development of ecotourism in India. *Journal of Travel and Tourism* 2(1), 137–140.

Richter, L.K. (1989) *The Politics of Tourism in Asia*. University of Hawaii Press, Honolulu.

Sen, J. (1989) *Darjeeling: a Favoured Retreat*. Indus Publishing Co., New Delhi.

Sengupta, N.K. (1997) Tourism and balance of payments crisis. *Journal of Travel and Tourism* 1(1), 14–21.

Shackley, M. (1998) The Camel Safari Industry of Jaisalmer, Thar Desert (Rajasthan). *Journal of Travel and Tourism* 2(1) April 1997–March 1998: 71–89.

Sherring, M.A. (1975) *Benares: the Sacred City of the Hindus*. B.R. Publishing Corporation, Delhi.

Singh, S. (1997) Developing human resources for the tourism industry with reference to India. *Tourism Management* 18(5), 299–306.

Singh, S. and Singh, T.V. (1996) Preface. In: Singh, S. (ed.) *Profiles of Indian Tourism Industry*. Ashish Publishing Corporation, New Delhi, pp. v–vii.

Singh, T.V. (1975) *Tourism and Tourist Industry in U.P.* New Heights, New Delhi.

Singh, T.V. (1989) On developing Himalayan tourism ecologically. In: Singh, T.V. and Kaur, J. (eds) *Studies in Himalayan Ecology*. Himalayan Books, New Delhi, pp. 227–238.

Singh, T.V. and Singh, S. (2000) Tourism in India: development, performance and prospects. In: Hall, C.M. and Page, S. (eds) *Tourism in South and South East Asia*. Butterworth-Heinemann, Oxford, UK, pp. 225–232.

Singh, T.V. and Kaur, J. (1985) *Integrated Mountain Development*. Himalayan Books, New Delhi.

Singh, T.V. and Kaur, J. (1989) *Studies in Himalayan Ecology*, revised edn. Himalayan Books, New Delhi.

Tyagi, N. (1991) *Hill Resorts of U.P. Himalaya: a Geographical Study*. Indus Publishing Company, New Delhi.

WTO (1998a) Asia crisis hits Africa. *WTO News* 4 (July–August), 7.

WTO (1998b) Andhra Pradesh signs for sustainability. *WTO News* 5 (Sept–Oct–Nov), 12.

WTO (1998c) *Tourism Market Trends – South Asia: 1988–97*. World Tourism Organization, Madrid.

WTO (1998d) Asia warned about too much red tape. *WTO News* 5 (Sept–Oct–Nov), 13.

10

The Journey: an Overview of Tourism and Travel in the Arab/Islamic Context

Heba Aziz

Introduction

Edward Said's seminal *Orientalism* (1991) charts the construction of an imaginary landscape – the fabulous East. This fantasy of luxurious splendour and cruel depravity was a projection of the repressed European imagination, fuelled by exotic reports from early traders, adventurers and warriors, from Marco Polo to Lawrence of Arabia. In the footsteps of such near-mythical pioneers have followed a more recent and mundane traveller: the modern tourist.

For the purpose of this chapter, the 'Middle East', or 'Arab world', is defined as the Arabic-speaking Middle East and North Africa (MENA), and is taken to be Algeria, Bahrain, Egypt, Iraq, Jordan, Kuwait, Lebanon, Libya, Morocco, Oman, Qatar, Saudi Arabia, Syria, Sudan, Tunisia, the United Arab Emirates and the Yemen. It is a region that Western tourists have visited in relatively low numbers, largely because of prevailing socio-political, cultural, psychological and religious factors in both the generating and receiving markets (Aziz, 1991). However, at the time of writing, the MENA region was witnessing a significant expansion in the number of visitors. In the following pages there is, first, a discussion of Arabic/Islamic perspectives on such concepts

as travelling, journeying and tourism, which have influenced regional attitudes towards the development of the tourist industry, and this is followed by a brief overview of recent trends in tourist movements in the region. The main focus of this chapter is an analysis of the *Hajj* (the annual Muslim pilgrimage to the Holy City of Mecca) in terms of its tourist features, for the *Hajj* constitutes the largest voluntary and regular mass movement of population in the world. Although often overlooked in Western studies of travel and tourism, and virtually excluded from data sources, it clearly shares many features of travel for recreational purposes, and must be understood if Western perspectives on tourism are not to underestimate and distort the significance of travel and tourism in the region.

Travel and Tourism in the Arab/Islamic Context

The image of the Arab world in the popular media of the West is largely negative. Islamic society tends to be painted from a palette consisting mostly of stereotypes of patriarchal oppression, harsh environments, religious fundamentalism, political unrest, cultural intolerance and irrational violence. Unsurprisingly, such stereotypes have inhibited the growth of mass tourism – a situation that has not disappointed those in the Arab world who fear its impact on traditional Islamic culture, for there is a widely held counter-stereotype of Western tourists as shameless hedonists corrupting local morals through empty promises of economic benefit, a view seemingly confirmed by the actions of some Arab tourists, who similarly behave 'out of their culture' while on of holiday. These stereotypes neither adequately reflect the realities of lived experience, nor do justice to the complex ambivalence registered by early explorers in a region that for centuries has been a hub for generating and receiving travellers. From a Western perspective, for example, the chroniclers of the Crusades saw divine intervention behind Christian victories and at the same time held up such 'infidel' warriors as Saladin as shining examples of chivalry. Similarly, in the 19th and early 20th centuries, the writers on the region who made the most impact were soldiers and administrators who, although deeply implicated in the colonial enterprise, had nevertheless (to some extent) 'gone native'. The journeys of Doughty (1908), Stark (1936), Burton (1937), Thesiger (1964) and Lawrence (1976) were all undertaken within the context of imperialism, but their writing reveals a fascination with a culture in which the concept of the journey was at the core of both spiritual and practical existence. It is an Islamic ideal of travel that continues to be of importance, even if individual Muslim travellers do not always live up to it, and is explored further in this chapter.

Islamic doctrine explicitly endorses travel. Spiritually, all Muslims are obliged to undertake pilgrimage to Mecca if they can afford the expense, and the experience of the *Hajj* is one of the five pillars of the faith. Other forms of religious travel include *Hijra* (the obligation to migrate from lands where Islam cannot be freely practised) and *ziyaras* (visits to local shrines). Moreover, Islam does not recognize a radical distinction between the religious and secular spheres. As a consequence, it endows forms of travel that in the West would not be regarded as specifically religious with a spiritual dimension, explicitly endorsing travel in

search of knowledge (*rihla*) or trade as being 'in the route of God' (*Fi sabeel Allah*). More specifically, some journeys have been especially significant in the political and religious history of Islam. The Islamic calendar (*Hijri*) takes as its starting point the resettlement of the Prophet and his followers from Mecca to Medina, and the term *Hijri* itself derives from *Hijra* (religious migration).

Traditionally, the Arabs of the Peninsula have been nomadic Bedouin, who travelled in search of water and pasture, and their concepts regarding rules of hospitality and the rights and duties of hosts and guests were well advanced even prior to Islam. The Quran and the examples of the Prophet (*sunna*) and the sayings attributed to him (*hadith*) are the formal source of the jurisprudence for Muslim societies. In all three sources there is a clear emphasis on developing concepts and rules relating to travel and the offering of hospitality. Respect for the home of the host and offers of hospitality were not simply matters of choice, but a religious duty and a means to moving closer to God by following the lead of His Prophet.

The Quran exhorts Muslims to travel in the land of God to experience His creation more widely, to acquire knowledge, and to meet people and spread the word of God among Muslims and non-Muslims. Travel is also meant to consolidate the notion of the *Ummah* (the nation of Islam) promoted by Islam (Quran, 2: 164; 3: 137, 10: 22, 11: 40–48), an emphasis apparent even in the standard subject index of the Quran (Rehman, 1991), where there are no fewer than 19 entries under the sub-heading of man's travel over land and sea.

Prior to Islam, hospitality in Arabia was based on the concept of reciprocity, which owed much to the harsh environments in which Bedouin used to travel. Food, drink and lodging were generously provided to passers-by, whether strangers or tribesmen, and thus ensured reciprocal hospitality at a future date. It was generally agreed that such hospitality should be offered unconditionally for at least 3 days. Islam built on such concepts and granted travellers a distinguished status in their own right. Guests became guests of God, and hospitality ceased to be a choice and became a duty, based not on the hope of future reciprocity but on religious principle. In a sense, it illustrated the many ways in which God is generous with His subjects. Rather than believing they are dealing only with passers-by, hosts believe that, in a wider divine context, they are meeting God's needs, and it is from God that their rewards will come. For their part, guests are asked not to enter houses without permission and to respect the rules of the houses in which hospitality is provided.

Travellers are considered closer to their Creator while travelling, and it is believed their prayers are responded to more readily than when at home. Further manifestation of travellers' special status in the Islamic faith is indicated by concessions they are accorded in the performance of religious duties and rituals. Quoting the *Sahih al Bukhari*, Din notes that they are allowed to shorten their prayers and postpone fasting during the month of Ramadan. They are to be treated compassionately and granted religious endowments, and must be welcomed personally and offered 'superior food for at least three days'. For their part, travellers must help one another on their journeys – for example, by sharing water and the burden of luggage (Din, 1989: 552).

Not surprisingly, the Arab world has produced a remarkable body of travel literature. The journeys of Ibn Djubayr (1145–1217) and Ibn Battouta (1304–1368) recorded the rich diversity and the cultural cohesion of Islamic societies. These journeys provide further evidence of the lack of distinction between the secular and the religious. Pilgrimage was the primary impulse (or excuse) for the journeys of both travellers. Ibn Djubayr's *rhila*, for example, was prompted to atone for drinking wine that had been forced on him by Almohad, governor of Granada. Similarly, Ibn Battuta made pilgrimage the excuse for what proved to be a virtual lifetime of globe-trotting, and his accounts became classics of travel writing (Anon., 1986: 528).

According to Din (1989: 552), Islamic doctrine considers travel an instrument for fostering unity among the nation of Islam. It eschews the hedonism and emphasis on consumption in modern tourism and enjoins gen-uine, humane, equitable and reciprocal cross-cultural communication. Unlike modern mass tourism, the relationship between hosts and guests is a personal one, which is directed towards submission to the way of God.

Islamic rules governing the relationship between host and guest are by no means simply a relic of the past. When modern tourism was introduced into regions inhabited by Bedouin communities, it resulted in genuine confusion. The Bedouin of the Sinai desert, for example, have had to differentiate between guests and tourists, who increasingly provide most of their income. The dilemma is especially acute because, in this region, Bedouin have increasingly found themselves providers for the hospitality industry, a term which is itself contradictory for them. While the Bedouin do not own the major international hotels that have sprung up in the region, they do own and operate most of the small coffee shops, camp sites and taxi services. Others perform versions of 'staged authentic hospitality', receiving tourists and offering tea and dates, as is traditional in the region. In this case, however, financial reward rather than God's blessing is the motivating factor.

At the same time, though, Bedouin still welcome genuine guests, whether friends from nearby villages or visitors outside the tourist industry, according to their traditional rules of hospitality. As a consequence, they tend to make a strong distinction between tourists and guests, associating tourists with the beach and guests with the interior. It is a distinction that has become increasingly problematic. The tourist stranded in his four-wheel drive in the interior will be rescued without expectation of reward and treated as a guest, even if the day before they had haggled over the price of a taxi ride to the beach (Aziz, 1999: 239–246).

Recent Trends in Tourism in the Arab/Islamic World

Modern tourism in the Arab world began with visits to the archaeological sites of Egypt, and other centres of cultural interest soon became popular. In the 1960s, Morocco, in particular, became a destination for low-budget travellers. However, the wide difference in these two societies, and the type of tourists they attract, illustrates a more general problem. It also surfaces in the way that the region is categorized by the World Tourism Organization (WTO), which divides the 'Expanded Middle East' (EME) into three sectors. The first is Northern Africa (Algeria, Morocco, the Sudan and Tunisia), the second is Mediterranean Europe (Cyprus, Israel and Turkey) and the third is the Middle East (Bahrain, Egypt, Iraq, Jordan, Kuwait, Lebanon, Libyan Arab Jamahiriya, Oman, Qatar, Saudi Arabia, Syrian Arab Republic, the United Arab Emirates and the Yemen) (WTO, 1998). In fact, there are major variations among the three sub-regions, and the East Mediterranean Europe sector, for example, accounts for more than half the total receipts of the EME.

The position taken in this chapter, where the Arab Islamic world is treated as synonymous with the MENA, is not without its own difficulties. Although the Arab world has numerous intra-regional political organizations – for example, the Arab League, which has a Higher Council for Tourism, and the Gulf Cooperation Council (GCC) – they appear not to produce statistics of tourist movement within the MENA region. Even with this restricted definition of the Middle East, huge socio-economic variations in the region are soon revealed, which have a radical influence on the way that the area's tourism has developed. Because of oil, the United Arab Emirates (UAE) and Qatar, for example, are among the richest countries in the world, and thus have no obvious economic reason to develop incoming tourism (even though the UAE and Bahrain are seriously attempting to promote tourism as a form of public relations).

By contrast, the Sudan and the Yemen are among the poorest and most politically unsettled (Burns and Cooper, 1997). Political unrest has also played a major role in preventing tourism development in Algeria, Palestine and (until the latter part of 2000) Lebanon, and security issues have been crucial in Egypt (Aziz, 1995). When it is also recognized that no Islamic country has yet managed to accommodate the needs of Western tourists

without compromising the religious and cultural expectations of most of its own people, it is evident that tourism development for much of the region is still some distance away.

Analysis of data on tourist arrivals and receipts for the EME (Table 10.1) confirms, first, that the East Mediterranean accounts for a large percentage of the arrivals in the EME region, as indicated earlier. Secondly, it is noteworthy that the ratio of receipts to arrivals varies widely across countries. Tourists visiting Egypt, for example, spend more per capita than those who go to North Africa, a sub-region whose proximity to Europe has enabled it to maintain steady growth, but which appeals primarily to low-spending package tourists and backpackers. Visitors to Saudi Arabia also spend relatively little, but here the reason is different: most are pilgrims, who use facilities subsidized by the authorities.

Thirdly, although the WTO considers the Middle East sub-region to be the least within the EME (WTO, 1998), statistics can be misleading. Citizens of member states of the GCC (Saudi Arabia, Kuwait, Bahrain, Qatar, Oman and the UAE) visiting other member states are not subject to immigration or passport control and thus their visits go unrecorded. It is also necessary to take population size into account, for even though absolute arrivals and departures are low, a high percentage of the population may still be tourists. In 1994, for example, from a population of 18.1 million in Saudi Arabia, 6.5 million travelled to international destinations, and account should also be taken of the large percentage of expatriate workers in Saudi Arabia (Travel and Tourism Analyst, 1996).

In 1997, within the sub-region of the Middle East, Egypt alone accounted for 24.7% of arrivals, followed by Saudi Arabia, which took 24.3%. Except for Egypt, which is popular among holidaymakers from Europe, the leisure market is less important than for North Africa, and business travel is the major market main segment, along with religious tourism. Independent statistics for these two segments are not available. The relative share of Europe is also increasing in some of the Gulf countries, e.g. Oman, Bahrain and UAE (WTO, 1998).

Table 10.1. Tourist arrivals and receipts in the Expanded Middle East (EME),1996–1997.

EME	Tourist arrivals (000)		Change (%)	Tourists receipts (US$, 000)		Change (%)
	1996	1997	97/96	1996	1997	97/96
Turkey	7,966	9,040	13.48	5,962	7,000	17.41
Tunisia	3,885	4,263	9.73	1,451	1,450	6.13
Egypt	3,528	3,657	3.66	3,204	3,847	20.07
Saudi Arabia	3,458	3,594	3.93	1,308	1,420	8.56
Morocco	2,693	3,115	15.67	1,381	1,200	–13.11
Cyprus	1,950	2,060	5.64	1,670	1,613	–3.41
Israel	2,100	2,003	–4.62	2,942	2,800	–4.83
Bahrain	1,757	1,848	5.18	258	260	0.78
UAE (Dubai)	1,768	1,792	1.36	–	–	–
Jordan	1,103	1,127	2.18	744	760	2.15
Syria	830	842	1.45	1,206	1,250	3.65
Algeria	605	635	4.96	24	20	–16.67
Lebanon	424	558	31.60	715	1,000	39.86
Qatar	327	425	29.97	–	–	–
Oman	349	375	7.45	99	108	9.09
Iraq	345	346	0.29	13	13	0.00
Libya	88	94	6.82	6	6	0.00
Yemen	74	84	13.51	42	69	64.29
Sudan	65	64	–1.54	8	8	0.00
Kuwait	33	35	6.06	144	140	–2.78
Total	33,348	35,957	7.8	21,177	23,054	8.9

UAE, United Arab Emirates.
Source: WTO (1998: 16).

Despite the huge numbers of arrivals to Saudi Arabia, it is not yet considered to have a major tourist industry, it does not issue tourist visas, and it is perceived to be culturally opposed to inbound international leisure tourism (Burns and Cooper, 1997). However, it is one of the world's centres of religious tourism, a topic that is discussed in the remainder of this chapter.

The *Hajj*

Exact figures of pilgrims to Saudi Arabia are difficult to calculate. According to one source, in 1983 a record 2.5 million pilgrims went to Saudi Arabia to perform the *Hajj* (Travel and Tourism Analyst, 1996: 28) but such numbers were not maintained, possibly because it was soon after this time that the Saudi authorities restricted the number of visitors by imposing quotas. Saudi authorities indicate that over the period 1988–1997, pilgrims performing the *Hajj* over the designated 4-day period increased to over a million, (Table 10.2).

However, pilgrims arriving on *Umra* (a visit to the holy sites) outside the specified month of *Hajj* (and thus not performing a ritual prescribed as one of the five pillars of Islam) along with business and other visitors over the rest of the year accounted for an additional 2 million (Table 10.3).

Although they spend less than recreational tourists, the *Hajj* is the largest voluntary mass movement and the largest concentration of people for any event in the world, and is enough to make Saudi Arabia especially significant in the study of travel and tourism. It is a moot point as to whether or not the *Hajj* is a form of tourism, and debate on this topic is ongoing. Christians going on pilgrimage to Europe's sacred sites, such as Lourdes, Fatima and Lisieux, are routinely classified as tourists, whereas the Saudi authorities refuse to consider the *Hajj* even as a type of religious tourism, associating tourism with the stereotypical hedonistic behaviour of Western tourists.

However pilgrims are defined, the number of people performing the annual *Hajj* is rou-

Table 10.2. Pilgrims making the *Hajj* to Mecca: 1988–1998ᵃ.

Year AH	Year AD	No. of pilgrims
1409	1988/89	774,600
1410	1989/90	827,200
1411	1990/91	720,100
1412	1991/92	1,015,700
1413	1992/93	992,800
1414	1993/94	997,400
1415	1994/95	1,046,307
1416	1995/96	1,080,465
1417	1996/97	1,168,600
1418	1997/98	1,132,300

ᵃThese figures refer only to the offical 4-day period of the *Hajj*, and do not include pilgrims and other visitors for the rest of the year.
Sources: Saudi Arabia Central Department of Statistics (1997); Chamber of Industry and Commerce (1999).

tinely high, and much of the action occurs in a concentrated period, the exact time of which, at least from a Western perspective, varies from year to year. The date is determined by the *Hijri* calendar, which itself relates to a journey, the migration of the Prophet from Mecca to Medina in AD 622. Indeed, *Hijri* derives from *Hijra* (migration). The calendar is based on lunar months and thus does not correspond to the Gregorian calendar, producing a difference of some 11 days every year. In terms of the Gregorian calendar, then, the *Hajj* is a movable feast that can occur in any month of the year.

Saudi Arabia restricts the numbers of pilgrims that can visit the country at any one time. To this end, there is a Ministry of the *Hajj* in Saudi Arabia, which implements quotas for the various Islamic states, assisted by Islamic leaders or government ministries for religion in Islamic countries. No reliable figures for quotas have been made available but it was widely reported in the Arab press that permission was

given to 60,000 Egyptian pilgrims to travel to Mecca for the *Hajj* of the year 2000. Airlines allocate special flights, and Jeddah airport has a special terminal to cope with the numbers.

Even with the quotas, such vast numbers, concentrated over 4 days in and around Mecca, present unique and extraordinary challenges for special event management and require the maintenance of order and safety while yet preserving the spiritual significance of the events (Al-Yafi, 1993). The logistics of moving and accommodating so many pilgrims, performing the same rituals at the same time and place, are impressive. As guardians of the holy city of Mecca, the Saudi government considers providing for the pilgrims a duty, and spends nearly US$500 million annually in the process (Travel and Tourism Analyst, 1996: 28). Pilgrims must be accommodated, transported and protected from health and other hazards, an effort that does not always succeed. In 1997, a fire occurred during the *Hajj* that left many dead and injured, and a few years previously the sheer weight of numbers led to a blockage in an underground tunnel.

Governments in most Islamic countries help their citizens to make the pilgrimage. Many arrange loans for employees to go on *Hajj* and some government and other public organizations contribute directly towards the costs of the journey, while television and radio quiz shows give out *Hajj* and *Umra* trips as prizes. In 2000, the United Nations realized the importance of the *Hajj* to Iraqis and allocated a fund for Iraqi citizens to go on the *Hajj* and arranged special transport for them. Muslims from all social classes aspire to go on *Hajj* once in their lifetime, often spending their life savings to fulfil this religious requirement. For Muslims from lower socio-economic groups, it is usually the only chance to travel overseas, to meet Muslims from all over

Table 10.3. International tourist arrivals and receipts to Saudi Arabia, 1988–1997.

Year	1988	1989	1990	1991	1992	1993	1994	1995	1996	1997
Arrivals (000s)	2137	1677	2209	2094	2582	2869	3229	3325	3458	3594
Change (%)	−4.21	−21.53	31.72	−5.21	23.30	11.12	12.55	2.97	4.00	3.93
Receipts (US$ million)	2066	2050	1884	1000	1000	1121	1140	1210	1308	1420
Change (%)	−20.54	−0.77	−8.10	−46.92	0.00	12.10	1.69	6.14	8.10	8.56

Source: WTO (1998: 59).

the world, and to be re-created in a spiritual and practical sense. Expenditure for such trips is considered to be for a divine purpose, enabling the pilgrim to be closer to God.

The concept of pilgrimage in Islam, however, allows for the satisfaction of human as well as religious needs (Quran, 2: 198). Muslims are encouraged to engage in trade while on pilgrimage, albeit not to the detriment of the religious purpose of their journey, and African pilgrims, for example, finance their journey by taking with them trade goods for sale and barter. Alongside the religious rituals of the *Hajj*, mundane daily life continues.

Such a mass movement of population attracts the same agencies as those catering for conventional tourism. For tour operators and travel agencies, the *Hajj* is a lucrative source of income. Many have identified a niche market and promoted packages that replace tents with air-conditioned marquees, and ensure that the entire journey takes no more than 5 days. Such 'executive pilgrimage' attracts affluent pilgrims and those with little time to spare and, despite the argument of some religious leaders that such 'package tours' contradict the principles of humility and equality for all races and classes that are a fundamental tenet of the *Hajj*, they remain popular.

For Muslims, going to Mecca is a return to the centre of Islam, the birth and burial place of the prophet Muhammad, where the Quran was bestowed upon him. They also perceive it as a return to the centre of the Abrahamic faiths. This symbolic notion is illustrated by the very first ritual that pilgrims undertake upon their arrival to Mecca: the circumambulation (*Tawaf*) of the *Kaa'ba*, a site believed by Muslims to be the house of God built by the Prophet Abraham, the father of all prophets. The rituals of *Hajj* are a representation of the life story of Abraham and pilgrims take pride and honour in attempting to relive and crystallize this important stage of their history and religion. The fact that Islam prohibits representation and imagery makes the *Hajj* (and to a lesser extent *Umra*) one of the primary ways of accessing the intangible.

The *Hajj* takes place in the 11th month of the *Hijri* year, *Dhul-Hijjah*, but months before it starts pilgrims begin arriving at Mecca, having assumed the condition of *Ihram*, wearing simple white cloth wrapped around the body rather than finished items of clothing. They thus demonstrate that all Muslims are equal before God, irrespective of differences in wealth. Many pilgrims first go to Medina to visit the Mosque of the Prophet, but the majority go straight to Mecca to perform the initial *Tawaf Al Qudum* (the circumambulation of the Arrival). On the 8th day of the month, about a third of the pilgrims go to Muna to stay in tent camps, while most of those remaining stay in Mecca.

On the 9th day of the month, when the sun has risen, pilgrims proceed to the plain of Arafat for the ritual of *Wukuf*, standing on the Mountain of Mercy, believed to be the site on which Abraham offered to sacrifice his son in response to God's commandment. They then move to *Muzdalifia*, where they throw pebbles at the symbolic devils in the valley of Muna, sacrifice an animal (also symbolic of the story of Abraham) and return to Mecca for another circumambulation of the *Kaa'ba*. After this, they move between the hills of Safa and Marwa (the act of *Sa'ee*) to symbolize events in the life of *Hajer* (Abraham's wife) and make a last circuit around the *Kaa'ba* before being released from *Ihram* cloths.

As Muslims believe that they must make the pilgrimage to Mecca once in their lifetime, they do so as soon as the opportunity arises. However, it is common to go relatively late in life, because only then have many saved up sufficient funds to make the journey. The process of leaving home is always accompanied by a series of celebrations, resembling weddings. Lights are hung on the house of the individual preparing for the journey, there are ululations (*zaghrouda*) expressing happiness felt at the occasion, and cars and taxis taking pilgrims to the airport or port display white flags to symbolize purity. Friends and relatives gather at the house, asking the pilgrim to remember them when in the house of God.

The journey to Mecca is not only a religious journey. Pilgrims engage in other activities and, after the *Hajj* rituals are complete, most engage in trade and shopping, often purchasing souvenirs for friends and relatives. These include white woven hats worn by men, prayer mats and prayer beads (worry beads), and other items commonly sold during the season of the *Hajj*. Some also take jerry cans filled with water from the spring of Zemzem, which dates back to the Prophet's time. Such items are given as presents on the pilgrims' return and are especially valued by recipients, as they are souvenirs of the Holy Cities.

Pilgrims return from the *Hajj* with their status enhanced, especially if they are from rural villages where few can afford the journey. Returnees are perceived as pure and free from sins, and men receive the title of *Hajj* before their name, and women that of *Hajja*.

The process and rituals of the *Hajj* have certain aspects of liminality, especially when placed in the wider context of the rules of the Islamic faith. The *Ihram* cloths that denote equality before God are first worn just before the performance of pilgrimage rituals, quite literally on the outskirts of Mecca. In the circuits around *Kaa'ba*, men and women are mixed – a process considerably at variance from other religious duties in Islam, where they are usually segregated. The uniformity of dress and movement allows participants to experience a feeling of unity and oneness that reaches its peak during the *Hajj* but is supposed to be observed in the Muslim's daily life.

For those who undertake it, going on the *Hajj* is far more significant than any other journey. It is a life-changing experience and, as indicated earlier, its spiritual importance is recognized by Muslim states and by the Saudi government. At the same time, except for citizens of oil-rich states, most Muslims enjoy little discretionary income. For them, the *Hajj* is a substitute for what, in other circumstances, would be recreational travel. Given the history of tourism, and the role that religion has played in motivating people to travel, this is not surprising. The terminology of tourism, religion and pilgrimage illustrates the connec-

tions among them, as numerous references to 'holy days' and 're-creation' testify (Graburn 1977; Cohen, 1979, 1992).

Conclusions

Western concepts and definitions tend to dominate discussions of the nature and extent of international tourism. These relate uneasily to notions of travel in the Islamic faith and culture, where life itself is seen as a journey, to be spent serving God. Indeed, travel is central to the culture of the Arab Islamic world, both conceptually and physically, and the tensions and complexities of tourism in the region must be seen in this context. At the same time, the notion of purposeful travel promoted by Islam contrasts with Western tourism, and Islamic states take pride in distancing themselves from the hedonism and self-indulgence it is felt to represent. Nevertheless, at the time of writing, such views appear to be changing, and many countries in the Gulf region, including Saudi Arabia and the Sultanate of Oman, are developing national plans for tourism, albeit along Islamic lines.

The phenomenon of the *Hajj* provides a spectacular example of a type of tourism not yet fully recognized in Western studies of tourism. It is a form of intra-regional and inter-regional tourism that within MENA boundaries fulfils both spiritual and material requirements of Muslims without compromising their religious principles. Muslims are encouraged to engage in purposeful travel and the *Hajj* provides the means through which this purposefulness is dedicated to God. Yet despite the arrival of at least 1 million pilgrims a year to Saudi Arabia, the country is still criticized in the West for not opening its doors to international tourism.

References

Al-Yafi, A. (1993) *Management of Hajj Mobility Systems, a Logistical Perspective*, Joh. Enshede, Amsterdam BV.

Anon. (1986) *Encyclopaedia of Islam*. E.J.Brill, Leiden, The Netherlands.

Anon. (1997) *Year Book*. Saudi Arabia Central Department of Statistics, Jeddah.

Anon. (1999) *Study on the Development of Tourism Facilities in Saudi Arabia*. Chamber of Industry and Commerce, Jeddah.

Aziz, H. (1991) The image of Egypt in the British media. MSc thesis, University of Strathclyde, Glasgow, UK.

Aziz, H. (1995) Understanding attacks on tourists in Egypt. *Tourism Management* 16(2), 91–95.

Aziz, H. (1999) Negotiating boundaries and reconstructing landscapes: a study of the relations between Bedouin, tourists and the state. PhD thesis, University of Surrey, UK.

Burns, P. and Cooper, C. (1997) Yemen tourism and a tribal-Marxist dichotomy. *Tourism Management* 18(8), 555–563.

Burton, Sir Richard (1937) *A Pilgrimage to Meccah and Medina*. H. Joseph, London.

Cohen, E. (1979) A phenomenology of tourists experiences. *Sociology* 13, 179–201.

Cohen, E. (1992) Pilgrimage centers, concentric and excentric. *Annals of Tourism Research* 19(1), 33–50.

Din, K. (1989) Islam and tourism, patterns, issues and options. *Annals of Tourism Research* 16(4), 542–563.

Doughty, C.M. (1908) *Wanderings in Arabia: being an abridgment of 'Travels in Arabia Deserta'*, Vol. 1. Duckworth, London.

Graburn, N. (1977) Tourism: the sacred journey. In: Smith, V. (ed.) *Hosts and Guests: the Anthropology of Tourism*. University of Pennsylvania Press, Philadelphia, Pennsylvania, pp. 16–31.

Lawrence, T.E. (1976) *Seven Pillars of Wisdom: a Triumph*, 5th edn. Cape, London.

Quran (*The Holy Quran*), translated by Abdullah Yusuf, Dar Al Arabia, Beirut.

Rehman, A. (1991) *Subject Index to the Holy Quran*. Noor Publishing House, Delhi.

Said, E. (1991) *Orientalism: Western Conceptions of the Orient*. Penguin Books, London.

Stark, F. (1936) *The Southern Gates of Arabia: a Journey in the Hadhramaut*. Murray, London.

Thesiger, W. (1964) *The Marsh Arabs*. Longmans, London.

Travel and Tourism Analyst (1996) Outbound markets. *Saudi Arabia Outbound* 4, 20–34.

WTO (1998) *Tourism Market Trends: Expanded Middle East, 1988–1997*. World Tourism Organisation, Madrid.

11

Mass Tourism and Alternative Tourism in the Caribbean

David B. Weaver

Introduction

Within the 'less developed world', the Caribbean stands out as a region of exceptionally high levels of tourism development and dependency. The primary purpose of this chapter is to analyse the Caribbean tourism sector in terms of the contemporary status of mass tourism and small-scale tourism options such as ecotourism, and to position this discussion within the dynamics of sustainability. Following a brief overview of the Caribbean tourism sector, a broad context model of tourism possibilities for destinations in general, based upon variations in scale and regulation, is presented as a framework for the subsequent analysis of Caribbean destinations. The four categories that constitute this model are then used sequentially as a basis for examining tourism within the region. This examination also considers the transformations that may occur among those four categories. The chapter concludes by presenting a generic model of tourism development appropriate for most of the region's states and dependencies.

Overview of Caribbean Tourism

The Caribbean is an archipelagic region defined in this chapter as including all insular states and dependencies located within the Caribbean Sea. Bermuda, and those islands which fall under the jurisdiction of Central or South American states such as Colombia (e.g. Isla de Margarita) and Honduras (e.g. Roatan), are excluded (Fig. 11.1). All qualifying states and dependencies are listed in Table 11.1, along with their resident populations and basic data pertaining to their tourism sectors. As defined above, the Caribbean accounted for 0.6% of the world's population in 1996, but fully 2.3% of all international stayovers, thereby giving the region a fourfold over-representation as a destination region relative to its resident population. This over-representation is even more apparent when cruise ship excursionists are taken into consideration, since the Caribbean accounted for 53.6% of all such activity in 1995, in terms of bed-days spent on cruise ships (Sobers, 1996: 73).

With tourism accounting for about one-quarter of all regional export earnings (compared with 7% worldwide), the Caribbean can legitimately be described as the world's most tourism-dependent region (Holder, 1996). This general statement, however, disguises the existence of significant internal variations. At one extreme, the Dutch dependency of St Maarten (a component of The Netherlands Antilles) and the UK dependency of the Turks

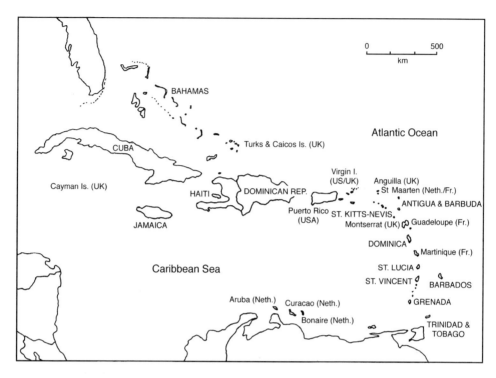

Fig. 11.1. The Caribbean. Island names in full capitals (e.g. DOMINICA) are independent states; those with initial capitals only (e.g. Aruba) are dependencies (Fr. = France, Neth. = The Netherlands).

and Caicos Islands may be characterized as 'hyper-destinations' whose economies depend almost entirely on tourism, and who receive almost 20 inbound stayovers each year for every local resident. By way of comparison, the USA would need to host almost 5 billion inbound stayovers per year to achieve a comparable level of tourism penetration. At the opposite end of the spectrum, Haiti and Cuba host far fewer stayovers relative to their resident populations, and realize a relatively low 5–7% contribution from tourism to their national economies (which is, however, still comparable to the global contribution level of tourism). The general pattern discernible within the Caribbean is that smaller states or dependencies tend to be relatively more dependent on tourism than larger entities. Among other factors, this is the result of limited resource endowments that have historically hindered the formation of a diverse economic base. Hence, tourism contributions to gross national product (GNP) in the magnitude of 20–50% are normative among the region's smaller states and dependencies, a level matched elsewhere only by isolated countries or dependencies within the South Pacific (e.g. Guam, Northern Marianas), the Indian Ocean (Maldives, Seychelles) and the Mediterranean (Malta, Cyprus).

The Caribbean as a Pleasure Periphery Component

Although specific locations such as Havana were already well-developed as tourist destinations prior to the Second World War, it is the post-war period that is associated with the widespread diffusion of mass tourism in the Caribbean. Since 1950, various demand-based or 'push' factors (e.g. increased discretionary time and income, demographic and technological change) have combined with supply-based or 'pull' factors (e.g. provision of high quality 3S – sea, sand, sun – resources and open investment climates) to facilitate a

Table 11.1. Tourism-related data for Caribbean destinations.

| Destination | Resident population 1996 | Stayovers (000) | | | 1996 | | |
		1982	1992	1996	Cruise ship excursions	Stayovers per resident	Tourism as % of GNP
Anguilla	10	N/A	32	37	N/A	3.7	75
Antigua and Barbuda	65	87	210	220	300	3.4	55
Aruba	68	220	542	641	316	9.4	36[b]
Bahamas	259	1,101	1,399	1,633	1,686	6.5	40
Barbados	257	304	385	447	510	1.7	38
Bonaire	11	N/A	51	65	15	5.0	N/A
British Virgin Islands	18	114	117	244	160	13.6	75[c]
Cayman Islands	35	121	242	373	771	10.7	N/A
Cuba	10,951	N/A	455	999	2	0.1	7
Curacao	150	174	219	219	170[c]	1.5	8[a]
Dominica	83	19	47	63	193	0.8	16[c]
Dominican Republic	8,089	480	1,415	1,926	111	0.2	13
Grenada	95	23	88	108	267	1.1	21[c]
Guadeloupe	408	189	341	625	611	1.5	N/A
Haiti	6,732	158	90	150	N/A	0.02	5[c]
Jamaica	2,595	468	1,057	1,162	658	0.4	28[c]
Martinique	399	178	321	477	408	1.2	N/A
Montserrat	12	15	17	9	7	0.8	36[b]
Puerto Rico	3,802	1,564	2,657	3,065	1,045	0.3	6[c]
Saba	1	N/A	25	10	N/A	10.0	N/A
St Eustatius	2	N/A	30	24	N/A	12.0	N/A
St Kitts and Nevis	41	35	88	84	86	2.1	31[c]
St Lucia	158	70	181	238	182	1.5	50[c]
St Maarten	33	213	551	351	657	19.9	N/A
St Vincent and the Grenadines	118	37	53	58	128	0.5	21[c]
Trinidad and Tobago	1,272	184	235	266	22	0.2	2
Turks and Caicos Islands	14	N/A	47	88	N/A	6.3	N/A
US Virgin Islands	105	340	478	279	1,316	2.7	N/A
Total	35,762	6,094	11,373	13,861	9,621	0.4	

GNP, gross national product.
[a]1992
[b]1994
[c]1995
Sources: WTO (1987, 1998).

fundamental restructuring of the regional economy away from the primary sector, and plantation-based agriculture in particular, toward tourism (McElroy and de Albuquerque, 1998). The subsequent description of the region as part of an emerging global 'pleasure periphery' (Turner and Ash, 1975) alludes to its economically marginal or less developed status, and to the increasing mobilization of this periphery for leisure-based tourism purposes by the core metropolitan countries.

However, just as the actual importance of tourism varies from one island to another, this concept of pleasure periphery is itself something of an oversimplification that requires clarification. First, with regard to the 'periphery' component, it is true that countries such as Jamaica, the Dominican Republic and especially Haiti personify the stereotype of the less developed Third World country. Yet the Cayman Islands, British Virgin Islands, Puerto Rico, Bahamas, Barbados and Trinidad and Tobago, in particular, display per capita GNP levels and social indicators that are more characteristic of the developed world. Secondly, the characterization of the Caribbean as a strictly leisure/pleasure-based destination region is also an oversimplification. In fact, the regional tourism sector can best be described as a three-tier structure, where 3S-centred beach resorts and cruise ship excursionist tourism occupy the top and most important tier. The middle tier is occupied in roughly equal proportions by visiting friends and relatives (VFR) and business tourism, while historical, cultural and environmental tourism is positioned at the bottom of this hierarchy (Fig. 11.2). In general terms, the lower two tiers tend to be relatively more important as components of the tourism sector in countries where tourism is less important.

Generic Tourism Modes

Figure 11.3 provides a framework for categorizing and analysing the diverse Caribbean tourism sector by proposing four generic modes of tourism development that are applicable to all destinations. These modes are obtained by combining the scale of tourism development with the extent to which regulations are in place to ensure adherence to principles of sustainability. Dotted lines are used to separate the four categories, in recognition of the fact that the actual positioning of Caribbean destinations along both axes

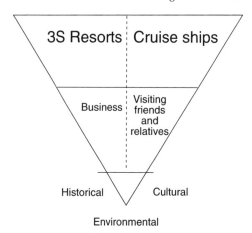

Fig. 11.2. Structure of Caribbean tourism. (Source: Weaver, 1998.)

occurs on a continuum rather than within discrete categories.

Briefly, unsustainable mass tourism (UMT) occurs where the level of tourism development is large-scale, and the accompanying regulatory environment minimal or non-existent in terms of its ability to minimize the negative impacts of the sector (Weaver, 2000). Accordingly, existing economic, socio-cultural and environmental carrying capacities of the destination are breached by the tourism sector. In contrast, sustainable mass tourism (SMT) is regulated internally (i.e. by the industry) or externally (i.e. by government) to ensure that existing carrying capacities are not exceeded, and that the latter are adjusted, if necessary, to accommodate further tourism-related development. This could be achieved, for example, by implementing strict waste disposal and recycling procedures within a large resort hotel, conforming the architecture of these hotels to local vernacular styles, hiring a quota of local residents, supporting community development programmes, and 'naturalizing' hotel properties to accommodate native vegetation.

At the less intensive end of the scale, circumstantial alternative tourism (CAT) is non-regulated, small-scale tourism that exists as such only because the destination happens to be situated within the incipient stages of the destination life cycle – as represented, for example, by the Exploration and Involvement stages of Butler's well-known S-shaped sequence (Butler, 1980). Hence, local ownership, adherence to vernacular architectural norms, robust inter-sectoral linkages and other characteristics associated with alternative tourism occur merely as a 'circumstance' of pre-development dynamics, and not as a consequence of deliberate planning and management decisions. In contrast, where such a small-scale alternative to mass tourism is consciously maintained through appropriate regulations, the destination can be described as having deliberate alternative tourism (DAT). DAT, in turn, can be differentiated between socio-cultural alternative tourism and ecotourism, the latter being commonly associated with three essential characteristics: (i) an emphasis on the natural environment (or some element thereof) as the primary basis of attrac-

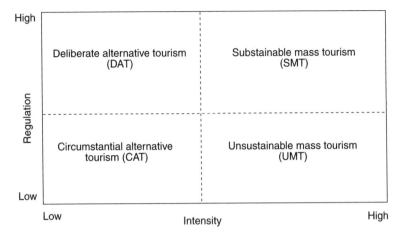

Fig. 11.3. Destination tourism possibilities. (Source: Weaver, 2000.)

tion (with associated cultural attributes constituting a secondary element of attraction); (ii) an appreciative or educative relationship with the attraction, rather than one where the natural environment is simply a setting for other types of activity (as in adventure tourism or beach-bathing); and (iii) a reasonable intent to be environmentally, socio-culturally and economically sustainable (Blamey, 1997).

Application of the Model to the Caribbean

The following section considers the applicability of the four tourism categories to the Caribbean tourism sector, and also examines the possible transformations and relationships that can and do occur among the categories.

Unsustainable mass tourism

There is a great deal of evidence to suggest that large-scale tourism in the Caribbean, in the main, has developed along an environmentally, socially and economically unsustainable trajectory from a destination perspective (e.g. Edwards, 1988; Robbins, 1994; de Albuquerque and McElroy, 1995; Holder, 1996; Pattullo, 1996; Olsen, 1997; France, 1998). These costs are now briefly outlined.

Environmental costs

Environmentally, large-scale tourism has been implicated as a major factor in the destruction of the region's coral reefs, as well as in the deterioration of offshore water quality, sand mining, the appropriation of high quality farmland, and the clearance of mangrove and other sensitive littoral vegetation. While there is some evidence of improvement in recent years (see the section on SMT, below), the basic problems persist due to a combination of lenient regulations, irregular enforcement of these regulations, and the relentless expansion of tourism development within and beyond existing high density resort areas. To illustrate, a major survey of 68 hotels and resorts in the eastern Caribbean, conducted in the mid-1990s, showed little compliance with the basic criteria for effluent disposal, with most waste matter simply being dumped into the sea (Holder, 1996: 159). With regard to volume, accommodation capacity in the Caribbean study area continues to expand unabated, having risen from 131,852 rooms in 1990 to 173,406 in 1995 (Devas, 1997: 62) and almost 180,000 in 1996 (WTO, 1998).

It is simplistic to argue that these continuing environmental problems are strictly the result of stupidity or corruption, although both factors do play a role in many situations. Clearly, a more sophisticated understanding of the surrounding issues is necessary if the problem is to be effectively gauged and resolved. In the first instance, environmental destruction is the almost inevitable outcome resulting from the collision of two basic factors. One of these is the inherently fragile nature of beaches, coral reefs, dunes, estuaries, mangroves, and other coastal and littoral environments. The second factor is the imperative for resort-based tourism developers to locate their projects as close as possible to the beach and sea in order to maximize their profitability, given that resort patrons generally want to be as close as possible to these 3S tourism resources. Clearly, such development must be attended by the strictest regulations if it is to have any chance of being sustainable in the long term. Hotels, not surprisingly, may seek to avoid these regulations, given that the associated costs threaten profit margins that are already extremely narrow.

For their own part, governments are also reluctant to implement or enforce such regulations. This reticence must be understood in the context of the need for each island to compete effectively with its neighbours in the one area (i.e. tourism) where most islands have a relatively strong competitive advantage. If environmental regulations are perceived by developers to be too strict in one island, then another is usually available to attract the resort project with lax environmental laws and other incentives. In weighing the decision to relax its own laws in order to be as competitive, the original island might consider a number of factors, including the indisputable correlation that exists between intensively developed tourism sectors and high per capita incomes (especially on the smaller islands), the relative attractiveness of large resorts over small projects as employment generators, and the need to generate foreign exchange to redress escalating levels of external debt. The foreign debt of Antigua, for instance, increased from US$54 million in 1984 to US$268 million in 1990, while the comparable figure for Jamaica was US$2071 million and US$4152 million (Holder, 1996: 155). Governments are also disposed toward larger-scale tourism development by differential lags between cause and effect. In economic terms, the positive effects of a large resort are almost immediately realized. However, in environmental terms, the costs of that same project may not be fully

apparent until the arrival of a 100-year hurricane event, or until a large number of indiscernible effects eventually accumulate into a major environmental problem.

Socio-political and economic costs

Mass tourism in the Caribbean has socio-political and economic dimensions of unsustainability that interact with the environmental perspective described above. Early articulations of these dimensions were based mainly on the Dependency paradigm, as for example in the 'plantation model' of tourism development which argued that the post-Second World War sectoral transformation of Caribbean economies was not accompanied by any fundamental structural change. Thus, while the plantation itself may have been replaced in coastal areas by resorts, the latter have retained many elements of the plantation system that serve to retain the destination in a dependent state. These include the retention of control by the expatriate and local elite, the differentiation of space into a resort-dominated coast and local-dominated interior, and the maintenance of hierarchical power structures (Weaver, 1988).

While aspects of the Dependency framework are still considered in discussions of the socio-political and economic sustainability of Caribbean tourism (e.g. France, 1998), it is becoming increasingly common to frame this issue in the context of globalization. This perspective emphasizes the footloose nature of international capital, which is able to operate and migrate to its own advantage within an increasingly homogenized world where national sovereignty poses less of a constraint to the business of making a profit. Small island states in the Caribbean and elsewhere are seen as being especially susceptible to such macro-forces, especially given that their fragile economies have always absorbed significant negative impacts as a result of tourism. During the mid-1990s, Caribbean destinations spent US$4 billion each year in importing goods from outside the Caribbean for the tourism industry, reflecting the lack of intra-regional linkages among economic sectors. Exacerbating these import costs are revenue leakages associated with the repatriation of corporate profits and non-resident wages, a problem which in turn results from the high levels of offshore control and expatriate labour inputs that characterize many of the larger resorts. Large-scale tourism in the Caribbean is also especially susceptible to seasonality effects, wherein the low summer season is accompanied by widespread employee lay-offs and net revenue losses.

Sustainable mass tourism

There is debate over whether the growing interest in sustainable tourism is indicative of a fundamental shift toward a 'green' paradigm (e.g. Knill, 1991) or merely a cynical ploy by companies to enhance their public image (e.g. Wheeller, 1997). There is considerable evidence that the tourism industry within the Caribbean and elsewhere has been paying more serious attention to the issue of sustainability in recent years, especially since the early 1990s. This concern may seem somewhat ironic in light of the conventional tourism industry's role in fostering UMT over the past four decades. However, the same corporations that control the mega-resorts are probably in the best position to effect the transition toward sustainability, relative to their smaller counterparts. This is owing to the critical mass that allows them to allocate significant resources specifically for environmental and social purposes. In addition, they generate enough waste to justify sophisticated recycling and waste disposal systems, and they can exert a positive influence on suppliers to act in a similar manner (Clarke, 1997). From a corporate perspective, the incentive to implement sustainable tourism derives not just from the direct profitability associated with energy efficiency, recycling and other 'environmentally friendly' practices, but from the fundamental fact that most tourists are repelled by polluted and aesthetically unpleasant destination surroundings. To despoil these surroundings is therefore to undermine the very 'foundation assets' upon which the sector, and hotel profitability, depends.

Several levels of commitment to sustainable tourism can be identified, ranging in credibility from rhetoric to institutionalization and, finally, actual practice. With regard to the former, there is no doubt that Caribbean businesses and governments, as with businesses and governments worldwide, have publicly embraced the rhetoric of sustainable development. This was indicated by the adoption of the Agenda 21 programme for sustainable development by virtually all Caribbean governments at the 1992 United Nations Conference on Environment and Development, an event that was personally addressed by six Caribbean heads of state (UNCED, 1993). At the sectoral level, rare indeed is the national tourism master plan that does not proclaim adherence to this concept.

A more tangible level of commitment is indicated by the establishment of institutions related to sustainable tourism, or membership in such existing organizations. As of 1998, 112 Caribbean hotels or other businesses and organizations, most of them larger resorts, were registered as members of Green Globe, a programme initiative of the World Travel and Tourism Council (WTTC) designed to foster the implementation of sustainable environmental practices among its members. Especially high levels of involvement were evident in Jamaica (23 members), Barbados (14) and Aruba (13). A major regional effort to institutionalize sustainable large-scale tourism is the Caribbean Action for Sustainable Tourism (CAST), which was established in 1997 by the Caribbean Hotel Association (CHA), the regional hotel industry's major sector organization, to provide environmental guidance and assistance to its member hotels. Concurrently, the CHA has introduced an annual CHA/American Express Green Hotelier Awards programme to recognize exemplary practice within the industry (Clean Islands International, 1997).

The litmus test of commitment is actual adherence to principles of sustainability. It is possible to cite large resorts that are making significant and tangible progress in the direction of sustainability, even though the ideal of sustainable development and sustainable tourism implementation is admittedly handicapped by a variety of major problems. These include difficulties associated with indicator identification, measurement and monitoring, problems in identifying critical impact thresholds, and difficulties in separating tourism-related impacts from those attributable to other forces. Notwithstanding these shortcomings, facilities such as the Half Moon Golf, Tennis and Beach Club in Jamaica's Montego Bay, Club St. Lucia (in St. Lucia), and the Casuarina Beach Club in Barbados have all earned respect for their efforts to practise sustainable tourism. Especially notable is the 6071 ha Punta Cana Beach Resort in the Dominican Republic, which has, among other measures: (i) provided jobs for workers from the local charcoal-producing sector, which has been cited as a major factor in local deforestation; (ii) allocated 707 ha for the establishment of the Punta Cana Ecological Foundation; (iii) inaugurated a sea turtle protection programme; (iv) supported community development projects, including schools and crafts production, for employees who live on the resort property; (v) incorporated elements of the local vernacular architecture in the hotel design; (vi) constructed an incinerator to dispose of solid wastes; (vii) established on-site gardens, employing 40 full-time gardeners, to provide local fruits and vegetables for the resort; and (viii) established a programme to divert local fishers away from the nearby coral reef, which was being negatively affected by local fishing activity (Rainieri, 1995).

Some of these initiatives may be criticized as paternalistic, though the point remains that the Punta Cana innovations represent a great improvement over conventional resort operations and impacts within the Caribbean. However, the Punta Cana model is by no means common within the region, where UMT is still normative.

Circumstantial alternative tourism

Despite its reputation for being a tourism-intensive region, most of the Caribbean is actually occupied by CAT activity. This is obviously true for countries such as Haiti and Cuba, but also applies to intensively developed destinations such as the Bahamas and Antigua, where resort tourism occupies only a very small proportion of the national territory, and DAT options have yet to be widely implemented. CAT landscapes are associated mainly with rural areas where a rudimentary and informal tourism sector is based upon a few small local guesthouses, and hiking/driving activity by a variety of tourist types. Urban areas such as Nassau (Bahamas) and St John's (Antigua) also accommodate CAT through the presence of similar guest houses in 'local' neighbourhoods (Weaver, 1993). To a large extent, the business sector, and particularly the VFR sector (Fig. 11.2) also fall within the CAT sector.

Deliberate alternative tourism

The Caribbean has hosted a number of pioneering DAT strategies, including Jamaica's 'Meet the People' project, established in the 1970s to foster positive and equal relationships between locals and tourists by hosting the latter in the homes of ordinary Jamaicans. This programme, however, like similar initiatives in other less developed countries, has never accounted for more than a tiny fraction of Jamaica's tourism sector (Dernoi, 1981). Since the early 1990s, DAT-like strategies have become more common in the Caribbean. It is now useful to distinguish between those that are comprehensive, in so far as they apply to entire states or dependencies, and those that are localized, or restricted to particular environments within a destination that is otherwise dominated by mass tourism.

Comprehensive DAT

The best regional example of comprehensive DAT is Dominica, which in the early 1970s abandoned its futile attempts to attract large-scale resort tourism. Since then, Dominica has consciously positioned itself as the 'Nature Island of the Caribbean', differentiating itself from its neighbours by publicizing and marketing its mountains, forests, and lack of development as tourism assets rather than liabilities (Weaver, 1991). In addition, a tourism strategy has been developed which encourages small-scale facilities, local ownership, and an emphasis on environmental, historical and cultural attractions. Another country that seems to be moving in a similar direction is St Vincent, which is physically and economically similar to Dominica. The government of St Vincent has established an Advisory Group on Ecotourism to advise the administration on the establishment of ecotourism, and has also created the position of Ecotourism Coordinator to lead such an effort (Weaver, 1998: 193). At the same time, funding was secured from the European Union in the late 1990s to develop specific sites in the island's interior for nature tourism purposes (Department of Tourism, St Vincent and the Grenadines, 1998, personal communication). Another destination to display a similar tendency was the British dependency of Montserrat, prior to the virtual destruction of its tourism industry by the eruptions of its long-dormant volcano after 1995 (Weaver, 1995). In all of these cases, it is interesting to note that intensive 3S tourism would likely have been pursued had it not been for their unfavourable physical settings, indicating comprehensive DAT's status as a 'default' rather than preferred option.

Localized DAT

For most of the states and dependencies that continue to be dominated by mass tourism, there is a growing awareness that DAT, and ecotourism in particular, constitutes a potentially beneficial option for non-resort areas otherwise unsuited for 3S tourism because of unfavourable physical conditions, unsuitable location, or extreme environmental sensitivity. The largest scale form of DAT occurs where one or more peripheral islands are designated, planned and managed for small-scale tourism. The best emerging examples include the Out or 'Family' islands of the Bahamas, Little Cayman and Cayman Brac islands (relative to Grand Cayman Island) and St John island, relative to the main US Virgin Islands of St Thomas and St Croix (CEP, 1994). Saba and St Eustatius may also qualify, relative to the larger Netherlands Antilles entity to which they both belong (Weaver, 1998). Other venues suited toward DAT include mountainous interiors (e.g. northern Trinidad, central Grenada and St Lucia, and the Cordillera Central of the Dominican Republic), offshore coral reefs (e.g. Grand Cayman Island, Bonaire) and coastal areas unfavourable for resort development (e.g. Trinidad's Caroni swamp and the mouth of Jamaica's Black River).

The most tangible manifestations of DAT are found in national parks and other formally protected areas. Traditionally regarded as an area largely devoid of such entities, most Caribbean states and dependencies are now in the process of establishing their national protected area systems. Alternative types of tourism, and ecotourism in particular, are almost always recognized as the most desirable and compatible form of economic activity that can be accommodated within such systems. The logic of a strong linkage between DAT and protected areas is based on the existence, at least in theory, of park regulations that ensure outcomes consistent with the core principles of alternative tourism, including the preservation of the natural environment. One of the best examples of a new protected areas system is found in Jamaica, where recently established units range in size from the 128 h Montego Bay National Marine Park to the 78,529 h Blue and John Crow Mountains National Park. Among countries with more established systems, both the Dominican Republic (Nature Conservancy, 1996) and Cuba (Santana, 1991) have been seriously considering the introduction of ecotourism as an integral component of park master plans. Cuba's protected areas system consists of some 200 units that occupy 12% of the nation's territory, and therefore constitutes an especially significant potential DAT venue.

Within the private sector, DAT is represented by a small but expanding number of 'eco-resorts' that cater to a more specialized ecotourist clientele. A considerable number of these already operate in comprehensive DAT destinations such as Dominica, while significant examples within localized DAT areas include the Maho Bay Campgrounds on the US Virgin Island of St John, and the Asa Wright Nature Centre in the northern rainforests of Trinidad. Possibly related to ecotourism are the Atlantis Submarines of Barbados, which explore reefs, shipwrecks and marine life, while providing passengers with educational talks. If responsible diving is recognized as a legitimate form of ecotourism, then this again would expand the scope for DAT by incorporating offshore areas (e.g. off most major Caribbean resort beaches) where such activity is a common component of 3S tourism.

The annual ecotourism conferences sponsored by the Caribbean Tourism Organization reflect a broad regional institutional interest in this sub-sector. However, comparable levels of formal recognition are not as apparent at the scale of individual destinations. In 1994, the Caribbean Environment Programme (a component of the United Nations Environment Programme) sought to determine the status of ecotourism among individual destinations by sending a questionnaire to all countries and dependencies in the region. Of the 28 listed in Table 11.1, only six responded to this survey (Bahamas, Barbados, Dominican Republic, Martinique, St Vincent and the Turks and Caicos Islands), and all proffered their own idiosyncratic and divergent definitions of 'ecotourism'. Notable was Martinique's inclusion of golf as a form of ecotourism. Furthermore, few agencies had been established at the national level to foster ecotourism initiatives; among the few exceptions were the aforementioned initiatives in St Vincent, and the Ecotourism Department of the National Parks Commission of the Dominican Republic. The surveys also revealed a complete lack of ecotourism-related training programmes, standards or

benchmarks (CEP, 1994). Among agencies that are not ecotourism-specific, National Trusts (NT) in many Caribbean countries have played an important role in developing localized ecotourism opportunities. This is especially apparent in Barbados and Bahamas, and in St Lucia, where the local NT has been instrumental in having the island labelled as a Nature Heritage Tourism destination, and in including ecotourism in regional management plans for St Lucia's watersheds and coastlines (Popovic, 1997).

Transformations

Tourism is an evolutionary rather than a static phenomenon, and it is therefore necessary to consider avenues of probable evolution. Figure 11.4 depicts a range of potential transformations that may occur among the four stages of the model. It should be noted that the much discussed Butler sequence is but one of several possible scenarios. None of the depicted transformations involves movement from high to low intensity, as such transitions are highly unlikely. Of the seven proffered one-stage transformations, only the four options more pertinent to the Caribbean are outlined below.

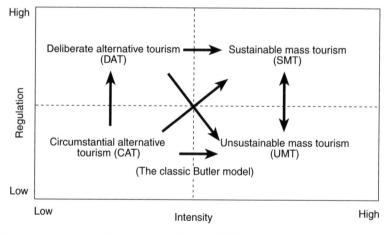

Fig. 11.4. Transformation possibilities. (Source: Weaver, 2000.)

CAT to UMT

The progression of a destination from CAT to UMT is the classic sequence described in the Butler S-curve, and accurately describes the evolution of the most intensively developed Caribbean resort concentrations. Much of the tourism literature creates the impression that such a progression is inevitable for all parts of the Caribbean, a perception that is abetted by continual increases in the number of tourist arrivals and tourism-related facilities throughout the region. However, most of land currently occupied by CAT in the Caribbean is likely to remain as such, or at most undergo a change to some sort of DAT structure. This is due to the simple fact that such space has been and will probably remain unsuitable for large-scale resort development because of its location or unfavourable site characteristics. Attention should therefore be focused on the identification and management of those CAT locations that are most likely to undergo an evolution toward UMT. In the Caribbean, these are likely to include undeveloped beachfronts and their hinterlands, and local settlements located near existing resort areas. In such areas, a transition to either DAT or SMT is more desirable, depending upon community attitudes and other factors.

CAT to DAT

The scope for CAT to DAT transformations within the Caribbean is considerable, especially in the venues described earlier as being suitable for the latter, including island interiors, offshore islands, etc. A complicating factor is the extent to which the natural environments of some Caribbean destinations (e.g. Haiti and 'sugar islands' such as Barbados and Antigua) have already been severely degraded by subsistence or plantation agriculture or other forces unrelated to tourism, suggesting circumstances that are already unsustainable in the broader sense. An alternative strategy in these cases is to use the potential revenues obtained from DAT as an incentive to restore selectively the environmental integrity of such degraded regions.

DAT to UMT

The long-term maintenance of an area as a DAT destination should not be taken for granted. A deliberate transition toward SMT may be deemed desirable if intensification is feasible on economic, social and environmental grounds, and if this conforms to community wishes. More worrisome is a possible movement toward UMT resulting from internal (tourism-related) and external factors. Both of these are evident in Dominica. With regard to internal factors, concerns have been raised over the sustainability of escalating cruise ship arrival numbers, which increased from 90,000 in 1992 to 193,000 in 1996 (WTO, 1998: 57). In sectors external to tourism, the transnational mining corporation BHP is planning the construction of a copper mine in the largely undisturbed central forests of the island, following the passing of the Mines and Minerals Act in 1996. This legislation makes environmental impact assessments discretionary, repeals indigenous land and mineral rights, and allows for only token fines for acts of environmental pollution (Project Underground, 1996). The potential negative repercussions for Dominica's tourism industry are considerable, illustrating the fact that no tourism planning can occur in isolation from such external environments.

UMT to SMT

Despite the growing interest in DAT-type options, the Caribbean tourism industry of the future will almost certainly remain grounded in the more intensive tourism models (Holder, 1996). Hence, the wholesale transition of this sector from a UMT orientation to an SMT orientation is the 'great imperative' of Caribbean tourism as a whole if the latter is to serve as a vehicle for the long-term economic development of the region. The greatest difficulty in bringing about this imperative will be the reversal of the environmental, economic and socio-cultural damage already created by unsustainable mass tourism. However, efforts to effect such a transition in European destinations such as Jersey and Magaluf (on Mallorca) may serve as a prototype for Caribbean islands wishing to undertake a similar process.

Tourism Model for Caribbean Destinations

Currently, most Caribbean states and dependencies display a pattern wherein varying degrees of coastal resort UMT give way to CAT as one moves into the island interior. If coral reefs and peripheral islands are taken into account, then the CAT scenario also extends into the offshore. Currently, there is little or no deliberate interaction between the two zones, aside from the incidental and systemic fact that the CAT interior may serve as a local labour reservoir for the coastal resorts. Further, the emergence of tourism along the coast has been a major contributor to the demise of plantation agriculture in the interior (Weaver, 1988). The preferred option involves a combination of two of the above scenarios: that is, a coastal conversion from UMT to SMT, and the conversion of space elsewhere from CAT to DAT. A corollary to this is the need to integrate the SMT and DAT regions into a synergetic relationship, wherein soft ecotourism options in the DAT sphere help to diversify the mainstay 3S product base. Concurrently, the presence of a soft ecotourism clientele in DAT areas serves as a stimulant to local economic development, and as an economic incentive to preserve and restore natural assets in those regions.

Such a synergy is consistent with Ayala's (1996) assertion of an emerging convergence between mass tourism and ecotourism. This is occurring as the growing soft ecotourist market demands a higher level of creature comfort and affiliated services, while the resort market concurrently moves toward a greater awareness of 'green' issues and increased interest in ancillary environmental, cultural and historical attractions (Poon, 1993). There are various dangers, however, which could attend an SMT/DAT synergy. These include the possibility that the ecotourism component will become too much like mass tourism, yet with limited scope for an upward adjustment in carrying capacity thresholds because of remoteness and the nature of the resource base. It may not be possible, for example, to provide a remote location visitors' centre with an efficient waste disposal system to cope with increased visitation by soft ecotourists from the resorts. Within the Dependency context, the danger also exists that the large resorts, as a consequence of their integration with DAT environments, will appropriate and gain control over tourism in these areas to the exclusion of local communities. The cumulative effect could be a significant penetration of the global capitalist economy into the remotest parts of the Caribbean islands, a process similar to that described by Zurick (1992) in the context of Nepal's Himalayan region.

Conclusions

The Caribbean is one of the world's most tourism-dependent regions, although significant variations in the intensity of tourism and in development levels are apparent at the level of individual states and dependencies. The regional tourism industry is dominated by large-scale resort and cruise ship tourism that has generally proved to be unsustainable. Although the continued expansion of this sector can be seen as further evidence of this unsustainable character, initiatives are being taken at the institutional and individual level to implement sustainable tourism practices. At present, such measures are by no means universal. Most of the Caribbean landscape, ironically, is occupied by CAT, although there are indications of DAT implementation at both a localized and comprehensive scale, Dominica being the best example of the latter, and scattered protected areas the best indicator of the former. Currently, a UMT-to-CAT transect from coast to interior is normative among most Caribbean destinations. For tourism to be viable in the long-term as an effective agent of regional development, a transition to an integrated SMT-to-DAT transect is imperative, except in destinations that opt for comprehensive DAT.

References

Ayala, H. (1996) Resort ecotourism: a paradigm for the 21st century. *Cornell Hotel and Restaurant Administration Quarterly* 37(5), 46–53.

Blamey, R.K. (1997) Ecotourism: the search for an operational definition. *Journal of Sustainable Tourism* 5(2), 109–130.

Butler, R.W. (1980) The concept of a tourist area cycle of evolution: implications for management of resources. *Canadian Geographer* 24(1), 5–12.

CEP (1994) *Ecotourism in the Wider Caribbean Region – an Assessment.* CEP Technical Report No. 31. Caribbean Environment Programme, Kingston, Jamaica.

Clarke, J. (1997) A framework of approaches to sustainable tourism. *Journal of Sustainable Tourism* 5(3), 224–233.

Clean Islands International (1997) CAST: CHA's environmental arm. [URL document] http://www.islands.org/cii/cwart3.htm (visited 29 December 1998).

de Albuquerque, K. and McElroy, J.L. (1995) *Antigua and Barbuda: a Legacy of Environmental Degradation, Policy Failure and Coastal Decline.* Supplementary Paper No. 5. USAID, EPAT/MUCIA, Washington, DC.

Dernoi, L.A. (1981) Alternative tourism: towards a new style in North–South relations. *International Journal of Tourism Management* 2(December), 253–264.

Devas, E. (1997) Hotels in the Caribbean. *Travel and Tourism Analyst* 2, 57–76.

Edwards, F.N. (ed.) (1988) *Environmentally Sound Tourism Development in the Caribbean.* University of Calgary Press, Calgary, Canada, 143 pp.

France, L. (1998) Local participation in tourism in the West Indian islands. In: Laws, E., Faulkner, B. and Moscardo, G. (eds) *Embracing and Managing Change in Tourism: International Case Studies.* Routledge, London, pp. 222–234.

Holder, J.S. (1996) Maintaining competitiveness in a new world order: regional solutions to Caribbean tourism sustainability problems. In: Harrison, L.C. and Husbands, W. (eds) *Practising Responsible Tourism: International Case Studies in Tourism Planning, Policy, and Development.* John Wiley & Sons, Chichester, UK, pp. 145–173.

Knill, G. (1991) Towards the green paradigm. *South African Geographical Journal* 73(1), 52–59.

McElroy, J.L. and de Albuquerque, K. (1998) Tourism penetration index in small Caribbean islands. *Annals of Tourism Research* 25(1), 145–168.

Nature Conservancy (1996) Caribbean conservation action. [URL document] http://www.tnc.org/infield/int-programs.html (visited 29 December 1998).

Olsen, B. (1997) Environmentally sustainable development and tourism: lessons from Negril, Jamaica. *Human Organization* 56, 285–293.

Pattullo, P. (1996) *Last Resorts: the Cost of Tourism in the Caribbean.* Cassell, London.

Poon, A. (1993) *Tourism, Technology and Competitive Strategies.* CAB International, Wallingford, UK, 370 pp.

Popovic, C. (1997) Protecting our natural assets. *Visions of St Lucia* 8, 30–33.

Project Underground (1996) Issue alert: BHP threatens Waitukubuli. [URL document] http://www.moles.org/ProjectUnderground/motherlode/dom/dominica.html (visited 26 June 1998).

Rainieri, F. (1995) If you build it they will come: sustainable tourism. [URL document] http://www.earth-pledge.org/projects/wpapers/wppunta.htm (visited 31 December 1998).

Robbins, E. (1994) Trouble in Paradise. *Environmental Magazine* 5(3), 36–40.

Santana, E. (1991) Nature conservation and sustainable development in Cuba. *Conservation Biology* 5(1), 13–16.

Sobers, A. (1996) Market segments: USA to the Caribbean. *Travel and Tourism Analyst* 3, 65–77.

Turner, L. and Ash, J. (1975) *The Golden Hordes: International Tourism and the Pleasure Periphery.* Constable, London.

UNCED (1993) *Report of the United Nations Conference on Environment and Development,* Vols 1–3. United Nations Conference on Environment and Development, New York.

Weaver, D.B. (1988) The evolution of a 'plantation' tourism landscape on the Caribbean island of Antigua. *Tijdschrift voor Economische en Sociale Geografie* 79(5), 319–331.

Weaver, D.B. (1991) Alternative to mass tourism in Dominica. *Annals of Tourism Research* 18(3), 414–432.

Weaver, D.B. (1993) Model of urban tourism for small Caribbean islands. *Geographical Review* 83(2), 134–140.

Weaver, D.B. (1995) Alternative tourism in Montserrat. *Tourism Management* 16(8), 593–604.

Weaver, D.B. (1998) *Ecotourism in the Less Developed World.* CAB International, Wallingford, UK, 258 pp.

Weaver, D.B. (2000) A broad context model of destination development scenarios. *Tourism Management* 21, 217–224.

Wheeller, B. (1997) Here we go, here we go, where we go eco. In: Stabler, M.J. (ed.) *Tourism and Sustainability: Principles to Practice.* CAB International, Wallingford, UK, pp. 39–49.

WTO (1987) *Compendium of Tourism Statistics,* 8th edn. World Tourism Organization, Madrid, 225 pp.

WTO (1998) *Compendium of Tourism Statistics 1992–1996,* 18th edn. World Tourism Organization, Madrid, 270 pp.

Zurick, D. (1992) Adventure travel and sustainable tourism in the peripheral economy of Nepal. *Annals of the Association of American Geographers* 82(4), 608–628.

12

Resort-based Tourism on the Pleasure Periphery

Brian King

Introduction

This chapter examines the role that resorts play in tourism in the 'less developed countries' (LDCs). The term itself accommodates a wide range of societies, ranging from those that are rapidly industrializing to those characterized by chronic aid dependence and poverty. Reference to 'resorts' is similarly varied, ranging from vast integrated developments to boutique eco-resorts. In view of this diversity, why do resorts in LDCs merit especially close attention? One reason is that the typical resort complex powerfully symbolizes the economic dualism of LDCs. Epitomizing capital intensity, an integrated resort conveys tangible evidence of free-spending international tourists, bringing the prestige of such international brand names as Shangri-La and Hyatt to capital-starved LDCs and their leaders. For critics, resorts exemplify stark disparities between Western élites, able to enjoy leisure and conspicuous consumption in exotic locations, and the local workforce, which must behave with neocolonial servility towards white guests in compound-like settings from which they would otherwise be excluded. Whilst it is difficult to generalize about resorts in LDCs without sacrificing something of the truth, the fact that they

embody (or are perceived to embody) the contradictions of tourism makes them worthy of study.

Like tourists, resorts have been the butt of jokes and criticism and make easy targets. With commodities such as jewellery and luxury cars, they exemplify conspicuous consumption when presented ostentatiously in glossy lifestyle magazines and other upmarket media. Top-of-the-range properties, especially, attract attention for their self-conscious exclusivity, and are alleged to be examples of what MacCannell (1992: 174) has described as 'empty meeting grounds' squeezing 'the local people out of every role except the menial positions that they have always occupied'. As part of a broader critique of consumerism, such targeting has some validity, but too narrowly focuses on consumers rather than on destinations and residents. It is also important to ask what meaning resorts have in countries or regions where they are located, and how far they are integrated with their physical, socio-cultural and economic environments.

The chapter examines various resort definitions and distinguishes between types of resort property and resort development. Particular attention is paid to the relationship between the scale of resort development and the extent to which such properties achieve integration with the adjoining environment. Small island countries are especially considered, because large-scale resort developments are so conspicuous in such settings. As the author has researched the attitudes of the travel trade, consumers and local communities towards resorts in Pacific island countries, examples from the region are incorporated in this chapter.

Approaches to the Study of Resorts in LDCs

There is an extensive and growing literature on the nature and characteristics of tourism in LDCs. A common theme is the relationship between the principal generating countries for resort tourism (predominantly in the developed countries) and the world's tropical and subtropical destinations (predominantly in the LDCs). Such studies have included examinations of centre–periphery relations (Hoivik and Heiberg, 1980), sustainability and the 'new tourism' (Mowforth and Munt, 1998), the role of transnational corporations (Dunning and McQueen, 1982), imagery (Britton, 1979), the marketing of authenticity (Silver, 1993) and the role of the tour operator. Several authors have evaluated resort tourism in small island destinations (Britton and Clarke, 1987; Cazes, 1987), and others have studied the links between tourism, dependency and underdevelopment in Fiji (Britton, 1983). Much of the literature noted above makes only passing reference to resorts, but they constitute an important tourist setting to explore many of these broader themes.

Though resorts have often tried to be fully self-contained, researchers have examined the resort phenomenon from various perspectives, often attempting to understand the relationship between resorts and destinations. Such studies have included resort development (Dean and Judd, 1985; Stiles and See-Tho, 1991), planning (Smith, 1992), assessment of local attitudes (Witter, 1985), marketing (King and Whitelaw, 1992), the resort life cycle (Butler, 1980), resorts as communities (Stettner, 1993), architecture (England, 1980) and landscaping (Ayala, 1991), to name but a

few. In some of these studies, and notably in Butler's seminal work on the resort life cycle, the distinction between what constitutes a resort and what constitutes a destination is blurred. A significant feature in this literature is the role of resorts as 'enclave' developments, separated from everyday life in adjacent areas or regions (Freitag, 1994). Resorts in LDCs have been used as case studies in many general examinations of resort tourism, but have been the subject of relatively few theoretical investigations (Oppermann and Chon, 1997: 56–70). While many resorts studied have been in developed countries, it is their role in LDCs that seem to offer the most startling insights into the nature and paradoxes of tourism.

Resort definitions are applied inconsistently in the literature. Sometimes reference is to a specific property, as with 'integrated resorts', which usually denotes developments satisfying a very specific criterion of capital intensity. Alternatively, a broader categorization is intended, when 'resort' is used to describe a destination region, as when large conurbations choose to portray themselves as resorts in their promotional literature. According to the wider use of the term, virtually any tourist destination can qualify as a resort, but coastal cities seem to offer the best fit with the resort concept. Somewhere between single resort properties and urban destinations is the 'resort zone', an intermediate category that is sometimes applied to a cluster of several resorts, and at others to resorts adjoining pre-established communities. Such resort zones often constitute an important component in the national tourism development plans of LDCs.

Perhaps because resorts can be studied at the micro level, as well as in the wider tourism context, they have attracted researchers from diverse disciplines. Operational and technical analyses have been undertaken by specialists in such fields as business operations, construction, design and environmental planning, and the large scale of transnational investment in resorts has attracted the attention of lawyers, financial planners, architects and designers, some of whom have contributed to the resort literature.

Social scientists, too, have shown considerable interest in the broader context within which resorts operate. To many, resorts epito-mize the archetypal package tour-based tourism. This view arose as a result of the experience of Mediterranean resorts during the 1960s and 1970s. Such resorts were geared almost exclusively to satisfying the expectations of package holidaymakers from northern Europe. The later evolution of tourism makes the link between resorts and mass package destinations less obvious, as markets have moved away away from standardized mass-produced products and placed greater emphasis on more customized holiday experiences. A number of authors have observed that resort-based tourism and tourist behaviour typify many characteristics of modern life. Krippendorf (1987: 70–71), for example, described resorts as 'therapy zones for the masses', referring to 'sun–sea therapy' in coastal resorts and 'snow–ski therapy' in the mountains. He also referred to 'self-sufficient holiday complexes, designed and run on the basis of careful motivation studies as enclaves for holidaymakers. Total experience and relaxation. Fenced off and sterilised'. Resorts are a particular target for his acerbic analysis of contemporary tourism, and he proposed a 'humanisation of travel' to counter excesses experienced in resorts. Krippendorf's critique was not applied exclusively to LDCs, but many of his observations about the limitations of resorts are particularly germane to such settings.

O'Grady is another vigorous critic of resorts as they are presently constituted. His overall argument is that the development of resorts in LDCs is acceptable only when resort tourism is kept separate from the daily lives of local people (O'Grady, 1981). He proposed a form of enclave tourism, accompanied by improved education, enhanced income and economic benefits for the local population, in preference to the more conspicuous and intrusive resort development.

The view that resorts embody many excesses of modern tourism has attracted geographers, social anthropologists, planners, sociologists, economists and historians. That 'resort' may be used a noun or a verb has been exploited by some authors. Craik (1991: vii) used the word resort in a pejorative way, considering tourism 'resorted to' in the absence of any viable alternative. Lea (1988) adopted a similar approach in his text on tourism in the Third World, viewing tourism as a 'last resort,' rather than a development priority in such countries. Krippendorf, O'Grady, Craik and Lea represent a school of thought that is highly critical of the way in which most resorts currently operate.

Defining Resorts in LDCs

According to the *Oxford Dictionary*, a resort is 'a place resorted to, a popular holiday place'. Academic definitions have also tended to be general, descriptive and pragmatic and are rarely applied exclusively to LDCs. For Gunn (1997: 74), 'the modern resort is similar to the organization camp in its relative independence and tight linkage with attraction clusters'. Whilst more specific in its reference to tourism, Burkart and Medlik (1981: 45, 46), too, focused on general features, suggesting that a resort is 'any visitor centre to which people resort in large numbers'. Indeed, they encompassed capital cities within this definition on the grounds that such centres function 'as centres of commerce and government'.

It is clear that resorts may be defined narrowly (as hotels offering a comprehensive range of recreational facilities on site) or broadly (as any recreational destination where tourists congregate, including capital cities). Mieczkowski (1991) provided a useful summary of these sometimes contradictory definitions. He based his classification on the work of Grunthal (1934), who typologized human settlements as those without tourism, as those with tourism and, finally, as 'tourism settlements'. Using the criteria of resources and function, Mieczkowski distinguished between cities and resorts as key types of tourism settlements. He positioned resorts along a continuum, ranging from small scale to large scale, for example, with a 100–200 room hotel at one end and, at the other what he described as 'resort towns' or 'resort cities' such as Waikiki Beach, Hawaii (Mieczkowski, 1991: 318). Whilst useful, this typology ignores small-scale boutique resorts, which are becoming a more prominent component of the resort field, but the definition goes some way to accommodating micro and macro levels of analysis. Nevertheless, Mieczkowski does not manage to accommodate fully the various loose references to resorts as tourism regions that are found throughout the literature.

For the purposes of the current chapter, the definition of a resort is as follows:

> A complex of tourism facilities incorporating accommodation, food and beverage and recreational provision. The destination is incorporated in inclusive tour programmes offering the option of at least one meal per day plus other ancillary services. By offering sufficient range of activities and attractions within the resort complex, it lends itself to an extended length of stay.

The Pleasure Periphery

The view that resort zones constitute 'a pleasure periphery' has played an important role in the development of tourism theory. The concept first gained currency when Turner and Ash (1975: 127), referring to the Club Méditerranée Group, noted that resorts were concentrated in LDCs offering an appropriate climatic and resource base (such as sandy beaches) and were close to metropolitan tourism-generating countries. Since then, the perspective has been used in numerous empirical studies, including an article by Ferreira and Hanekom (1995) that evaluated the Warmbaths spa resort area in South Africa as an example of a pleasure periphery. At a macro level, Cazes (1992) took the concept further by regarding tourism in LDCs as a *de facto* transformation of sovereign states into holiday resorts, as indicated by the subtitle of his book on tourism and the Third World: '*les nouvelles colonies de vacances*' (the new holiday camps).

A more positive view regards mass tourism in the pleasure periphery as a key catalyst in improving standards of living, bringing them closer to those in tourism-generating countries. Indeed, it has been argued that mass resort tourism helped to bring internationalism and democratic pluralism to dictatorships in Spain and Portugal. They were not LDCs but, before the period of resort development, had lagged behind much of Europe economically in the 1950s and early 1960s (Davidson,

1998; Valanzuela, 1988). The argument exemplifies the positive outlook for the pleasure peripheries that adjoin the developed world (the Mediterranean and Europe, the Caribbean and North America, the Indian Ocean and South America).

LDCs are predominantly found in Asia, Africa, Latin America and the Pacific, and it is perhaps unsurprising that the largest tourism 'pleasure peripheries' are close or adjacent to major generating countries. Mexico, for instance, is near the vast North American market, and its tourism industry has, in stages, culminated in large-scale, capital-intensive, internationally managed developments providing a standardized tourism product for package tourists. The role of *Fondatur*, Mexico's tourism development corporation, has prompted discussion of the state's role in determining the shape of resort development in LDCs. Mexico has interesting examples of highly planned resort development (for example, Cancun and Ixtapa-Zihuatenejo) and of relatively spontaneous and unplanned development (Acapulco). As in China (Richter, 1989: 31), there is considerable resistance in Mexico to the threat of foreign dominance. The vastness of the US market adds to the sense of a neocolonial foreign invasion in some of the Mexican resorts, particularly package destinations such as Acapulco and those in the Baja California close to the US border (Gormsen, 1983: 149).

Other resort studies have also focused on tourism in LDCs. Hartmann (1994) examined the opportunities for resort development in Latin America, and King and McVey (1996) provided an overview of resort development in Asia, with particular emphasis on the comparative experience of Indonesia, Malaysia and Thailand. In the Caribbean, a negative feature of tourism development is its association with an earlier colonial era characterized by slavery, and Taylor (1993) examined racial tensions in the development of Jamaica's resort tourism.

Most LDCs aspire to rapid economic development, even if their achievements fall short of the ambition, and the role tourism plays in this process is an interesting strand in the literature. China, for example, has experienced rapid economic development, and in some parts of the country, notably Hainan Island, government-planned resort developments have played a major role. This process has attracted research (Zhang *et al.*, 1995; Zhang, 1996; Yu, 1998), and Meyer (1996) has documented the rapid expansion of resorts along the Chinese coastline and planning problems associated with such expansive development. Resorts characterized by dense concentrations of foreigners prompt debate about the sense of (real or perceived) exclusion experienced by local people, an issue critical in such LDCs as China, which has a history of suspicion towards foreigners and a desire to do things the 'Chinese way'.

China has also been the focus of studies evaluating the extent and speed with which resort destinations should internationalize their markets. Should resorts target overseas or domestic tourists? If overseas markets are targeted, how fast should this direction be pursued? Gang (1998: 43) has argued that a stronger emphasis on domestic tourism would be appropriate in China, and that the country is moving too fast to attract international markets. However, in poorer countries the greater spending power of international visitors is always a temptation, despite the merit of making prime tourism resources accessible to residents of the host country.

Resorts and Their Regions

Coastal beach resorts are the dominant category in LDCs, though mountain resorts, safari and wildlife resorts and spas are also important. Beach resorts can play a significant role in the spatial distribution of tourism development and Wong (1993) has examined the relationship of tourism and the coastline, principally though not exclusively in LDCs. Oppermann (1992) examined Malaysia as an example of a less developed country with an extended coastline suited to beach resort development. Despite the wide spatial dispersal of resorts in Malaysia, he argued that more adventurous tourists are preferable because they disperse more widely than resort tourists, whose habits are more sedentary – a view held despite the remote location of many resorts. In fact, resorts located away from

major population centres generally draw their workforce from some distance and are often hailed as catalysts for regional economic development. This role can be particularly valuable in LDCs characterized by rapid rural-to-urban migration.

Cukier-Snow and Wall (1994) examined migration into the southern resort area of Bali. They noted employment practices in the informal sector, specifically among beach and street vendors in Kuta, Bali, and also highlighted the lack of training provision in resort areas (relative to cities), suggesting that migration by resort employees needs to be accompanied by adequate training and education provision. Cukier and Wall (1995: 399) also focused on the importance of gender in the resort workforce, concluding that it influences access to resort employment.

Many coastal resorts are located away from major conurbations, and exacerbate ribbon development by prompting inflation in land values along a narrow coastal strip. This can sometimes lead to excess visitor-carrying capacity, a danger that should be avoided by integrated resorts developed within an overall strategic plan. This advantage is not always evident in the case of established communities, which increasingly assume the characteristics of resorts. A study by Sen (1993), for example, concluded that the Dudhia resort in the Darjeeling area of West Bengal in the Himalayas exceeded its natural carrying capacity as a tourist destination.

It is not surprising that resort development in LDCs indicates great diversity, ranging from the spontaneous and anarchic to meticulous planning under rigid central control. The extent to which resorts have been subject to a formal planning process will influence the level of integration with the existing infrastructure and superstructure. LDCs are often typified by a high level of subsistence agriculture and by underemployment and unemployment outside the metropolitan areas. Major capital investment can lead to significant structural change, as indicated in Kermath's (1992) article on resorts in the Dominican Republic. He pointed to a substantial literature on the dual nature of Third World economies generally, including the concepts of centre–periphery relations and metropolis and sub-metropolitan bases, which suggest that less developed countries follow a mode of development largely determined by previous colonial masters. According to this view, while some selected sites have been allowed to assume the outward trappings of development, other areas have been exploited for mineral or other extraction development. However, Kermath claimed that little of this research was specifically applied to tourism, especially to the interface between subsistence agriculture and tourism development. He proposed a spatial dynamics model linking the formal and informal tourism sectors, and concluded that displaced individuals involved in the informal sector were unlikely to be absorbed in the expanding formal resort economy. This implies the emergence of a sort of 'buffer zone' separating the stricter organization of the resort itself from the less formal employment arrangements prevalent in surrounding areas. Whilst Kermath viewed this as a negative characteristic that limits employment opportunities, there is little consensus in the broader literature on the desirability of such separation. Like Kermath, many authors are attracted by the concept of 'integration', but others regard the existence of barriers as a means of minimizing negative impacts on the adjoining community.

The respective roles of the formal and informal sectors are critical to the debate about the benefits of integrated versus enclave development. Examining participation in tourism in the Dominican Republic, Freitag (1996) highlighted the marginalization of the poor in communities close to resorts and has shown elsewhere that operators of enclave resort developments may deliberately minimize economic exchange between tourists and local businesses to increase resort profit margins (Freitag, 1994: 538). Such empirical evidence supports critics who accuse resorts in LDCs of fostering alienation amongst the local population, for the physical segregation of resorts may exacerbate the sense of displacement felt by local people, in an environment which they perceive to be their own.

To counteract the criticism that resorts amount to foreign enclaves, many LDC governments have attempted to integrate them into national and regional planning strategies.

However, such countries are characterized by poorly developed administrative structures, particularly at local and regional levels, and thus considerable responsibility is placed on planners at national level. Governments have adopted different approaches to the development of resort precincts. In Bali (Indonesia) and Fiji, the extent to which such areas are properly integrated as precincts influences the visitor experience and the competitiveness of the destination. McDonnell and Darcy (1998) explored a critical link in the relationship between resorts and their regions, and concluded that the emergence of clearly designated 'resort precincts' in Bali had made that destination more appealing to Australian tourists than Fiji, where resorts are typically more widely dispersed. Innskeep (1994: 42) has outlined the advantages of zoning to ensure compatibility between resorts and the adjoining environment. He also warned against an excessively technical approach to planning for resorts in LDCs and noted the importance of featuring culture and environment as attractions in their own right. His suggestion that tourism plans should encapsulate the unique character of a destination and not succumb to a formula approach has been given surprisingly little coverage by other authors.

Most literature on resort development in LDCs has concluded that tourists prefer larger scale developments and are prepared to pay for this type of experience. However, the work of Poon (1993) on 'new tourists' is particularly relevant to resorts. Arguing that they need to understand the changing needs and preferences of consumers and to embrace technology and diagonal integration, she played down the differences in circumstances in developed countries and LDCs, and proposed instead that LDCs should embrace the opportunities presented by the 'new tourist'. In support of this view, recent literature on market trends, especially on ecotourism, has identified a growing consumer preference for smaller-scale developments. In Java, for instance, increased tourist awareness of social and cultural issues has been noted, and Gunawan (1997: 52) observed that there is some evidence of a move away from the large-scale resort enclaves previously favoured from the 1960s to the 1980s. Her work is an example of a growing body of work by authors from the LDCs, which provide a stronger destination perspective, though it should be acknowledged that many authors emanating from and based in less developed countries were trained in developed countries.

The Social and Cultural Context

The implications of resorts in the study of culture have received little attention. This is especially surprising, in view of Valene Smith's outline of concepts that could usefully be brought to bear on resort settings (Smith 1977). A number of anthropological perspectives were proposed by various contributors to Smith's book *Hosts and Guests*, notably the anthropological approach of Nunez (1997: 213) distinguishing between 'resort tourism' and 'off-the-beaten-track tourism'. There has been minimum debate over how far local and regional cultures should be conveyed to guests and, if this is desirable, how far 'authenticity' is an issue. An exception is Eastman's research on the marginalization of Swahili in Kenya, where the conclusion was that beach resorts of Kenya fail to project the reality of Swahili coastal culture (Eastman, 1995: 181). Harrison (1998: 136) has argued that, in Fiji, resorts do embrace indigenous cultural imagery, but on a highly selective basis, with Indo-Fijian imagery virtually non-existent and Fijian images highly prominent. In general, critics of resort development depict tourists as occupying an 'ecological bubble' (Cohen, 1972: 172; Jenkins and Likorish, 1997: 77), oblivious to the cultural characteristics of the destination, whereas others suggest that tourists are becoming increasingly sophisticated and increasingly willing to visit resorts that set out to convey concepts of local or regional identity. Sceptics show less faith in the willingness of consumers to transform their behaviour, and stress the negative impacts associated with tourism growth (Craik, 1991: 5).

Attempts to assess the social and cultural impacts of resorts alongside the economic repercussions of development have struggled to find objective criteria that may be applied. Relatively few studies have taken a multi-disciplinary approach, and most have focused on a single dimension – for example, economic impacts. Poirier's study of Tunisia acknowledged the economic benefits of resort development but also outlined the clash between Islamic and European values (Poirier, 1995). More generally, there is no agreement among researchers on what constitutes an 'appropriate' pace of socio-cultural change in the meeting of tourist and host culture. However, many social impact assessments have been undertaken in resort areas. Resident perceptions were evaluated in Montego Bay, Jamaica (Frater, 1998), and in Nadi, Fiji (King *et al.*, 1993). Focusing on the future, Hernandez *et al.* (1996) examined resident attitudes to a planned enclave resort in Puerto Rico as opposed to an existing development. An important dimension of resort assessment is the extent of linkage between resort properties and the areas that adjoin them.

Other studies have focused more narrowly on resort management and its relationship to local cultures. Dwyer *et al.* (1998), for example, examined organizational culture and strategic management in a resort property and the implementation of organization-wide communication and participation, and the chapter by Leiper (1995) on a resort in Vanuatu highlighted the use and ultimate failure of an experimental style of management and organizational culture. Harrison (1998: 134) emphasized the limits to social and cultural interaction arising from management structures, suggesting that 'the physical situation and organization of many island resorts in Fiji tends to ensure that the closest interaction occurs between and among guests, rather than between "guests" and their official "hosts"'. Using a rather different approach, King (1997) referred to island resorts as 'total communities' and examined intimacy and integration between members of the workforce and visitors. He also examined the relevance of post-modern concepts to resorts in Fiji, depicting them as consumption-focused communities where elements of the pseudo-traditional are combined with ultra-modern conveniences, as demonstrated by the fact that resort visitors may be accommodated in (albeit suitably modernized) *bures* (traditional thatched cottages). His study of the Mamanuca Islands in Fiji concluded that, despite the strong commercial ethos of the resorts, integration with local Fijian communities was occurring on a significant scale (King, 1997: 237). Harrison (1997: 175), however, outlined a process of conflict in one of the same islands, where resort owners moved deliberately to exclude visitors from an adjoining backpacker development owned and operated by the local community.

Studies of resort failure provide useful lessons about management strategies. Sofield's (1996) investigation of a resort that failed in the Solomons exemplified what can occur when developers misunderstand local social and cultural values. The research highlighted the need for sensitivity over land tenure issues in LDCs generally, and South Pacific island countries in particular. Confrontation led ultimately to the elimination of the resort. The extent to which employment practices in resorts mirror deeper cultural tensions is examined in a chapter on Fiji by Burns (1995), where resorts are treated as a mirror for wider inequalities within society.

Some researchers have explored visitor perceptions of resort quality, while others have examined issues of quality from a management perspective. Tourist perceptions of resort quality were the focus of a study by Ekinci *et al.* (1998). Tribe and Snaith (1998) applied the so-called HOLSAT (holiday satisfaction) technique as a way of measuring satisfaction, as an alternative to SERVQUAL (the service quality model applied widely in the management and marketing literature). Dann (1996) studied perceptions of visitors to Barbados, with particular reference to environmental attributes and the extent to which experience matches expectations. An interesting component of such studies is the extent to which perceptions of resort quality are equated with views of the destination as a whole. In this context, resorts are more significant than hotels, which are typically a single component of a holiday package rather than a complete destination. For tourists, the distinction between the resort and the destination country can become quite blurred. It is clear that many tourists are unaware that the island of Bali is part of Indonesia (Craig-Smith and French 1994: 147) or that the capital city of Noumea is part of a larger entity called New Caledonia.

Issues of Scale in Resort Management

What is 'appropriate' development, from a destination point of view? Taking Schumacher's (1974) 'small is beautiful' approach, Lee *et al.* (1998) prepared a scenario to compare the economic impact of an 'ecotourism area' in South Korea with or without ski and golf resort development and concluded that mainstream resort development would result in economic loss, and that less developed ecotourism is more appropriate. By contrast, Middleton and Hawkins (1995: 76) concluded that properties managed by large hotel groups are often best placed to implement environmentally responsible practices because of the superior amount of resources at their disposal. They also argued that the more enlightened environmental policies of larger hotel management groups make them more suitable in certain conditions. While smaller developments may appear 'eco-friendly', in reality they may adopt a less responsible approach to their surroundings (King, 1997: 229).

Though resorts are widely regarded as somewhat separate from their surroundings, the linkages that do exist are worth detailed examination. Sack (1992: 2) concluded that, compared with such commercial developments as shopping centres, resorts depend heavily on the quality of their setting and on the adjoining landscape. Whereas shoppers will be attracted to a centre on the basis of the merchandise on display and the facilities within the centre itself, resort tourists will be strongly influenced by the appeal and attractiveness of the resort setting. A link between agriculture generally, and plantations in particular, was the focus of a study by Mohamad (1997) of the Tekam Plantation Resort and Kampung Guntong (Setiau) Agrotourism Project in Malaysia. Agrotourism in Malaysia was also studied by Abdullah and Isa (1994). As many resort developments occur in rural agricultural areas, it is important that linkages are subject to detailed examination to assist planners with the next wave of resort development in LDCs. The Namibian study by Shackley (1993: 253) is another investigation of agrotourism, though she eschews this expression in favour of the term 'guest farms'. These are seen as a means of linking resort tourism with farmers needing to diversify in times of economic and climatic uncertainty.

The development of supply chains linking resorts with nearby agricultural producers is important but problematic in LDCs. Resorts tend to rely heavily on imported foods, and as a consequence leakages are high. Telfer and Wall (1996), who examined the linkages between tourism and food production in Lombok, Indonesia, identified the importance of securing a regular and reliable supply of fresh produce for the resorts and the mismatch between the expectations of food producers and tourism sector purchasers. Resort developments often attract their workforce from those previously employed nearby in agriculture. The need to stem such rural depopulation is sometimes viewed by governments as a reason to strengthen local supply chains.

Resort management takes many different forms and types of accommodation vary considerably. One approach, a growing component of the resort field, is timeshare. According to Dean (1993: 74; 1997: 38), LDCs in Asia have been slow to adopt this emerging management approach compared with such developed countries as Australia. The symbiotic relationship between traditional tourist accommodation and time-sharing in various resort settings, including LDCs, has been investigated (Centre d'Etudes de Tourisme, 1987: 1). While timeshare developments constitute only a small component of total resort development, such studies indicate the multifaceted operational characteristics of resorts, where a range of accommodation types and management practices are incorporated within a single complex. In a sense, LDCs are more vulnerable to the type of sharp timeshare management practices involving hard-sell techniques and questionable real estate projects (Pearce et al., 1998: 293).

However, the fact that timeshare development is occurring later in LDCs at least provides an opportunity to learn from mistakes made elsewhere.

How can resorts bolster existing settlements? A study on Korea by Kang et al. (1997) concluded that inadequate social infrastructure may impede tourism development. The integration between resorts and adjoining communities has been analysed in the case of Bali, Indonesia, where large-scale boutique-style resorts are closely linked to adjoining communities. Wall (1996) has examined the extent to which attitudes to tourism in Bali vary according to the proximity of resorts. This project, spanning several years, has closely documented the role played by resorts in tourism development in Bali, showing that resort development is not necessarily antipathetic to the development of cultural tourism, though the large scale of some resorts individually, and of resort development overall, does pose a threat to the integrity of Balinese culture.

Ayala (1997) has advocated the development of close linkages between properties and adjoining areas, with particular reference to the physical environment. She argued that resort features such as swimming-pools and gardens should complement the features of the area outside the resort, rather than trying to outdo nature in scale, and cited the 'tourism–conservation–research masterplan' in Panama as a model for appropriate development, as a catalyst for national and regional partnerships, and for 'resort ecotourism'. Others have followed, advocating the benefits of eco-resorts through 'best practice' case studies. The study of resorts in the Andaman and Nicobar islands by Khatri (1996), for instance, praised the 4Rs approach (reduce, recycle, reuse and rethink) and attempts by resorts to educate tourists about the fragile island ecosystems. Weaver (1998: 188), less deliberately polemic in his approach, addressed the more challenging question of how principles of ecotourism can be made relevant in destinations characterised by established resorts based on attracting '3S' (sea, sand, sun) tourism. He proposed three alternatives for the adoption of ecotourism principles, in place of or as an adjunct to established resort-based tourism in the

Caribbean. The interface between idealists, who regard small-scale ecotourism as a potential panacea for the excesses of mass tourism, and pragmatists, who stress the beneficial economies of scale from large-scale resort development, is critical. Such authors such as Ayala and Weaver bring realism to the idealists and some lateral thinking to exponents of the traditional approach.

In their article on new destinations for developed countries, Doswell and Quest (1990) took the view that, while resort markets are diversifying and the tourist-generating potential of many Third World countries is expanding, the solid mass market is composed mainly of people seeking comprehensive holiday hotels and other types of smart tourist accommodation, near to or on a beach and preferably part of a resort complex. Here, the transformative potential of resort-based tourism is considered limited, especially in the short term, and such tourism is seen as reflecting market preferences. Along with Innskeep (1994), Doswell has contributed to definitive studies on resort design, planning and development (Doswell, 1970, 1997; Doswell and Gamble, 1981).

The academic literature includes a number of resort project assessments. Some are distinguished from the predictable 'excellence/best practice' case studies in embracing the broader political and socio-economic setting and the attempt to offset social and cultural costs against economic benefits. An interesting study by Fish and Rudolph (1986) outlined the rates of return provided by resort development in LDCs using several different assumptions. This is relevant to a variety of LDCs and is one of only a few academic contributions to the study of the financial aspects of resort development. Jenkins (1982), too, examined issues of scale as they apply to resorts in LDCs, showing that larger-scale development may be the only viable option for countries that lack basic infrastructure and need to attract a cluster of development projects, if the provision of basic infrastructure is to be made viable.

In a seminal article, Gray (1981) outlined the key economic advantage of resort development in LDCs: infrastructure is geographically concentrated and capable of providing economies of scale. Against this, he also noted that the resort product is highly substitutable and leads to intense price competition between destinations. As evident in Gray's work, there is vigorous debate about how far very large-scale developments are appropriate for LDCs. Much criticism has been directed at large-scale resort development. In the 1970s, the World Bank received widespread criticism for supporting mega-resort projects. An interesting review outlined the experience of the Bank in four projects in Mexico, Tunisia, Yugoslavia and the Ivory Coast (Davis and Simons, 1982). The article is of historic interest, because the World Bank closed its specialized tourism department in the early 1980s, but the debate about what constitutes an appropriate scale of development remains unresolved almost 20 years later.

Resort Types

Until recently, resort tourism has been considered synonymous with mass, 3S tourism, generally focused on large hotels, and especially attractive to 'package' tourists. This, at any rate, was the common perception at the time of de Kadt's edited volume on tourism that appeared in the late 1970s, well before the current trend towards small-scale boutique resorts and ecotourism. It was this perception that underpinned the debate on the social and cultural impacts of mass tourism (de Kadt, 1979: 7).

More recently, the extent to which resorts embrace concepts to create particular settings or themes has also been the subject of analysis. Yuanxiang examined the linkages between resorts and surrounding environmental assets; he focused on issues of afforestation and referred to 'plant scenic window' and to 'beautified garden-like hamlets and villages' (Yuanxiang, 1993: 34). Less polemically, Trapasso (1994: 449) outlined the negative and positive impacts of ecotourism resorts on the adjoining rainforest in Brazil and Belize, observing that ecotourism resorts in Amazonian Brazil contributed to local conservation efforts, whereas slash-and-burn agriculture in the rainforests of Belize was destructive to the environment. He concluded that resorts could play a constructive conservation role. As mentioned previously, resort tourism may also be linked to agrotourism, and marine tourism and cruising are obviously linked to the environment, with many resorts concentrating on such nature-based activities. Kim (1996) undertook an investigation of such linkages in South Korea. As an indication of the almost endless range of concepts used as resort themes, Sharma (1995) evaluated 'jungle resorts' in Chitwan (Nepal), and Thomas and Fernanadez (1994) examined what they described as 'mangrove resorts'.

Resorts specializing in a particular type of activity are increasingly popular. Golf resorts in South-East Asia, for example, have been particularly successful in attracting Japanese visitors, as well as research interest. Such resorts, often targeted exclusively at the needs and expectations of overseas visitors, are environmentally questionable because of the vast quantities of water they consume and the amount of land involved in their development. While golf resorts in developed countries attract a local clientele, this is not so in such destinations as the Middle East, Vietnam, Malaysia and Thailand (Sullivan, 1996). Pleumarom (1992) has outlined Thailand's emergence as the centre of Asian golf tourism, claiming that expansion of golf courses is likely to increase even more as land becomes increasingly scarce in developed countries. Like most upmarket resorts, golf resorts are criticized because of their apparent irrelevance to local needs, as well as their use of scarce natural resources.

As resorts diversify from sporting and passive activity into fantasy concepts, the literature on theme parks is becoming increasing relevant to resort settings. Such major developments as Disneyworld in Florida clearly combine the characteristics of theme park and resort. The work of Turner (1996) on waterparks has examined the world's latest waterpark projects, many incorporating resort hotels as well as retail and other components. Many of these developments are located in Asia, notably in South Korea, Thailand and China. Despite this evidence of region-wide trends, surprisingly few studies have provided detailed analysis of resort development of any kind in different countries. Exceptions include the comparison by King (1997) of resorts in a developed country (Australia) and a less developed country (Fiji), and those by J.D. Kim (1996) and Y.J.E. Kim (1996) on resort development in Japan and Korea.

Modifying Marx's original maxim about capitalism, it can be argued that 'tourism carries with it the seeds of its own destruction'. Burac (1996) concluded from his examination of tourism development in Martinique and Guadeloupe that practising sustainable tourism actually enhanced the destination and attracted an increased number of tourists, thus leading to difficulties in accommodating the extra arrivals. This poses a dilemma, in that 'responsible' behaviour may exacerbate the very problem it seeks to counter. Issues of carrying capacity have been addressed by Hawkins and Roberts (1994), who suggested that continued expansion of coastal tourism is incompatible with the reef resources of the Red Sea; Kocasoy (1995) focused on the links between resorts, pollution and environmental carrying capacity in Turkey. While contemporary resource management techniques have improved the ability of resort destinations to cope with increasing visitor numbers, a combination of limited resources and fragile ecologies (particularly obvious in island micro-states on coral atolls) is a particular threat to less developed countries.

Resort Detractors and Resort Boosters

There are many polemics on the evils of resort development in LDCs. Equally, others are keen to document the benefits that resorts bring to destinations. At a macro level, resorts receive very favourable treatment – for example, in Payne (1993); other studies, though more cognisant of challenges and problems to be faced, propose techniques that can be adopted by destinations generally and resorts in particular to enhance their competitiveness. The study of winter resorts by Weiermair (1993), evaluating the features most attractive to tourists that constitute critical success factors, could be applied equally to LDCs or to developed countries.

Clearly, resorts arouse strong passions, especially when they are located in vulnerable environments. The LDCs most dependent on tourism tend to be small island nations and they face particular challenges. They are relatively inaccessible, for example, and can rarely take advantage of economies of scale. Baum and Mudambi (1995: 115–120) suggested that damaging competition in the accommodation sector can be avoided if property owners (perhaps as members of hotel associations) collaborate to ensure that individual promotional and development activities are consistent with the aims agreed for the destination as a whole. Most tropical islands have been subject to resort development, so any studies giving an overview of tourism in such destinations will provide some insights into resort development.

The best studies of resort areas take a longitudinal approach and document the application of both successful and unsuccessful strategies. One such example (Singh, 1994) examined development in the Goa resort area in India, where increasing conflict was addressed by the implementation of a Coastal Regulation Zone, with beneficial results and improved cooperation between various groups. Sharpley (1994) examined tourism development in the Gambia, highlighting the development of negative social impacts associated with the resort life cycle process. The more thoughtful studies encourage those contemplating resort development to learn from the pitfalls of previous experience. A good example of this is found in Farrell (1982), where a model is provided for LDCs in particular, based on the Hawaiian experience.

There are innumerable accounts of the destruction wrought by resort developers. One example is given by Seethi (1995), who claimed to document the social and environmental destruction caused by the Goshree Island Development Project in Maharashtra Province in India. Publications such as *Tourism in Focus* (published by Tourism Concern) and *Contours* document numerous cases of resorts said to have had negative impacts on those who live nearby. A typical example is entitled 'A new fear strikes Bali; Bali's 80 million rupiah monstrosity' (Anon., 1994). It appears that resorts in LDCs will continue to be criticized into the foreseeable future.

Conclusions and Opportunities for Further Research

Debate about the role that resorts should play in tourism development in LDCs is evolving. Whilst criticism lingers that many function as neocolonial enclaves, the evidence is certainly not one-sided. As destinations diversify, the origins of tourists and the sense of dependency on the patronage of former colonial masters become less obvious. As visitors show increasing interest in the culture and environment of destinations, the type-casting of resort tourists as interested exclusively in the three Ss seems increasingly outdated. The emergence of new design concepts, some involving a postmodern melange of local tradition and contemporary styles, makes the type-casting of 'concrete monstrosities' less universally applicable. There are numerous examples of bad practice, but other resorts show evidence of making genuine attempts to operate responsibly.

The emergence of eco-resort concepts may provide resorts in LDCs with an element of respectability that was previously lacking. The growing popularity of smaller-scale developments proclaiming their sustainability credentials must, however, be seen in the context of globalization and the centralization of power in the hands of a declining number of private corporations. Some have more power than many host governments. Where major hotel management groups are involved in resort operations, commercial motives will tend to prevail over the concerns of residents at the destination (Dunning and McQueen, 1982). In some cases, governments may be unable or even unwilling to protect the interests of the host population against the wishes of a powerful international company. The growing popularity of vast mega-resorts managed by transnational corporations, notably in South-East Asia, is thus of ongoing concern, despite the emergence of boutique eco-resorts and the 'small is beautiful' ethos.

The debate has clearly moved beyond a simple choice between the enclave approach to resorts or the integrated approach. If we are to gain a better understanding of the critical role that resorts play in tourism in LDCs, further research is needed. This might examine the extent to which properties of various sizes in different settings and countries are integrated with their adjoining regions. To what extent does the level of economic development in the destination country affect the attitudes and behaviour of developers? Such research would start to provide us with a better understanding of how resorts affect countries at different stages of development.

References

Abdullah, N.M.R. and Isa, A.H.M. (1994) Revitalizing the agricultural sector through agrotourism. *Options-Serdang* 9(1): 14–16.

Anon. (1994) A new fear strikes Bali; Bali's 80 million rupiah monstrosity. *Contours* 6(6), 12–15, 16–18.

Ayala, H. (1991) Resort hotel landscape as an international megatrend. *Annals of Tourism Research* 18(4), 568–587.

Ayala, H. (1997) Resort ecotourism: a catalyst for national and regional partnerships. *Cornell Hotel and Restaurant Administration Quarterly* 38(4), 34–40.

Baum, T. and Mudambi, R. (1995) Managing demand fluctuations in the context of island tourism. In: Conlin, M.V. and Baum, T. (eds) *Island Tourism. Management, Principles and Practice.* John Wiley & Sons, Chichester, UK, pp. 115–120.

Britton, R. (1979) The image of the Third World in tourism marketing. *Annals of Tourism Research* 6(3), 318–329.

Britton, S.G. (1983) *Tourism and Underdevelopment in Fiji.* Monograph No. 13, ANU Development Studies Centre, Canberra.

Britton, S.G. and Clarke, W.C. (eds) (1987) *Ambiguous Alternatives: Tourism in Small Developing Countries.* USP, Suva, Fiji.

Burac, M. (1996) Tourism and environment in Guadeloupe and Martinique. In: Briguglio, L., Butler, R., Harrison, D. and Filho, W.L. (eds) *Sustainable Tourism in Islands and Small States: Case Studies.* Pinter, London, pp. 63–74.

Burkart, J. and Medlik, S. (1981) *Tourism Past, Present and Future.* Heinemann, London.

Burns, P. (1995) Sustaining tourism under political adversity: the case of Fiji. In: Conlin, M.V. and Baum, T. (eds) *Island Tourism: Management Principles and Practice.* John Wiley & Sons, Chichester, UK, pp. 259–272.

Butler, R. (1980) The concept of a tourist resort life cycle of evolution: implication of management of resources. *Canadian Geographer* 34(1), 5–12.

Cazes, G. (1987) *L'Isle Tropicale, Figure Emblematique du Tourism International.* Les Cahiers de Tourism, Series C, No. 112.

Cazes, G. (1992) *Tourisme et Tiers-monde: un Bilan Controversiale: les Nouvelles Colonies de Vacances.* Editions L'Harmattan, Paris.

Centre d'Etudes de Tourisme (1987) Station touristique et temps partage: deux formes de villegiature. *Notes du CET* 7(8), 1–4.

Cohen, E. (1972) Towards a sociology of international tourism. *Social Research* 39(1), 164–182.

Craig-Smith, S. and French, C. (1994) *Learning to Live with Tourism.* Pitman, Melbourne.

Craik, J. (1991) *Resorting to Tourism: Cultural Policies for Tourist Development in Australia.* Allen and Unwin, Sydney.

Cukier, J. and Wall, G. (1995) Tourism employment in Bali: a gender analysis. *Tourism Economics* 1(4), 389–401.

Cukier-Snow, J. and Wall, G. (1994) Tourism employment in Bali, Indonesia. *Tourism Recreation Research* 19(1), 32–40.

Dann, G.M.S. (1996) Tourists' images of a destination – an alternative analysis. *Journal of Travel and Tourism Marketing* 5(1/2), 41–45.

Davidson, R. (1998) *Travel and Tourism in Europe,* 2nd edn. Longman, London.

Davis, H.D. and Simons, J.A. (1982) World Bank experience with tourism projects. *Tourism Management* 3(4), 212–217.

de Kadt, E. (ed.) (1979) *Tourism: Passport to Development?* Oxford University Press, Oxford, UK.

Dean, J. and Judd, B. (eds) (1985) *Tourism Development in Australia.* Royal Australian Institute of Architects Education Division, Red Hill, Australia.

Dean, P. (1993) Timesharing opportunities for the hotel sector. *Travel and Tourism Analyst* 4, 74–94.

Dean, P. (1997) The timeshare industry in the Asia-Pacific Region. *Travel and Tourism Analyst* 4, 38–45.

Doswell, R. (1970) *Towards an Integrated Approach to Hotel Planning.* New University Education for the University of Surrey, London.

Doswell, R. (1997) *Tourism: How Effective Management Makes the Difference.* Butterworth-Heinemann, Oxford, UK.

Doswell, R. and Gamble, P. (1981) *Marketing and Planning Hotel and Tourism Projects.* Hutchinson, London.

Doswell, R. and Quest, M. (1990) New destinations for developed countries. In: *Horwath Book of Tourism.* Macmillan, London, pp. 35–45.

Dunning, J.H. and McQueen, M. (1982) Multinationals in the international hotel industry. *Annals of Tourism Research* 9(1), 69–90.

Dwyer, L., Teal, G. and Kemp, S. (1998) Organisational culture and strategic management in a resort hotel. *Asia Pacific Journal of Tourism Research* 3(1), 27–36.

Eastman, C.M. (1995) Tourism in Kenya and the marginalization of Swahili. *Annals of Tourism Research* 22(1), 172–185.

Ekinci, Y., Riley, M. and Fife-Schaw, C. (1998) Which school of thought? The dimensions of resort hotel quality. *International Journal of Contemporary Hospitality Management* 10(22/3), 63–67.

England, R. (1980) Architecture for tourists. *International Social Science Journal* 32(1), 44–45.

Farrell, B.H. (1982) *Hawaii, the Legend that Sells.* The University Press of Hawaii, Honolulu.

Ferreira, S.L.A. and Hanekom, F. (1995) Tourism and the local economy of Warmbaths, Northern Transvaal. *Development Southern Africa* 12(2), 249–257.

Fish, M. and Rudolph, P. (1986) The impact of changing conditions on international resort returns: a case study in a developing country. *International Journal of Hospitality Management* 5(2), 63–69.

Frater, J.L. (1998) The economic impact of tourism: Jamaican residents' perceptions. *Visions in Leisure and Business* 17(1), 23–36.

Freitag, T.G. (1994) Enclave tourism development. For whom the benefits roll? *Annals of Tourism Research* 21(3), 538–554.

Freitag, T.G. (1996) Tourism and the transportation of a Dominican coastal community. *Urban Anthropology* 25(3), 225–258.

Gang, X. (1998) Domestic tourism and its economic effect in Beidaihe, the largest seaside resort of China. *Pacific Tourism Review* 2(1), 43–52.

Gormsen, E. (1983) International tourism, a new frontier in Third World countries. *Geographische Zeitschrift* 71(3), 149–165.

Gray, H.P. (1981) Wanderlust tourism: problems of infrastructure. *Annals of Tourism Research* 8(2), 285–290.

Grunthal, A. (1934) *Probleme des Fremdenverkhehrs – Geographie.* Heft. 9. Schiftreihe des Forschungs Institute für den Fremden Verkehr, Berlin.

Gunawan, M.P. (1997) National planning for Indonesia's tourism. *Pacific Tourism Review* 1(1), 47–56.

Gunn, C. (1997) *Vacationscape. Developing Tourist Areas,* 3rd edn. Taylor & Francis, New York.

Harrison, D. (1997) Globalisation and tourism: some themes from Fiji. In: Oppermann, M. (ed.) *Pacific Rim Tourism.* CAB International, Wallingford, UK, pp. 167–183.

Harrison, D. (1998) The world comes to Fiji: who communicates what and to whom? *Tourism, Culture and Communication* 1(2), 129–138.

Hartmann, G.P. (1994) Segmenting Latin America. *Hotel Valuation Journal* Winter, 1–4.

Hawkins, J.P. and Roberts, C.M. (1994) The growth of coastal tourism in the Red Sea: present and future effects on coral reefs. *Ambio* 23(8), 503–508.

Hernandez, S.A., Cohen, J. and Garcia, H.L. (1996) Resident attitudes towards an instant resort enclave. *Annals of Tourism Research* 23(4), 755–779.

Hoivik, T. and Heiberg, T. (1980) Centre-periphery tourism and self-reliance. *International Social Science Journal* 32(1), 69–98.

Innskeep, E. (1994) *National and Regional Tourism Planning. Methodologies and Case Studies.* Routledge, London.

Jenkins, C.L. (1982) The effects of scale on tourism in developing countries. *Annals of Tourism Research* 9(2), 229–249.

Jenkins, C.L. and Likorish, L. (1997) *An Introduction to Tourism.* Butterworth-Heinemann, Oxford, UK.

Kang, B.S., Oh, D.S., Kim, J.H. and Choi, Y.I. (1997) The connection between county centre and residents' settlement in mountain village; with relevance to the tourist resort type. *Journal of Forest Science* 55, 90–104.

Kermath, B.M. (1992) Spatial dynamics of resorts: Sosua, Dominican Republic. *Annals of Tourism Research* 19(2), 173–190.

Khatri, N. (1996) A '4R' environmental model for Andaman and Nicobar. *Cornell Hotel and Restaurant Administration Quarterly* 37(5), 62–66.

Kim, J.D. (1996) A comparative study on resort development of Korea and Japan. *Bulletin of the Tokyo University Forests* 95, 1–64.

Kim, Y.J.E. (1996) Overview of coastal and marine tourism in Korea. *Journal of Tourism Studies* 7(2), 46–53.

King, B.E.M. (1997) *Creating Island Resorts*. Routledge, London.

King, B.E.M. and McVey, M.J. (1996) Resorts in Asia. *Travel and Tourism Analyst* 4, 35–50.

King, B.E.M. and Whitelaw, P. (1992) Resorts in Australian tourism. A recipe for confusion? *Journal of Tourism Studies* 4(1), 41–48.

King, B.E.M., Pizam, A. and Milman, A. (1993) Social impacts of tourism. Host perceptions. *Annals of Tourism Research* 20(4), 650–665.

Kocasoy, G. (1995) Waterborne disease incidences in the Mediterranean region as a function of microbial pollution and T90. *Water Science and Technology* 32(9–10), 257–266.

Krippendorf, J.C. (1987) *The Holidaymakers*. Heinemann, London.

Lea, J. (1988) *Tourism and Development in the Third World*. Routledge, London.

Lee, C.K., Lee, J.H. and Han, S.Y. (1998) Measuring the economic value of ecotourism resources: the case of South Korea. *Journal of Travel Research* 36(4), 40–46.

Leiper, N. (1995) *Tourism Management*. RMIT Publishing, Melbourne.

MacCannell, D. (1992) *Empty Meeting Grounds. The Tourism Papers*. Routledge, London.

McDonnell, I. and Darcy, S. (1998) Tourism precincts: a factor in Bali's rise in fortune and Fiji's fall from favour – an Australian perspective. *Journal of Vacation Marketing* 4(4), 353–367.

Meyer, R.A. (1996) China will try destination resorts, but planning vagueness is evident. *Journal of Travel and Tourism Marketing* 5(4), 85–93.

Middleton, V.T.C. and Hawkins, R. (1993) Practical environmental policies in travel and tourism – Part 1. *Travel and Tourism Analyst* 6, 63–70.

Mieczkowski, Z. (1991) *World Trends in Tourism and Recreation*. Peter Lang, New York.

Mohamad, S. (1997) Agrotourism in Malaysia: conceptual issues, typology and social participation. *Akademika* 50, 103–121.

Mowforth, M. and Munt, I. (1998) *Tourism and Sustainability. New Tourism in the Third World*. Routledge, London.

Nunez, T. (1977) Touristic studies in anthropological perspective. In: Smith, V. (ed.) *Hosts and Guests. The Anthropology of Tourism*. University of Pennsylvania Press, Philadelphia, Pennsylvania, pp. 207–216.

O'Grady, R. (1981) *Third World Stopover. The Tourism Debate*. World Council of Churches, Geneva, Switzerland.

Oppermann, M. (1992) International tourism and regional development in Malaysia. *Tijdschrift voor Economische en Sociale Geografie* 83(3), 226–233.

Oppermann, M. and Chon, K.S. (1997) *Tourism in Developing Countries*. International Thomson Business Press, London.

Payne, M. (1993) *Tourism in the Pacific Rim: Growth in a Region of Opportunity*. Financial Times Business Information, London.

Pearce, P.L., Morrison, A.M. and Routledge, J. (1998) *Tourism. Bridges Across Continents*. McGraw Hill, Sydney.

Pleumarom, A. (1992) Course and effect: golf tourism in Thailand. *Ecologist* 22(3), 104–110.

Poirier, R.A. (1995) Tourism and development in Tunisia. *Annals of Tourism Research* 22(1), 157–171.

Poon, A. (1993) *Tourism, Technology and Competitive Strategies*. CAB International, Wallingford, UK.

Richter, L. (1989) *The Politics of Tourism in Asia*. University of Hawaii Press, Honolulu.

Sack, R.D. (1992) *Place, Modernity and the Consumer's World*. The Johns Hopkins University Press, Baltimore, Maryland.

Schumacher, F.E. (1974) *Small is Beautiful: a Study of Economics as if People Mattered*. Sphere, London.

Seethi, K.M. (1995) Destruction of unique ecosystem of Kochi backwaters. *Economic and Political Weekly* 30(29), 181–183.

Sen, J. (1993) Socio-economic landscape of Dudhia in Darjeeling Himalaya. *Indian Journal of Landscape Systems and Ecological Studies* 16(2), 12–19.

Shackley, M. (1993) Guest farms in Namibia: an emerging accommodation sector in Africa's hottest destination. *International Journal of Hospitality Management* 12(3), 253–265.

Sharma, P.R. (1995) Culture and tourism: defining roles and relationships. *Discussion Paper Series – Mountain Enterprises and Infrastructure – ICIMOD* 95(2).

Sharpley, R. (1994) The tourist–host relationship. In: *Tourism, Tourists and Society.* Elms Publications, Huntingdon, UK, pp. 162–188.

Silver, I. (1993) Marketing authenticity in Third World countries. *Annals of Tourism Research* 20(1), 302–318.

Singh, S. (1994) Problems of tourism development in coastal Goa. *Tourism Recreation Research* 19(1), 65–67.

Smith, R.A. (1992) Beach resort evolution: implications for planning. *Annals of Tourism Research* 19(2), 304–322.

Smith, V. (1977) Introduction. In: Smith, V. (ed.) *Hosts and Guests: the Anthropology of Tourism.* University of Pennsylvania Press, Philadelphia, Pennsylvania, pp. 1–14.

Sofield, T.H.B. (1996) Anuha Island resort, Solomon Islands: a case study of failure. In: Butler, R. and Hinch, T. (eds) *Tourism and Indigenous Peoples.* International Thomson Business Press, London, pp. 176–202.

Stettner, A.C. (1993) Commodity or community? Sustainable development in mountain resorts. *Tourism Recreation Research* 18(1), 3–10.

Stiles, R.B. and See-Tho, W. (1991) Integrated resort development in the Asia Pacific Region. *Travel and Tourism Analyst* 3, 22–37.

Sullivan, M. (1996) The Japanese golf holiday market. *Travel and Tourism Analyst* 2, 58–70.

Taylor, F.F. (1993) *To Hell with Paradise: a History of the Jamaican Tourism Industry.* University of Pittsburgh Press, Pittsburgh, Pennsylvania.

Telfer, D.J. and Wall, G. (1996) Linkages between tourism and food production. *Annals of Tourism Research* 23(3), 635–653.

Thomas, G. and Fernandez, T.V. (1994) Mangrove and tourism: management strategies. *Indian Forester* 120(5), 406–412.

Trapasso, L.M. (1994) Indigenous attitudes, ecotourism and Mennomnites: recent examples in rainforest destruction/preservation. *Geojournal* 33(4), 449–452.

Tribe, J. and Snaith, T. (1998) From SERVQUAL to HOLSAT: holiday satisfaction in Varadero, Cuba. *Tourism Management* 19(1), 25–34.

Turner, A. (1996) Water world. *Leisure Management* 16(8), 66–69.

Turner, L. and Ash, J. (1975) *The Golden Hordes. International Tourism and the Pleasure Periphery.* Constable, London.

Valenzuela, M. (1988) Spain: the phenomenon of mass tourism. In: Williams, A.M. and Shaw, G. (eds) *Tourism and Economic Development. Western European Experience.* Belhaven Press, London, pp. 40–60.

Wall, G. (1996) Perspectives on tourism in selected Balinese villages. *Annals of Tourism Research* 23(1), 123–130.

Weaver, D. (1998) *Ecotourism in the Less Developed World.* CAB International, Wallingford, UK.

Weiermair, K. (1993) Some reflections on measures of competitiveness for wintersport resorts in overseas markets. *Tourist Review* 48(4), 35–41.

Witter, B.S. (1985) Attitudes about a resort area: a comparison of tourists and local retailers. *Journal of Travel Research* Summer, 14–19.

Wong, P.P. (1993) *Tourism vs Environment: the Case for Coastal Areas.* Kluwer Academic Publishers Group, Dortrecht, The Netherlands.

Yu, L. (1998) China's hotel industry: assessment and prospects. *Journal of Vacation Marketing* 4(4), 368–380.

Yuanxiang, L. (1993) Afforesting research of Wu Lin Yuan scenic resort. *Journal of Shanghai Agricultural College* 11(1), 34–40.

Zhang, Y.W. (1996) Tourism resource development in China: an overview of the growth, prospects and problems. *Tourism Recreation Research* 21(1), 19–27.

Zhang, G.R., Lew, A.A. and Yu, L. (1995) China's tourism development since 1978: policies, experiences, and lessons learned. *Tourism in China: Geographic, Political and Economic Perspectives.* Westview Press, Boulder, Colorado.

13

Child Sex Tourism in Thailand

Heather Montgomery

Introduction

In monetary and statistical terms, the rise of tourism in Thailand has been phenomenal. The number of tourists visiting Thailand has been rising since the early 1970s. In 1973 there were 1 million; there were 2 million in 1981, 4 million in 1988 (ECPAT, undated) and more than 7.5 million in 1998 (Anon., 1999: 1) – an increase of more than 7% compared with 1997. Growth is expected to continue in 1999. At the time of writing (January–March 1999, the last months for which figures were available), there were 2,279,122 tourist arrivals, compared with 2,043,292 over the same period the previous year. Visitors are also staying longer (Anon., 1999: 2) and tourism is now the country's highest source of foreign currency revenue (Lewis and Kapur, 1990). The collapse since October 1997 of the Thai currency, the baht, made Thailand an even cheaper destination for tourists and it continues to be the most visited country of South-East Asia. On 2 June 1997, the Thai government floated the baht and called in the International Monetary Fund (IMF). The exchange rate plummeted and Thailand was effectively bankrupt, while for tourists the cost of travelling in Thailand became extremely cheap (Chalongphob, 1999: 1).

Thailand also continues to be the country where tourism remains most controversial, and many have claimed that these figures mask a heavy social cost to the country in the form of environmental damage, prostitution and AIDS (e.g. ECTWT, 1983, 1990; Asia Partnership for Human Development, 1985; Richter, 1989; ASA Social Responsibilities Committee, 1993; Gonzales, 1993). In this chapter, the focus is on prostitution and sex tourism, especially involving children. The debate around tourism in Thailand is becoming increasingly focused on the issue of prostitution and whether there is a direct causal relationship between the two.

It is undeniable that prostitution and Thailand have become indelibly linked in many people's minds, so much so that 'sex tourism' and Thailand have become almost synonymous. In 1995, there was a minor scandal in Bangkok when Longman's published an English dictionary that described Bangkok as 'the capital city of Thailand. It is famous for its temples and other beautiful buildings, and is also often mentioned as a place where there are a lot of prostitutes' (Mukdawan, 1993). Reactions in Thailand to this dictionary were marked – for example, *The Nation*, which carried articles entitled 'Government will try to educate Longman'

(*The Nation*, July 1993, p. 15) or 'Silver lining in Longman's stormy cloud' (*The Nation*, July 1993, p. 8) – but the description caused great offence and led to protests outside Longman's as well as outrage in newspaper editorials in both the Thai and English language press in the country. For many years, Thai women's groups had been running campaigns against the image of brothel Thailand with slogans such as 'Thailand not Sexland' and the unquestioned assumptions behind the Longman's description angered many.

There is a strong perception that tourism, by its very nature, must lead to prostitution and that in many forms one is simply a reflection of the other. Graburn (1983: 441) has articulated this most clearly, drawing explicit parallels between tourism and prostitution and claiming that, conceptually, there is no difference between the two.

> As host nations, they may have little to sell but their 'beauty' which is often desecrated by (sacrificed to) mass tourism. The men of such countries are forced into pimp roles … At a psychological level [poor] nations are forced into the 'female' role of servitude, of being 'penetrated' for money, often against their will: whereas the outgoing, pleasure seeking 'penetrating' tourists of powerful nations are cast in the 'male' role.

For Graburn, prostitution is not an unfortunate and unforeseen consequence of mass tourism but is at the heart of the tourism industry and cannot be disentangled from it. The assumption that prostitution is fundamentally bad means that tourism is likewise condemned. The two are not only linked; they are interchangeable.

In the case of Thailand, it is hard to disagree with much of this. There are whole areas, such as Patpong in Bangkok or 'The Strip' in Pattaya, which cater brashly and exclusively for the foreign sex tourist (Montgomery, 1996: 91). There are bars that will not allow Thai men into them and, although technically illegal in Thailand, prostitution flourishes openly in these places. There is obvious collaboration with the Thai authorities but equally the Western tour operators know what they are marketing. Coy hints in holiday brochures that certain hotels in Pattaya are 'unsuitable for families' suggest that tour operators are quite happy to collude in selling the sex industry. Thailand is now so well known for prostitution, not least through the many documentaries and newspaper articles on the nature and extent of the sex industry, that travel agents need do little to promote the country as a place for male sexual fantasy.

Sex Tourism

The tourist and the prostitute have become powerful images with which to condemn mass travel and package tourism. There is something deeply unpleasant about the idea of foreign men, with all their assumed superiority of class, age, race and sex, buying the sexual services of poorer, younger Asian women. It is perhaps worth pointing out that women, too, can be sex tourists but there was very little evidence of this in Thailand when I was conducting research. However, others have discussed the role of female tourists in sex tourism in Africa and the Caribbean (ECTWT, 1983; de Albuquerque, 1998). While this might say more about Western sensibilities about sex and the rigid distinctions drawn in the West between paid sex and that exchanged in a 'proper' relationship, it still has the ability to disturb. For this reason, the usual stereotype of a sex tourist is of an old, fat, balding and unattractive man who has to buy sex in Thailand as no one in his home country will willingly agree to have sex with him for free. It is easy to despise a man like this; not only is he using his structural (financial, racial, political and social) power to have sex with a much younger, more attractive woman, but he is openly flaunting that power.

When dealing with the issue of child prostitution, these issues are even more intense. Sexual morality has changed in the West and various sexual behaviours that were previously condemned publicly and viewed as matters for state intervention, such as homosexuality and adultery, are now tolerated, or at least recognized as private behaviour, in which the state has no right to interfere. However, as strictures around these have loosened, such other issues as children's sexuality and prostitution have become more problematic and have commanded greater attention.

The explosion of interest in, and concern about, child abuse, especially child sexual abuse, has been overwhelming in the past decade and has brought calls for the greater protection of children. In a less obvious way, prostitution remains a cause for concern and is still criminalized and stigmatized. While the two issues cannot be easily compared, prostitution and child sex remain the two areas that demand government intervention and criminal prosecution. Given this, it is unsurprising that those who seek out child prostitutes carry such a huge social stigma and have been demonized so effectively.

The issue of adult prostitution remains a controversial one. While many continue to condemn it as exploitation or as a form of neocolonialism, others who have worked with sex workers have pointed to the complexity of the situation and the various levels of exploitation at work. Sociologists and anthropologists (e.g. Cohen, 1986; Fordham, 1995) have argued that many sex workers are skilled manipulators who hold the balance of power in individual relationships, even though they are powerless on the larger political and economic stage. Others, such as Kempadoo (1998) and Alexander (Delacoste and Alexander, 1988), have argued for a woman's right to choose prostitution and have argued that a woman's rights over her body include the right to exchange sex for money.

The issue of sex tourism, therefore, is far from simple and it cannot be proved that tourism leads to prostitution and that, because the latter is invariably morally wrong, so is the former. The issue of child prostitution, however, encounters no such difficulties. By definition, children are under the age of consent, and therefore do not have a right to exchange their sexuality for money. They also have little individual autonomy and have no room to negotiate or gain power in individual relationships (Finkelhor, 1979). There can be no mitigating factors for those who use child prostitutes and no ambiguities. While there can and should be debate about who is exploiting whom when an adult tourist has sex with an adult, sex with a child means sex without consent. The morality of tourism as it relates to adult prostitution is ambiguous; for child prostitution it is not.

For those who condemn tourism, especially non-governmental organizations (NGOs) from developing countries who resent, often with some justification, the intrusion of large numbers of foreign tourists, the issue of child prostitution is central. By continually emphasizing the connections between child sex tourism and more general tourism, a link between the two is established and the assumption made that any tourist is a potential child sex tourist. One of the largest campaigning groups against child prostitution, End Child Prostitution in Asian Tourism (ECPAT, 1993: 11), claimed that:

> while much of the industry might not actively, deliberately or consciously organise sex tourism, they are still providing the vehicle in the form of an aeroplane or a bus or whatever. In a symbolic way also they provide a vehicle in the industrialised or wealthy countries through creating the mood in society, the general expectation that part of life can be a trip overseas. The environment that makes tourism possible and in which tourism flourishes is a kind of vehicle.

The existence of child sex tourism automatically contaminates all tourists. If only a few tourists are committing crimes against children, the risk is considered serious enough to target all tourists as potential child abusers and to take steps against everyone who travels. In Sweden, for example, all international airline tickets contain a leaflet warning against child sex tourism. There have been widely publicized efforts by tourist-receiving countries to stamp out child prostitution. Their efforts have been matched by tourist-sending countries, some of which have passed new laws to allow for the prosecution of extra-territorial crimes against children. Men who escape justice in countries such as Thailand or the Philippines can now be tried in their country of origin. The Australian government has been particularly critical of child sex tourism and has passed a law that would imprison its citizens for up to 17 years if they were found guilty of sexual offences against children abroad. Norway, Germany, France, Belgium, New Zealand and Sweden have similar laws. In Britain, despite the government's initial opposition, The Sex Offenders Bill was passed in March 1997, which empowered the UK courts to prosecute people who commit sex offences against children abroad, if they commit a crime that is an offence in both countries. To date, successful prosecutions have been obtained in 1990 in Norway, in June 1995 in Sweden, in April 1996 in Australia and in October 1997 in France. At the time of writing, the UK has not yet prosecuted anyone under the new Act. Nevertheless, although the number of successful prosecutions has been relatively small, there is a new will to eradicate child prostitution and several countries have prosecuted their own nationals for crimes against children.

Child Sex Tourists

Despite this new determination to stamp out child prostitution, there is still very little information on who buys sex with children abroad and why. With only stereotypes and a handful of cases to go on, it is impossible to know who child sex tourists are and whether or not the threat of prosecution will lead to a decrease in the number of men travelling thousands of miles to have sex with children. There is little information on how many child sex tourists there are, how they travel, or on their sexual preferences. Likewise, there is next to no information on the identity of the children who prostitute themselves or what is expected of them by clients. There are too many assumptions about these children and their clients that need to be problematized. The lack of relevant information on the subject means that much of the debate is based on speculation and unproved assumptions that need to be questioned.

It is claimed, for example, that there are 1 million child prostitutes in Asia, or even that one million children every year become prostitutes in Asia. However, although the figure of 1 million child prostitutes in Asia seems to have been accepted by NGOs worldwide, it has little basis in fact or in research. Rather, it is based on a statement made by the Norwegian government to the Council of Europe which read: 'Every year, one million children are kidnapped, bought, or in other ways forced to enter the sex market' (Black, 1994: 12). No source was given for this figure, nor was there any indication of how it was calculated.

Such a random use of numbers was quite unnecessary; in 1989, the same year as when the statement was first made, the Norwegian Save the Children (Redd Barna) published a full report on what was known of the nature and extent of child prostitution. Funded by the Norwegian Agency for International Development (NORAD), the report deliberately gave no numbers and statistics and acknowledged the difficulty in defining and counting child prostitutes. It also emphasised the unreliability of many sources for these numbers (Narvesen, 1989:24). The Norwegian government then appeared to ignore its own research and, as a result, its estimate has taken on a life of its own and is now the most commonly quoted statistic.

In fact, the extent of the problem remains unclear, as does (more importantly) the number of children who cater to Western tourists. There are thriving indigenous sex industries of Asia, especially in Thailand, where the demand is for young Burmese girls (Asia Watch, 1993), or in India, where there is evidence of Nepalese girls being trafficked into the brothels of Bombay and Delhi (e.g. Mukherji, 1986; Rozario, 1988; Patkar, 1991; Sleightholme and Sinha, 1997). What is not known is how many of these children regularly or even occasionally have Western clients or how many Westerners deliberately go on holiday to these places to seek them out for sex. In her study of children in the tourism industries of Thailand and the Philippines, Black (1995: 21) claimed:

> A sober analysis of the evidence does not bear out the claim that tourism is 'the main factor in the explosion in numbers of children recruited, enticed, and brought into prostitution', as reliable commentators recently pointed out. ... In Thailand, under-age girl prostitutes mainly serve local customers; one estimate places the proportion serving foreigners at less than 10%, and suggests that Western tourists mainly patronize women aged above 18. What can be stated on the basis of the available – inadequate – information is that demand for commercial sex among visitors, including those from neighbouring Asian countries, exerts pressures in the market generally, drawing in young newcomers at the cheaper end.

It is unlikely that tourists have created a market for child sex, though they are certainly the most visible clients. They are also the most disturbing, precisely because they are foreigners and therefore a problem for countries that receive and send tourists. It is difficult for those outside Thailand or the Philippines to condemn indigenous child prostitution without being accused of unwarranted interference, whereas when Western men travel abroad to have sex with children it becomes an international problem. Although the numbers of successful prosecutions have been small, there is clearly a greater awareness of the problem and a greater willingness to tackle it. Previously, offenders caught by the Thai police were released on bail and left the country (Drummond and Chant, 1994) whereas now they are likely to be prosecuted in the country where the crimes were committed.

Despite the growing number of cases of men being arrested for child prostitution offences, there is still little information on these men, especially how they travel to the country, how they arrange meetings with children and why they do so (Montgomery, 1996: 116). Again, there are stereotypes and assumptions: that the paedophile is a middle-aged man, part of a 'ring' of men meeting secretly to plot their next conquest. Yet those arrested have been individuals who arrived in Thailand or the Philippines on their own. The process by which they met the children and had sex with them has not been made explicit. This does not discount the possibility that they did have contacts in Thailand, who bought children for them, but the mechanics of the transactions remains unclear. Linked to this is the assumption that clients are tourists who travel for the explicit purpose of buying sex with children. Once again, some men undoubtedly fall into this category, but many documented cases involve men who have lived for some time in the countries concerned, either setting up businesses (for example, travel firms) or even running social or charitable projects. In 1989, for instance, Mark Morgan, a Mormon from Utah, was arrested in Thailand for the sexual abuse of children in a shelter that he had set up for indigent boys. It was later proved that he and two associates had been systematically abusing the boys and arranging sexual meetings between their friends and the children in their

care (Ruff, 1992: 35). As far as the abuse of children is concerned, these distinctions may seem rather academic but, in terms of prevention of abuse and also the links between tourism and child prostitution, there are important differences which should be noted.

Other received wisdom about child sex tourists is that younger and younger children are being drawn into the sex industry in response to the threat of AIDS (Heyzer, 1986; Lee Wright, 1990; Hiew, 1992; Muntabhorn, 1992; ECPAT – Philippines, 1994). In this scenario, tourists are aware of the AIDS risk and therefore demand young children, believing they will have had fewer partners and are therefore likely to be AIDS-free. It is also claimed that in some Asian cultures (for example, China) sex with a virgin is alleged to cure AIDS and other venereal diseases, and that tourists from China or Taiwan actively seek out very young children. There is no ethnographic evidence for either of these beliefs (Ennew et al., 1996: 10). In the absence of any detailed study of the clients of child prostitutes, they remain assumptions that, although sounding reasonable and certainly prompting further research, are currently without empirical support. Indeed, research on Thai clients of prostitutes has produced contradictory evidence. Fordham (1995) claimed, for example, that knowledge of the risk of AIDS is high but gambling with that risk is part of a ritualized construction of masculinity. The age of the prostitute is irrelevant, and men will usually choose an older girl who looks healthy, i.e. is plump, with clear skin and shiny hair. Children much younger than 16 may well look too skinny and undeveloped and are therefore assumed to be at greater risk from AIDS. Another study of Thai men (Sittitrai and Brown, 1994: 4) claimed that 'many males felt that child prostitutes between 15 and 18 were more desirable than adults, but that it was wrong to sleep with younger ones' (under 14). There have been no similar studies among the Western clients of child prostitutes and it is impossible to know if Western men use similar criteria.

The final category claimed to frequent child prostitutes is the 'casual sexual experimenter' (O'Grady, 1992: 81). These are people who would never actively seek out a child for sex and may well be appalled at the thought of child prostitution. Nevertheless, on holiday they may be tempted to experiment sexually and such loosening of codes of behaviour may include sex with a child. Given the availability of sex in such countries as Thailand, and the liminal state of tourists on holiday, such experimentation seems plausible but, however likely the scenario, there is a dearth of evidence of the subject. The unpublished study by O'Connell Davidson (1994) of sex tourists in Pattaya, Thailand, suggested that many sex tourists retain their dislike of such 'abnormal' sexualities as homosexuality and paedophilia. That said, what tourists tell researchers and how they actually behave in private may not coincide and, in other circumstances, tourists have admitted to experimenting with young prostitutes (Kennedy, 1996).

Little can be said with any certainty about men who travel to abuse children sexually. There is no convincing profile of a typical sex tourist and the term 'tourist' itself may be misleading. Prosecuted cases indicate a problem that must be addressed, but solutions are not easily available when so little is known about how and why the sexual abuse of children overseas occurs. Clearly, some assumptions may be more reasonable than others and both Ennew (1986: 112) and Ireland (1993: 29) quoted studies that suggest tourists are more likely to follow paedophile urges when away from home, because exotic and unusual surroundings encourage the view that differences in climate and culture will be accompanied by differences in morals. O'Grady (1992: 82) painted a lurid picture of such casual sexual experimenters:

> Recently, a young Australian couple went to Bangkok. They belong to the young professional set with more money and freedom than they can handle responsibly. During their time in Thailand they were able to test their freedom to the maximum and after the usual round of massage parlours, sex shows and partners in the room, they spent two evenings when they brought two child prostitutes to their hotel. The young girl and boy were required to take part in a variety of sexual experiments to satisfy the desire of the older couple.

As a contrast to this picture of the jaded sexual experimenter, willing to try anything once

as long as he (or she) is abroad, the other image of the child sex tourist is of the obsessive and sinister paedophile. This image derives from the literature on paedophilia in Western countries which highlights the predatory nature of the child sex abuser and the lengths to which he will go to find children. Unlike the sexual experimenter who may have sex with a child if it is offered, but whose sexual preference is not for children, the preferential child sexual offender actively seeks out sex with children of a particular age (Ennew, 1986: 83; Finkelhor and Araji, 1986; Wilson and Cox, 1986; Lanning, 1987: 7; Ireland, 1993: 25). Many cases coming to court fit this model well. In 1994, for example, Bradly Pendragon, an Australian, was arrested in the northern Thai city of Chiang Mai after trying to develop photographs clearly depicting the sexual abuse of a young girl. Not only was the abuse graphically shown, but the sacrilegious use of a Buddhist figure was also visible, compounding the offence. Pendragon had the classic paedophile profile and his extensive and secret preparations for overseas trips were accompanied by such paraphernalia as videos or cameras. It was unlikely to have been his first offence and he had clearly travelled with the intent to target and to abuse Thai children.

The case of Pendragon showed clearly that child sex tourists posed a real threat and that some men were prepared to go to extreme lengths to indulge their sexual fantasies. Nor was he an isolated case. In recent years, Thai newspapers have run a steady stream of articles about child prostitution, documenting many cases of child abuse by foreigners; for example: 'German engineer arrested on "perverted sex" charge' (*The Nation*, 3 March 1994, p. 2); 'Child Molester Flees Thailand' (*Bangkok Post*, 31 January 1995, p. 3); 'German couple recruiting kids for sex photos' (*Pattaya Mail*, 4 January 1993, p. 15); 'Swiss caught with small boy' (*Pattaya Mail*, 23 March 1994, p. 12. Whatever the extent of the problem and whatever its nature, it cannot be denied that the commercial sexual exploitation of children in Thailand does have links with the tourism industry and that some tourists travel to Thailand explicitly to have sex with children. The ready availability of paid sex in Thailand and the ease of the transaction have created an atmosphere where many tourists assume that places such as Patpong or The Strip are as much a part of Thai culture as its temples and markets. The freedom of tourists to indulge in sexual behaviours not permitted in their home countries – for example, visiting prostitutes or watching sex shows – has led to a belief among some tourists that prostitution is different in Thailand: the women are not 'really' prostitutes and paid sex is less sleazy and more romantic than its counterpart in the West (Cohen, 1982: 410–412). Equally, this belief enables men to see themselves as lovers and boyfriends rather than clients. As O'Connell Davidson (unpublished, 1994) pointed out,

> for British men, the non-contractual nature of the exchange conceals its commercial nature. It makes it possible for them to buy sexual services without having to see themselves as the kind of men who use prostitutes.

Tourism and Prostitution

Tourism in Thailand must stand heavily condemned. It has undoubtedly proved extremely lucrative for some investors and for the Thai economy. Richter (1989: 87) claimed that 'a study done in 1982 discovered that of the entire trade deficit, 40 percent was reduced by tourism revenues'. However, tourism in Thailand has always relied heavily on sexual tourism and the sexuality of Thai women, whether air hostesses with the national airline or bar girls, has been heavily promoted. In areas such as Pattaya, this sexualization has been taken to the extreme and children, too, have become commercialized and their sexuality sold in response to tourist demand. In this context, it is hardly surprising that Thailand has a vigorous anti-tourism campaign which has demanded an end to sexual tourism and severe curbs on all tourism (e.g. Srisang, 1990).

Nevertheless, the easy conflation of tourism with prostitution is problematic. Other countries have high levels of tourism without the same degree of sex tourism and child prostitution. The question must be asked whether Graburn (1983) is right, and tourism and prostitution are so intimately linked that

the former automatically causes the latter, or if specific features of the Thai tourism industry have allowed sex tourism to flourish. The assumption that all tourism leads inevitably to prostitution, and that wherever there are tourists there will be clients of prostitutes and men seeking children for sex, must be questioned. Despite attempts to reduce their impact, horror stories of child abuse by foreigners have undoubtedly tarnished the reputation of Thai tourism, but how far the Thai experience can be used as a model for other tourist contexts is disputable and such comparisons should be carefully handled.

The lack of research on child prostitution has left many questions unanswered and, in many cases, unasked. Its extent remains unknown, as do the numbers of indigenous and foreign clients. Similarly, the links between adult and child prostitution, including the degree to which adult prostitution encourages child prostitution, have not been established. In addition, apart from a few cases of travel agents actively promoting child sex trips, the role played by the general tourist industry in promoting overseas prostitution is unknown and unquantifiable. The World Tourism Organization, with many national travel and tourism authorities, has been vociferous in condemning child sex tourism, and is determined to break any links between child prostitution and the tourism industry.

With all tourism under suspicion of aiding and abetting child prostitution, campaigns against child sex tourism have targeted all tourist-receiving countries regardless. Even if they currently lack a child prostitution problem, it is assumed one will develop in the future. At the time of writing, the situation in islands of the South Pacific (for example, Fiji, Tonga and Samoa) is of special concern and the New Zealand government has funded projects to study the extent of child sex tourism there, even though there have been no reports of its existence. Whilst there was indeed an Australian paedophile, resident in Fiji for some years, who had sexually abused Fijian children and taken pornographic pictures of them, the research in question was based on the assumption that, with crackdowns in Thailand and the Philippines, paedophiles must be looking for other places where children are easily available and would move their operations there. Yet this is speculative. Paedophiles *might* turn their attention to Fiji if child sex is known to be available, but this assumption is as yet unproved and ignores the differences between the types of tourist who visit Fiji and those who visit Thailand. It also ignores the very different history and cultural context of tourism in these two areas, thus indicating the danger of transposing one model of tourism on to another country and assuming that all tourism follows the same pattern. It is indeed necessary to be vigilant, but the Thai model is not necessarily predictive.

Profiles of Tourism

In order to challenge these assumptions, it is worth examining the different contexts in which tourism has occurred in Fiji and in Thailand and the implications that this has for assumed links between child prostitution and tourism. The history of tourism, especially sex tourism, in Thailand must start in the late 1960s, when the Vietnam war began to spill over into Cambodia, Thailand's neighbour. The Thais recognized the necessity of accommodating the Americans and not only allowed the US to station troops in Thailand, but also (and more importantly) permitted American servicemen to use Thailand as an 'R and R' station (Rest and Recreation, more commonly referred to as 'I and I' – Intoxication and Intercourse). Given the huge numbers of young men with large amounts of money to spend, the foreign sex industry quickly became organized with bars and brothels set up explicitly catering to foreign men. Based around Western music and Western food, the women who worked there were encouraged to learn English and to attend exclusively to foreign men. Many women became very mobile, leaving their home provinces and moving to Pattaya or Bangkok to find lucrative work among the Americans (for an autobiographical example see Malee, 1986).

Thailand quickly gained a reputation as a sex paradise and became a byword for cheap, blatant, commercially available sex. By 1975, most troops had gone, leaving behind the infrastructure of the sex industry and an illusion and stereotype of beautiful, pliant and docile Oriental women, who offered much more than paid sex. That these fantasies were fuelled by men and drew on Orientalist stereotypes was never questioned, and in time they became self-fulfilling. Thai women and children had to be docile and subservient because that was what was expected of them. Some servicemen simply did not give up the dream and stayed on in Thailand, especially in places like Pattaya and Bangkok, running bars. One of the major red light districts in Bangkok is a lane called Soi Cowboy, named after an American who bought and operated many bars there at the end of the Vietnam war.

Sexual services were therefore built into the very fabric of the tourism industry. Tourism in Thailand was set up to cater for single men with a high disposable income and an appetite for sex. The military presence in Thailand was integral to the development of a tourist industry and what was previously arranged for soldiers was simply provided to tourists at the end of the war. That the tourists who were thus encouraged were no longer young men hardly changed what was on offer. Hundreds of compliant young women were prepared to fulfil sexual fantasies at a bargain price. A similar pattern emerged in the Philippines, and large numbers of US soldiers at such bases as Olongapo Bay provided a foundation for sexual tourism (Asia Partnership for Human Development, 1985: 45; Miralao *et al.*, 1990). Services for the tourists and the military overlapped in these places and an entire sub-sector of the service and hospitality industry was set up, centred on the sale of sex. It would be naive to think that children are unaffected by the sex industry, or that their bodies are immune from commercialization, and it is inevitable that they become caught up in the process. They sell their bodies simply because they can and because prostitution is, and always will be, an industry putting a premium on youth.

As Ennew (1986: 11) pointed out, 'an old prostitute is a redundant prostitute'. In a job that requires beauty, which is often synonymous with youth, prostitutes are invariably young, and if we follow the United Nations and define children as anyone under the age of 18, rates of child prostitution will always be high. Other children in the tourist industry will also be affected. Even if their work is not sexual, in places such as Pattaya or Olongapo Bay, their labour is ultimately connected to the tourist trade, which is largely indistinguishable from the sex trade (Black, 1995: 5). Their labour is crucial in keeping the resort running and their dependence on the tourist industry is total. For example, the mayor of Pattaya once said in a newspaper interview, 'Every morsel eaten by Pattaya's population of 200,000 is provided by tourists' (*Pattaya Mail*, 12 November 1993, p. 1).

Tourism in Fiji, and more widely in the South Pacific, has no such history. Despite the image (often popularized by anthropologists) of the South Pacific as a sexually liberated and sensuous place, there has been little sexual tourism there. In Fiji, the most visited country of the region, tourism's impact is most visible, but the number of tourists in Fiji is significantly smaller than in Thailand, and Fiji attracts very different types of tourist. Tourism in Fiji has been controlled and the assumption that sex tourism must exist there, either now or at some time in the future, seems unwarranted. The emphasis on the single male, so evident in Thailand, does not exist in Fiji. It is a particularly popular location for weddings and honeymoons, and many other tourists, often middle aged, come in couples. Other tourists are backpackers on round-the-world trips, and they are generally more interested in snorkelling or surfing than sex tourism (Tracey Macintosh, Department of Sociology, University of the South Pacific, 1997, personal communication). There is no large military presence or nearby base, and the number of visitors is significantly smaller.

It has been suggested (Turner and Ash, 1975: 197) that

the Tahitian or Fijian soon comes to value her/his sexuality in money terms, hence prostitution and the 'gigolo' soon appear in tourist-intruded communities, even where they had not existed before.

but there is little evidence available from Fiji to support such a view. In September 1997, the author carried out a series of interviews in Suva, Fiji's capital, and respondents were women's groups, the police, non-governmental organizations and government depart-

ments. No one mentioned sex tourism as an area for concern, even though child abuse, incest, domestic violence and women's rights were high on their agendas. This is not to suggest that tourism in Fiji is problem-free, but it has not experienced the social tensions connected with tourism in Thailand and has not led to an influx of men seeking sex with local women or to an epidemic of commercial child abuse. If shadowy rings of paedophiles are seeking a new tropical paradise where they can have sex with children, it is unlikely they will find it in Fiji.

Conclusion

In some instances, tourism, prostitution and the commercial sexual exploitation of children have clearly become indistinguishable from one another, and increased tourism has facilitated the abuse of children by paedophiles. However, it would be wrong to view this as a function only of tourism and to set it apart from wider political, social and historical factors. There have been specific features of Thai tourism that have enabled the sex industry to develop but these are not common to all forms of tourism. The problem of child sex tourists is real but, despite all the rhetoric, it remains under-researched. The most certain aspect of the use of child prostitutes by tourists is that very little is known about it. It exists in certain countries and, despite laws and the intense social stigma against child sexual abuse, some men (and possibly some women) continue to travel overseas to have sex with children, just as they continue to abuse them in their own countries. However, it is not known whether the problem is increasing, decreasing or staying the same, and it is not known whether the extra-territorial laws are proving a deterrent (Ennew, 1997: 4).

Child sexual abuse, especially when it is a commercial transaction involving rich Europeans and poor Asians, is an emotive subject and should be treated with a great deal of sensitivity. It is of concern to many people and is finally being treated with the attention and urgency it deserves. However, when dealing with such issues, there is a tendency to overestimate their extent and find problems where they do not exist. The seach for child prostitutes wherever there are tourists does not help children in Thailand and the Philippines, where the risk of child abuse is greatest. Such risks are not evenly spread throughout tourist-receiving countries and it is possible to calculate which children are most at risk, in which countries, and to target resources accordingly. While it is clearly important to take the threat of child prostitution seriously, this means dealing with it rationally and basing predictions on what is known or what can be reasonably assumed.

The prosecution of individual tourists or travel agents is a worthy goal that makes these people accountable for their actions, but to emphasize tourism alone leaves the wider social structures untouched and unstudied. Child prostitution will not be ended by punishing individual tourists, or even by blaming the tourism industry for creating the monster of child prostitution. The tourist industry is not a monolithic structure forcing all developing countries to follow the same pattern, and individual governments have very different priorities. For some, sexual tourism is unthinkable, while for others it is the necessary price of economic development. In 1980, the Deputy Prime Minister of Thailand justified sex tourism because it encouraged tourists and created jobs. He acknowledged (Ennew 1986: 99) that there were 'some forms of entertainment that some of you might consider disgusting and shameful because they are forms of sexual entertainment that attract tourists [but] … we must do this because we have to consider the jobs that will be created'.

Many factors explain the existence of child sex tourists and all must be taken into consideration when analysing the threat posed by these tourists. Tourism is just one of several variables which, in conjunction with other circumstances, may cause child prostitution, but tourism alone does not necessarily promote the sexual exploitation of children. The real and terrible cases of abuse that have come to light in Thailand should be treated as a sign of the seriousness of the issue and the need for certain countries to crack down harshly on those who break the law. They are not, however, conclusive proof that prostitution and tourism cannot be conceptually separated or that tourism is simply rape by another name.

References

Anon. (1999) *International Tourist Arrivals: Bangkok.* Tourist Authority of Thailand, Bangkok.

ASA Social Responsibilities Committee (1993) *Pleasure in Paradise?* Anglican General Synod, Sydney.

Asia Partnership for Human Development (1985) *Awake.* APHD, Sydney.

Asia Watch (1993) *A Modern Form of Slavery: Trafficking of Burmese Women and Girls into Brothels in Thailand.* Human Rights Watch, New York.

Black, M. (1994) Home truths. *New Internationalist* February, 9–13.

Black, M. (1995) *In the Twilight Zone, Child Workers in the Hotel, Tourism and Catering Industry.* International Labour Organization, Geneva.

Chalongphob, S. (1999) *Economic Crisis and Recovery in Thailand: the Role of the IMF.* Thailand Development Research Institute (TDRI), Bangkok.

Cohen, E. (1982) Thai girls and Farang men – the edge of ambiguity. *Annals of Tourism Research* 9(3), 403–442.

Cohen, E. (1986) Lovelorn Farangs; the correspondence between foreign men and Thai girls. *Anthropological Quarterly* 59(3), 115–127.

Delacoste, F. and Alexander, P. (1988) Sex *Work: Writings by Women in the Sex Industry.* Virago, London.

de Albuquerque, K. (1998) Sex, beach boys, and female tourists in the Caribbean. *Sexuality and Culture* 2, 87–111.

Drummond, A. and Chant, A. (1994) Child sex Britons freed with bribes. *Evening Standard* 7 March, p. 20.

ECPAT (undated) *Report on International Conference to End Child Prostitution in Asian Tourism.* Unpublished manuscript, End Child Prostitution in Asian Tourism, Bangkok.

ECPAT (1993) *Report on International Consultation.* End Child Prostitution in Asian Tourism, Bangkok.

ECPAT – Philippines (1994) *Tourism and Child Prostitution in Cebu.* ECPAT – Philippines, Manilla.

ECTWT (1983) *Tourism, Prostitution, Development.* Ecumenical Coalition on Third World Tourism, Bangkok.

ECTWT (1990) *Caught in Modern Slavery: Tourism and Child Prostitution in Asia*. Ecumenical Coalition on Third World Tourism, Bangkok.

Ennew, J. (1986) *Sexual Exploitation of Children*. Polity Press, Cambridge, UK.

Ennew, J. (1997) *Extraterritorial Legislation in Response to the International Dimension of Child Sexual Exploitation*. Public Hearings – Centre International de l'Enfance et de la Famille (CIDEF), Château de Longchamp, Paris, France, 30 September–2 October, 1997.

Ennew, J., Gopal, K., Heeran, J. and Montgomery, H. (1996) *The Commercial Sexual Exploitation of Children: Background Papers and Annotated Bibliography*, for the World Congress on the Commercial Sexual Exploitation of Children. Childwatch International and UNICEF, Oslo.

Finkelhor, D. (1979) What's wrong with sex between adults and children? Ethics and the problem of sexual abuse. *American Journal of Orthopsychiatry* 49(4), 692–697.

Finkelhor, D. and Araji, S. (1986) *A Sourcebook on Child Sexual Abuse*. Sage, London and Delhi.

Fordham, G. (1995) Whisky, women and song: alcohol and AIDS in Northern Thailand. *Australian Journal of Anthropology* 6(3), 154–177.

Gonzales, P. (1993) *Social, Political and Ecological Impacts of Tourism*. ECTWT, Bangkok.

Graburn, N.H. (1983) Tourism and prostitution. *Annals of Tourism Research* 10(3), 437–442.

Heyzer, N. (1986) *Working Women of South-East Asia – Development, Subordination and Emancipation*. Open University Press, Milton Keynes.

Hiew, C.C. (1992) Endangered families in Thailand: Third World families affected by socio-economic change. In: Albee, G., Bond, L. and Cook Monsey, T. (eds) *Improving Children's Lives: Global Perspectives on Prevention*. Sage, New Delhi and London.

Ireland, K. (1993) *Wish You Weren't Here*. Save the Children Fund, London.

Kempadoo, K. (1998) *Global Sex Workers: Rights, Resistance and Redefinition*. Routledge, New York.

Kennedy, D. (1996) Child abuse tourists boast to undercover researchers. *The Times* 30 August, p. 10.

Lanning, K. (1987) *Child Molesters: a Behavioral Analysis*. National Center for Missing and Exploited Children, Arlington, Virginia.

Lee-Wright, P. (1990) *Child Slaves*. Earthscan Publications, London.

Lewis, J. and Kapur, D. (1990) An updating country study – Thailand needs and prospects in the 1990s. *World Development* 18(10), 1363–1378.

Malee (1986) *Tiger Claw and Velvet Paw: the Erotic Odyssey of a Thai Prostitute*. Headline, London.

Miralao, V., Carlos, C. and Santos, A. (1990) *Women Entertainers in Angeles and Olongapo*. Rainbow, Manila.

Montgomery, H. (1996) Public vice and private virtue: child prostitution in Thailand. PhD Dissertation, Department of Social Anthropology, University of Cambridge, Cambridge, UK.

Mukdawan, S. (1993) A silver lining on Longman's stormy cloud. *The Nation* 18 July, p. 8.

Mukherji, S.K. (1986) *Prostitution in India*. Advent Books, New York.

Muntabhorn, V. (1992) *Sale of Children*. Report submitted by the Special Rapporteur. E/CN.4/1992/55. United Nations, New York.

Narvesen, O. (1989) *The Sexual Exploitation of Children in Developing Countries*. Redd Barna, Oslo.

O'Connell Davidson, J. (1994) British sex tourists in Thailand. (Unpublished manuscript.)

O'Grady, R. (1992) *The Child and the Tourist*. ECPAT, Bangkok.

Patkar, P. (1991) Girl-child in the Red Light areas. *The Indian Journal of Social Work* 52(1), 71–80.

Richter, L. (1989) *The Politics of Tourism in Asia*. University of Hawaii Press, Honolulu.

Rozario, R.M. (1988) *Trafficking in Women and Children in India*. Uppal Publishing House, New Delhi.

Ruff, H. (1992) Action for change. In: *Children in Prostitution: Victims of Tourism in Asia*. End Prostitution in Asian Tourism (ECPAT), Bangkok.

Sittitrai, W. and Brown, T. (1994) *The Impact of HIV on Children in Thailand*. Thai Red Cross Society, Bangkok.

Sleightholme, C. and Sinha, I. (1997) *Guilty Without Trial: Women in the Sex Trade in Calcutta*. Rutgers University Press, New York.

Srisang, S. (1990) National report on tourism and child prostitution: Thailand. In: *Caught in Modern Slavery: Tourism and Child Prostitution in Asia*. ECTWT, Bangkok.

Turner, L. and Ash, J. (1975) *The Golden Hordes: International Tourism and the Pleasure Periphery*. Constable, London.

Wilson, G.D. and Cox, D.N. (1986) *The Child Lovers – a Study of Paedophiles in Society*. Peter Owen, London and Boston.

14

Community-based Ecotourism, Social Exclusion and the Changing Political Economy of KwaZulu-Natal, South Africa

Frank Brennan and Garth Allen

Introduction

In its Rural Development Strategy (RDS) (Government of National Unity, 1995), the South African government unequivocally supported community-based ecotourism as a developmental strategy. The authors of the RDS argued that tourism had hitherto been developed on a racial basis, by whites for a white elite, and that new policies must ensure environmental sustainability and fairness in the distribution of benefits. Proactive, democratic community involvement must be facilitated, and new partnerships nurtured to link conservation with economic development. Small ecotourism enterprises were to be integrated in the structure of the national tourism industry, and special attention given to the role of women and other marginalized groups in South African society. Scenery and wildlife were considered the most important attractions for most foreign visitors, and therefore the vital conservation of biodiversity within South Africa's national parks and other state protected areas has been retained under the supervision of statutory bodies. Ecotourism development is enthusiastically supported by various government departments and official agencies, including the South African Tourism Board (Satour), and by numerous environmen-

tal groups throughout the country. Articles and programmes on ecotourism feature frequently in the press and on television, and among the white minority, at least, there is a high general awareness of the subject.

In 1994, the Chief Director of Tourism Promotion for Satour proposed a 'new tourism' in South Africa, reasoning that by the end of the 1990s tourism would have become an entirely new phenomenon. Growing environmental awareness and concern, along with the evolution of more sophisticated consumer expectations, were driving changes in the global tourism market and a 'new wave' of tourism activity was emerging. South African tourism had to adapt to meet the demands of the more individual and discerning visitor, and competition in this sector was expected to be severe. As a consequence, agencies closest to the source areas of tourist demand needed to be vigorous in presenting quality and value in the South African tourist experience, and success would be contingent upon the demonstrably sustainable use of the environment and upon the construction of a dynamic private sector (Heath, 1994: 3).

Satour's definition of ecotourism reflects the environmental concerns of this higher-spending market segment (Satour, 1994: 6):

Ecotourism implies tourism practices that would benefit all concerned parties rather than that benefit some concerns and neglect others. The term 'ecotourism' has therefore come to include concepts such as planning before development; sustainability of resources; economic viability of a tourism product, no negative impact on the environment and local communities; responsibility for the environment from both developers, the tourism industry and tourists; environmentally friendly practices by all parties concerned; and economic benefits flowing to local communities.

This definition places more emphasis on the protection of the tourism product, the environment, and on the market viability of ecotourism than on human rights and democratic empowerment identified by the new political dispensation in South Africa. However, by providing political support for ecotourism and recognizing its commercial potential, policies for developing rural areas in the Republic are clearly reinforced.

The New South Africa was born at a time when old certainties in development theory had lost much of their authority. During the period of transition from 1990 to 1994, leaders of the apartheid regime and moderates in the opposition settled on political, economic and legislative compromises that ensured the survival of conservatism. Although it was claimed at the time that such measures were necessary to prevent the political transformation in South Africa from developing into a chaotic and vengeful cataclysm (Levin and Weiner, 1996: 94), others criticized the leaders of the African National Congress (ANC) for being over-conciliatory in their drive towards capitalism and for their reluctance to adopt costly welfare programmes (Munck, 1994: 204–206).

Sustainable development now seems to offer an ethos and an economic policy which transcend old divisions and heal the sores of separate development. What is being argued is the need for a paradigmatic shift in development theory and practice (Cook, 1995: 279). None of this is new, and Chambers (1985, 1986) has long advocated a more people-centred, bottom-up approach. However, these changes in development theory emerged when the forces of apartheid were at their most brutal and comprehensive in South Africa, and neighbouring countries were

already adopting more radical redistributionary policies which were contributing to major economic crises. It was left to the new South African government to overcome the social exclusion so rigorously institutionalized under the apartheid regime.

Advocates of sustainable development in South Africa highlight the social and environmental benefits anticipated from synergistic strategies that focus on the *quality* of growth, rather than on quantitative indicators of national economic expansion (Munslow, *et al.*, 1995). In the *Reconstruction and Development Programme* (RDP), the ANC (1994: 5) clearly stated its support for the philosophical, humanitarian and environmental principles of sustainable development:

> Development is not about the delivery of goods to a passive citizenry. It is about active involvement and growing empowerment. In taking this approach we are building on the many forums, peace structures and negotiations that our people are involved in throughout the land.

It is axiomatic that development of the human-resource base cannot be achieved without establishing appropriate and enabling democratic institutions to facilitate participation at all levels of South African society. This particular governmental model, with its emphasis on the humanitarian elements of democracy, empowerment and communal upliftment, provides the conceptual basis for the comparative analysis of the ecotourism initiatives discussed in this chapter.

Chambers (1986: 1) defines a paradigm as 'a coherent and mutually supporting pattern of concepts, values, methods and action, amenable to wide application'. Whether or not the model of ecotourism outlined above constitutes a paradigm for future practice in South Africa is of major interest in this chapter.

Tourism in South Africa

Prior to the publication of the White Paper on Tourism by the Ministry for Administration and Tourism (Anon., 1992), the sector was not a major source of foreign exchange and its development had been left almost entirely in private hands. Overseas demand had constantly fallen short of its potential, largely because of the low international status of the apartheid regime, but also because of national protectionism over flights to South Africa, which kept ticket prices high at a time when deregulation elsewhere was bringing fares down (TTI, 1999: 79).

However, political transformation was accompanied by marked changes in overseas tourism demand. From 1990 until 1994, international arrivals grew by 73%, as indicated in Table 14.1, and during the late 1990s there was a general increase in visitors to South Africa, as shown in Table 14.2. Even so, despite the deregulation of air travel to the country and the rand's devaluation, the increase in tourist arrivals did not match predictions that South Africa was to experience a boom in international tourism (Satour, 1994). That this did not occur is generally attributed to international news coverage of the widespread violence which occurred during and after the elections of 1994 (Koch, 1994: 12).

At the time of writing, tourism accounted for only 2.6% of the gross domestic product of South Africa, against a global average of 4.2% (TTI, 1999: 80), and politicians and other decision-makers took little interest in the industry. In fact, receipts from domestic tourism are more significant than those from overseas arrivals. During 1996, some 16 million South Africans took at least one leisure trip away from home and an estimated 82% of South Africa's white population travelled for pleasure within the country's borders. It is also claimed that 60% of non-whites also took

leisure trips, a figure that reflects the high tendency among black South Africans to visit friends and relatives away from their place of work (TTI, 1999: 82).

The research in progress

Research by the authors into ecotourism entailed repeated visits to the province of KwaZulu-Natal during the period 1994–1999. Numerous tourism locations were visited and many interviews held with various stakeholders, including officers in conservation authorities, academics, *ndunas* (headmen), consultants, and representatives of non-governmental organizations (NGOs) and the private sector. An email network was also established to maintain the flow of information. A central aim of this research has been to consider ecotourism within the context of the province's political economy, and the extended time involved has allowed the authors to identify a cluster of historical, political and social factors that contributed to ecotourism's evolution in KwaZulu-Natal.

The political economy of rural society in South Africa

South Africa remains one of the most unequal societies in the world, and access to employment, education, land, housing, health services and other essential resources is still divided more or less clearly along lines of race. The spatial distribution of the population

Table 14.1. South Africa's international arrivals and tourism receipts, 1990–1998.

Year	Arrivals (000)	Annual change (%)	Receipts (US$ million)	Annual change (%)
1990	1029	–	N/A	N/A
1991	1710	66.2	N/A	N/A
1992	2703	58.1	N/A	N/A
1993	3093	14.4	N/A	N/A
1994	3669	18.6	1424	N/A
1995	4488	22.3	1595	12.0
1996	4944	10.2	1995	25.1
1997	5530	11.9	2297	15.1
1998 (provisional)	5700	3.1	2366	3.0

Source: Travel and Tourism Intelligence (1999: 83).

Table 14.2. Trends in tourist arrivals in South Africa (000s), 1993–1998.

Market	1993	1994	1995	1996	1997	1998 (estimated)
Africa	2474	2964	3816	3771	4050	4100
Europe	411	445	698	771	950	1000
Other	208	260	374	402	530	600
Total	3093	3669	4888	4944	5530	5700

Source: Travel and Tourism Intelligence (1999: 84).

has also been determined by skin colour. During the apartheid era, rural areas were officially designated as either white-dominated areas of the four provinces of the Republic of South Africa, or artificially created 'homelands' or bantustans, where 85% of the black population lived on 13% of the land (Meer, 1997: 133). At the time of writing, 70% of the population of the former homelands were classified as living below the poverty line (Motteux *et al.*, 1999: 262). In homelands such as KwaZulu, land-hunger is keenly felt and autocratic dictatorships have denied rural populations any genuine political voice (Motteux *et al.*, 1999: 262).

A far-reaching programme of land restitution has been prepared to ameliorate the plight of the historically disadvantaged, but there are major obstacles to its successful implementation. Along with the political and economic strength of the landed classes, who can be expected to resist changes in the landholding pattern of South Africa, there are constitutional constraints surrounding property rights. Moreover, land reform is hampered by the same crisis in funding that affects other government actions. Rural communities are often inexperienced in representing their own interests, and there are frequently conflicting claims among communities or individuals for the same piece of land. The government itself is inexperienced in dealing with problems of such magnitude and complexity, and the actual amount of cultivable land available is insufficient to meet all claims and needs.

The dangers to many of the world's conservation areas arise primarily from the poverty of their surrounding populations (Ghimire, 1994; Barrett and Arcese, 1995). In the past, managers of protected areas have focused on security and have rigorously excluded local people – a militaristic approach that in some

countries has led to severe sanctions, fines, prison sentences and even the death penalty. Not surprisingly, local residents have reacted with hostility, seeing themselves excluded from economic opportunities in hunting, farming and tourism (Wells and Brandon, 1992, ix).

In South African agrarian society there is a deep mistrust of the conservation movement (Koch, 1994: 18), which has its roots in the evictions of African families throughout this century. When reserves were established to protect the hunting interests of the whites, Africans were commonly denied access to game and were even prohibited from killing animals damaging their crops. Such restrictions were particularly advantageous to the white population, generating a dispossessed labour force for the mines and for commercial farming (Koch, 1994: 19). Frequently illegal and sometimes destructive encroachments were the result, as were acrimonious relationships between conservation agencies and their neighbours. More recently, it has been recognized that conservation goals can be achieved only with support from and direct involvement of local populations, and that environmental issues are indeed political. In fact, concern for environmental protection has highlighted the necessity to meet communities' basic needs and provide real alternatives to illegal land invasions and poaching.

The general exclusion of the impoverished and vulnerable in Zulu society from decision-making processes is linked to the prevalence of criminal and communal violence in the province. During the period of transition, when state violence showed signs of abating and the politics of negotiation were emerging, seemingly pointless massacres and atrocities, many committed in KwaZulu-Natal, dominated media coverage (du Toit, 1993: 1). The frequent and often fatal clashes between rival groups, which led to more than 500,000 people being displaced in KwaZulu-Natal (Carver, 1996: 4), were allegedly supported and sometimes led by key personnel in the Inkatha Freedom Party (IFP) in collusion with right-wing groups comprising a third force (Gwala, 1992: 55). The leader of the IFP, Chief Buthelezi, who before and after the 1994 elections headed the repressive administration of the homeland of KwaZulu, certainly exploited his relationships with the police and security forces in his political and territorial struggles with the supporters of the United Democratic Front and the ANC (S. Taylor, 1995). Moreover, Buthelezi's links with powerful organizations and individuals allowed a dangerous culture of impunity to flourish within the province. Unsurprisingly, public perceptions of KwaZulu-Natal as a dangerous destination led to disappointing growth rates in tourism demand in the province. Much of the literature concerned with the welfare of African communities in northern KwaZulu-Natal focuses, reasonably enough, on the debilitating and chronic poverty that characterizes the region's tribal life, but this does not always convey the tangle of processes and institutional factors that sustain extremely vulnerable communities. The concept of social exclusion, often used in the study of European and North American politics, is preferred here because of its usefulness in analysing social processes that block progress of the deprived and marginalized (Evans, 1998: 42). These may include restricted access to land, unemployment, low incomes, little or no welfare support, gender inequalities, ethnic rivalries and social monopolies (Evans, 1998; Gaventa, 1998).

In northern KwaZulu-Natal, violence and the fear of it, the resurgence of chieftainship, political venality, the slow development of an appropriate institutional framework to support communal empowerment, and a shared memory of apartheid's injustices also prevent the black rural population from progressing. With few property rights, and a weakened identity with place (itself the product of forced migration under apartheid), black rural communities in KwaZulu-Natal generally display low self-esteem, and an intensified sense of social exclusion. Such social anomie is a major challenge to developmental initiatives among remote and disempowered tribal groups in the northern regions of the province. Moreover, the democratizing influence of developmental planning, based on notions of social empowerment, may not be well received by traditional powerholders such as Zulu chiefs. The sometimes evangelical support for community-based ecotourism and democratic participation ignores these concerns, and in doing so encourages naive speculation on an approach that has yet to prove it can deliver.

It is not the intention here to provide another tidy developmental narrative. Instead, this chapter focuses on conflicting needs and aspirations of the various stakeholders, and on the tangle of factors in the local and national political economy that inform the development of ecotourism in KwaZulu-Natal. For concerned white South Africans, the discourse of sustainability is compelling, but the immediacies of rural African life deny many Zulus the privilege of adopting such considered and long-term assessments of their own economic opportunities.

Tourism in KwaZulu-Natal

KwaZulu-Natal (Fig. 14.1) consists of the former homeland of KwaZulu and the former province of Natal, which together became a single administrative unit after the elections of 1994. The province is the third smallest in the country but it has the highest population (over 9 million, predominantly Zulus in rural areas) and the third highest incidence of poverty in South Africa – 74% of the rural population live below the poverty line (May, 1995: 4). Nevertheless, KwaZulu-Natal has major scenic attractions, all-year-round sunshine, long beaches, the warm Indian Ocean, and vast protected areas with substantial numbers of the 'big five' – elephants, rhinos, buffaloes, leopards and lions. The Drakensberg Mountains and the rolling countryside of the Midlands attract walkers and climbers and, most importantly for this chapter, the northern region of the province is rich in wetlands and other special ecosystems that are internationally recognized and valued. Because of these

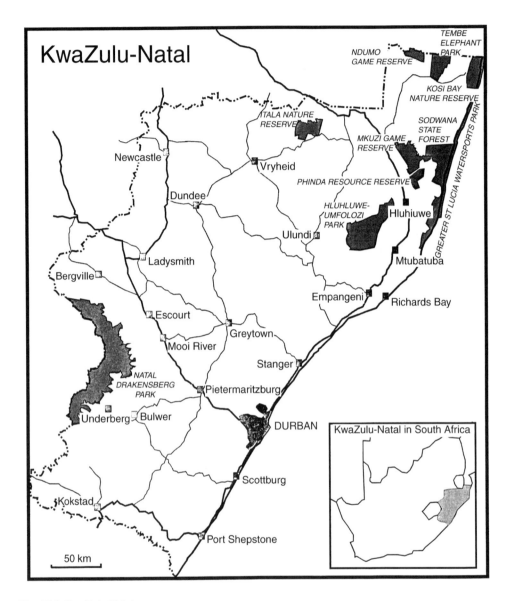

Fig. 14.1. KwaZulu-Natal.

attributes, the province is a traditional destination for domestic holidaymakers.

In 1996, 406,000 visitors (almost a third of all international arrivals to the Republic) spent at least part of their holiday in the province. Although this was a 4.1% increase from the previous year, it was considerably lower than the national rate (Table 14.1) and KwaZulu-Natal lost ground to the provinces of the Western Cape and Gauteng. According to the KwaZulu-Natal Tourism Authority (KZNTA), the Durban beachfront is by far the strongest attraction, followed by Zulu 'cultural villages', and the game parks (KZNTA, 1997: 29). Several factors constrain tourism development in the province, including a fragmented and underfunded marketing approach, seasonal demand, malaria (particularly in the north), and fears for personal safety (KZNTA, 1997: 30).

Domestic tourists are especially important.

Most come from the province of Gauteng (32%) or from KwaZulu-Natal itself (30%) (KZNTA, 1999: 8). Between October 1997 and September 1998, nearly 6 million adult domestic tourists spent an average of 4.9 nights in the province (KZNTA, 1999: 11). More than half were visiting friends and relatives, 45% spent time on the beach at Durban, 18% visited townships and 8% visited the nature parks (KZNTA, 1999: 21). While Durban attracted more than half the domestic visitors, northern KwaZulu-Natal (where all of the following case studies are located) appealed to only 2% of South African tourists (KZNTA, 1999: 18).

The expanding role of the conservation authority in ecotourism development

Biodiversity in KwaZulu-Natal is protected by the official conservation agency, the KwaZulu-Natal Nature Conservation Service (NCS), formed on 1 April 1998 by the amalgamation of the former Natal Parks Board (NPB) with the poorer and smaller KwaZulu Department of Nature Conservation. A parastatal organization, the NCS is responsible to the provincial cabinet via the KwaZulu-Natal Conservation Board, which reports, in turn, to the Minister of Traditional and Environmental Affairs (D. Münster, Pietermaritzburg, 31 March 1999, personal communication). In this chapter, where discussion focuses on developments prior to April 1998 the conservation authority will be referred to as the NPB, whereas for later dates it will be referred to as the NCS.

One of the best known and internationally respected conservation agencies in Africa, the NPB won numerous awards for its innovatory work in protecting the flora and fauna of KwaZulu-Natal. However, under the new political dispensation, and within the parameters of the RDP, a profound change is required of the Board. Neighbouring Zulu communities, previously considered major threats to park security, are to be consulted on the future role of the parks in rural development. Social responsibility has become an important criterion by which the progress of projects is to be assessed. In particular, the government argues that collaboration with local communities in

ecotourism initiatives is required if black South Africans are to make a living and to understand the value of conservation.

The Board addresses its responsibility towards its neighbours through its Community Conservation Programme, which during 1996/97 covered over 150 local projects of community upliftment, in support of which R20 million had been raised from outside donors (NPB, 1997: 6). Since early 1998, another source of funds has been the Community Levy, paid by visitors entering some of the protected areas under the authority of the Board. The additional charge is justified in terms of the benefits it provides local people; by May 1999 a substantial amount had been collected but none had been invested in community projects (D. Münster, Pietermaritzburg, 31 March 1999, personal communication). Examples of achievements under the Community Conservation Programme include the establishment of market gardens, the manufacture of concrete blocks, craft stalls, and improvements to water supplies and sanitation systems.

The NPB especially promoted its Community-based Tourism Programme, considering ecotourism a key contributor to sustainable development and a means of eliminating the rancour that characterized relationships between the Board and communities that suffered most from the historical expansion of protected areas in the province (Morrison, 1997: 11). Going beyond the former tokenistic practice of periodically allowing strictly controlled access to thatch and herbs, NPB advocates of the new approach claimed that the Board's neighbours could now negotiate the utilization of natural resources on an empowered and genuinely equitable basis. Around the perimeter fence of the large Hluhluwe-Umfolozi Park in northern KwaZulu-Natal, for example, the authority cooperated with local people in small tourism ventures. These included a bed-and-breakfast enterprise and the establishment of two curio stalls close to entrances to the Park (Morrison, 1997: 12). One senior NPB officer felt that, through such contacts and the employment provided in the everyday operation of the reserve, the Park's neighbours were beginning to appreciate the links between conservation and community upliftment (NPB, Hluhluwe-Umfolozi, 24 March, 1998, personal communication).

However, the community-based work of the NPB was not without its critics. Members of one NGO active in community development and conflict resolution in KwaZulu-Natal suggested that many of the Board's social amelioration projects had been supplementary rather than integral to the main business of conservation (Interface Africa, 24 March, 1998, personal communication). Furthermore, most improvements in services and infrastructure had allegedly been slight and short-lived, and community participation in the NPB's ecotourism development far short of that envisaged by the authors of the RDP and other commentators on sustainable development in South Africa (Munslow and Fitzgerald, 1994; Cook, 1995; Picard and Garrity, 1995). In the Hluhluwe-Umfolozi examples, benefits remained potential rather than actual, and the lack of business acumen among the participants constrained economic progress (Morrison, 1997: 11). Others observed that the NPB had always been ambivalent towards tourism and tourists and that, in the past, it had not made optimum use of the natural resources under its authority (Interface, Durban, 24 March, 1998, personal communication). According to such viewpoints, the main focus of NPB planning continued to be conservation, and ecotourism more of a public relations exercise than a sincere attempt to promote local economies (NPB, Pietermaritzburg, 23 March, 1998, personal communcation).

It was clear during interviews that senior officers of the NPB doubted the wisdom of allocating strategic responsibilities to professionally inexperienced and untrained members of local communities. Moreover, although there were numerous community improvement schemes, they could not meet the needs of everyone concerned. They had not been integrated into the wider economy of KwaZulu-Natal and, because funding was provided by outside sources, the connection with conservation was not explicit. Some community leaders asked for more transparency and accountability in the Board's operations, and questioned the NPB's prefer-

ence for projects based on ecotourism. However, the fundamental assumptions underpinning such plans remained untested, and Zulu communities, dangerously poor already, had most to lose if ecotourism failed to deliver (Carruthers and Zaloumis, 1995). Some communities close to the protected areas suspected that the Board's endeavours were a subtle means of extending its authority beyond the fences, and little more than a pretext for pursuing an obsession with conservation at all costs (Interface Africa, Durban, 24 March, 1998, personal communication).

Case Studies in Ecotourism Development

Ecotourism, the Natal Parks Board, and the struggle for resources in St Lucia

They will try to convince us of the value of tourism, but once they win they will chase us away.
(Settler in Dukuduku Forest, quoted in CROP, 1995a: 4)

The NPB has been confronted with particularly complex problems over plans for ecotourism development and environmental protection in one of its major protected areas, the Greater St Lucia Wetland Park (GSLWP). The Park, situated on northern KwaZulu-Natal's subtropical coastline some 250 km north of Durban, consists of a large and beautiful estuarine and lake system, and contains a remarkable variety of eco-niches and habitats, including grasslands, mangroves, dunes and coral reefs. Two areas of wetland are registered as regions of international status by the Ramsar Convention. Hippos, flamingo, crocodiles and pelicans abound in the wetland, along with rare species of antelope and migratory birds (R.Taylor, 1995: 4).

In 1989, the Park became the subject of a bitterly fought dispute over land use when Richards Bay Minerals (RBM), a subsidiary of Rio Tinto Zinc, shocked South African environmentalists by applying to dredge-mine a 12 km stretch of dunes in the south-eastern corner of the GSLWP. These vegetated beach dunes on the eastern shore of the lake contain rich sources of titanium and other heavy minerals. RBM claimed that the proposed mining would not cause any lasting damage to the ecology of the dunes, that disruption would be minimal, and pointed to its record of environmental reparation work (for which it had won an award). It further argued that mining would provide jobs for local people and foreign exchange for the country as a whole (Preston-Whyte, 1995: 151).

Despite the political and economic strength of the mining industry in South Africa, the NPB and a consortium of around 150 environmental groups mounted a sophisticated and high-profile campaign against RBM's application. It proposed, instead, an integrated ecotourism development strategy (Koch, 1994: 2), incorporating a range of community-based ecotourism projects which, it claimed, would provide more and longer lasting jobs than those generated under RBM's plan. The NPB argued that the revegetation envisaged by RBM after mining was completed was unlikely, that changes in the soil structure would alter the hydrology of the local ecosystem, and that the loss of income from potential ecotourism receipts would exceed the anticipated but short-term local benefits from dredge-mining the dunes (May, 1995: 20).

Extensive public concern and the National Party's waning confidence in its own authority resulted in chronic indecision, and a huge environmental impact assessment (EIA) was requested. In 1993, after the EIA was published, the review panel appointed to make recommendations unequivocally rejected the mining application, basing its decision not on the wealth of scientific evidence made available by the EIA, but on the grounds that mining would destroy St Lucia's 'unique and special sense of place' – a feature the GSLWP considered essential in its attraction for 'higher order' ecotourism (Baskin and Stavrou, 1995: 5). Reluctant to decide on such a sensitive and fiercely debated matter, the National Party shelved the problem until after the 1994 elections. In March 1996, the new South African government finally rejected the application to mine the dunes, preferring an inte-

grated development and land-use programme, based on ecotourism (Derwent, 1996).

The threat to the eastern dunes was not the only land-use problem faced by the conservation authority in the GSLWP. From 1988, several thousand displaced African subsistence farmers, including some claiming to have been removed from the GSLWP when it was initially declared a nature reserve, settled illegally in the nationally important and protected coastal state forest of Dukuduku, south of the St Lucia–Mtubatuba road. Dukuduku comprises 5960 ha of coastal lowland forest, grassland and swamp, and contains many Red Data plants and animals. Formally incorporated into the GSLWP in 1994, the forest plays a crucial role in the functioning and survival of the wetland system and is considered by the NPB and environmentalists an integral component of the Park (W. Menne, St Lucia, 2 October, 1998, personal communication). An educational and ecotourism resource, Dukuduku is viewed by many as a national treasure.

The illegal occupation caused widespread damage to the fragile environment of the forest, and large areas were cleared by slash-and-burn farming. Some settlers laid claim to eastern shore dunes that were targeted by RBM, and were unhappy about being excluded from the largely white middle-class debate over the dunes. They refused to move from the forest until land claims had been settled (CROP, 1995a: 3). Others occupied Dukuduku to obtain jobs if RBM's application were granted, and yet others claimed the forest itself as their ancestral land, strongly rejecting the NPB's authority over Dukuduku. Living conditions in the forest generally were characterized by environmental health problems (there was no sanitation system in a near-swamp environment), high levels of crime and violence, intimidation, poaching, and all the symptoms of extreme poverty and insecurity (Münster, 1996: 1). Furthermore, Dukuduku's nearness to the GSLWP led to poaching of game animals, and rival chiefs encouraged occupation of the forest to enlarge their own support base (Carnie, 1997).

At first, the NPB refused to negotiate with the settlers until they moved out of the forest, and the Natal Provincial Administration attempted to resolve the problem by some-times heavy-handed intimidation. Later, set-tlers were promised secure tenure and services at an alternative 3000 ha site on the north side of the St Lucia–Mtubatuba road (Carnie, 1993a). By May 1993, many of the 1040 half-hectare family sites had been allo-cated, and a school and community centre completed. The superior living conditions and promise of legal rights to land persuaded some 6500 people to relocate to the new site (now called Khula) and to seek opportunities for economic advancement in the new com-munity. To this end, the Dukuduku Development and Tourism Association (DDTA) was formed and a committee elected. As a consequence, the NPB argued that it was making positive and supportive moves towards settlers who had relocated, and was introducing members of the DDTA to the complexities of integrated conservation and developmental planning (Münster, 1996: 5). Because of this more conciliatory and open approach, officers of the NPB felt that advances had been made in building trust between the community in Khula and the conservation agency (NPB, 23 March 1998, personal communication). Subsequently, an ambitious plan for ecotourism development in the GSLWP, the Gateway Project, was opti-mistically considered by both parties.

Despite improved conditions in Dukuduku north, many settlers in Dukuduku south refused to move to the new settlement. Those who stayed accused the others of 'selling out' and relationships between the two communi-ties soured. To compound the problem, many new settlers occupied the space vacated by the residents of Khula, taking the estimated number of illegal occupants to around 20,000 (Münster, 1996: 2). Widespread violence among the settlers, between settlers and police, and between settlers and the NPB, became major problems for the provincial authorities (Carnie, 1993b), to the extent that NPB officials, mandated to protect the forest, were ordered not to enter it.

In 1994, the NPB produced a plan to reset-tle the occupants of Dukuduku south on an area of farmland near to the town of Monzi, with a forest strip (a buffer zone for the GSLWP) to be made available to the settlers

for their own ecotourism projects. Access to part of the forest would be retained by the set-tlers and a camp of 200 beds would be estab-lished alongside the St Lucia–Mtubatuba road, also for further ecotourism development. By December 1998, it appeared that agreement had been reached whereby settlers in Dukuduku south would be relocated on the proposed site and the Dukuduku Declaration was signed in Durban by the national Minister for Water Affairs and Forestry and the provin-cial Minister for the Environment. At the same time, government made it clear that it would not negotiate on the issue of land invasion, and that settlers would have to leave the forest (N. Barker, St Lucia, 2 December 1998, per-sonal communication). A process of register-ing the forest dwellers would begin, and the South African Police Service and the South African Defence Force were to be deployed to prevent further encroachments in the forest.

The mood of the settlers had been wholly misinterpreted and they rejected the Declaration in its entirety. At a meeting con-vened to assess community reactions, it was apparent that they strongly objected to being labelled 'squatters' by the press and in official documentation, and still regarded the forest as their rightful home. They especially resented the national government's intervention in the dispute, continued to reject the authority of the conservation agency (now the NCS) over the forest and felt that acceptance of the alter-native site at Monzi would be shameful (N. Barker, St Lucia, 14 December, 1998, per-sonal communication). Press reports later sug-gested that activist protesters were intimidating settlers considering the move and preventing them from registering for plots in the new site at Monzi. By April 1999, only 270 families had submitted their names to the register (Anon., 1999a).

Phinda Resource Reserve: ecotourism and the private sector

Not all ecotourism developments in KwaZulu-Natal depend on state leadership and public resources. Phinda Resource Reserve, which is adjacent to the GSLWP, is owned by Conservation Corporation Africa, a highly successful private company which offers luxurious accommodation and services at all five of its reserves in South Africa (Linscott, 1991). The enterprise originated in the late 1980s, when the company bought 7500 ha of largely uncultivatable land, and further purchases enlarged the property to around 17,000 ha. Two upmarket lodges were built, and the stock of game animals was enlarged. The company has managed to attract enormous investment from overseas, even during the period of transition when there was a continuing, and largely effective, investment boycott (Grossman and Koch, 1995: 25) – a success it attributes to its emphasis on sustainability and social responsibility in developmental planning.

Phinda is promoted as an outstanding example of the social and developmental potential of well-managed ecotourism (Conservation Corporation, Phinda, 17 April, 1998, personal communication). The reserve is neighbour to three especially impoverished and isolated communities of approximately 30,000 people, which have few services and poor access to water (Carlisle, 1997: 6). The Corporation acts as a conduit for donations made to the Rural Investment Fund – established by the company – which channels capital from sources outside South Africa into community development programmes (L. Carlisle, Phinda, 28 March, 1998, personal communication), thus linking conservation and tourism to communities in the vicinity of the Phinda Reserve. Access to the company's communication facilities is offered to local people establishing small businesses, along with the services of two full-time members of staff whose work is dedicated entirely to community welfare. Plans have been made to encourage and assist local people to become directly involved in ecotourism by constructing their own lodges in the more remote parts of the reserve.

In making these efforts, the company has cooperated with the NPB, local tribal chiefs, NGOs and civic leaders under the auspices of the Southern Maputaland Development Forum. However, local people have no voice in the administration of the conservation and tourism activities of the Phinda Resource Reserve. Their roles are passive, and major benefits are jobs and infrastructural improve-

ments (L. Carlisle, Phinda, 28 March, 1998, personal communication). Within the organization, it is held that impoverished local communities rarely have the resources and technical knowledge to develop their own projects and that development initiatives must be managed to attain optimum economic and environmental benefits (Carlisle, 1997: 7).

Kosi Bay: community participation and the role of NGOs

The complexity of the issues surrounding democratic participation can be usefully examined through another case study carried out during the current research. Kosi Bay, situated in far northern KwaZulu-Natal close to the border with Mozambique, was designated a nature reserve in 1988, when there were already plans of the KwaZulu administration and the private sector for a luxury resort that would necessitate the eviction of the tribal inhabitants, whose livelihood was based partly on fishing with traditional wooden kraals in the lakes and estuary, and partly on migrant labour (Munnik, 1995). Most eventually moved out under the harassment of the KwaZulu Department of Nature Conservation, but about 130 families (from the Kwadapha, eMalangeni and Nkovukeni tribes) refused to leave and were subsequently fenced in. Their plight attracted the attention of the Community Resources Optimization Programme (CROP), a small NGO active in community development and conflict resolution in northern KwaZulu-Natal. CROP, while working to improve relationships between the community and the various stakeholder authorities, began to consider the feasibility of setting up a small-scale and wholly community-based ecotourism project within the boundaries of the nature reserve (CROP, Kosi Bay, 16 November, 1995, personal communication).

Once an atmosphere more conducive to developmental planning was achieved, CROP initiated successful fund-raising, and a four-wheel-drive vehicle and a motorized inflatable dinghy for ferrying personnel and tourists across the lakes to a tented camp were purchased (CROP, Kosi Bay, 16 November, 1995, personal communication). From the outset, the initiative (now called KEN, from the initial letter of each tribe's name) was based on the fundamental principles of empowerment through proactive participation, and emphasis was placed on the importance of incorporating the most disadvantaged, including women (CROP, Durban, 10 March, 1999, personal communication). Institutional support for the enterprise was provided by democratically elected committees. The highly dedicated members of the NGO saw themselves only as facilitators in the process of training the community in hospitality and business skills. The first tourists arrived in December 1994 and bookings from various interested groups soon followed (Munnik, 1995). The Wildlife Society of South Africa was a major supporter of the project, which it saw as a low-impact, nonconsumptive alternative to the environmentally threatening activities of tourists elsewhere in the region (Carnie, 1996). However, crucial decisions had to be made about the future operation of KEN. It was accepted that further funding was needed, and that contractual arrangements with external investors would have to be made, but CROP was anxious to ensure that tribal groups retained their decision-making role, that they would not be displaced by more powerful agencies, and that sustainability and the meeting of basic needs should remain paramount (Grossman and Koch, 1995: 63).

The fact that KEN did not own the land upon which it was based made its legal position ambiguous, discouraged investors, and restricted its access to low-interest RDP loans (Munnik, 1995). The project's small scale meant that tourism receipts were few, and discontent increased among tribespeople impatient for an improved standard of living. CROP representatives were apprehensive at the possibility of a longer lease, feeling that communities might be tied to goals that would later prove irrelevant, or would restrict subsequent efforts to diversify (CROP, 1995b: 5). Sadly, even early in the operation, the KEN project encountered difficulties of another sort. Rivalries between committee members began to emerge and crystallize. Some individuals made demands on facilities that conflicted with the wider needs of the ecotourism project, and tourists were concerned at the

presence of strangers in and around the camp (CROP, 1995b). Relationships between members of KEN and the conservation authorities had soured over the former's demand for a new access road within the nature reserve, and large sections of the perimeter fence were substantially damaged (Shepherd-Smith, 1995). In fact, the project was faltering because of poor management and worsening relationships among its members, leading to a general inability to adopt effective decision-making procedures. Members of CROP, for their part, were profoundly disillusioned with KEN. They recognized that personal obligations of participants in such initiatives should be clarified, and advocated a more professional and commercially orientated approach for future initiatives (CROP, Durban, 10 March, 1999, personal communication).

Issues Arising from the Case Studies

In South Africa, there has been a swing from almost total exclusion of black communities from decision-making to an insistence that they have a central and proactive role in all issues affecting their own interests. However, Boshoff (1996) argued that – despite the moral imperative of the discourse of participation – conflicts of interests within communities, and the lack of educational and professional experience among members of civil organizations and NGOs, have led to inefficient prioritizing of needs and misallocation of resources. It is also proving difficult to keep communities to agreements already reached. Evidence from programmes of community development undertaken in other parts of the world indicates that consensus is particularly difficult to sustain in regions with a history of conflict, and that in these situations traditional power-holders typically feel threatened by notions of democratic decision-making (Gaventa, 1998: 55). According to Boshoff (1996: 71), grassroots organizations in South Africa tend to be dominated by powerful local interest groups, and impoverished communities might be more productively (and ultimately more equitably) served if local authorities took full control and operated in an accountable way within the guidelines of the RDP, while heeding the advice of civil organizations and NGOs.

While the language of justice and empowerment is seductive, experience in KwaZulu-Natal shows that participation is a slow and costly exercise. The case studies indicate a range of participation by community stakeholders in ecotourism development. At Dukuduku, the conservation authority took positive steps to bring communities into the decision-making arena, but to an extent determined by itself and other official agencies. In disputes over land use in Dukuduku and over the eastern dunes, planning and negotiations were steered by environmental lobby groups, by the conservation authority, by the provincial administration and by the national government. Although genuine participation by African communities has grown, it remains modest and is regarded as contingent upon behaviour that accords with the aspirations and strategies of official agencies.

By contrast, local people at Phinda are expected to enjoy many benefits of conservation and ecotourism, but largely as passive beneficiaries in terms of services and jobs provided. Jobs that do become available tend to go to the most educated rather than the most needy (Grossman and Koch, 1995: 34). Local residents do not participate in managerial operations or become shareholders in the company (L. Carlisle, Phinda, 23 March, 1998, personal communication). For the moment, and at best, the Corporation appears to be filling a supportive role that in other locations would be occupied by local government.

In the KEN project at Kosi Bay, the level of participation enjoyed by the stakeholder communities is high and most closely reflects the principles of the RDP. However, internal rivalries have impeded economic progress, and tourists have been dissatisfied with the quality of hospitality and security. In such circumstances, the highly principled stand of CROP on participation, democracy and sustainability, and strict adherence to the tenets of the RDP, could ultimately be a disadvantage. Access to decision-making has led to some abuse and CROP is possibly asking too much of ecotourism. Taking the spirit of socially

responsible development to its logical conclusion may well restrict choice and limit opportunities to expand. If the principles themselves prove to be unsustainable, the best could be the enemy of the good.

At the heart of the problem of participation is the assumption that community members share interests and are likely to pursue shared aspirations as a group. The evidence in this chapter strongly demonstrates the need for developmental models based on notions of self-interest and diversity within communities, rather than on notions of community spirit and stability. Olson (1977), too, doubts that individuals will always work for the common economic good if they are unlikely to benefit themselves. Such cooperation occurs only in special circumstances, where there are strong negative or positive sanctions, or where the group itself is small. Assuming that there are always opportunity costs to participation, Olson's basic argument is that where the benefits of collective action cannot be ring-fenced by those who have actually invested in the cause, then those who will benefit in any case have no rational incentives to bear the cost of active involvement (Olson, 1977).

Public authorities and private companies continue to set the agenda for negotiations, and the existence of RDP forums and civil organizations is no guarantee of a fair representation of the most disadvantaged in KwaZulu-Natal. In particular, the rights of women in Zulu society have changed little since the 1994 elections. Their empowerment – a central tenet of the RDP – would entail a radical transformation of the patrimonial structure of rural society in South Africa, including new restraints on the powers of tribal chiefs. Notwithstanding the Communal Properties Association Act (1996), which insists upon their fair representation, women have been effectively muted in committees established to expedite the land reform programme, an exclusion considered by Ritchken (1995: 205) to be inevitable.

There is no single explanation of the recurrent violence in KwaZulu-Natal. Contributory factors include mass poverty, political rivalries, conflict between traditional and modern political systems, warlordism, historical intra-tribal feuds over contested land and other resources

(J. Argyle, Durban, 20 November, 1995, personal communication), covert encouragement and support of the Inkatha Freedom Party by right-wing groups, and the active complicity of a corrupt and partial police force (Olivier, 1992; S. Taylor, 1995; Carver, 1996). Much antagonism arises when young Zulus, tired of old systems of patronage, reject the traditional authority of chiefs and look for personal benefit to the putatively more democratic ANC. While attempts to explain the violence are legion, the consequences are also manifold, including widespread insecurity, lost productivity, failure of investor confidence, and an intensified sense of exclusion and alienation (Olivier, 1992: 2). The resulting social volatility leads to a general failure to develop democratic institutions necessary for community-based ecotourism, and the crime and violence reputedly found in the GSLWP area has contributed to the sluggish performance of the tourism sector (V. Barker, St Lucia, 2 December, 1998, personal communication).

Land rights continue to dominate the discussion of ecotourism development in the GSLWP. The harsh treatment sometimes inflicted on settlers in Dukuduku reflects a lack of understanding of traditional ties to land and attachment to ancestral graves (Carnie, 1991). Ecotourism development will not attract sufficient public resources or private investment until rival land claims are settled. Meanwhile, many settlers in Dukuduku are convinced that the conservation authority's plans for ecotourism and community amelioration are little more than pretexts for retaining control over contested land areas. Environmentalists fear that if ecotourism fails to deliver on its promises, the mining application might be revived (Barker, 1997). In Kosi Bay, the KEN initiative has suffered from the outset because it has no legal claim to the natural resources upon which it was established. By contrast, at Phinda the lack of ambiguity over land ownership has contributed to the Conservation Corporation's successful appeals to investors and to the RDP for low-interest credit. If land rights are in doubt, community-based projects are at a disadvantage.

The government has set itself the enormous task of addressing the problems of rural poverty and disadvantage in a complex pro-

gramme of land reform but it is not clear whether the state has sufficient resources to meet its pledge to provide poor claimant families with grants to support their applications (Meer, 1997: 136). A land reform pilot programme in KwaZulu-Natal has already demonstrated the inadequacy of government grants, and has led to recipients overloading themselves with debt in order to make up the shortfall (Meer, 1997: 136). Rival land claims in KwaZulu-Natal have resulted in extreme violence between claimant groups, and the slow pace of land reform exacerbates old territorial enmities (Gibson, 1997). Under the Zulu customary communal system, land-use rights are dispensed by chiefs to male heads of households (Billy, 1996) but in recent years some chiefs have sold land to outsiders, or have used it to secure political support (Vanderhaeghen, 1998). Many chiefs have been able to straddle civil society and state political structures, gaining access to developmental resources in a way that does not conform to the RDP's model of democratic development (Ritchken, 1995: 219). The state's efforts to develop the appropriate institutional and legislative framework to tackle the politically dangerous issues of land rights, and create an equitable model for new land-holding patterns, have been muddled and inconclusive (Levin and Weiner, 1996: 110).

The role of the state in the development of ecotourism has attracted considerable attention (de Kadt, 1994; Jenkins, 1994; Leslie, 1994; Smith, 1994; Preston-Whyte, 1995). Jenkins (1994) disapproved of state intervention in tourism planning and management, suggesting that the commercial ineptitude of state departments and their ignorance of the special dynamics of tourism make the incorporation of local interests all the more difficult and unlikely. By contrast, Leslie (1994) emphasized the need for government control. For Lea (1993), the tourism industry could not be relied upon to regulate itself, or to arrive at an appropriate code of practice. Drawing lessons for tourism from development studies as a whole, de Kadt (1994) suggested that only the state has sufficient authority to offer necessary incentives, impose negative sanctions, and ensure that companies fulfil their environmental and social responsibilities. Similarly,

Wells and Brandon (1992), in their wide-ranging study of integrated conservation and development projects, insisted that initiatives operating without full government support have the least chance of being integrated into the wider economy, and therefore the least chance of success. However, much support for ecotourism in South Africa ignores the bald fact that none of the conservation areas under state protection are profitable. All depend on state subsidies (Grossman and Koch, 1995: 71). By contrast, only those game reserves in private hands are financially successful and thus (financially) sustainable.

What is certain is that the successful implementation of the RDP requires a new organizational culture in both the public and private sector (Cook, 1995: 294). The institutional framework reflects and is informed by wider political and cultural values. In KwaZulu-Natal, the cluster of organizations directly or indirectly involved in tourism development is a structural legacy of the apartheid era. The racial and class partiality of the institutional framework of tourism in the province has contributed enormously to its lack of legitimacy in the eyes of the black population. Although the need for a 'people-friendly' system is self-evident, changes so far have been minor and curricular rather than fundamental and ethical (Schutte, 1995: 298). The prioritization of apartheid over developmental goals has contributed to the proliferation and survival of a considerable number of ineffective agencies in the province (J. Barnes, University of Natal, 11 November, 1995, personal communication). Professionally trained and qualified officials are competent in procedures but ill-equipped to deal with the legacy of separate development.

Compounding these problems, and like public services elsewhere in Africa, state organizations in South Africa, including the South African Tourism Board (Cokayne, 1997) and the provincial administration of KwaZulu-Natal, have been prone to corrupt practices (Lodge, 1998: 169). While much of this was inherited from the apartheid era, particularly in departments responsible for the homelands, reports of financial graft at every level of government feature regularly in the national and provincial press (e.g. Anon., 1999b). Such publicity gives little incentive to African communities to trust official policies and procedures.

Despite the undoubted natural beauty of the GSLWP, and its potential as a major tourist attraction, progress in community-based ecotourism initiatives has been minimal and there are fears that the stagnant nature of the local economy will leave the GSLWP vulnerable to any revived application that might be made to mine the eastern dunes (Barker, 1997). In addition, there are strong doubts over the ability of the NCS to operate effectively in the commercial world of tourism. Niki Barker (St Lucia, December 1998, personal communication) pointed to the long chains of command in the organization, which often leave central decision-makers out of touch with local circumstances. In the field, officers are committed conservationists rather than profit-motivated managers, and are often unavailable when tourists require assistance. The authority has been criticized for its failure to tackle the occupation of Dukuduku with sufficient haste and clarity of purpose (W. Menne, St Lucia, 2 October, 1998, personal communication). There are also strong doubts that positive and productive relationships can be established between the NCS and the settlers in Dukuduku, who associate the authority with so many past and present injustices. Many members of the white community, hoping that tourism will provide a way forward for the economy of the region, look to the private sector rather than to the conservation authority to pilot a more dynamic, market-based sector (N. Barker, St Lucia, 2 December 1998, personal communication).

The scale of tourism operations is important. In a seminal paper on the lessons that tourism can learn from development as a whole, de Kadt (1994) contended that a general scaling down of operations at least reduces the risk of environmental damage and maintains the ecological appeal of the location in question. However, the size of an ecotourism initiative is clearly reflected in the extent and nature of the direct benefits received by local people. In fact, community involvement in tourism accounts for only 1% (11,200) of all tourism beds in KwaZulu-Natal (Van Duffelen and Delport, 1996) – a tiny proportion of touristic activity in the province – and income from attempts to marry conservation with development remains slight. In addition, the adoption of ecotourism as a developmental strategy does not guarantee biodiversity. As the Dukuduku case shows, when confronted by neighbours with increasing (and increasingly impoverished and politicized) populations, protected areas are likely to come under severe pressure.

Conclusion

The South African government has to promote new developmental policies while dealing with crises in the fields of health, crime, access to land, employment and other major problems inherited from the apartheid system. However, existing and reluctant institutions, irredentism, political volatility and the continuing power of important vested interests are all obstacles to administrative transformations. It is fair to criticize the RDP for being high in ideas but low in mechanisms. New legislation alone cannot overcome the chronic and deeply institutionalized exclusion of vulnerable and poor members of rural society in northern KwaZulu-Natal, and the smell of poverty dominates memories of the authors' research visits to rural African settlements.

Much has been asked of ecotourism. The definition provided in the introduction to this chapter – travel to protected areas which does not damage the environment and brings benefits to local people – amounts to a Utopian vision of perfect development. In practice, the costs and benefits of economic and social change are rarely shared equally, and improvements in the welfare of people living close to perimeter fences of protected areas are yet to be achieved. Similarly, opportunities for Zulu communities to participate in decision-making procedures in ecotourism initiatives have been patchy and limited, and there are exclusions within exclusions; there is little evidence, for example, that the lives of Zulu women have improved as a result of the state's intentions of establishing an enabling institutional framework.

The evidence provided here questions the feasibility of attempting to link conservation with development in the context of dire needs, a history of extreme violence, political venality and an expanding population. Many infrastructural improvements in African villages have been funded by outside charitable sources, not from ecotourism itself, and there is thus little perception of a direct link between the protection of the environment and improved services and infrastructure. For community-led ecotourism to become sustainable, it must be able to support itself, and despite the arguments of many environmentalists in KwaZulu-Natal, conservation involves power over the distribution of resources. It is a political issue. Agencies that mediate access to natural resources continue to hold the power to set agendas. In KwaZulu-Natal, parks and other protected areas are painful reminders of apartheid's injustices, and of the continuing privilege of whites who enjoy looking at wildlife while Africans suffer from land starvation. Community-based ecotourism has achieved little in securing the protected areas for the future, and divided rural communities have few grounds for optimism over plans of the conservation sector. Community participation has been elusive and minimal, and may even prove to be a wasteful and misguided goal in itself.

At the same time, while it is essential to keep chiefs and headmen involved, they do not represent everyone in their deeply divided communities. Indeed, the ability of chiefs to so influence new committees and civil organizations that their activities reflect traditional patterns of patronage has impeded the emergence of a new balance of power in northern KwaZulu-Natal. As things stand, policies of empowered participation may entail a degree of social engineering that is unrealistic.

Despite enthusiasm for ecotourism in the province, this research over 5 years has found disparities between rhetoric and actual opportunities, and between the desirable and the affordable. Social exclusion involves disadvantage and problems of different orders. The relationships between such factors as poverty, illiteracy, poor health, inadequate public resources, low employment prospects, land hunger, fear of violence, a resurgence of traditional politics and a shared memory of apartheid are not always clear. These variables are associated, but direct causal links are hard to determine. Links between poverty and health, for example, are complex and problematic. Nevertheless, such factors constitute a huge barrier to the implementation of empowered and sustainable community development. Despite high-sounding principles, it is doubtful if community-based ecotourism in KwaZulu-Natal amounts to anything like a paradigm as defined by Chambers (1986). Ecotourism is essentially an ideal, promoted by well-fed whites. As the case studies indicate, there have been many genuine efforts to link conservation with human rights in KwaZulu-Natal, but the benefits have been few, and existential conditions in the province expose weaknesses in a theory that so far has not travelled well. Unless discussion of ecotourism in the province situates its development in the prevailing conditions of the political economy, ecotourism can be little more than a pipe dream.

References

African National Congress (ANC) (1994) *The Reconstruction and Development Programme.* Umanyano Publications, Johannesburg.

Anon. (1992) *White Paper on Tourism.* Ministry for Administration and Tourism, Pretoria, 18 pp.

Anon. (1999a) Dukuduku walkout. *The Mercury* 13 April.

Anon. (1999b) Boesak jailed. *Daily News* 24 March.

Barker, N. (1997) The Battle for St Lucia is far from over. *Mail and Guardian* 14–20 November.

Barrett, C.B. and Arcese, P. (1995) Are integrated development projects (ICDPs) sustainable? On the conservation of large mammals in sub-Saharan Africa. *World Development* 23(7), 1073–1084.

Baskin, J. and Stavrou, A. (1995) *Synthesis Report on the Issues Related to Various Land Use Options in the Greater St Lucia Area.* Written for Land and Agricultural Policy Centre, 21 pp.

Billy, A. (1996) The plight of rural women. *Natal Witness* 26 September.

Boshoff, G.B. (1996) Beating the participation trap: ensuring sustainable community development in marginalized communities: a South African perspective. *Sustainable Development* 4, 71–76.

Carlisle, L. (1997) An integrated approach to ecotourism. In: Creemers, G. (ed.) *Research on Community Involvement in Tourism.* Natal Parks Board, Pietermaritzburg, pp. 6–8.

Carnie, T. (1991) Only months to save Dukuduku. *Natal Mercury* 1 May.

Carnie, T. (1993a) New home for the forest people. *Natal Mercury* 14 July.

Carnie, T. (1993b) Solution hopes still running high. *Natal Mercury* 23 May.

Carnie, T. (1996) Kosi patch of paradise. *Natal Mercury* 29 June.

Carnie, T. (1997) The Dukuduku tragedy gains momentum. *Natal Mercury* 17 January.

Carruthers, J. and Zaloumis, A. (eds) (1995) *People and Parks, Parks and People Conference, Summary Proceedings,* Durban, 8 pp.

Carver, R. (1996) KwaZulu-Natal: Continued Violence and Displacements, [online] [1st edn,Writenet Country Papers (accessed 26 September 1999), 27 pp.

Chambers, R. (1985) *Rural Development: Putting the Last First,* 4th edn. Longman, Harlow, UK, 246 pp.

Chambers, R. (1986) New professionalism, new paradigms and development. *IDS Discussion Paper* 227, 39 pp.

Cokayne, R. (1997) SATOUR undertakes to expose corruption. *Natal Mercury* 1 July.

Cook, J. (1995) Empowering people for sustainable development. In: Fitzgerald, P., McLennan, A. and Munslow, B. (eds) *Managing Sustainable Development in South Africa.* Oxford University Press, Cape Town, S. Africa, pp. 279–296.

CROP (1995a) *Greater St Lucia Wetland.* Community Resource Optimization Programme, Durban, 19 pp.

CROP (1995b) *The CROP Experience in Maputaland.* Community Resource Optimization Programme, Durban, 12 pp.

de Kadt, E. (1994) Making the alternative sustainable. Lessons for tourism from development. In: Smith, V.L. and Eadington, W.R. (eds) *Tourism Alternatives.* John Wiley & Sons, Chichester, UK, pp. 47–75.

Derwent, S. (1996) Land claims on St Lucia come to fore. *Daily News* 8 March.

du Toit (1993) *Understanding South African Political Violence: a New Problematic?* United Nations Research Institute for Social Development (UNRISD), 31 pp.

Evans, M. (1998) Behind the rhetoric: the institutional basis of social exclusion and poverty. *IDS Bulletin* 29(1), 42–49.

Gaventa, J. (1998) Poverty, participation and social exclusion in north and south. *IDS Bulletin* 29(1), 50–57.

Ghimire, K. (1994) Parks and people: livelihood issues in national park management in Thailand and Madagascar. In: Ghai, D. (ed.) *Development and Environment: Sustaining People and Nature.* Blackwell, Oxford, UK, pp. 195–230.

Gibson, H. (1997) Death for Christmas. *Sunday Tribune* 7 December.

Government of National Unity (1995) *Rural Development Strategy.* Pretoria, 42 pp.

Grossman, D. and Koch, E. (1995) *Nature Tourism in South Africa: Links with the Reconstruction and Development Programme.* Written for South African Tourism Board, Pretoria, 82 pp.

Gwala, Z. (1992) Natal conflict under the microscope: a case-study approach, In: Bekker, S. (ed.) *Capturing the Event: Conflict Trends in the Natal Region 1986–1992.* Indicator SA, University of Natal, Durban, South Africa, 34–45.

Heath, E. (1994) Into the 'New' tourism. *SATOUR Quarterly Review* 3(1), 2–3.

Jenkins, C. (1994) Tourism in developing countries: the privatisation issue. In: Seaton, A.V., Jenkins, C.L., Wood, R.C., Dieke, P.U.C., Bennett, M.M., MacLellan, L.R. and Smith, R. (eds) *Tourism: the State of the Art.* John Wiley & Sons, Chichester, UK, pp. 3–9.

Koch, E. (1994) *Reality or Rhetoric? Ecotourism and Rural Reconstruction in South Africa.* United Nations Research Institute For Social Development (UNRISD), 87 pp.

KZNTA (1997) *International Tourism Market Trends with Specific Reference to KwaZulu-Natal.* KwaZulu-Natal Tourism Authority, 31 pp.

KZNTA (1999) *KwaZulu-Natal's Domestic Tourism Market: October 1997–September 1998.* KwaZulu-Natal Tourism Authority, 41 pp.

Lea, J.P. (1993) Tourism development ethics in the Third World. *Annals of Tourism Research* 20(4), 701–715.

Leslie, D. (1994) Sustainable tourism or developing sustainable approaches to lifestyle? *World Leisure and Recreation* 36(3), 30–36.

Levin, R. and Weiner, D. (1996) The politics of land reform in South Africa after apartheid: perspectives, problems, prospects. *Journal of Peasant Studies* 23(2, 3), 93–119.

Linscott, G. (1991) Game reserves eco-tourism venture. *Natal Mercury* 16 August.

Lodge, T. (1998) Political corruption in South Africa. *African Affairs* 97, 157–187.

May, J. (1995) *An Assessment of Alternative Economic Opportunities for the Greater St Lucia Region.* Written for Data Research Africa, 27 pp.

Meer, S. (1997) Gender and land rights: the struggle over resources in post-apartheid South Africa. *IDS Bulletin* 28(3), 133–144.

Morrison, P. (1997) Community involvement in tourism near the Hluhluwe-Umfolozi Park. In: Creemers, G. (ed.) *Research on Community Involvement in Tourism.* Natal Parks Board, Pietermarizburg, South Africa, pp. 11–14.

Motteux, N., Binns, T., Nel, E. and Rowntree, K. (1999) Empowerment for development: taking participatory appraisal further in South Africa. *Development in Practice* 9(3), 261–273.

Munck, R. (1994) South Africa: the great economic debate. *Third World Quarterly* 15(2), 205–217.

Munnik, V. (1995) Turning the tide. *Sunday Tribune* 12 November.

Munslow, B. and Fitzgerald, P. (1994) South Africa, the sustainable development challenge. *Third World Quarterly* 15(2), 227–241.

Munslow, B., FitzGerald, P. and McLennan, A. (1995) Sustainable development: turning vision into reality. In: FitzGerald, P., McLennan, A. and Munslow, B. (eds) *Managing Sustainable Development in South Africa.* Oxford University Press, Cape Town, 630 pp.

Münster, D. (1996) *Planning with People: a Transactive Planning Case Study.* Natal Parks Board, Pietermaritzburg, South Africa, 10 pp.

NPB (1997) *Annual Report 1996/97.* Natal Parks Board, Pietermaritzburg, South Africa, 30 pp.

Olivier, J. (1992) Political conflict in South Africa: a resource mobilisation approach. In: Bekker, S. (ed.) *Capturing the Event: Conflict Trends in the Natal Region 1986–1992.* Indicator SA, University of Natal, pp. 1–14.

Olson, M. (1977) *Logic of Collective Action: Public Goods and the Theory of Goods,* 1st edn. Harvard University Press, Cambridge, Massachusetts, 186 pp.

Picard, L. and Garrity, M. (1995) Development management in Africa: In: Fitzgerald, P., McLennan, A. and Munslow, B. (eds) *Managing Sustainable Development in South Africa.* Oxford University Press, Cape Town, pp. 63–85.

Preston-Whyte, R. (1995) The politics of ecology: dredge mining in South Africa. *Environmental Conservation* 22(2), 151–156.

Ritchken, E. (1995) The RDP, governance and rural development. In: Fitzgerald, P., McLennan, A. and Munslow, B. (eds) *Managing Sustainable Development in South Africa*. Oxford University Press, Cape Town, pp. 195–221.

Satour (1994) *Satour Fact Sheet No. 1*, August. South African Tourism Board, Pretoria, 12 pp.

Schutte, L.B. (1995) New training approaches: exploring the paradigm shift. In: Fitzgerald, P., McLennan, A. and Munslow, B. (eds) *Managing Sustainable Development in South Africa*. Oxford University Press, Cape Town, pp. 297–314.

Shepherd-Smith, J. (1995) Reserve fence torn down. *Sunday Tribune* 19 November.

Smith, V.L. (1994) Privatization in the Third World: small-scale tourism enterprises: In: Theobald, W. (ed.) *Global Tourism: the Next Decade*. Heinemann, Oxford, UK, pp. 163–173.

Taylor, R. (1995) *Greater St Lucia Wetland Park*, 1st edn, Struik, Cape Town, 48 pp.

Taylor, S. (1995) *Shaka's Children*. Harper Collins, London, 416 pp.

TTI (1999) South Africa. *TTI Country Reports*, No. 2. Travel and Tourism Intelligence, London, pp. 79–100.

Vanderhaeghen, Y. (1998) A war the government doesn't need. *Natal Witness* 28 February.

Van Duffelen, L. and Delport, D. (1996) The Lubombo Initiative. *Sunday Tribune* 20 October.

Wells, M. and Brandon, K. (1992) *People and Parks*. World Bank, Washington, DC, 99 pp.

15

Wallace's Line: Implications for Conservation and Ecotourism in Indonesia

Sheryl Ross and Geoffrey Wall

Introduction

The Indonesian archipelago is one of the most complex geological zones on earth (Audley-Charles, 1981). Continental movements over millions of years have resulted in a distribution of volcanic mountains, islands and coastlines, and unique flora and fauna which are attractive to travellers and sources of invaluable information to biogeographers.

In the second half of the 19th century, Alfred Russel Wallace was one of the first to recognize the great significance of unusual floral and faunal distributions in the Indonesian archipelago (Wallace, 1855, 1859, 1863, 1869, 1876). Since then, many scientists have devised theories to account for the tremendous biological diversity found on these islands. Current technology is beginning to unravel the mysteries of the islands' origins through an enhanced ability to trace the movements of tectonic plates. Unfortunately, although an understanding of underlying processes is being expanded and although Indonesia is increasingly acknowledged as one of the earth's most significant sources of endemic biodiversity, many of these evolutionary products are perishing.

This chapter provides a brief overview of developments in biogeographic theory as they apply to Indonesia in general and Sulawesi in particular. The implications of the area's complex origins for conservation and ecotourism will then be discussed.

Wallace and his Line

From 1854 to 1862, Wallace travelled throughout the Indonesian archipelago and collected sufficient material to fuel a lifelong career pursuing biogeographic origins. He covered over 22,000 km from Sumatra to New Guinea, collecting specimens of flora and fauna for his own and for museum collections (George, 1979), discovering significant zoogeographical phenomena, and compiling data to support his theory that 'every species has come into existence coincident both in space and time with a pre-existing closely allied species' (Wallace, 1855). He believed that the patterns he observed in the geographical distribution of plants and animals reflected aspects of both geological and biological history, and his research on the distribution of islands and the origins of their fauna presents some of the most significant theory and practice of biogeography to date (Fichman, 1977).

By studying the floral, faunal, volcanic and bathymetric features of the Indonesian islands,

Wallace (1863) developed a well-supported theory that certain islands had either Australian or Asian affinities and were once connected with the precursors of these continents. A general distinction was made between Australia's substantial marsupial and parrot fauna and the Asian region's abundance and variety of large mammals, noting at the same time the latter's lack of marsupials and parrots. From this generalization, faunal characteristics were used to link observed distributions to either Asian or Australian origins. For instance, Wallace noted that marsupials (such as genera *Cuscus* and *Belideus*) were found throughout the Moluccas and Celebes (now Sulawesi) but were not detected further west. Conversely, species of squirrels (*Sciuridae*) in the western islands were not found further east than Celebes (Wallace, 1859). During a visit to Bali, Wallace noted many birds of common 'Indian' genera which were present throughout Java and Borneo. Upon crossing the 15 miles from Bali to Lombok, he discovered that these genera of birds were completely absent. Therefore, the Strait of Lombok was demarcated as a divide separating two of the 'great zoological regions of the globe' (Wallace, 1859) (Fig. 15.1).

The Sulawesi Puzzle

Wallace was most intrigued by the great biological diversity of the Indonesian archipelago, now known to house some of the richest tropical rainforest in the world. He recognized that the zoological differences between the islands far outweighed their geomorphological differences. However, when he went to Sulawesi, he soon discovered that its mix of floral and faunal inhabitants did not fit comfortably into the puzzle that he was ingeniously constructing. He noted (Wallace, 1876: 426) that it was

> in many respects, the most remarkable and interesting [island] in the whole region, or perhaps the globe since no other island seems to present so many curious problems for solution.

Sulawesi possessed not only a mixture of Australian and Asian species (in 1876, Wallace cited two Australian genera, *Cuscus* and *Mus*, and four Asian genera, *Cynopithecus*, *Anoa*, *Babirusa*, *Sciurus*), but also was home to many endemic species found nowhere else in the archipelago (e.g. *Sus babirusa*, now known as the endangered *Babyrousa babyrussa*). Wallace

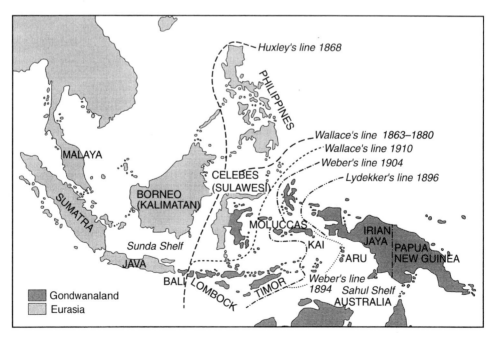

Fig. 15.1. Lines proposed to separate Asian and Australian biogeographic realms (after Audley-Charles, 1981; George, 1981).

then described the distribution of species on Sulawesi as 'anomalous', a description often used even today (cf. Cranbrook, 1987).

Undecided on the mysterious origins of Sulawesi and its flora and fauna, Wallace eventually changed the placement of his line. Originally placing Sulawesi to the east of the division, in 1910 (at 87 years of age) he decided that it was more likely to have had Asian origins (but must have separated and been isolated much earlier than other islands) and, therefore, should be to the west of the line. A relatively recent study of Sulawesian mammalian origins by Groves (1976, cited in Simpson, 1977) came to similar conclusions: Asiatic origins with long-term isolation.

Many other theories on island origins and biogeographic limits were promoted, using different parameters for analysis (for example, Huxley's Line, based on bird distributions in 1868, and Weber's Line, based on molluscs and mammals in 1904). These efforts have been reviewed by Simpson (1977). The resulting confusion and multiplicity of lines led to the creation of the term 'Wallacea' by Dickerson in 1928 (George, 1981). This was used to refer to islands between Wallace's original line and Weber's line, immediately to the east of the Moluccas (Fig. 15.1). The term 'Wallacea' is still used today (e.g. George, 1987; Whitten et al., 1987; Michaux, 1994) and conjures up an appealing image of islands with ancient origins and peculiar, unique and endemic flora and fauna. The detailed study of plate tectonics is generating further information resulting in refinement of understanding of the complex geological origins of the Indonesian archipelago.

Plate Tectonics

Wallace (1876: 438) suggested:

when we have before us such a singular phenomenon as are presented by the fauna of the island of Celebes (Sulawesi) we can hardly help endeavouring to picture to our imaginations by what passed changes of land and sea (in themselves not improbable) the actual condition of things may have been brought about.

Wallace's imagination and his research resulted in the development of a theory that

has stood the test of time, but the study of plate tectonics has resulted in a set of evolving, complementary ideas. Contemporary technology has combined with palaeontology, biogeography and modern earth science research methods to develop current theories on the origins of the Indonesian islands. It is now widely accepted that, for the last 15–25 million years, various islands of Indonesia have emerged and subsided due to complex vertical crustal movements. Similarly, parcels of land have been separated and reunited due to plate movements and rising and falling sea levels (Audley-Charles, 1981).

Audley-Charles (1981) summarized the monumental land movements that led to the creation of the archipelago and George (1987) complemented this summary with biogeographical analyses. The following statement is a general consensus based primarily on these sources. Preceded by India's separation approximately 140 million years ago (140 Ma), Australia and New Guinea broke away from Gondwanaland (the continental mass that originally contained Antarctica, South America, Africa, India and Australia) about 53 Ma and began to drift northwards. Approximately 15 Ma, Gondwanaland's Australia and New Guinea land mass collided with its counterpart Laurasia (North America, Europe and parts of Asia) at or near present-day Sulawesi. Australia and New Guinea's upper extension, the Sula platform (an Australian plate) is believed to have collided with a submerged eastern arm of Sulawesi (which was part of a South-East Asian plate known as the Sunda Shelf). This collision constituted a significant connection between the two supercontinents and it eventually created a chain of islands that linked Australia to South-East Asia (Fig. 15.1).

Some theorists suggest that this initial collision might have enabled Australian fauna to migrate as far west as Sulawesi, but geologists have strong evidence to suggest that the western part of Sulawesi was submerged at the time of the collision. Palaeozoological studies of invertebrates and vertebrates led to similar findings; that is, an eastern arm of Sulawesi was sutured to a west and central province (Hutchison, 1989; Duffels and De Boer, 1990; Vane-Wright, 1990; all cited in Michaux, 1994), with the result that the flora and fauna of modern Indonesia could have originated from three possible sources: Laurasia, Gondwanaland via Australian north-west migrations, or Gondwanaland via Indian south-east migrations (Whitmore, 1982). This variety of possible zoological origins has implications for Indonesia's genera and species.

The greatest challenge to scientists continues to be the origins of Sulawesi. Large-scale crustal movements have resulted in Sulawesi's composition of highly differentiated geological provinces. Groups of rocks once widely separated are believed to have been brought together in late Cenozoic time (10–20 Mya) (Audley-Charles, 1981). A belief that eastern and central Sulawesi were once joined to Kalimantan is linked with evidence that the Makassar Strait opened, closed and re-opened during the Cenozoic. Haile (1978) attributes Sulawesi's odd shape to the collision of its eastern province, which caused a counter-clockwise movement of its western side and a shifting around of the north end.

Biogeographical and palaeozoogeographical evidence suggests some similar origin theories, though these theories vary according to which parameter is traced (for example, palms by Dransfield and mammals by Groves, 1976, cited in Whitmore, 1987; vertebrates by Cranbrook, 1981). However, the historic isolation of Sulawesi is evident, due to its extraordinarily high degree of mammalian endemism, and is not disputed (Michaux, 1994). Musser's (1987) study of Sulawesian 'ancient character' mammals revealed that 98% of its non-volant mammals are endemics. Regardless of which scientific methods are used, the questions focus on Sulawesi. In tracing vertebrate faunal connections, Cranbrook (1981: 67) suggested that 'if any zoogeographical line is to be drawn, it should circumscribe Celebes ... to emphasize its peculiar isolation from the east as much as from the west'.

Conservation and Tourism

Biodiversity: assets, threats and responses

Present-day Indonesia, which consists of approximately 17,000 islands spanning a dis-

tance of 5200 km (2,000,000 km^2), is rich in natural resources. Its biological diversity is perhaps its greatest wealth. Because of the archipelago's ancient origins, many of its individual islands harbour unique flora and fauna found nowhere else in the world. For example, it contains 10% of the earth's tropical moist forest biome and the second richest expanse of tropical rainforest in the world next to Brazil (Whitmore, 1990). It holds 17% of all the earth's known species, including 11% of all known flowering plants, 12% of all mammals, 15% of all amphibians and reptiles, and one of the earth's ten tallest trees (of some 70 m, in the ancient forests of Sulawesi). It also possesses the greatest number of mammalian species, the second largest number of endemic mammalian species and the second greatest occurrence of primate endemism and diversity. In addition, Indonesia's marine habitat includes some of the earth's most important continuous coral reefs (World Conservation Monitoring Center, 1992). The country's importance in its contribution to biodiversity is globally significant and Indonesia has been labelled as one of the top four 'megadiversity' countries of the world (Mittermeier, 1988).

Unfortunately, Indonesia also contains the most species threatened with extinction (Caldecott, 1994). Its economies rely heavily on forestry, agriculture and livestock grazing, fisheries, water resources for irrigation and power and, of course, natural resources considered attractive by tourists (McNeely et al., 1994). At the same time, its tropical forests have been disappearing faster than those of almost any other country in the world. High-density human populations have encroached on natural habitats, with the result that forests have been destroyed (often illegally) for fuel, cultivation and livestock grazing.

The destruction of Indonesia's natural ecosystems has serious consequences. For example, the removal of 10,000 ha of lowland tropical forest in Sumatra could lead to the loss of 30,000 squirrels, 5000 monkeys, 15,000 hornbills, 900 siamang, 600 gibbons, 20 tigers and ten elephants (Whitten et al., 1984), not to mention local extinctions of invertebrates and plants. Reduced ecological diversity is not the only result. Uncontrolled tropical habitat destruction has implications for shrinking gene pools, disruption of evolutionary processes, the permanent loss of otherwise sustainable resources, depletion of water supplies, global climatic changes and reduced opportunities to maintain wildlands for recreation, education, science and tourism. The urgent need for sustainable development, particularly with respect to deforestation, is evident.

Indonesia's global significance has put the country under tremendous pressure to conserve its natural land and incorporate sustainable practices. Many international organizations are cooperating with Indonesia for badly needed conservation efforts. These include: the World Bank; United Nations (UN) Educational, Scientific and Cultural Organization World Heritage Fund and Biosphere Program; the UN's Food and Agriculture Organization; United States Agency for International Development; Birdlife International; the International Union for Conservation of Nature (IUCN); the World Wide Fund for Nature (WWF); The Nature Conservancy; and Conservation International. A new act, the Conservation of Living Natural Resources and their Ecosystems, was passed in 1990, and in 1992 the country committed itself to the UNCED Convention on Biological Diversity. As a result, Indonesia was encouraged to develop a Biodiversity Action Plan, which was published in 1993 by BAPPENAS. The government now has an ambitious 17.2% of its land under protected area status, recognized by IUCN's Commission on National Parks and Protected Areas (CNPPA). Unfortunately, although policy framework seems impressive, little implementation of the effective management required to protect these designated areas has so far been apparent (BAPPENAS, 1994).

Ecotourism opportunities

Faced with declining oil revenues, Indonesia has turned with considerable success to international tourism as a growing source of foreign exchange. In fact, in 1995, over 4 million international visitors were received and tourism was exceeded only by forest products

and textiles as a non-oil generator of export income. However, tourism, like the level of economic development as a whole, is extremely unevenly distributed. Wallace's line now roughly separates the more densely populated and developed western islands (approximately two-thirds of the human population live on Bali and Java) from the less inhabited, economically less developed eastern islands. Transmigration programmes are being used to relocate people from densely populated areas to such sparsely inhabited islands as Sulawesi and Irian Jaya, and it is hoped that more tourists can be attracted to the eastern islands to stimulate development and thus reduce the economic gulf between east and west. Ecotourism based on the rich ecological resources of eastern Indonesia is viewed as a means of diversifying Indonesia's tourism product and stimulating economic development in otherwise disadvantaged areas. This may be a timely opportunity for, according to the World Tourism Organization, destination trends reveal a significant shift in favour of developing countries where flora and fauna are most diverse, and the potential for ecotourism is highest (Filion et al., 1994).

Indonesia's biogeographical history has created many unique ecotourism opportunities, 'so that in a few hours we may experience an amount of zoological difference which only weeks or even months of travel will give us in any other part of the world' (Wallace, 1876: 174). Its endemic mammalian diversity allows the promotion of many singular species simultaneously as ecotourism attractions and as targets for conservation. For example, on the west side of Wallace's Line, ecotourists can travel to the lowland forests of Kalimantan to view the orang-utan (*Pongo pygmaeus*), the 'great man-like ape of Borneo' that was fascinating naturalists even in the early 1800s (Wallace, 1869). Travelling east across the Makassar Strait to Sulawesi, to the core of 'Wallacea', one can witness *Tarsius spectrum*, one of the world's smallest primates, labelled by primatologists as a 'living fossil' (Musser, 1987). A glimpse of the Komodo dragon (*Varanus komodoensis*), the world's largest lizard, with a close resemblance to a dinosaur, can be gained further east at Komodo National Park.

Primates, in particular, are sometimes considered to be 'charismatic megavertebrates', or flagship species for conservation (Mittermeier, 1988), because they are often highly visible in the wild. They appeal to tourists, are important to humans for study of human origins and for biomedical research, and play an important ecological role in their own ecosystems. Indonesia boasts a high diversity of primates (over 28 species, according to Marsh, 1987) but many are threatened by habitat loss, especially from hunting, commercial logging and shifting agriculture (Marsh, 1987; Mittermeier, 1988). Opportunities for promoting primates for forest conservation and simultaneously reaping economic benefits from ecotourism should be further investigated. Taking the threatened Brazilian rainforest habitat as an example, the golden lion tamarin (*Leontopithecus rosalia*) has been used as a key flagship species for promoting conservation. WWF's successful golden lion tamarin campaign created a high profile for this appealing primate and it was used to promote support to protect Brazil's dwindling tropical forests. However, ecotourism and management strategies are often only implemented as a last resort with species already threatened with extinction, as with Sumatra's critically endangered rhinoceros, *Dicerorhinus sumatrensis*. Unfortunately, several of Indonesia's primate species, including gibbons, macaques, leaf monkeys and tarsiers, are believed to be declining and in need of closer monitoring (Mackinnon and Mackinnon, 1986; Whitten *et al.*, 1987).

Ecotourism in North Sulawesi: potentials and obstacles

The Government of North Sulawesi has identified four major priority sectors in its development plans: agriculture, fisheries, mining and tourism. As described in a recent brochure, the potential for nature-based tourism is considerable:

> To witness the results of two ancient supercontinents colliding ... to visit prehistoric rainforests and volcanic landscapes harboring unique plants and animals that have been evolving there for 15 million years ... to experience some of

the world's finest coral reefs ... to observe one of the Earth's smallest primates – a living fossil of ancient times ... to walk in Wallace's footsteps along the north eastern shores and envision the sights he might have seen ...

The island of Celebes, which fascinated Wallace over a century ago and still constitutes one of the greatest challenges to zoogeographers, thus has much to offer tourists. During the summer of 1859, Wallace was charmed by the villages and 'savage' life of North Sulawesi, and tourists today might be equally charmed by its unique qualities. Ecotourism in North Sulawesi, especially, has been recognized by the government to have important potential for economic development. The first international flights from Silk Air, a subsidiary of Singapore Airlines, landed in North Sulawesi early in 1995. By December 1996, a Novotel and an Ibis Hotel were under construction in the main city of Manado, and have since been completed, and the 320-room, five-star Paradise Resort opened in February 1996 (Simpson and Wall, 1999a,b). The number of international visitors to the province of North Sulawesi in 1994 was a little over 13,000 but double-digit annual rates of growth have been achieved in recent years, albeit from a small base, and such trends are expected to continue. Annual international tourist arrivals in the province were projected to approach 50,000 by the year 2000 (BAPPENAS, 1993) but political uncertainties make continued growth an uncertain proposition.

With its coral reef coasts, its tropical forest habitats and its indigenous communities, Sulawesi also warrants concern for protection and conservation of its assets and character. Economic growth is often accompanied by a reduction in biodiversity (McNeely *et al.*, 1994), as has occurred in such densely populated tourist areas as Bali. In an ideal ecotourism development, natural resources are not compromised and local communities benefit from the industry (Boo, 1992). Well-managed ecotourism would offer visitors a quality experience and provide locals with economic benefits that act as an incentive to maintain the natural habitat that surrounds them.

Sulawesi's northern province possesses three special opportunities for ecotourists, all within reasonable distance from its main city and airport in Manado (Fig. 15.2). These areas – Bunaken National Park, Tangkoko-Duasudara Nature Reserve and Bogani National Park – are all recognized under the CNPPA's protected area systems. However, all three attractions present challenging situations requiring careful management if resources are not to be appropriated from relatively poor indigenous peoples to satisfy the demands of relatively rich visitors.

1. Bunaken National Park consists of five islands off North Sulawesi's north-west shores and a small area of mainland. It encompasses pristine coral reefs, which have become increasingly popular among divers. While a growing number of dive establishments have been built on the mainland, some uncontrolled illegal cottage development has unfortunately occurred within the park, which is home to a large resident population. A management plan for the park has been recently formulated but does not include an ecotourism strategy.

2. Tangkoko-Duasudara Nature Reserve consists of low montane/volcanic tropical forest habitat; it offers glimpses of *Tarsius spectrum* and hikes up Dua Sudara volcano. Only 60 km from Manado, it is in the early stages of tourist development. Reached by a challenging road, which can become impassable during the wet season, its facilities are rudimentary and, although a draft management plan was prepared in 1995, it has not yet been officially operationalized (Kinnaird and O'Brien, 1995). In 1993, the Reserve received an estimated 1000 international tourists in 9 months (BAPPENAS, 1993). A 20-room guest house has recently been constructed on Tangkoko's eastern beach. Further information on the ecology of Tangkoko can be found in O'Brien and Kinnaird (1996) and the current status of ecotourism is detailed by Ross and Wall (1997, 1999b).

3. Bogani National Park (formally known as Dumoga-Bone) encompasses 300,000 ha of rich tropical rainforest and is recognized as an important reserve for primate conservation and a rich habitat for butterflies. The park was established in 1982 and began with many difficulties. Deforestation of a water catchment had

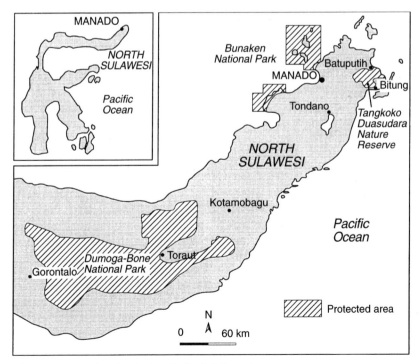

Fig. 15.2. Selected ecotourism destinations in North Sulawesi.

to be prevented and 400 farmers were evicted. Fortunately, Bogani has been part of a pilot project run by Indonesia's Forest Protection Agency and the World Bank to link park management with local economies through Integrated Conservation and Development Projects (ICDP) (BAPPENAS, 1994).

A framework to assess the status of ecotourism in the three locations described above was developed and is discussed in detail elsewhere (Ross and Wall, 1999a). The nature of ecotourism is, in fact, a contested subject and there is a diversity of opinion on its attributes which range all the way from considering it as a mere marketing device to more rigorous definitions of ecotourism, incorporating the protection of biodiversity, the stimulus of local economic development and the provision of high quality tourism experiences, as well as such factors as the promotion of environmental education and stewardship (Wight 1993a,b, 1996). As the definitions become more complex and demanding, they become increasingly difficult to achieve in reality. The work reported here is based upon a demanding definition incorporating the provision of high quality tourism experiences in natural areas, preservation of biodiversity and benefits to local people. While it is not an easy task to achieve such objectives simultaneously, they do constitute goals to which one might aspire and they can be used as criteria against which the present status of places can be assessed. This is the approach adopted here and the results of this evaluation are summarized and tabulated in Fig. 15.3. Dotted lines in the diagrams indicate that links between components are rudimentary, and missing connections show where relationships have yet to be established, suggesting priorities for action (Ross and Wall, 1999b). It can be seen that much still needs to be done if the full potential of ecotourism in North Sulawesi is to be achieved.

At present, impacts on North Sulawesi's above-mentioned protected areas are almost wholly from local communities in and adjacent to the reserves. In all three parks, aspects of agricultural and fishing practices conflict with resource conservation. As in other regions characterized by human population growth and poverty, it is difficult to reduce or elimi-

nate local usage. Even though Indonesia has designated these parks as protected areas, the impacts of local illegal activities currently outweigh the impacts of relatively light tourism use. Illegal practices in North Sulawesi include the use of fishing nets and traps close to shore, coral extraction, hunting of species within the parks, removal of park flora and fauna, cutting mangroves and other trees for fuelwood, and invasive agricultural practices. 'Dilarang, dilarang, dilarang!', (meaning 'not allowed, not allowed, not allowed!') are the local impressions of poorly coordinated park protection efforts (BAPPENAS, 1992). It appears as though North Sulawesians are not yet familiar with the potential benefits of ecotourism and, as a result, have yet to embrace it as a means to diversify their restricted economies, to support protected area designation, and to accept it as a sustainable use of their precious resources.

This is perhaps not surprising when, according to Whitten *et al.* (1987), most formally educated Indonesians have never heard of Alfred Russel Wallace and are not familiar with his works.

Conclusions

Over a century ago, Wallace spent eight productive years collecting countless specimens in the Indonesian archipelago and theorizing over their implications. As Wallace studied the products of 15 million years of geological dynamics and biological evolution, he could not have foreseen the recent fate of many of the archipelago's natural resources. Perhaps nowhere is the struggle to protect and manage the Earth's biological diversity more pressing and challenging than in Indonesia. Indonesia appears fully committed to conservation at the policy level but, for a variety of reasons, including scarce financial resources and a lack of skilled personnel and political will, much less has been achieved on the ground. Development and conservation objectives for parks and protected areas will not be achieved unless they also address the needs of local populations, the traditional users of the resources.

Can appreciation of Indonesia's ancient origins and unique zoological attributes help to

Fig. 15.3. An overview of the overall strengths, weaknesses and potentials for ecotourism at Bunaken, Bogani and Tangkoko, North Sulawesi, Indonesia.

	Strengths	Weaknesses	Potentials
Bunaken	• Locals benefit from protected resources (non/use zones) • Management focuses on local resource users • Locals begin to benefit from tourism • Community outreach in progress • Good NGO involvement	• No provision of environmental education/interpretation • No revenue-capturing from tourism • No environmental advocacy from locals • No on-site active or passive management	• Development of tour-operator cooperative to provide interpretation • Development of collective body to capture tourist revenues (e.g. entrance fees) • Enlisting locals and NGO to monitor resource use • An on-site management team (being done)
Bogani	• Locals benefit from protected resources (water for irrigation; minerals?) • Management addresses locals through community outreach, and maintains biodiversity records • Tourism managed through guiding • Research attention	• No revenue-capturing from tourism • Inadequate interpretation • No local participation in conservation or tourism (no environmental advocacy) • More consistent field management of illegal activities required	• Capture revenues from entrance and guiding fees • Local participation through existing community outreach • Trained guides and development of visitor centre • Additional field management of illegal activities • Hiring of trained, skilled park ecologist
Tangkoko	• Tourism managed through reserve guiding • Minimal positive inter-cultural interaction beginning • NGO involvement and acquired resources/skills	• No revenue-capturing from tourism • Inadequate interpretation • No local participation in conservation or tourism • Inadequate active and passive management (poor patrolling, no ongoing biodiversity monitoring)	• Capture revenues from entrance and guiding fees • Enlist NGO for community education and capacity-building (particularly tourism development) • Trained guides and clarification of PHPA field duties (regular monitoring and patrolling) • Compile interpretation resources from existing ones

preserve its evolutionary treasures? Indonesia's appeal to naturalists and biogeographers is now being matched by its appeal to a growing number of tourists. However, while Indonesia has rich resources with the potential to attract ecotourists (as has been described briefly for North Sulawesi), little has been done to date to transform these resources into products that can be sold to tourists or to ensure their long-term viability. Clearly, the future of biodiversity and economic growth through tourism can both benefit from international support. At the same time, their success will largely depend on the receptivity and cooperation of local Indonesians who gain a precarious livelihood from these same resources.

Indonesia has recently drafted a Biodiversity Action Plan that not only addresses protection needs but also investigates other strategies to promote biodiversity, including the creation of inventories of pharmaceutical and biomedical values. Indonesia's proposed *Terrestrial Biodiversity Management Program* suggests that conservation of its terrestrial, coastal and marine habitats will require US$190 million annually for *in situ* management (such as upgrading management skills and implementing priority projects of the ICDP similar to the one at Bogani) and another US$100 million annually for such *ex situ* measures as national zoological inventories, documentation and storage of research materials, captive breeding and propagation of resources (Caldecott, 1994). Is it possible that environmentally appropriate, economically viable and culturally sensitive ecotourism could help to defray such costs while improving the lifestyles of local people and helping maintain the rich flora and fauna that constitute a global legacy in Indonesia's care?

References

Audley-Charles, M.G. (1981) Geological history of the region of Wallace's Line. In: Whitmore, T.C. (ed.) *Wallace's Line and Plate Tectonics.* Clarendon Press, Oxford, UK, pp. 24–36.

BAPPENAS and Ministry of Forestry (1992) *Livelihood Strategies and Marine Resource Use Among Residents of Bunaken National Park, North Sulawesi.* Report No.14, USAID, Jakarta.

BAPPENAS and Ministry of Forestry (1993) *Ecotourism Development in Bunaken National Park and North Sulawesi.* USAID, Jakarta.

BAPPENAS and Ministry of Forestry (1994) *Policy Towards Protected Areas in Indonesia.* Report No. 38, USAID, Jakarta.

Boo, E. (1992) *The Ecotourism Boom. Wildlands and Human Needs.* WHN Technical Paper. WWF and USAID, Washington, DC.

Caldecott, J.O. (1994) *Terrestrial Biodiversity Management in Indonesia: Study and Recommendations.* EMDI, Halifax, Nova Scotia.

Cranbrook, Earl of (1981) The vertebrate fauna. In: Whitmore, T.C. (ed.) *Wallace's Line and Plate Tectonics.* Clarendon Press, Oxford, UK, pp. 59–69.

Fichman, M. (1977) Wallace: zoogeography and the problem of land bridges. *Journal of History of Biology* 10, 45–63.

Filion, F.L., Foley, J.P. and Jacquemot, A.J. (1994) The economics of global ecotourism. In: Munasinghe, M. and McNeely, J. (eds) *Protected Area Economics and Policy.* IUCN and World Bank, Washington, DC, pp. 235–252.

George, W. (1979) Alfred Wallace, the gentle trader: collecting in Amazonia and the Malay Archipelago 1848–1862. *Journal of the Society for the Bibliography of Natural History* 9, 503–514.

George, W. (1981) Wallace and his line. In: Whitmore, T.C. (ed.) *Wallace's Line and Plate Tectonics.* Clarendon Press, Oxford, UK, pp. 3–8.

George, W. (1987) Complex origins. In: Whitmore, T.C. (ed.) *Wallace's Line and Plate Tectonics.* Clarendon Press, Oxford, UK, pp. 119–131.

Haile, N.S. (1978) Reconnaissance paleomagnetic results from Sulawesi, Indonesia and their bearing on paleogeographic reconstructions. *Tectonophysics* 46, 743–771.

Huxley, T.H. (1868) On the classification and distribution of the Alectoromorphae and Heteromorphae. *Proceedings of the Zoological Society of London* 294–319.

Kinnaird, M. and O'Brien, T. (1995) *Tangkoko Duasudara Nature Reserve, North Sulawesi Draft Master Plan.* WCS and PHPA, Indonesia.

Mackinnon, J. and Mackinnon, K. (1986) *Review of the Protected Areas System in the Indo-Malayan Realm.* International Union for Conservation of Nature (IUCN)/United Nations Environment Programme (UNEP), Morges, Switzerland.

Marsh, C. (1987) A framework for primate conservation priorities in Asian moist tropical forests. In: Marsh, C. and Mittermeier, R. (eds) *Primate Conservation in the Tropical Rain Forest.* Alan R. Liss, New York, pp. 343–354.

Marsh, C.W. and Mittermeier, R.A. (1987) *Primate Conservation in the Tropical Rain Forest.* Alan R. Liss, New York.

McNeely, J.A., Harrison, J. and Dingwall, P.P. (eds) (1994) *Protecting Nature. Regional Reviews of Protected Areas.* Morges, Switzerland.

Michaux, B. (1994) Land movements and animal distributions in East Wallacea (Eastern Indonesia, Papua New Guinea and Melanesia). *Palaeogeography, Palaeoclimatology, Palaeoecology* 112, 323–343.

Mittermeier, R.A. (1988) Primate diversity and the tropical forest: case studies from Brazil and Madagascar and the importance of the megadiversity countries. In: Wilson, E.O. (ed.) *Biodiversity.* National Academy Press, Washington, DC, pp. 145–154.

Musser, G. (1987) The mammals of Sulawesi. In: Whitmore, T.C. (ed.) *Biogeographical Evolution of the Malay Archipelago.* Clarendon Press, Oxford, UK, pp. 83–93.

O'Brien, T. and Kinnaird, M. (1996) Changing populations of birds and mammals in North Sulawesi. *Oryx* 30, 150–156.

Ross, S. and Wall, G. (1997) Opportunities and constraints to ecotourism development in North Sulawesi, Indonesia: the case of Batuputih. *Journal of Travel and Tourism* (Indian Institute of Tourism and Travel Management) 2, 106–114.

Ross, S. and Wall, G. (1999a) Ecotourism: towards congruence between theory and practice. *Tourism Management* 20, 123–132.

Ross, S. and Wall, G. (1999b) Evaluating ecotourism: the case of North Sulawesi, Indonesia. *Tourism Management* 20, 673–682.

Simpson, G.G. (1977) Too many lines; the limits of the oriental and Australian zoogeographic regions. *Proceedings of the American Philosophical Society* 121(2), 107–120.

Simpson, P. and Wall, G. (1999a) Environmental impact assessments for tourism: a discussion and an Indonesian example. In: Pearce, D., Butler, R. and Din, K. (eds) *Contemporary Issues in Tourism Development.* Routledge, London, pp. 232–256.

Simpson, P. and Wall, G. (1999b) Consequences of resort development. *Tourism Management* 20, 283–296.

Wallace, A.R. (1855) On the law which has regulated the introduction of new species. *Annals and Magazine of Natural History* 16, 184–196.

Wallace, A.R. (1859) On the zoological geography of the Malay Archipelago. *Journal of the Linnean Society of London (Zoology)* 4, 172–184.

Wallace, A.R. (1863) On the physical geography of the Malay Archipelago. *Journal of the Royal Geographic Society* 33, 217–234.

Wallace, A.R. (1869) *The Malay Archipelago, the Land of the Orang-utan and the Bird of Paradise.* Harper and Brothers Publishers, New York.

Wallace, A.R. (1876) *The Geographical Distribution of Animals,* Vol. 1. Macmillan and Co., London.

Whitmore, T.C. (1982) Wallace's line: a result of plate tectonics. *Annals of Missouri Botanical Garden* 69, 668–675.

Whitmore, T.C. (1987) *Biogeographical Evolution of the Malay Archipelago.* Clarendon Press, Oxford, UK.

Whitmore, T.C. (1990) *Tropical Rainforests.* Clarendon Press, Oxford, UK.

Whitten, A.J., Damanik, S.J., Anwar, J. and Hisyam, N. (1984) *The Ecology of Sumatra.* Gadjah Mada University Press, Yogyakarta, Indonesia.

Whitten, A.J., Mustafa, M. and Henderson, G.S. (1987) *The Ecology of Sulawesi.* Gadjah Mada University Press, Yogyakarta, Indonesia.

Wight, P. (1993a) Ecotourism: ethics or eco-sell? *Journal of Travel Research* 31(3, Winter), 3–9.

Wight, P. (1993b) Sustainable ecotourism: balancing economic, environmental and social goals within an ethical framework. *The Journal of Tourism Studies* 4(2), 54–66.

Wight, P. (1996) North American ecotourism markets: motivations, preferences and destinations. *Journal of Travel Research* 35, 3–10.

World Conservation Monitoring Center (1992) *Protected Areas of the World; a Review of National Systems.* Vol. I (IVth World Congress on National Parks and Protected Areas). International Union for Conservation of Nature (IUCN), Morges, Switzerland.

16

Ecotourism Development in the Rural Highlands of Fiji

Kelly S. Bricker

Introduction

This chapter is about the introduction of eco-tourism into the rural hinterland of Fiji and the issues faced by the two villages and the tour operator involved. The area concerned (Fig. 16.1) is in the Highlands of Viti Levu, the largest island in Fiji, at a point where two river systems, the Wainikoroiluva ('Luva) and upper reaches of the Navua Gorge, flow through dense tropical rainforest. Focus is especially on the development of whitewater recreation and how it is perceived in the villages of Nakavika and Nabukelevu, which have hitherto relied primarily on subsistence farming and, in the case of Nabukelevu, the sale of timber. Fiji is a South Pacific island nation of approximately 330 islands covering a region of 1.3 million km^2 lying nearly 1900 miles north of Sydney and just over 3,000 miles southwest of Honolulu. The total land area of Fiji is approximately 18,333 km^2 which is slightly larger than Hawaii. Nearly one-third of the total number of islands are inhabited and Suva, the capital, is on the largest island of Viti Levu, which accounts for 59% of the land area and 70% of Fiji's population of 780,000.

Ecotourism in Fiji

The tourism industry in Fiji has grown substantially over the past 50 years. During 1999, more than 409,955 overseas visitors spent F\$600 million in foreign exchange (Fiji Visitors Bureau, 1999) and tourism is directly or indirectly responsible for over 40,000 jobs in the formal sector, where it is the most important business, followed by sugar.

The recognition of 'ecotourism' is relatively new in Fiji. However, in February 1999, the government adopted an ecotourism policy, *Ecotourism and Village-based Tourism: a Policy and Strategy for Fiji* (Ministry of Tourism and Transport, 1999), and the definition of ecotourism provided there is also used in this study:

A form of nature-based tourism which involves responsible travel to relatively undeveloped areas to foster an appreciation of nature and local cultures, while conserving the physical and social environment, respecting the aspirations and traditions of those who are visited, and improving the welfare of the local people.

The policy incorporates five main principles. It is recognized that ecotourism should complement but not compete with more conventional tourism, that tourism should take second place to conservation and, at times,

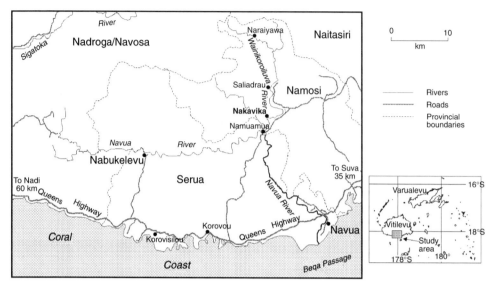

Fig. 16.1. Highlands of Viti Levu, the largest island in Fiji.

may be banned or restricted in areas considered especially vulnerable, and that successful implementation of the policy can be achieved only through social cooperation. In addition, information on village-based tourism should be centrally available and regularly monitored, and successful implementation of the policy will be based on the existence of strong and effective institutions.

Amongst other matters covered in the policy document is the need to develop an awareness of the physical and cultural environment. Since most tourism development occurs in the islands and major urban areas, the policy also focuses on rural areas and the need to enhance the quality of life in more remote villages, advocating fiscal and other incentives to assist village-based projects and the development of necessary skills. The policy also commits the government to clarify rights of ownership and thus avoid conflicts over tourism development.

At the time of writing, the Department of Tourism has encouraged the rejuvenation of the Fiji Ecotourism Association, which is beginning to address some policy issues, including the understanding of hosts and guests of ecotourism, and is forming a centralized association as a springboard for information and educational programmes. Government has also appointed a strategic planning committee for ecotourism to assist in developing a formal evaluation programme, perhaps involving a national accreditation or best-practice scheme.

Rivers Fiji

Rivers Fiji (RF) originated in a previous agreement between a Fijian and a North American to build whitewater boats. This business relationship eventually led to the formation of RF, with a sole Fijian partner (owning 51% of the company) and two Americans, resident in the USA (holding the balance). As the second American partner owned and operated a successful whitewater operation in the western USA, he was able to contribute knowledge of over 27 years of commercial whitewater operations to the Fiji Islands. Another North American subsequently became managing director and moved to Fiji to develop and implement day-to-day operations. In his view, using the boats in a whitewater operation seemed a creative way to 'complete the circle' and establish a unique company that purchased the key programme elements (the boats manufactured in Fiji). The American managers (the author and her spouse) had over 18 years experience in adventure travel and overseas operations. They went to Fiji to set up and manage the operations of RF for a minimum of 3 years.

After 2 years of exploration and pre-approval meetings in the interior of Fiji, RF formed an ecotourism adventure company and in December 1997 received approval from the Fiji Trade and Investment Board (FTIB) to operate on the Wainikoroiluva ('Luva) and Upper Navua rivers, which are located in Namosi and Serua provinces, respectively.

The role of Government

Permission from the FTIB is required before overseas investors can form a business in Fiji, a process that can take some time. As FTIB was unwilling to allow another business to operate if it competed with or resembled any current tourism programmes in the Navua River region, several enquiries were made to see if a similar operation existed in either Namosi or Serua Province.

It was also necessary for the RF managers to discuss the project with landowning patrilineages (*mataqali*) who controlled access to the rivers, and the company consulted with all the villages along each corridor. At the request of the provincial leaders (*Roko Tuis*) of each Provincial District office (Namosi and Serua), a second series of meetings with villages of Nakavika and Nabukelevu occurred after FTIB approval. The primary focus of these meetings was again to secure signatures of approval by relevant *mataqali* for RF to begin business. The fact that these meetings were held again was somewhat confusing to each village, for they had assumed the first round of approvals was adequate.

RF also discussed the project with the Fiji Visitors' Bureau (FVB), the Department of Tourism, the Ministry of the Environment (including the Department of Forestry), local tour operators and the World Wide Fund for Nature. In general, government bodies were unaware of the economic and ecotourism potential of whitewater recreation, but they supported the project, primarily because it would take tourism opportunities to remote areas.

Once established, RF continued to liaise with government entities, provincial offices, and landowners, and found an especially enthusiastic ally in the FVB. It was at the behest of the FVB that a meeting was held in July 1998 with several ministers and directors from the Departments of Environment, Tourism and Transport, Fijian Affairs, and Women and Culture, at which RF outlined a proposal for developing Fiji's hinterland, an area not included in the sun, sand, and sea (3S) tourism for which Fiji tends to be better known. At the meeting, RF also explained the need for a conservation area on the Upper Navua.

In the course of the meeting, which was a turning point in RF's attempts to establish its operation in Fiji, government officials emphasized the importance of continued dialogue with, and involvement of, local communities. Importantly, after more than 2.5 years in developing the RF ecotourism project, the suggestion was first made that the Native Lands Trust Board (NLTB), a parastatal organization set up in 1940 to administer native land for the benefit of Fijian owners, should be involved.

In retrospect, the omission of the NLTB from previous discussions had been fundamental. More than 80% of land in Fiji is communally owned by *mataqali* and, as such, is reserved for their special use and cannot be leased without their consent (FTIB, 1998). It was because of this that RF was advised to reach formal agreements through NLTB with *mataqali* in the areas they wished to use, to maintain long-term access to the river. This type of legal agreement, it was felt, was the only way to protect RF's long-term investment.

Local communities and landowners

The land along both river corridors is native land, and before anyone outside the landowning group could use it (commercially or otherwise), permission by the *mataqali* or other kinship groups had to be obtained. When whitewater specialists from America visited Fiji to explore the rivers and assess their commercial potential, they therefore had to be introduced through traditional welcoming ceremonies (*sevu sevu*). Such meetings involved sitting with community elders, discussing the project and the fees to be paid to gain access to the river. After two river canyons were identified as potential ecotourism operations, the consultation process formalized into several meetings with associated *mataqali* to discuss the future potential of a commercial river operation and low-impact tourism development. Crucially for RF, any future investment required villagers' agreement on several points. Firstly, RF should have long-term access to the river corridor for commercial whitewater activities (kayaking and rafting) and camping activities. Secondly, local people should have an interest in running and guiding the operation; and, finally, the *mataqali* would support RF in conserving the river and the surrounding area. As a result of these discussions, the villagers agreed and the project continued.

Partnerships and agreements: the leases

RF wanted an equitable partnership with government and local landowners to enable the business to remain viable and productive for many years and bring benefits to local people. At the same time, the structure and interests of villages and needs of the communities vary, and arrangements with *mataqalis* also differ according to circumstance. Agreements cannot be 'rubber-stamped'. In the case of Nabukelevu village, for example, formal leases were necessary to protect RF's investment in roads, bridges and product development, whereas arrangements with the village of Nakavika were arrived at during the welcoming meetings and accepted through less legalistic but shared understanding by RF, the village and the Provincial Council. This process involved the presentation of a *tabua* (whale's tooth) by RF to the village of Nakavika and associated *mataqali*. Traditionally presented to distinguished guests, or exchanged at weddings, funerals and birthdays, the *tabua* is also presented at the conclusion of agreements and contracts.

The Upper Navua Gorge

This element of the operation, described here as the Upper Navua River project, and based at the village of Nabukelevu, was created through agreements involving the NLTB

(which managed the lease on behalf of the landowning *mataqali*), the villagers and RF. RF's first proposal included leasing a 5 km road used in the past for transporting timber, and which provided access to the village, but it soon became evident that access to the upper section of the river was not enough. While it was possible to begin the river trip at the village, there were inherent problems in creating a commercially sustainable whitewater tourism product. Operations on the upper section of the river depended on consistent rain and water flows, but it transpired that sometimes the river flooded to dangerously high levels, while at other times it was low and difficult to 'run'. After a year of drought and another of 'average' rainfall, RF decided that the upper section of river was not commercially viable for the tourists whom they felt would be attracted (ranging from novices to advanced river runners) and it was therefore considered necessary to gain access to the lower section of the river, which would also provide an alternative exit for safety purposes.

Upgrading the logging road and constructing a bridge to secure access to the lower reaches of the river involved RF in unexpectedly heavy investment. As a result, the company decided that if these investments in infrastructure were to proceed, they required exclusive long-term 'tourism' use of the road. Their lawyers recommended a legally binding formal lease, a hurdle that was to pose considerable problems for RF. Such a lease was unusual, as the lessee was not to be engaged in extracting resources, but simply needed access and sole use. While approvals from the *mataqali* were quickly obtained, prolonged negotiations with the NLTB delayed the start of the company's operation by 18 months.

According to NLTB, the delays occurred because of the peculiar nature of the lease request. It was finally issued in November 1999, 18 months after RF had been advised to approach NLTB and 22 months after the FTIB had given permission for RF to begin its operation. The lease of the road, which was for 50 years, involved a one-off payment to NLTB, which was distributed, after the deduction of administrative costs and other fees, to three *mataqali*. In addition, RF was to pay an annual fee, in return for which it could operate whitewater programmes and have exclusive use of the road.

Other problems surfaced. Work on the road and the construction of the bridge lasted into the rainy season and led to additional delays, and it also seemed that external factors would have a detrimental effect on the new business. At the time of writing, the law of Fiji permits logging within 30 m of waterways, and roads in the whitewater rafting area sometimes come within 2 km of the river's edge. It was learned that a proposal existed for a road to the river to extract gravel for other logging roads in the area, and the proposed extraction site was directly opposite one of the largest waterfalls on the river and in the middle of RF's proposed operation. Such threats from the logging industry led RF to seek the establishment of a linear biosphere reserve in future lease agreements.

Logging is dangerous to whitewater rafters if carried out in close proximity and the proposed reserve would considerably reduce the risks to RF's clients. There would also be long-term benefits for both RF and the *mataqali*, as it would protect the canyon from felled trees and other debris from logging, enhance the tourist experience, enable RF and landowners to evaluate the nature and growth of ecotourism in the area, and provide jobs for rangers and guides. At the time of writing, the concept of a protected linear biosphere reserve had been approved by the relevant *mataqali* along the river and the proposal was finally accepted by the NLTB in November 2000.

The Wainikoroiluva river

The arrangement with *mataqali* of the village of Nakavika, where the 'Luva River is located, was arrived at differently. The NLTB was not involved, but agreements still required signatures of approval from heads of all the relevant *mataqali*. While many discussions centred on the initial project, subsequent meetings focused on payments for daily operations. Community meetings were held to outline a plan of action and proposed activities operated by RF. At one benchmark community meeting, RF asked the village

(including the *mataqali* whose land provided access to the river) if they would like to involve the NLTB in drawing up a formal lease. However, villagers preferred to retain the existing agreements with RF, arrived at by 'traditional' negotiations. As a consequence, all parties, including the Provincial council, the Chief of Nakavika and relevant *mataqali*, signed documents confirming RF as the sole operator for the sections of river outlined in their programme.

Once support from the villagers and the Provincial office had been secured, RF felt confident about investing further in training guides, developing trails, building thatched huts (*bures*), marketing, and programme expansion. Indeed, after nearly 2 years of operation, the company expanded its operations to include a 2-day whitewater experience and overnight camp. However, soon after agreement with the villagers had been reached, RF's position was challenged by another operator interested in the same stretch of the river. Despite numerous attempts to persuade the *mataqali* to break the agreement, the sole right of RF to operate on the designated stretch of the river was reaffirmed. However, the other operator continues to try to use sites incorporated in the RF programme, even though special agreements have been made with associated *mataqali*. As part of this agreement, fees are paid to landowners for areas incorporated into the programme of activities, for disembarking tourists at the village (put-in and take-out fees), for the use of sites for lunch, for a trek to a waterfall, and for take-out areas (where RF ends the trip).

Monitoring the RF operation

At the time of writing, 1-day trips run at least three times a week on the 'Luva, and they have introduced a 2-day river trip, including an overnight camp and a visit to Nakavika. Because of the delay in upgrading the road and constructing the bridge, operations on the Upper Navua are less advanced. One-day trips for youth groups began in July 2001, but when the road and bridge are completed (estimated September 2001) RF will schedule 1- and 2-day programmes for the general public.

The value of the agreements lies not on the paper on which they are written, but the relationships between the tour operator and the villagers. If they disapproved of the actions of RF, even with the most formal of agreements, villagers could always resort to road blocks to hinder the operation. Building such relationships takes time and understanding on the part of the operator and the villagers. In several instances, for example, villagers had to educate the tour operators in the culture of the village, and the villagers in turn needed to be informed about the ways of tourism and tourists.

One method of furthering this process of mutual understanding was the use of focus groups in both villages, and these were started at the end of 1998. In Nakavika, they were set up 6 months after commercial operations were under way, while on the Upper Navua Gorge they commenced with the first training trips from the village of Nabukelevu. Initial meetings were held in both villages to seek permission, discuss the purpose of the study, introduce research assistants and schedule meetings, and someone from each village was recruited to assist in scheduling and organizing the focus groups. After discussions with the chiefs, the *Turaga Ni Koro* (the village speaker and representative of the District Council), elders and research assistants, it was decided to split focus groups by gender and age. Men and women were divided, and two age groups, covering the range 18–30 and 31 years and after, were set up. The local assistant in each village recruited volunteers from each *mataqali* and four focus groups were formed, numbering from ten to 16 people, from each village, totalling 45 in Nakavika and 26 in Nabukelevu.

Interviews in the local Fijian dialect were conducted by two research assistants from the University of the South Pacific, and groups met twice a week at times convenient to the villagers, in the evenings and at weekends. Discussions were recorded and later translated into English. The results show how villagers perceived tourism, its costs and benefits, how they viewed what they had to offer tourists, and their perception of other issues that follow from opening the region to tourism (Bricker, 1999).

Perceived village attractions

Focus groups in both villages felt that the traditional Fijian way of life was unique and would be appreciated by tourists. As one man remarked, 'tourists come to experience our way of life, behaviour, and warm hospitality of which we are renowned for'. Another villager discussed the importance of showing visitors 'their culture':

> For those of us who live in the village [pause] there exists the proper and genuine Fijian way of life or norms and behaviour which could be shown to tourists. For example, the *mekes* [dances] – these are traditional genuine *mekes*, which is unique here, and one that we learn which could be shown to tourists. Another example is the preparation of the traditional *yaqona* ceremony. The tourists also have their own unique culture and ceremonies, which we often see on TV. So we can also show them our culture and ceremonies.

At the time of writing, guests on 1-day trips did not visit Nakavika. However, as previously noted, RF is planning to introduce a 2-day programme, which may include a visit to Nakavika village. The villagers discussed this and referred to guests coming to see their way of life:

> Another thought is for the tourists to actually come to the village and experience the Fijian way of life. They get to taste traditional Fijian delicacies and come to know some Fijian herbal medicine, which might be beneficial to them. They [tourists] can't understand or appreciate our culture and traditions if they just arrive and depart from our village. They have to spend time with us. What I'm trying to say here is that they have to take some treasured memories with them when they depart from here ... They can't do that if they don't spend time with us!

Nabukelevu villagers also believed it was important to share the Fijian 'way of life' with tourists and implicitly to recognize cultural differences:

> Here in Nabukelevu, our Fijian way of life is very much intact – that is, love and respect for all, good interpersonal relationships. When the tourists visit our main urban centres, it is still like the life they live in their country of origin. These tourists want to see something different, experience, taste, touch and feel something different. They want to come to villages for their holidays – to experience something different.

In addition to whitewater rafting and kayaking, villagers listed several activities they felt would be appropriate to offer guests. Examples included visiting caves and ancient fortresses, bird-watching, hiking or trekking, dances and preparation of traditional foods, handicrafts, storytelling, myths and legends, and horse-riding. Villagers from Nabukelevu and Nakavika also considered their natural surroundings to be an 'attraction' for tourists:

> Another aspect of their visit is that in their countries they are surrounded by white concrete jungle. When they come to our place they see the mountain ranges, breath of fresh air, the unbounded and pristine forest where they will realize that it has been untouched since the creation of the world.

Up to the time of writing, river trips are RF's primary focus, but there have been occasions when visitors have paid fees to stay overnight in the village, lodging with acquaintances of RF staff. At a meeting of community leaders and RF managers in September 1999, villagers in Nakavika expressed a wish for more such guests and proposed that RF should manage the details in conjunction with other villagers. In response, the company set up a camp area near the river on land belonging to one of the *mataqali* Villagers expressed an interest in developing the site: they plan to provide tents for accommodation and traditional meals cooked in underground ovens (*lovo*, food).

Perceived benefits of tourism

Villagers in Nakavika and Nabukelevu identified several communal and individual benefits that could result from tourism development. Increased revenues were clearly important. For example, at the time of writing, RF paid a fee for every guest travelling down the 'Luva River. Of the total amount paid, 18% went directly to the village community fund, 18% to the caretaker of the waterfall, and the remainder to the *mataqali* owning land used in the course of the trips. From information given at the focus groups, funds thus obtained by Nakavika were to be used to build schools, improve the village facilities (for example, by upgrading footpaths), and develop spin-off businesses. As one community member reported:

> with the development of tourism, the potential is there to achieve greater things, such as going into new business ventures, trucks and shops for example. Most importantly, is our quest for giving our children the very best education.

Other village groups also benefited from the tourist dollar. Rugby teams, youth groups and school groups have worked on individual projects to earn cash for fund-raising projects. During 1998, for example, the community needed funds to complete their church and RF needed a substantial trail to the river. After a meeting with the *Turaga Ni Koro*, a price was agreed and a 100 m trail to the river was built in 2 days. The village rugby team contributed its labour, and used the money it received to purchase new team strips.

Villagers recognized that ecotourism allowed them to improve their standard of living:

> I think the proceeds we receive from tourism will dramatically transform our village to a better one in terms of the structure, fittings and fixtures and design of our homes. We all know it is only money that will generate development, nothing else. Therefore, in terms of the future development, I think it will move from good to better.

Another remarked, 'I welcome the development of tourism to our village because we will be able to further develop our school, our village, and our standard of living'.

Thirdly, employment and training were seen to derive directly from tourism. At the outset of the project, RF anticipated a need to train four individuals from each village as whitewater guides. Meetings were held with village elders in Nakavika to discuss guidelines, job descriptions and anticipated days of work per month. Then the elders selected four individuals (one from each of the four *mataqalis* in the village) for training, a decision which, according to one of the guides, brought the *mataqali* and the community more 'together'. Those chosen subsequently received a 4-month whitewater guiding course and in-service training, and also participated in annual Red Cross cardiopulmonary resuscitation, first aid and swiftwater rescue training courses.

Delays in formalizing the lease, upgrading the road and building the bridge meant that RF's operation in Nabukelevu advanced more slowly than in Navakika, but a similar process of hiring guides was implemented. After several meetings with village elders, for example, it was decided, as in Nakavika, that a man from each *mataqali* would train as a white-water guide.

RF also employs men from Nakavika to carry equipment, develop trails and build traditional *bures*. Instead of only a few individuals being porters, the chiefs, elders and other villagers organized a system whereby families took turns in providing porters, and the proceeds were used to buy fuel for the generator, which had been purchased in February 1999. In this way, families did not have to purchase a month's supply of fuel, and the entire community benefited from tourism employment, with lighting supplied to every home in the village. The villagers of Nakavika were pleased with the employment of their young men and the guides took pride in their role. Although the new work opportunities required them to manage their time to meet the demands of the job, families and friends, which clearly prompted a process of adjustment, their kin and other villagers considered the results to be positive, suggesting that guides spent less time around the *kava* bowl (which involves communal drinking of a Fijian non-alcoholic brew made from *kava, Piper methysticum*) and were thus more reliable and responsible. For their part, the guides realized that their opportunities to socialize were reduced, and sometimes they even had to miss a game of rugby (which is hugely popular throughout Fiji). However, they liked earning money because it allowed them to visit relatives, buy goods and gain access to preventive medical care. Villagers also acknowledged that the guides spoke English more proficiently.

According to some villagers, contact with tourists had involved them in a more general learning experience, and focus groups from Nakavika commonly stressed the benefits of cultural exchange. As one group member remarked:

> I really appreciate the tourists' visits. I often ask them where do they come from and it fascinates me just to look at them, especially their smiling

faces. When I see all these tourists from all over the world it's like I'm actually living in their place of origin.

Indeed, as a result of meeting tourists, some individuals expressed interest in one day travelling overseas:

> I know that these tourists come from developed countries whereby they have good jobs and enjoy high salaries. If they need some people to be employed in their home country then it would be nice for us to go and work there.

Villagers from Nabukelevu also felt there was an opportunity to learn from other cultures:

> I think tourists will bring a lot of good things and changes to our community. We will learn from them – new ways of doing things, perhaps.

Finally, villagers felt that tourism could benefit their children and future generations because it was sustainable. This view is summarized by a young man from Nabukelevu, which has experienced considerable logging over the last 10 years:

> Tourism is very different from other industries such as the logging industry or the fishing industry. The logging and the fishing industry will take away from our land our resources, in a way depriving us of our resources. Whereas for tourism, tourists would not take away any of our resources. They will just come, watch and experience our resources that also include our culture, and us the people. When the logging company departed from here, they departed with our forests. The land is stripped bare. When the fishing company departed from our waters, they departed with our marine life and our waters are scarce or even extinct with marine life. Our resources must be safeguarded so that our future generations can also utilize them.

Clearly, villagers from Nakavika and Nabukelevu approached tourism positively. According to Taukeinikoro (1999), close ties among the villagers, and the monitoring of all developments by RF, created a sense of trust and expectation in the benefits of tourism. The pace of development has been slow and villagers have had time to adjust, and because guides work on a part-time basis, they are still able to attend to village and family needs. Finally, as the guide's role requires them to interpret surroundings familiar to them, they develop confidence in their presentation and a pride of place in their home environment.

The perceived costs of tourism development

Residents of both villages were also aware, though, that tourism could have negative impacts. In particular, they felt that tourists might disrupt village life and offend local dress codes, and that tourism could lead to an unequal distribution of wealth. They clearly recognized that the regular routines of village life would be put under some pressure by tourism, and emphasized the need for discussions within the communities over tourist activities, the time and the duration of visits, and the rules that tourists should follow. As one male villager remarked:

> [With] further development of tourism in our village we have to meet and discuss the days that the tourists should visit our village so that it does not clash with other village activities. We welcome the development of tourism to our village; we just have to decide the time and day of their visit.

It was felt that tourists should not visit the villages every day, and commonly argued that Sunday 'should be free … because it is a day of worship', and 'Monday is a day devoted to community work'. When RF first started in Nabukelevu, Mondays and Wednesdays were set up as training days for the guides. However, the village then levied a fee on the guides, whose time spent on the river took them away from their communal obligations. As a result, training activites were quickly transferred from Monday to Friday.

Both villages required advance notice of tourist visits, and expected to greet them with the traditional ceremony (*sevu sevu*). As one villager remarked, 'People of Nakavika do not like tourists who walk into the village unannounced or they [tourists] do not have the courtesy to ask for permission from the *Turaga Ni Koro*'.

For most villagers, rules regarding dress and behaviour are important.

> Tourism would be a problem if the tourists just roam around our area and that there are no guidelines or rules for them to follow. If we [in Nabukelevu village] stick to our way of life and the tourists follow what they are supposed to do and how they are supposed to behave, then I do not see any problems.

It was generally felt that young people might imitate tourists and thus come into conflict with 'the Fijian way of life'.

> I would like to emphasize the point of dressing to developers – to wear clothing suitable or proper for the village community and behaviour that they display not to influence the young children or youth that may lure them away from the norms, values, morals that they were brought up with and which holds society together.

It was also believed that such problems could be overcome by establishing rules for visitors to the village, asking them to wear a *sulu* (sarong) and, if necessary, to avoid actions that might influence young people unduly.

Finally, villagers were concerned that incomes derived from tourism should be equally distributed. As one remarked:

> Tourism is the source of income for the four tour guides and for the village. Money has both good and bad advantages and is seen to be the root of all evil. With increasing wealth within the *mataqali* and village, there comes a time when there will be disharmony [and] this disharmony will lead to the barring of tourists to the village and the eventual closure of such enterprise.

To date, RF and the village of Nakavika have developed a system of recording payments made to the village, so that villagers always know how much has been paid to the community and associated *mataqali*. *Mataqali* are compensated whenever their land is used by tourists and, as indicated earlier, cash obtained from portering is shared. In Nabukelevu, where commercial operations have not yet started, equity was achieved by careful and equal distribution of training opportunities and employment to all the *mataqali* involved.

Infrastructure and access

Both villages were aware that the development of tourism necessitated a basic level of infrastructure and that access to the area was important if the ecotourism venture was to succeed. When the physical situation of the villages is understood, such concerns clearly have some validity. The village of Nakavika, for example, with its 57 houses and some 270 residents, and the portion of the 'Luva River used by RF, are in Namosi Province. Access to the village via the landing point on the river is by a gravel mountain road nearly 27 km long from Queen's Highway (the main highway on the island) over rugged, steep terrain. Transport to the main road for villagers is typically by overland carrier (usually a truck adapted to carry passengers) or by foot to the village of Namuamua, and then by motorized punt to Navua. Either way, trips from the village to the main road take at least 1.5 h and access to transport is irregular. The Public Works Department maintains the road, but since RF began operating on the 'Luva, unsafe road conditions, (for example, landslides and flooding), have made it necessary to cancel trips on several occasions.

By contrast, Nabukelevu is west of Namosi, in the province of Serua. The village, with 37 houses, has a population of 217. The road providing access to this village and the river is approximately 12 km from the Queen's Highway and its condition is often poor, as it is used periodically to transport timber. It normally takes about an hour to reach the landing point on the river, but occasional landslides and severe mud conditions can make access difficult.

Villagers in Nabukelevu and Nakavika felt that if tourism was to succeed, government assistance was essential, especially with roads, water, and schools and clinics:

> Government should improve our [Nakavika's] road, tar-seal our road because our road is very rugged. It could hinder the coming of more tourists to our village.

> Our village [Nabukelevu] needs the improvement of our water supply system. We have discussed and did some fund raising and were able to raise $12,000. Government contributed $32,000 for this project. As of today, nothing has materialized and we have not contacted Government's Water Supply Department – thus the delay.

Villagers in Nabukelevu were especially concerned about schools and health care:

> Government should improve the condition of our school in terms of building, text books and school equipment all in the effort to improve the education standard of our children.

> We need to improve the condition and facilities of our Dispensary.

Key Issues in Ecotourism Development in the Highlands.

In Fiji generally, native landowners undoubtedly control their resources and it is of major importance, certainly to the *mataqali* of Nakavika and Nabukelevu, that this situation continues. As the case study shows, villagers constrain the actions of RF in two distinct ways. Firstly, the company depends on the *mataqali* to gain access to the river; secondly, RF needs permission to have exclusive use of sites for camping, for meals and for embarking and disembarking tourists. However, as RF becomes established, villagers will need to determine the optimal level of growth and the point at which tourism begins to erode the structure of village life.

In Nakavika, villagers employed as guides and in related work demonstrated that part-time involvement has minimal negative implications for their social and family life (Taukeinikoro, 1999). However, tourism was new to both Nakavika and Nabukelevu, and both villages recognized the need to establish rules and protocol to be followed when tourists visit, and insisted that tourism was not to disrupt village routine. Furthermore, the villagers' participation in the project was crucial, in selecting guides, assisting with their work schedules, deciding who else should be involved in tourist-related activities, discussing the fee structure and creating new programme elements (for example, village visits and overnight camps).

At the same time, diplomacy on the part of RF was crucial. In the interests of equality, and to maintain good relations in the villages, it was necessary that each *mataqali* was represented by a guide. Although villagers selected the guides, they did so according to criteria provided by RF, which controlled the process of training and development and also decided who was ready to become a guide.

Control over future development also rests with the landowners. If RF is to progress with the conservation area, all ten *mataqali* must agree. In December1999, RF held a series of meetings to assess support for the buffer zone bordering a 17 km stretch of the Upper Navua. Agreement was unanimous and meant that logging and other forms of extraction would not be allowed for 200 m on either side of the river corridor. At the time of writing, though, uncertainties still exist. Agricultural and other activities on the part of the *mataqali* in the conservation area have yet to be agreed and RF also needs to establish that it can afford the cost of the lease.

Landowner control (and the relationships of trust developed through the focus groups) was also much in evidence when another tour company impinged on areas exclusively used by RF, as agreed with *mataqali* on the Wainikoroiluva Programme. The issue eventually went to the *Tui Namosi*, the highest chief in the province, who first sought the wishes of the *mataqali* and then instructed the other operator to leave the area of RF's operations.

The second key issue is the role of government. In Nabukelevu, delays by NLTB in developing the lease agreement for road access affected the village adversely and proved costly to RF. Arguably, if outsiders are to introduce ecotourism projects in rural areas, existing lease arrangements should be adapted and made more appropriate to new forms of tourism development. Without such support, small operators (whether Fijian Islander or expatriate) could find the cost of developing ecotourism too high. At the same time, negotiations must also be flexible enough to accommodate a range of partnerships and nature-orientated tourism activities.

Thirdly, ecotourism development in rural areas requires a supportive infrastructure – for example, ease of access, quality water supplies, adequate health care facilities and educational opportunities for villages. Like other forms of tourism, successful ecotourism involves the provision of food, catering services, accommodation and tour operations. However, in Fiji (at the time of writing) there are no operational standards or licensing arrangements for ecotourism ventures. As new areas are 'discovered', it will be increasingly necessary for government to confer with the tourism industry to develop standards for nature and cultural tourism operations. It is hoped that – as part of

the objectives of the Fiji Ecotourism Policy (Ministry of Tourism and Transport, 1999) – the Fiji Ecotourism Association, representing major stakeholders in the industry, and the Fiji National Ecotourism Committee, formed in December, 1999, will co-operate in developing such criteria.

Fourthly, it would seem advisable for government to review the structure of licensing for overseas investors in ecotourism projects. RF was not advised of the necessary inclusion of NLTB until after the licensing process was completed and the business was under way. It would seem preferable for the FTIB to address these issues with all stakeholders in the business proposal, including the local villages, provincial offices, and NLTB. Such communication with relevant organizations would help to ensure that deadlines developed by investors are based on a realistic assessment of the development process. Dollars would then be invested productively (and to the immediate benefit of villagers and landowners) much earlier, with a corresponding reduction in frustration for the operating company and local partners. At the time of writing, there are plans for NLTB to develop a tourism division, which would assist in promoting tourism at all levels, from large-scale resorts to ecotourism. Such a unit could play a crucial role in planning for and managing conservation in areas given over to nature-based tourism.

There are clear indications that the Fiji Government is actively planning support for the development of ecotourism. At the 1999 Fiji Tourism Forum, the Minister of Tourism announced government support for ecotourism development in Fiji, noting that indigenous ownership of natural resources provided an immediate avenue for rural participation in tourism development. She also suggested that the Fiji Development Plan took Fiji beyond the typical 'sun, sand, sea and smiles' resort and focused on culture, heritage, conservation and protection of the environment, and traditional land use practices (Mara-Nailatikau, 1999).

Finally, several key issues are centred on the role of RF and, by implication, the role of commercial ecotourism operators generally in conservation. In creating a new ecotourism product, the company wanted to develop a long-term plan to protect the river resources and thus preserve the experience for those who raft or kayak the remote river canyons. To this end, it entered into two quite different agreements with associated villages and *mataqali*: a traditional partnership with Nakavika and a lease agreement with NLTB. As previous sections indicate, negotiations with the latter were especially problematic, delaying commercial operations for more than a year, but it is hoped that the potential long-term benefits in protecting the Upper Navua Gorge will outweigh the costs in arriving at the operating agreement. For the company, future commercial success depended on protecting the environment and its investment, and developing and maintaining good relationships with villagers, who were partners in the project and part of the tourist 'product'. Whereas guides sometimes had to adjust their life style to meet family and community obligations, RF had to be prepared to monitor relationships with villagers, learn about operating in an unfamiliar cultural environment, and allow villagers a role in organizing the way work commitments were honoured. As indicated earlier, the company attempted to act responsibly and to respect the physical and social environment, but there were clear difficulties in combining ecotourism development with conservation.

Conclusions

It has been suggested that 'alternative' tourism that develops slowly and leaves control with local people is less likely to have negative implications (Butler, 1991) and this case study indicates that planning for a slow start, attention to education and training, maximizing local benefits and continued evaluation and feedback are crucial for ecotourism to be successfully introduced into a rural area that has no previous experience of tourism.

Planning for a gradual start

Clearly, delays that prevent any growth at all are commercially unacceptable, but research has demonstrated that when growth occurs gradually, some negative social impacts are minimized. (Butler, 1991; Stevens, 1991). The speed at which a project develops depends ultimately on the interest and understanding of the local community. To some extent by default, because of an unusual drought during the first year of operation, the RF project grew slowly. However, this allowed both the village and RF to adjust the training and timing of the operation. It also enabled villagers to assess the nature of tourism and the benefits it brought to the community, and to make plans for future developments.

Education and training

While human impact is considered one of the most destructive forces within national parks, advocates of ecotourism claim that education can minimize tourism's negative consequences (Pietri, 1992). Pre-departure information can facilitate more effective management of tourists in ecotourism programmes, and field personnel, especially, have a crucial role to play. 'Tour operators and guides must be particularly aware of and sensitive to the areas they promote because they develop the itineraries and are responsible for their clients' (Ziffer, 1989: 31). Wight (1993: 3) suggested that ecotourism should involve '*education among all parties* – local communities, government, non-governmental organizations, industry, and tourists (before, during, and after the trip)' (emphasis in the original).

RF took an active role to educate government, local communities and other non-governmental entities about whitewater programmes that they have developed. Visitors are provided with pre-departure fact sheets, while the training manual used in the company's whitewater school has been distributed to guides, some of whom have attended ecotourism workshops, subsequently disseminating the information in their village. Videos on the river project and ecotourism and information on the proposed conservation area have been a part of meetings with landowners and government officials; RF is also producing an interpretive guide for its area of operations. The company believes that this type of activity has enormous positive effects on the overall development of the programmes.

Maximizing local benefits

It is commonly accepted that ecotourism can provide long-term benefits 'to the resource, to the local community, and to the industry (e.g. benefits may be conservation, scientific, social, cultural, or economic)' (Wight, 1993: 3). However, although RF's company's philosophy is to 'leave no trace' of its operations, the introduction of a new type of tourism product has caused managers some concern. As the Managing Director commented:

> once we open these corridors up to the world, we open them up to the good and the bad ... As a result, we believe RF has an inherent responsibility to protect and conserve the resources in which we operate.

It is thus to encourage conservation, as well as for commercial reasons, that the proposed 'buffer zone' on the Upper Navua Gorge is so important. Such a plan, if formally accepted, would be the first of its kind in Fiji, where a private entity leases an area simply to protect it from extractive use and preserve the pristine quality of the experience, thus addressing economic, socio-political and environmental sustainability of the project.

Up to the time of writing, villagers had combined tourism with farming, and the logging activities of one company had also continued. As the focus group data indicate, they believed that tourism could bring additional economic and other benefits to their communities, and these are likely to increase in future. Women's groups, sports organizations and youth groups all expressed interest in special projects and ways of earning funds, and the women's groups also wanted to develop arts and crafts for sale to visitors.

Evaluation and feedback

If Fiji is to implement its own ecotourism policy successfully, it must evaluate, regulate and monitor competition and control the type of use that rural areas can potentially support. Guidelines for tourism operations in natural areas must be developed, with inputs from all stakeholders (including *mataqali*), and should be followed by a comprehensive plan to monitor all ecotourist activities on a regular basis. Whitewater recreation, for example, requires extensive knowledge and skill to operate safely, but successful operations are always likely to be imitated, often without respect for the environment and safety procedures implemented in the original product development.

As Ziffer (1989) noted, land management should be planned. Ideally, tourism development will incorporate both a comprehensive business plan and a land management scheme. However, the river corridors in which RF operates are neither part of a natural resource plan, nor the responsibility of any organized governing body. Their long-term care ultimately rests with the *mataqali* and with the businesses (RF and logging enterprises) leasing the land. Herein lies a crucial dilemma, with implications for all ecotourism development in Fiji, and indeed elsewhere, for one of the main issues surrounding this case study was how to protect river resources from over-exploitation, once a natural area becomes visible to the world. RF's long term goal was to protect and conserve the river corridor and the experience of those who raft, kayak or hike the remote canyons. If successful, this would ensure that the river experience (the 'tourism product') was both sustainable and economically viable, and would protect both the environment and the village way of life from the sometimes detrimental side-effects of poorly regulated competition.

Lindberg and McKercher (1997: 73) noted that a common method of increasing tourisms's economic benefits is to increase visitor numbers; they also suggested that economic benefits can be increased, and negative impacts minimized, through increased visitor spending, reduced leakages and more local participation in the industry. In fact, the continual struggle between preservation and conservation, on the one hand, and profit, on the other, is at the forefront of sustainable tourism development. Tourism growth is sometimes constrained by the destination itself, and lack of infrastructure, the possibility of overcrowding, a shortage of professional personnel, inadequate promotion and political instability all reduce the prospect of increased markets and development. As Hill (1990: 18) suggested, it is up to local communities 'to mitigate the environmental, social, and cultural impacts and take control of their local resources'. However, even when given control, villagers may lack the experience or knowledge to minimize such consequences and ultimately control the impacts of others. As Lindberg and McKercher (1997: 76) noted, 'the conventional wisdom regarding ecotourism's conservation and development benefits is being critically evaluated, and efforts will be needed to ensure that these benefits do, in fact, accrue'. As this case study shows, organizations such as the NLTB must be able to evaluate ecotourism projects and advise government according to recognized criteria of best practice. If this occurs, joint and effective responsibility becomes possible, and all is not then left to the good will and social conscience of the tour operator.

It is argued here that partnerships with rural people can succeed if ecotourism operators are knowledgeable and support the principles of ecotourism. Can ecotourism work if one company takes responsibility – however willingly – for environmental conservation and guardianship when it is simultaneously involved in running a business for profit? In fact, several resorts in Fiji take responsibility for the island environments that they lease or own, improving them and protecting them from further damage. This should occasion no surprise, for in nature-based tourism the environment is the key business asset. If it is damaged, the business is at risk. At the same time, in Fiji the long-term health of the environment is usually the responsibility of the *mataqali* and, with or without outside assistance, only the landowners can steer a sustainable course of action.

Finally, it can be concluded that partnerships in ecotourism cannot be based solely on good working relationships at the local level. They must also be supported by government and regional entities that monitor and regulate tourism. In the end, sustainability can be achieved only if all stakeholders cooperate in the endeavour and thread a common interest in sustainability into all new developments.

Acknowledgements

This case study is the result of the hard work and dedication of numerous individuals. The author would like to thank the villagers of Nakavika and Nabukelevu. Their enthusiasm and interest in tourism development in the rural highlands forms the basis of the study. Thanks are also due to Kasimoro Taukeinikoro and the guides of Nakavika, to the research assistants at the University of the South Pacific who transcribed and interpreted their dialect, and for the hard work and vision of George Wendt, Glenn Lewman and Colin Philip. A special *vinaka* to Dr Kerstetter for her push to develop this case study and continued mentoring. Finally, for help with copious notes, understanding of RF operations, wisdom, endless discussion, documentation and endless friendship, I am eternally grateful to Nathan Bricker.

References

Bricker, K. (1999) Sustainable rural tourism development: a case study of ecotourism in the Highlands of Fiji. (Unpublished manuscript), University of the South Pacific, Suva, Fiji.

Butler, R.W. (1991) Tourism, environment, and sustainable development. *Environmental Conservation* 18(3), 201–209.

FTIB (1998) *An Investor's Guide to Fiji*. Fiji Trade and Investment Board, Suva, Fiji.

Fiji Visitors Bureau (1999) *1999 Fiji International Survey*. Ministry of Tourism and Transport, Suva, Fiji.

Harrison, D. (ed.) (1999) *Ecotourism and Village-based Tourism: a Policy and Strategy for Fiji*. Ministry of Tourism and Transport, Suva, Fiji.

Hill, C. (1990) The paradox of tourism in Costa Rica. *Cultural Survival Quarterly* 4(1), 14–19.

Lindberg, K. and McKercher, B. (1997) Ecotourism: a critical review. *Pacific Tourism Review* 1, 65–79.

Mara-Nailatikau, A.K. (1999) *Minister of Tourism Address to the Forum*. The 1999 Fiji Tourism Forum, Nadi, Fiji.

Pietri, O.A. (1992) *The Ecotourism Dilemma*. The Ecotourism Society, p. 3.

Stevens, S.F. (1991) Sherpas, tourism, and cultural change in Nepal's Mount Everest region. *Journal of Cultural Geography* 12(1), 39–58.

Taukeinikoro, K. (1999) Nakavika: a guide's view of tourism. (Unpublished manuscript) University of the South Pacific, Suva, Fiji.

Wight, P. (1993) Ecotourism: ethics or eco-sell? *Journal of Travel Research* 31(Winter), 3–9.

Ziffer, K. (1989) *Ecotourism: the Uneasy Alliance*. Conservation International and Ernst and Young, Washington, DC.

17

Afterword

David Harrison

In the previous chapters, an attempt has been made to provide an overview of tourism in less developed countries (LDCs). It is argued that mass international tourism, which developed after 1945, continued processes already established with the rise of mass domestic tourism in western Europe during the second half of the 19th century. Several perspectives have been employed to understand the role of tourism in these processes of economic and social change. Some focused on tourism as a series of responses to changes in the nature of Western capitalist, industrial and post-industrial societies. Others linked it to various forms of religious travel or, at least, to travel that has a religious component, whereas geographers have analysed how tourist destination areas have physically evolved, or how landscape and place, community and nation, have been subjectively and collectively perceived by those caught up in changes brought about by international tourism.

The perspective adopted in the opening chapter of this book related the study of international tourism to processes of change broadly coming under the umbrella term, 'development'. Modernization theory, underdevelopment theory and environmentalism converged to contribute jointly to a wider perspective now commonly referred to as 'global-ization', in which tourism is both a cause and an effect. As forms of communication improved, tourism increased, and in turn prompted further developments. Indeed, tourists themselves are agents of change, bringing with them attitudes, patterns of behaviour, ideas and role models that have been variously admired and condemned by many – in less developed societies and elsewhere.

As Chapter 1 indicated, most international tourists travel to and from 'developed' societies, and intra-regional tourism is overwhelmingly the norm, but the share of at least some of the less developed countries in international tourism is increasing. Taking as a starting point the categories used by the World Tourism Organization (WTO), in every region there are specific LDCs with high levels of international tourist arrivals. In Europe they include Turkey, Cyprus and Malta; in East Asia and the Pacific: China, Hong Kong, Thailand, Singapore, Malaysia and Indonesia; in South Asia: India; in the Americas: Mexico, Puerto Rico and the Dominican Republic; in Africa: Tunisia, Morocco, Zimbabwe, Kenya and the Republic of South Africa; and in the Middle East: Egypt. At the same time, tourism's impacts and importance cannot be assessed only by examining the figures. Numerous small states, especially islands in the Caribbean and the Pacific, for example, depend on tourism for their well-being, and may be especially vulnerable to environmental degradation and social pressures, either from tourism or from alternative sources of economic development.

Chapter 2 focused on three key issues in the study of international tourism. First, it was argued that tourism could usefully be considered in the context of other forms of migration, that it frequently prompted the construction of second (holiday) homes and the development of substantial retirement communities, as well as sometimes reflecting the influence of migrants who had returned to their coutries of origin. Secondly, though, it was noted that migration itself occurred within the wider context of capitalist expansion, and that debates over commoditization, the alleged loss of 'authenticity', the ability or inability of people in LDCs to be entrepreneurs and the role of transnational corporations were perhaps best situated within this wider process, through which many of today's tourist destination areas have been increasingly (if only partially) incorporated into the global economy.

The third key issue discussed was the role of the state – another familiar topic in 'development debates' and one that continues to preoccupy many development agencies. That said, much of the crisis in development theory of the 1980s came about with the general realization that the state was a flawed agent in the promotion of 'development', a view certainly reinforced by an examination of its role in promoting tourism in LDCs. Yet, as indicated below, we cannot do without it.

As Linda Richter makes clear in Chapter 3, the political challenges of international tourism in the new millennium are not new. Poverty and the poor are still with us. Vast differences in wealth and income are still evident, either across societies or within them, and while many residents in developed societies peruse mail-order catalogues and weekend colour supplements for the latest consumer gadgets, the poor in less developed regions are still preoccupied with finding enough to eat. Such contrasts are often highlighted by international tourism. It is easy to

indulge in rhetoric about the urgent need for redistribution of wealth and resources, across societies and within them, but it is no easier in the 21st century than the 20th to make realistic and practicable suggestions as to how this can be achieved.

What, then, is to be made of the various contributions to this volume? How are they related to the 'development debate' and the issues raised in the opening chapters? Readers will undoubtedly draw their own conclusions, and perhaps criticize what they consider to be problematic emphases or surprising omissions. However, some common threads can be brought together to illustrate a more general pattern in tourism's relationship to development in less developed countries.

Inadequate Infrastructures

First, international tourism cannot occur on any scale if the overall infrastructure of transport and communication is inadequate. In Chapter 5, Guilherme Santana notes that poor telecommunication facilities and inadequate air and road transport facilities characterize much of the region covered by the South American Common Market (MERCOSUL). Shalini Singh makes a similar observation for India; Alan Lew points to the chequered history of air travel in China, and Derek Hall records the urgent need for post-communist governments in East and Central Europe to develop local and regional infrastructures, not least to facilitate their entry into the European Union. It is virtually a truism to assert that LDCs generally lack transportation systems able to carry people in bulk, in comfort and safety. Much the same might be said for the requirements that tourists have access to food and drink prepared and presented in hygienic conditions, and to reliable and efficient health care if they become ill. As several contributors to this volume indicate, when a region is considered unhealthy or unsafe for any reason, even if that perception is unjustified, it will attract few international tourists.

As Linda Richter notes, providing facilities for tourists may consume resources that could otherwise have been spent on meeting basic needs for the local population. In tourism, as in other economic sectors, who gets what is a political problem as well as an economic one. As a general rule, though, the introduction and development of international tourism is likely to be easier if attempts are made, at the same time, to meet the needs and aspirations of local residents. In this respect, it should be noted that they, too, want to travel. As several contributors to this volume have indicated, domestic tourism – in China, India, South Africa and post-communist societies, for example – is an important and growing feature of life in many less developed countries. It certainly involves more people than international tourism – though it may take different forms, as in visits to friends and relatives – and nationals whose travel facilities are improved are more likely to welcome international tourists than those feeling neglected and slighted. As Heba Aziz notes in Chapter 10, it cannot even be assumed that all pilgrims are exempt from such considerations; the 'executive pilgrims' she describes, at least, clearly enjoy their creature comforts.

Human Resource Issues

Secondly, previous chapters confirm the pervasiveness of what might be described as 'the human resource problem' in LDCs, and much of what Peter Dieke says about the need for education and training in Africa's tourism industry is universally applicable. There is also a dire need for trained and educated personnel in tourism in South America, India, Indonesia, the South Pacific, China and post-communist societies generally. As indicated in Chapter 2, this needs to be situated in a wider cultural context. Even among 'developed' societies, for instance, public attitudes to 'service' vary considerably, and where there is little general awareness or expectation of high quality service provision (at any level of the industry), it is unlikely to be provided. Similarly, if attending to customers' needs is considered demeaning, they are unlikely to be met. Arguably, the lack of a 'service culture' is at least as marked in most post-communist societies as in other LDCs, even if the historically specific reasons for it are different. And if international tourists are to be accommodated

according to international standards, those who work in the industry need to be socialized into at least some aspects of international culture. More narrowly, there is a clear need for training in specific skills at all levels of the tourism industry, from front desk operatives to household and bar staff, through to the highest tiers of management (which currently tend to be filled by expatriates). Where this training cannot be provided by government, it has to be provided by the private sector, either by small operators, such as the one described by Kelly Bricker in Chapter 16, or (perhaps more often) by transnational companies.

The Role of the State

Relatively low levels of skill and education, rather than being unique to the tourism industry, are among the defining characteristics of less developed societies. Much the same applies in relation to the role of the state, and most contributors to this volume reinforce what was said in Chapter 2 about its importance and the problematic nature of its performance. Unlike Japan, governments in LDCs have no financial interest in promoting outbound tourism (even though they might sometimes encourage other forms of migration) and in post-communist states, especially, where much recent effort has been put into reducing the role of the state and encouraging privatization and decentralization, there is a clear dilemma as to how far it is willing and able to plan tourism development (or, indeed, development of any kind). As Alan Lew indicates, this has posed special problems in China, where a long tradition of centralized government has to cope with pressures towards decentralization and individual freedoms. How far the result – a bureaucracy characterized by mismanagement, corruption and legal confusion – can be seen to represent (in Derek Hall's terms) a 'third way' remains to be seen, but the omens are hardly auspicious. What is certain, though, is that the public ownership and operation of hotels in China has been as unsuccessful as similar experiments elsewhere (CNTA, 1998).

The involvement of the state in international tourism in other LDCs seems to be no more efficient. Dieke points to the need for 'properly conceived' government intervention in providing institutional mechanisms to bring together private and public sector activities, but there is little evidence that this is happening in Africa. Indeed, according to Brennan and Allen in Chapter 14, the public sector in South Africa is riddled with inefficiency, inexperience and corruption, and Shalini Singh reports a similar situation in India, where poor policy formulation and implementation at national and state level are the norm, where cooperation with the private sector is tainted by corruption and where government bureaucrats (as elsewhere?) have had little or no experience in tourism or any other form of business activity. In the South Pacific, too, as Kelly Bricker notes, government departments are often at loggerheads with one another, and even if they are (relatively) free from corruption, it is hard to do business in a political environment which sometimes seems designed to make life difficult for investors. As Heba Aziz shows in Chapter 10 on tourism in the Middle East, it is not impossible for governments to organize tourism. Her description of the *Hajj* brings to mind the comment that 'a tourist is half a pilgrim, if a pilgrim is half a tourist' (Turner and Turner, 1978: 20), and even though it baulks at the comparison, the Saudi authorities have long experience of dealing with pilgrims to Mecca who, in many respects, are also tourists. In general, however, while a degree of scepticism is required when considering the state's role in international tourism, it must also be recognized that government involvement continues to be necessary, and it is argued here, not very originally, that governments should concentrate on doing relatively few things well. Clearly, ensuring the well-being of their citizens is their primary function but, in the specific context of tourism, governments must try to formulate and implement policies that enable the tourism industry, along with other economic sectors, to operate safely and successfully for the benefit of the country's population. If it is felt that economic and other benefits from the chosen types of tourism are not being spread fairly across the population, the state can use fiscal and other measures to redirect them to those it considers

should benefit most. Similarly, if the social and cultural effects of tourism are considered to be damaging, the state can act to reduce them. If it does not do so, it must (at least) share responsibility with other main players in the tourism industry for such neglect.

Such fine sentiments are easier to express than to translate into action. As indicated above, the state in LDCs generally is frequently inefficient and often criticized for being incompetent or corrupt. It is also held, like governments everywhere, to take more account of factional interests than the general welfare of its people. This is why ensuring the freedom of the mass media and raising levels of education are so important, for it is at least arguable that top-down development is more likely to be challenged if people know and understand what is going on. With specific reference to tourism, it is also the case that people will be more hospitable, and more willing to be educated and trained, if they feel that they and their families benefit, and are likely to go on benefiting, from the tourism industry. However, there is little evidence that such beliefs are widely held in LDCs. Until the message that conservation and tourism can bring benefits to local people reaches such places as North Sulawesi, discussed by Sheryl Ross and Geoff Wall in Chapter 15, and until the potentials start to be realized, tourism will continue to be an imperfect tool for development. It will continue to be so, until people believe it can offer them a sustainable future.

Sustainability

It is noticable that despite the increasing importance accorded to the environment in the literature on tourism development, as indicated in Chapter 1, few contributors to this volume focus on the issue of sustainable tourism development. Why should this be? The answer is not a lack of awareness on their part, but rather the nature of the state in many LDCs. Policies to bring about sustainable tourism development may figure in national development plans (especially if written by consultants well versed in the language of donor agencies) but conservation and the establishment of practices of sustainable tourism development require educated awareness, planning, a coherent regulatory framework, and the political will and ability to coordinate activities in the public and private sector and implement the rules successfully (Holden, 2000: 126–160) – characteristics notably absent from the state in many LDCs.

Where the state has failed, the private sector has fared little better, and although numerous voluntary codes of practice exist in the tourism industry, they are not much more than token gestures and marketing ploys. So far, their contribution to making international tourism more environmentally friendly has been minimal (Holden, 2000: 146–160) and, like codes of practice more generally, they can have unintended negative consequences (Heap, 2000: 102–129). Furthermore, successful projects require the active support of the bulk of the population, who are unlikely to embrace sustainability unless their current and future interests are best served in doing so. Putting it bluntly: hungry people are more likely to eat turtles, go 'poaching' or practise unsustainable logging than those who are well fed and whose continued prosperity is clearly linked to the survival of other species (Brandon and Wells, 1992).

This is not to suggest that forms of alternative tourism cannot be found in LDCs. David Weaver, in Chapter 11, focuses on the Caribbean. He distinguishes between sustainable and unsustainable mass tourism (SMT and UMT), on the one hand, and circumstantial and deliberate alternative tourism (CAT and DAT), on the other, but notes that (with some important exceptions) coastal resorts in the Caribbean are characterized by UMT, whereas destination areas inland are more likely to demonstrate CAT. By contrast, some larger tourism operators are seeing the commercial sense in developing SMT, and DAT is most likely to be found in terrestrial or marine environments that are protected, at least nominally, by government legislation.

As Weaver notes, even if it is possible to find examples of DAT, there is no reason to assume it will not develop into something that is *less* sustainable. Indeed, much of what is described and promoted as 'ecotourism' is likely (in Weaver's terms) to be CAT, simply

because difficulties of access or the vagaries of the climate restrict tourist arrivals. Given the chance, many practitioners of 'alternative' tourism would happily see a radical increase in arrivals – even the construction nearby of an international airport. Some evidence for this position is provided by contributors to this volume. In Chapter 9, for example, Shalini Singh notes the development of small-scale rural projects in the states of Rajastan and Haryana, both states that are unsuitable for mass tourism. The whitewater rafting project discussed by Kelly Bricker is also in an area where access is difficult; indeed, much of the hinterland of the Fiji Islands is similarly undeveloped, and it remains to seen how far the government, local communities and other interested organizations (Harrison and Brandt, forthcoming) will stand by the published policy to encourage small-scale ecotourism and village-based tourism when further confronted by the advocates of commercial logging.

Brennan and Allen, too, indicate in Chapter 14 the difficulties of promoting ecotourism in Kwazulu-Natal, South Africa, a region with a long history of oppression, political instability and domestic upheaval. They rightly note that in such circumstances the very idea of socially equitable, community-led ecotourism is Utopian. Indeed, tourism development – and all forms of development generally – is intimately linked to relationships of power, to government and the governed, and more often than not the impetus for change is from the top down.

Despite these reservations, which are considerable, small-scale 'alternative' forms of tourism are found in many LDCs, and the mass of literature on ecotourism, nature-based tourism, sustainable tourism and sustainable development generally provides ample evidence of a growing worldwide interest in such topics. There *are* resorts that care for their physical and social environment (e.g. Harrison, 1999), organizations that promote sustainable tourism, transnational companies that try to make their operations more environmentally friendly, and even nation states (for example, Dominica and Costa Rica) that strongly promote sustainable tourism development practices (e.g. Honey, 1999: chapters 4–10). That said, though, as Linda Richter remarks in

Chapter 3, despite the rhetoric of 'sustainability', examples of good practice are comparatively rare. As Weaver notes in Chapter 11, even in the Caribbean intense competition for the tourist dollar and a marked preference for large, prestigious tourism projects that bring in instant foreign exchange often outweigh longer-term environmental considerations.

It has to be recognized, too, that not all 'alternative' small-scale tourism is preferable to mass tourism. As Cater (1994: 76) noted, when ecotourism becomes popular, 'concentrated visitation may well result in an unacceptable level of degradation', a risk exacerbated in many ecotourism destinations by the lack of previous exposure to tourists. Indeed, the declaration by the United Nations that 2002 is to be the International Year of Ecotourism, and news that the initiative is to be led by the United Nations Environmental Programme (UNEP) and the WTO, produced fears of unsustainable increases in tourism in fragile environments and a less than enthusiastic response from a coalition of non-governmental organizations (NGOs) and pressure groups from developed and less developed countries (Pleumarom, 2000).

Child sex tourism is a more distressing case in point. As Heather Montogmery points out in Chapter 13 (and elsewhere), in so far as the demand for sex with children is related to tourism – an issue by no means settled – it is on a relatively small scale and involves close interaction with local people, even friendships with and regular visits to the children's families (Montgomery, 1996). Small in scale and interactive it may be, but child sex tourism is no less unwelcome for that.

Clearly, attempts to enhance the environmental credentials of small-scale tourism operators should continue, to their benefit and that of the wider community, and it is desirable that efforts are made to restrict tourism's growth to broadly agreed limits. There are certainly sufficient examples of 'good practice' in ecotourism (a small-scale variant of nature-based tourism) to provide key features of a model, or 'ideal type', against which actual operations can be assessed (Lindberg and Hawkins, 1993; Lindberg et al., 1998). In this regard, the work of Honey (1999: 21–26) provides an especially useful starting point.

However, mass tourism will never be replaced by 'alternative tourism', even of the acceptable, environmentally friendly variety, and all indications are that mass tourism will continue to increase, often preceded by 'alternative tourism' which, in Butler's (1992) terms, frequently representes the 'thin end of the wedge'. Rather than seeing this prospect (in reality a certainty) as a catastrophe, it should be seen as a challenge. Mass tourism can be made more environmentally appropriate, and there is evidence this is already under way, but it cannot be carried out by any one stakeholder alone. It is noteworthy that several contributors to this volume – including Richter, Dieke, Santana, Lew, Singh, Weaver, Ross and Wall, and Montgomery – discuss the role, in different contexts, of transnational companies, international agencies of various kinds, and national and international pressure groups. This should occasion no surprise, for in a period of increasing globalization, international tourism will inevitably involve international cooperation, as indicated below.

Towards a Framework for Understanding the Social and Cultural Impacts of Tourism

Undoubtedly, there will be regional wars and other catastrophes, and global warming is likely to have considerable impact on where tourists go and to have a marked effect on many destination areas (Brown, 2000), but absolute numbers of tourists will continue to increase. It is estimated that by 2020 there will be nearly 1.6 billion international tourist arrivals (WTO, 1997b: 1, 1999: 3), who will be transported across the world in planes capable of taking many more passengers than at present by a tourist industry increasingly reliant on technological means of communication (Tieman, 2000). At the same time, domestic tourism, commonly accepted to represent 10 times more arrivals than international tourism, will also increase. As standards of living rise and more free time and discretionary income become available to citizens of less developed countries, the more they will seek to travel for leisure purposes.

Tourism's growth will be more pronounced in some regions than others and, as suggested earlier, movements to, from and within Asia-Pacific (especially China) are likely to be greater than elsewhere. At the same time, if such countries as Saudi Arabi and Iran do successfully encourage non-Moslem tourism from the West, even a small increase in numbers could sometimes have a marked economic and social effect (especially if tourism development plans continue to marginalize social and cultural issues). While growth rates will not be as high, the absolute number of holidaymakers from developed societies will also increase, with the demand for more long-haul travel likely to continue to increase disproportionately.

Some types of tourism will grow faster than others. Futurologists envisage numerous scenarios, and in Chapter 3 Linda Richter notes the increasing importance of senior tourism (often known as the grey market, or empty nesters), a rise in tours with specific educational purposes, and increased provision for travel for those suffering from some form of disability. Others have noted different trends: shorter and more frequent holidays, an emphasis on city breaks, and other holiday-taking, including virtual tourism, cruising, cultural tourism and special interest tourism, along with more active, healthy holidays and ecotourism (Cheong, 1995; Jefferson, 1995; Williams and Hobson, 1995; WTO, 1996/1997, 1999; Macalister, 1999; Perry, 2000) and, space tourism has already started (Mckie, 2001). Those who predict the future always take hazards to fortune, but three features seem certain. First, international tourism will radically increase; secondly, it will pervade virtually every part of the globe and, thirdly, it will be characterized by the search for difference, for variety.

Although tourism is endlessly claimed to be the world's largest industry, the social and cultural impacts of international tourism are rarely analysed systematically. Indeed, such issues are scandalously marginalized in tourism development plans, even for such culturally sensitive areas as Islamic societies or small island states, and the major emphasis is placed, instead, on tourist numbers and the possible contribution their spending will make to the national economy. In a previous volume

(Harrison, 1992), a preliminary (and somewhat crude) examination of the social consequences of tourism focused on its role in spreading commoditization and on how it could lead to changes in the economic and social structures of tourist-receiving societies. Since then, understanding such changes has, if anything, become even more necessary, but a conceptual framework that would facilitate consistency in, and comparison of, social and cultural impact studies has yet to be produced. While it is not possible, in this final chapter, to detail such a framework, an indication can be given, at least in broad outline, of how it might appear, as indicated in Table 17.1.

New encounters and new forms of social interaction

At the risk of stating the obvious, tourism prompts social interaction across a range of people who might not otherwise have met, and has the potential to change radically the relationships of people and groups who are already associated. As a result of tourism, for example, residents of tourist-receiving societies may be brought into neutral, competitive or cooperative relationships with one another as they jockey for the economic benefits that tourism brings. At the same time, tourists meet other tourists, often forming relationships that endure for long after the holiday has ended. The resorts described by King in Chapter 12 as 'total communities' might profitably be analysed as 'total institutions', a term used by Goffman (1968: 13–115) to denote organizations where staff and visitors of various kinds live in a relatively closed social environment for an extended period of time. It is a perspective that emphasizes the uncomfortable similarity of many resorts, especially 'all-inclusives', cruise ships and holiday camps, to such apparently different organizations as hospitals and prisons.

Whereas host–host relations and guest–guest relations are often ignored in impact studies, this is less so for encounters of residents with visitors. Yet the nature of such interaction varies according to numerous factors, including: the type of tourism involved; the stage of development of the destination

Table 17.1. Levels of analysis for tourism's impacts.

Level of analysis	Features	Actors	
		Type	Examples
National and international arena	Nation states and national institutions in association with one another	Intra-government	UN Environmental Programme (UNEP) UN Development Programme (UNDP) UN Educational, Scientific and Cultural Organisation (UNESCO) European Union (EU) South American Common Market (MERCOSUL) Organization for African Unity (OAU) Organization for Economic Cooperation and Development (OECD) International Bank for Reconstruction and Development (World Bank) Asian Development Bank (ADB)
		Public/private sector	World Tourism Organization (WTO) Pacific Asia Travel Association (PATA) Other tourism promotion and marketing agencies.
		National organizations operating internationally NGOs operating internationally (often with local partners)	United States Agency for International Development (USAID) Department for International Development (DFID) (UK) World Wildlife Fund (WWF) Greenpeace End Child Prostitution in Asian Tourism (ECPAT) Ecumenical Coalition on Third World Tourism (ECTWT)
		Economic organizations operating internationally	Transnational hotels and tour operators World Travel and Tourism Council (WTTC)
Social structure	Individuals performing socially defined roles in social, cultural, economic and political institutions in regular relationship with one another	Social and cultural	Kinship groups Classes, ethnic and status groups Pressure groups against tourism (e.g. Tourism Concern) Arts and crafts associations Education and training institutions Churches and other religious organizations Non-governmental organizations operating at national level
		Economic	Companies in hospitality, travel and attractions Trade associations, and associated economic sectors
		Political	The state, local and central National tourism associations and/or tourist boards Political parties Trades unions and associations
interaction	Host–host, guest–guest and guest–host interaction in destination areas		Interaction varies according to age, gender, social and cultural difference (including language), historical context and type of tourism. The key role of culture brokers

area; tourist length of stay; material, cultural, status and power differences of host and guest; and the prior expectations and stereotypes held by participants in the interaction. This will also vary according to age and gender differences, and sex and romance tourism, along with criminal activities (of tourist and resident), may all form sub-categories of host–guest interaction.

It is also necessary to accord a special place to the role of 'guides', who may be trained and paid professionals or 'cultural brokers' of a less formal but nevertheless equally important variety. The nature of their activities also depends on numerous factors (especially their own status as insiders or outsiders in the 'host' community), as will the degree to which they mediate, facilitate or otherwise structure relationships between different visitors and guests (Cohen, 1982, 1985; Fine and Speer, 1985; Crick, 1992; Michaud, 1993; Gurung *et al.*, 1996; Adams, 1997; Wallace, 1997).

New and revised social institutions

Another way of looking at the impact of tourism is to examine its effects on the social, cultural and economic institutions of the tourist-receiving society. To do so is not to deny the importance of face-to-face interaction, but rather to hold it constant and to focus, instead, on the pattern of daily activities that residents are expected to maintain as part of their social order. In short, the focus shifts to the social structure. When tourists come into contact with local people they intervene in a system of interaction that is socially regulated, where social roles (clusters of expectations) are performed within social *institutions* that are culturally situated and perpetuated through a highly complex pattern of formal or informal, positive or negative sanctions. A waiter in the host society, for example, not only has an occupational role to perform, but also is a son, nephew or cousin in a family, a peer among his peers, a member of a social class, status or ethnic group, and perhaps a participant in a wider religious community – different roles, in short, that are all accompanied by cultural expectations and that, at times, may conflict with one another. It is thus a form of shorthand, but sometimes a necessary one, to refer to family, educational, economic, religious, cultural or political institutions as a prelude to trying to isolate the impact of different forms of tourism on a tourist-receiving society.

The social and cultural impact of tourist intervention in LDCs is not yet fully understood. Much research on tourism's impacts in less developed countries has focused on the extent to which the family, as a social institution, has been changed as a consequence of its members' contact with tourism (Harrison, 1992: 26–27). Tourism's effects on the role of women, in particular, have attracted considerable attention (Kinnaird and Hall, 1994; Swain, 1995; Sinclair, 1997) and – for reasons rarely, if ever, made explicit – they and younger members of societies have been considered especially vulnerable to 'demonstration effects' (Harrison, 1992: 30). Clearly, in so far as tourism does have an impact on the roles of women and younger generations, its effects are not restricted to the family, but will have ramifications for a wide range of activities within other institutions – for example, work, educational and religious practices. Much research has also been carried out on economic institutions, both national and transnational, related to tourism. That said, coherent research on tourism's impacts on other social institutions is much less in evidence, and in some cases has hardly begun.

As indicated elsewhere, tourism can prompt the development of new institutions and have a radical impact on those that predate it (Harrison, 1992: 27–29). When a tourist board or a department or ministry of tourism is introduced into a country's political life, for example, the political topography has changed and new actors emerge. If tourism then becomes an issue in political or religious debates (and the two may sometimes be difficult to separate), the practices and orientations of such institutions are affected. Similarly, the emergence of trades union activities among workers in the hospitality industry may signal the arrival of new forms of organization or the adaptation of old ones. By the same token, there may be changes in more specifically 'cultural' activities, such as arts and crafts associations, perhaps in conjunction with public or private education and training institutions.

Some indication of the kinds of social institutions involved in tourism-induced change are indicated in Table 17.1, but the nature of such organizations, and their relationships to tourism, must be established by research and cannot necessarily be predicted in advance. Again, much will depend on the society, the strength of the local culture and the solidity and flexibility of its institutions, as well as the links they have or can later form with groups, agencies and organizations elsewhere.

From social structure to world system

The nature of partnerships across national boundaries is immensely varied and includes those formed to develop, promote or market tourism – for example, local and transnational companies, hotel associations, and state, parastatal and private sector marketing agencies (Gee and Fayos-Solá, 1997: 303–319). Evidence from case studies elsewhere suggests that, along with access to local resources and a high level of community consensus, communities in less developed regions have adopted and adapted to tourism most successfully when in productive and sympathetic partnership with external agencies, including NGOs and players in the private sector (Harrison and Price, 1996: 8–14). Perhaps this point should be emphasized: while there is undoubtedly a role for NGOs in small-scale tourism enterprises, they are (like the state) not ideally positioned to act as entrepreneurs. In fact, many who work in them are likely to do so because they eschew the world of business, profit and loss! As a result, despite their increasing contribution to civil society in LDCs (Clayton, 1996), very few NGOs actively promote links with the private sector (Heap, 2000: 223). It is thus hardly surprising that many externally funded ecotourism projects, for example, cease to be economically viable when donor funding ends (Tourism Resource Consultants, 1999: 4–8), and yet sustainable tourism development cannot occur unless income exceeds expenditure.

This is not to suggest that the profit motive should reign supreme, and it is clear that tourism often contributes to situations generally deemed undesirable. As a consequence,

there are also partnerships, often across international boundaries, to publicize and resist aspects of tourism considered morally unacceptable – for example, the Ecumenical Coalition on Third World Tourism and Tourism Concern (O'Grady, 1990: Botterill, 1991; de Sousa, 1997), along with many others (O'Grady, 1990). As Heather Montgomery notes in Chapter 13, governments are increasingly cooperating to develop new legislation to counter crimes by tourists against children, and the tourism industry, too, is making efforts to follow suit (WTO, 1997a). The industry is also making efforts to bring about more environmentally sound (and sometimes more profitable) forms of tourism development, as in the case of the International Hotels Environment Initiative (1993). There are also broader-based organizations whose remit may include aspects of tourism, heritage and community development, such as the World Wide Fund for Nature (WWF, 2000), United Nations Educational, Scientific and Cultural Organization and the United States Agency for International Development. The plethora of national and international organizations and the many partnerships that emerge to promote or oppose different forms of tourism, are themselves key features of the globalization process. They also have their own internal organization, and their staff have their own interests (which may not coincide with the formal function of the institution). Indeed, they are but one of many impacts of international tourism and, in general, have been the subject of relatively little coherent research. Again, the specific organizations and the exact nature of their involvement cannot be predicted. However, the key function of the proposed framework for analysis is to draw attention to their existence and, by holding interactional aspects of tourism constant, to direct research to the nature of their involvement.

Closing Comments

There is no question that international tourism has economic, social and cultural impacts. They occur at the level of interaction, and also bring about change in local, regional and international institutions. However, the nature of these impacts cannot be predicted in advance. As with globalization generally, local responses to international tourism and the articulation of the local with the global vary according to numerous endogenous and exogenous factors. It is for this reason that the perennial debate over tourism's contribution to 'development' in less developed countries is so heated and, ultimately, so bound up with value judgements (Harrison, 1994: 252). In general, the argument that it brings economic benefits seems largely to have been accepted, but numerous juries are still deliberating its social and cultural effects. In the end, it is for the residents of less developed regions themselves, and not outsiders, however well intentioned, to decide whether or not the social 'problems' that tourism seems to bring actually *are* problems and, if they are, whether they are moral or political, and how far they can be solved through planning and the political process. It is also for them to decide what kind of tourism they want and how far it should be controlled. Ultimately, while such indices of 'progress' as television sets, mobile phones, doctors and schools can be counted, and gross national products and Gini coefficients calculated, there are no objective criteria for 'development'. Like beauty, it is in the eye of the beholder.

This book started by placing tourism in a historical context and will end in similar vein. The English seaside town of Brighton, which was mentioned in the first chapter, became a seaside resort in the 17th century. From the middle of the 19th century, like many other resorts in the UK, it increasingly catered for the masses, who went in their thousands by train, either as 'excursionists' going for the day or in family and other groups for longer periods. Throughout the second half of the 19th century, tourists (who would now be regarded as domestic tourists) were castigated for their drunkenness and immorality. They attracted prostitutes and criminals and other kinds of 'low life', and some local residents were scandalized by their behaviour. The town became noted for its urban squalor, and was much criticized for discharging sewage directly into the sea. Residents also complained that most of the money spent by the visitors did not ben-efit them, but went instead to outsiders (Gilbert, 1975: 103–105, 146, 205, 185–192, 220). Interestingly, such complaints are commonly expressed about the impact of tourism in LDCs.

At the time of writing, however, Brighton is often described as 'London-by-the-Sea' and (despite the English climate and some persistent social problems, many of which stem from its continued popularity) is generally considered one of the most lively and attractive seaside towns in the south of England. Its easy access to London and the rolling hills of the South Downs, its numerous leisure facilities and its seaside aspect (all of which made it a popular tourist destination), together with the efforts of its local government and citizens, make it a desirable place to live and have contributed to its continued success. Indeed, when Brighton, having merged with adjoining Hove to become Brighton and Hove, was awarded city status in December 2000, residents generally felt that the honour was no less than the new city deserved.

Clearly, the Brighton of today is a very different place from the Brighton of the late 19th century. However, it has adapted to changes in its external social and economic environment over the years, tourism continues to be a major industry, and its population is both viable and increasing. In these senses, at least, Brighton is an example of sustainable tourism development. This history may not always be repeated elsewhere, but the story of Brighton's evolution – and that of many other Western seaside resorts – may perhaps caution against hasty judgements for or against international tourism. In so far as it is perceived to create or exacerbate economic, social or cultural problems in less developed countries, those problems should be addressed; and the more that residents derive tangible benefits from tourism, the less acute the problems are likely to be. Tourism's immediate impacts should certainly not be ignored, but it is also important to recognize that destination areas alter over time, and changes that initially appear disruptive and damaging might later be viewed in a more positive light. Paradoxically, whether or not 'development' has occurred may often be decided only in retrospect.

References

Adams, K. (1997) Touting touristic 'primadonnas': tourism, ethnicity and national integration in Sulawesi, Indonesia. In: Picard, M. and Wood, R.E. (eds) *Tourism, Ethnicity and the State in Asian and Pacific Societies.* University of Hawai'i Press, Honolulu, pp. 155–180.

Botterill, D. (1991) A new social movement: Tourism Concern – the first two years. *Leisure Studies* 10, 203–217.

Brandon, K.E. and Wells, M. (1992) Planning for people and parks: design dilemmas. *World Development* 20(4), 557–570.

Brown, P. (2000) Europe told there is no choice but to adapt. *The Guardian* 2 November, p. 6.

Butler, R. (1992) Alternative tourism: the thin end of the wedge. In: Smith, V. and Eadington, W. (eds) *Tourism Alternatives.* University of Pennsylvania Press, Philadelphia, Pennsylvania, pp. 31–46.

Cater, E. (1994) Ecotourism in the Third World: problems and prospects for sustainability. In: Cater, E. and Lowman, G. (eds) *Ecotourism: a Sustainable Option?* John Wiley & Sons, Chichester, UK, pp. 69–86.

Cheong, R. (1995) The virtual threat to travel and tourism. *Tourism Management* 16(6), 417–422.

CNTA (1998) *The Yearbook of Chinese Tourism Statistics.* China National Tourism Administration, China Tourism Press, Beijing.

Clayton, A. (ed.) (1996) *NGOs, Civil Society and the State: Building Democracy in Transitional Societies.* International Non-governmental Organization Training and Research Centre (INTRAC), Oxford, UK.

Cohen, E. (1982) Jungle guides in Northern Thailand: the dynamics of a marginal occupation role. *Sociological Review* 30(2), 234–266.

Cohen, E. (1985) The tourist guide: the origins, structure and dynamics of a role. *Annals of Tourism Research* 12(1), 5–29.

Crick, M. (1992) The politics of tour guiding: Israeli and Palestinian guides in Israel and the Occupied Territories. In: Harrison, D. (ed.) *Tourism and the Less Developed Countries.* Belhaven, London, pp. 121–134.

Fine, E.C. and Speer, T.H. (1985) Tour guide performances as sight sacralization. *Annals of Tourism Research* 12(1), 73–95.

Gee, C.Y. and Fayos-Solá, E. (1997) *International Tourism: a Global Perspective.* World Tourism Organization, Madrid.

Gilbert, E.M. (1975) *Brighton: Old Ocean's Bauble.* Harvester Press, Hassocks, UK.

Goffman, E. (1968) *Asylums: Essays on the Social Situation of Mental Patients and Other Inmates.* Penguin, Harmondsworth, UK.

Gurung, G., Simmons, D. and Devlin, P. (1996) The evolving role of tourist guides: the Nepali experience. In: Butler, R. and Hinch, T. (eds) *Tourism and Indigenous Peoples.* Thomson Press, London, pp. 107–128.

Harrison, D. (1992) Tourism to less developed countries: the social consequences. In: Harrison, D. (ed.) *Tourism and the Less Developed Countries.* Belhaven Press, London, pp. 19–34.

Harrison, D. (1994) Tourism, capitalism and development in less developed countries. In: Sklair, L. (ed.) *Capitalism and Development.* Routledge, London, pp. 232–257.

Harrison, D. (1999) *A Cultural Audit of Turtle Island, Fiji.* University of North London, London.

Harrison, D. and Brandt, J. (2001) Ecotourism in Fiji. In: Harrison, D. (ed.) *Tourism in the South Pacific.* Cognizant, New York.

Harrison, D. and Price, M. (1996) Fragile environments, fragile communities? An introduction. In: Price, M. (ed.) *People and Tourism in Fragile Environments.* John Wiley & Sons, Chichester, UK, in association with the Royal Geographical Society, pp. 1–18.

Heap, S. (2000) *NGOs Engaging with Business: a World of Difference and a Difference to the World.* International Non-governmental Organisation Training and Research Centre (INTRAC), Oxford, UK.

Holden, A. (2000) *Environment and Tourism.* Routledge, London and New York.

Honey, M. (1999) *Ecotourism and Sustainable Development: Who Owns Paradise?* Island Press, Washington DC.

International Hotels Environment Initiative (1993) *Environmental Management for Hotels: the Industry Guide to Best Practice.* Butterworth-Heinemann, London.

Jefferson, A. (1995) Prospects for tourism: a practitioner's view. *Tourism Management* 16(2), 101–105.

Kinnaird, V. and Hall, D. (eds) (1994) *Tourism: a Gender Analysis.* John Wiley & Sons, Chichester, UK.

Lindberg, K. and Hawkins, D.E. (eds) (1993) *Ecotourism: a Guide for Planners and Managers,* Vol. 1. The Ecotourism Society, North Bennington, Vermont.

Lindberg, K., Epler Wood, M. and Engeldrum, D. (eds) (1998) *Ecotourism: a Guide for Planners and Managers*, Vol. 2. The Ecotourism Society, North Bennington, Vermont.

Macalister, T. (1999) White knight spoils the QE2 party. *The Guardian* 8 December, p. 31.

Mckie, R. (2001) Cosmic tourist blasts into space amid the usual holiday hold-ups. *The Observer* 29 April.

Michaud, J. (1993) Tourism as a catalyst of economic and political change. *Internationales Asienforum* 24(1–2), 21–43.

Montgomery, H. (1996) Public vice and private virtue: child prostitution in Pattaya, Thailand. PhD dissertation, Department of Social Anthropology, University of Cambridge.

O'Grady, A. (ed.) (1990) *The Challenge of Tourism: Learning Resources for Study and Action*. Ecumenical Coalition on Third World Tourism, Bangkok.

Perry, K. (2000) World's largest ocean liner, the Queen Mary 2, to herald new golden age. *The Guardian* 7 November, p. 9.

Pleumarom, A. (2000) International Year of Ecotourism. Greentour@egroups.com (27 October).

Sinclair, M.T. (ed.) (1997) *Gender, Work and Tourism*. Routledge, London.

de Sousa, D. (1997) Footprints. *Contours* 7(9), 32–36.

Swain, M.B. (ed.) (1995) Gender in Tourism. *Annals of Tourism Research* Special Issue, 22(2).

Tieman, R. (2000) The cruise ship of the skies. *Evening Standard* London, 18 November, pp. 46–47.

Tourism Resource Consultants (1999) *Report on the Pacific Ecotourism Workshop*, Taveuni, Fiji Islands, 28–31 July 1998. TRC, Wellington, New Zealand.

Turner, V.T. and Turner, E.L.B. (1978) *Image and Pilgrimage in Christian Culture: Anthropological Perspectives*. Columbia University Press, New York.

Wallace, V. (1997) Being a guide: keeping the peace? *Tourism in Focus* 24(Summer), 4–5

Williams, P. and Hobson, J.S.P. (1995) Virtual reality and tourism: fact or fantasy? *Tourism Management* 16(6), 423–427.

World Wide Fund for Nature (WWF) (2000) *Tourism Certification: an Analysis of Green Globe 21 and Other Tourism Certification Programmes*. WWF/Synergy, UK.

WTO (1996/1997) Eco-tourism: a rapidly growing niche market. *WTO News*, No. 5, December/January: 5.

WTO (1997a) Airlines join fight against child prostitution. *WTO News*, Issue 2: May: 1–2.

WTO (1997b) Travel to surge in the 21st century. *WTO News*, No. 5, November.

WTO (1999) *Tourism: 2020 Vision: Executive Summary Updated*. World Tourism Organization, Madrid.

Index

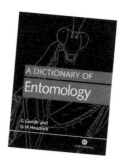

GUILDFORD **college**

Learning Resource Centre

Please return on or before the last date shown.
No further issues or renewals if any items are overdue.

- 2 MAR 2006   - 5 FEB 2008

2 2 APR 2008
- 4 JUN 2008

1 9 APR 2006

- 8 MAY 2006   1 8 JUN 2008

1 4 JUN 2006   1 2 MAY 2011

3 1 MAY 2012

- 4 JAN 2007
2 3 MAR 2007

2 7 JUN 2007   - 3 DEC 2013

Class: 338.4791 HAR

Title: Tourism and the less developed World

Author: Harrison, David